Accelerated C++

The C++ In-Depth Series

Bjarne Stroustrup, Editor

"I have made this letter longer than usual, because I lack the time to make it short."
—BLAISE PASCAL

The advent of the ISO/ANSI C++ standard marked the beginning of a new era for C++ programmers. The standard offers many new facilities and opportunities, but how can a real-world programmer find the time to discover the key nuggets of wisdom within this mass of information? The C++ In-Depth Series minimizes learning time and confusion by giving programmers concise, focused guides to specific topics.

Each book in this series presents a single topic, at a technical level appropriate to that topic. The Series' practical approach is designed to lift professionals to their next level of programming skills. Written by experts in the field, these short, in-depth monographs can be read and referenced without the distraction of unrelated material. The books are cross-referenced within the Series, and also reference *The C++ Programming Language* by Bjarne Stroustrup.

As you develop your skills in C++, it becomes increasingly important to separate essential information from hype and glitz, and to find the in-depth content you need in order to grow. The C++ In-Depth Series provides the tools, concepts, techniques, and new approaches to C++ that will give you a critical edge.

Titles in the Series

Accelerated C++: Practical Programming by Example, Andrew Koenig and Barbara E. Moo

The Boost Graph Library: User Guide and Reference Manual, Jeremy G. Siek, Lie-Quan Lee, and Andrew Lumsdaine

C++ In-Depth Box Set, Bjarne Stroustrup, Andrei Alexandrescu, Andrew Koenig, Barbara E. Moo, Stanley B. Lippman, and Herb Sutter

C++ Network Programming, Volume 1: Mastering Complexity Using ACE and Patterns, Douglas C. Schmidt and Stephen D. Huston

Essential C++, Stanley B. Lippman

Exceptional C++: 47 Engineering Puzzles, Programming Problems, and Solutions, Herb Sutter

Modern C++ Design: Generic Programming and Design Patterns Applied, Andrei Alexandrescu

More Exceptional C++: 40 New Engineering Puzzles, Programming Problems, and Solutions, Herb Sutter

For more information, check out the series Web site at http://www.aw.com/cseng/series/indepth/

Accelerated C++

Practical Programming by Example

Andrew Koenig
Barbara E. Moo

ADDISON–WESLEY

Boston • San Francisco • New York • Toronto • Montreal
London • Munich • Paris • Madrid
Capetown • Sydney • Tokyo • Singapore • Mexico City

The publisher offers discounts on this book when ordered in quantity for special sales. For more information, please contact:

Pearson Education Corporate Sales Division
201 W. 103rd Street
Indianapolis, IN 46290
(800) 428-5331
corpsales@pearsoned.com

Visit AW on the Web: www.awl.com/cseng/

Library of Congress Cataloging-in-Publication Data
Koenig, Andrew
    Accelerated C++ : practical programming by example / Andrew Koenig, Barbara E. Moo.
        p. cm.
    Includes index.
    ISBN 0-201-70353-X
    1. C++ (Computer program language) I. Moo, Barbara E. II. Title.
    QA76.73.C153 K67 2000
    005.13'3—dc21   00–040172

The authors typeset this book (`pic|eqn|troff -mpm|dpost`) in Palatino, Helvetica, and Courier, with assorted Sun Sparcstations, Hewlett-Packard laser printers, and three helper cats.

ISBN 020170353X

4 5 6 7 8 9 MA   04 03 02 01

4th Printing   November 2001

To our students,
who taught us
how to teach.

Contents

Preface

A new approach to C++ programming

We assume that you want to learn quickly how to write useful C++ programs. Therefore, we start by explaining the most useful parts of C++. This strategy may seem obvious when we put it that way, but it has the radical implication that we do not begin by teaching C, even though C++ builds on C. Instead, we use high-level data structures from the start, explaining only later the foundations on which those data structures rest. This approach lets you to begin writing idiomatic C++ programs immediately.

Our approach is unusual in another way: We concentrate on solving problems, rather than on exploring language and library features. We explain the features, of course, but we do so in order to support the programs, rather than using the programs as an excuse to demonstrate the features.

Because this book teaches C++ programming, not just features, it is particularly useful for readers who already know some C++, and who want to use the language in a more natural, effective style. Too often, people new to C++ learn the language mechanics without learning how to apply the language to everyday problems.

Our approach works—for beginners and experienced programmers

We used to teach a week-long intensive C++ course every summer at Stanford University. We originally adopted a traditional approach to that course: Assuming that the students already knew C, we started by showing them how to define classes, and then moved systematically through the rest of the language. We found that our students would be confused and frustrated for about two days—until they had learned enough that they could start writing useful programs. Once they got to that point, they learned quickly.

When we got our hands on a C++ implementation that supported enough of what was then the brand-new standard library, we overhauled the course. The new course used the library right from the beginning, concentrated on writing useful programs, and went into details only after the students had learned enough to use those details productively.

The results were dramatic: After one day in the classroom, our students were able to write programs that had taken them most of the week in the old course. Moreover, their frustration vanished.

Abstraction

Our approach is possible only because C++, and our understanding of it, has had time to mature. That maturity has let us ignore many of the low-level ideas that were the mainstay of earlier C++ programs and programmers.

The ability to ignore details is characteristic of maturing technologies. For example, early automobiles broke down so often that every driver had to be an amateur mechanic. It would have been foolhardy to go for a drive without knowing how to get back home even if something went wrong. Today's drivers don't need detailed engineering knowledge in order to use a car for transportation. They may wish to learn the engineering details for other reasons, but that's another story entirely.

We define abstraction as selective ignorance—concentrating on the ideas that are relevant to the task at hand, and ignoring everything else—and we think that it is the most important idea in modern programming. The key to writing a successful program is knowing which parts of the problem to take into account, and which parts to ignore. Every programming language offers tools for creating useful abstractions, and every successful programmer knows how to use those tools.

We think abstractions are so useful that we've filled this book with them. Of course, we don't usually call them abstractions directly, because they come in so many forms. Instead, we refer to functions, data structures, classes, and inheritance—all of which are abstractions. Not only do we refer to them, but we use them throughout the book.

If abstractions are well designed and well chosen, we believe that we can use them even if we don't understand all the details of how they work. We do not need to be automotive engineers to drive a car, nor do we need to understand everything about how C++ works before we can use it.

Coverage

If you are serious about C++ programming, you need to know everything in this book—even though this book doesn't tell you everything you need to know.

This statement is not as paradoxical as it sounds. No book this size can contain everything you'll ever need to know about C++, because different programmers and applications require different knowledge. Therefore, any book that covers all of C++—such as Stroustrup's *The C++ Programming Language* (Addison-Wesley, 2000)—will inevitably tell you a lot that you don't need to know. Someone else will need it, even if you don't.

On the other hand, many parts of C++ are so universally important that it is hard to be productive without understanding them. We have concentrated on those parts. It is possible to write a wide variety of useful programs using only the information in this book. Indeed, one of our reviewers, who is the lead programmer for a substantial commercial system written in C++, told us that this book covers essentially all of the facilities that he uses in his work.

Using these facilities, you can write true C++ programs—not C++ programs in the style of C, or any other language. Once you have mastered the material in this book, you will know enough to figure out what else you want to learn, and how to go about it. Amateur telescope makers have a saying that it is easier to make a 3-inch mirror and then to make a 6-inch mirror than to make a 6-inch mirror from scratch.

We cover only standard C++, and ignore proprietary extensions. This approach has the advantage that the programs that we teach you to write will work just about anywhere. However, it also implies that we do not talk about how to write programs that run in windowing environments, because such programs are invariably tied to a specific environment, and often to a specific vendor. If you want to write programs that will work only in a particular environment, you will have to turn elsewhere to learn how to do so— but don't put this book down quite yet! Because our approach is universal, you will be able to use everything that you learn here in whatever environments you use in the future. By all means, go ahead and read that book about GUI applications that you were considering—but please read this one first.

A note to experienced C and C++ programmers

When you learn a new programming language, you may be tempted to write programs in a style that is familiar from the languages that you already know. Our approach seeks to avoid that temptation by using high-level abstractions from the C++ standard library right from the start. If you are already an experienced C or C++ programmer, this approach contains some good news and some bad news—and it's the same news.

The news is that you are likely to be surprised at how little of your knowledge will help you understand C++ as we present it. You will have more to learn at first than you might expect (which is bad), but you will learn more quickly than you might expect (which is good). In particular, if you already know C++, you probably learned first how to program in C, which means that your C++ programming style is built on a C foundation. There is nothing wrong with that approach, but our approach is so different that we think you'll see a side of C++ that you haven't seen before.

Of course, many of the syntactic details will be familiar, but they're just details. We treat the important ideas in a completely different order from what you've probably encountered. For example, we don't mention pointers or arrays until Chapter 10, and we're not even going to discuss your old favorites, `printf` and `malloc`, at all. On the other hand, we start talking about the standard-library `string` class in Chapter 1. When we say we're adopting a new approach, we mean it!

Structure of this book

You may find it convenient to think of this book as being in two parts. The first part, through Chapter 7, concentrates on programs that use standard-library abstractions. The second part, starting with Chapter 8, talks about defining your own abstractions.

Presenting the library first is an unusual idea, but we think it's right. Much of the C++ language—especially the harder parts—exists mostly for the benefit of library authors. Library users don't need to know those parts of the language at all. By ignoring those parts of the language until the second part of the book, we make it possible to write useful C++ programs much more quickly than if we had adopted a more conventional approach.

Once you have understood how to use the library, you will be ready to learn about the low-level facilities on which the library is built, and how to use those facilities to write your own libraries. Moreover, you will have a feeling for how to make a library useful, and when to avoid writing new library code altogether.

Although this book is smaller than many C++ books, we have tried to use every important idea at least twice, and key ideas more than that. As a result, many parts of the book refer to other parts. These references look like §39.4.3/857, which refers to text on page 857 that is part of section 39.4.3—or at least it would do so if this book had that many sections or pages. The first time we explain each idea, we mention it in **_bold italic_** type to make it easy to find and to call your attention to it as an important point.

Every chapter (except the last) concludes with a section called _Details_. These sections serve two purposes: They make it easy to remember the ideas that the chapter introduced, and they cover additional, related material that we think you will need to know eventually. We suggest that you skim these sections on first reading, and refer back to them later as needed.

The two appendices summarize and elucidate the important parts of the language and library at a level of detail that we hope will be useful when you are writing programs.

Getting the most out of this book

Every book about programming includes example programs, and this one is no different. In order to understand how these programs work, there is no substitute for running them on a computer. Such computers abound, and new ones appear constantly—which means that anything we might say about them would be inaccurate by the time you read these words. Therefore, if you do not yet know how to compile and execute a C++ program, please visit http://www.acceleratedcpp.com and see what we have to say there. We will update that website from time to time with information and advice about the mechanics of running C++ programs. The site also offers machine-readable versions of some of the example programs, and other information that you might find interesting.

Acknowledgments

We would like to thank the people without whom this book would have been impossible. It owes much of its form to our reviewers: Robert Berger, Dag Brück, Adam Buchsbaum, Stephen Clamage, Jon Kalb, Jeffrey Oldham, David Slayton, Bjarne Stroustrup, Albert Tenbusch, Bruce Tetelman, and Clovis Tondo. Many people from Addison-Wesley participated in its publication; the ones we know about are Tyrrell Albaugh, Bunny Ames, Mike Hendrickson, Deborah Lafferty, Cathy Ohala, and Simone Payment. Alexander Tsiris checked the Greek etymology in §13.2.2/236. Finally, the idea of starting with high-level programs grew over many years, stimulated by the hundreds of students who have sat through our courses and the thousands of people who have attended our talks.

Andrew Koenig   Gillette, New Jersey
Barbara E. Moo   June 2000

0

Getting started

Let us begin by looking at a small C++ program:

```cpp
// a small C++ program
#include <iostream>

int main()
{
    std::cout << "Hello, world!" << std::endl;
    return 0;
}
```

Programmers often refer to such a program as a `Hello, world!` program. Despite its small size, you should take the time to compile and run this program on your computer before reading further. The program should write

```
Hello, world!
```

on the standard output, which will typically be a window on your display screen. If you have trouble, find someone who already knows C++ and ask for help, or consult our website, `http://www.acceleratedcpp.com`, for advice.

This program is useful because it is so simple that if you have trouble, the most likely reasons are obvious typographical errors or misconceptions about how to use the implementation. Moreover, thoroughly understanding even such a small program can teach a surprising amount about the fundamentals of C++. In order to gain this understanding, we'll look in detail at each line of the program.

0.1 Comments

The first line of our program is

```
// a small C++ program
```

The `//` characters begin a ***comment***, which extends to the end of the line. The compiler ignores comments; their purpose is to explain the program to a human reader. In this book, we shall put the text of each comment in *italic* type, to make it easier for you to distinguish comments from other parts of the program.

0.2 #include

In C++, many fundamental facilities, such as input–output, are part of the *standard library*, rather than being part of the *core language*. This distinction is important because the core language is always available to all C++ programs, but you must explicitly ask for the parts of the standard library that you wish to use.

Programs ask for standard-library facilities by using **#include** *directives*. Such directives normally appear at the beginning of a program. The only part of the standard library that our program uses is input–output, which we request by writing

```
#include <iostream>
```

The name iostream suggests support for sequential, or stream, input–output, rather than random-access or graphical input–output. Because the name iostream appears in an #include directive and it is enclosed in *angle brackets* (< and >), it refers to a part of the C++ library called a *standard header*.

The C++ standard does not tell us exactly what a standard header is, but it does define each header's name and behavior. Including a standard header makes the associated library facilities available to the program, but exactly how the implementation does so is its concern, not ours.

0.3 The main function

A *function* is a piece of program that has a name, and that another part of the program can *call*, or cause to run. Every C++ program must contain a function named main. When we ask the C++ implementation to run a program, it does so by calling this function.

The main function is required to yield an integer as its result, the purpose of which is to tell the implementation whether the program ran successfully. A zero value indicates success; any other value means there was a problem. Accordingly, we begin by writing

```
int main()
```

to say that we are defining a function named main that returns a value of type int. Here, int is the name that the core language uses to describe integers. The parentheses after main enclose the parameters that our function receives from the implementation. In this particular example, there are no parameters, so there is nothing between the parentheses. We'll see how to use main's parameters in §10.4/179.

0.4 Curly braces

We continue our definition of the main function by following the parentheses with a sequence of *statements* enclosed in *curly braces* (often simply called braces):

```
int main()
{                        //  left brace
                         //  the statements go here
}                        //  right brace
```

In C++, braces tell the implementation to treat whatever appears between them as a unit. In this example, the left brace marks the beginning of the statements in our `main` function, and the right brace marks their end. In other words, the braces indicate that all the statements between them are part of the same function.

When there are two or more statements within braces, as there are in this function, the implementation executes them in the order in which they appear.

0.5 Using the standard library for output

The first statement inside the braces does our program's real work:

```
std::cout << "Hello, world!" << std::endl;
```

This statement uses the standard library's *output operator*, `<<`, to write `Hello, world!` on the standard output, and then to write the value of `std::endl`.

Preceding a name by `std::` indicates that the name is part of a *namespace* named `std`. A namespace is a collection of related names; the standard library uses `std` to contain all the names that it defines. So, for example, the `iostream` standard header defines the names `cout` and `endl`, and we refer to these names as `std::cout` and `std::endl`.

The name `std::cout` refers to the *standard output stream*, which is whatever facility the C++ implementation uses for ordinary output from programs. In a typical C++ implementation under a windowing operating system, `std::cout` will denote the window that the implementation associates with the program while it is running. Under such a system, the output written to `std::cout` will appear in the associated window.

Writing the value of `std::endl` ends the current line of output, so that if this program were to produce any more output, that output would appear on a new line.

0.6 The `return` statement

A `return` statement, such as

```
return 0;
```

ends execution of the function in which it appears, and passes the value that appears between the `return` and the semicolon (0 in this example) back to the program that called the function that is returning. The value that is returned must have a type that is appropriate for the type that the function says it will return. In the case of `main`, the return type is `int` and the program to which `main` returns is the C++ implementation itself. Therefore, a `return` from `main` must include an integer-valued expression, which is passed back to the implementation.

Of course, there may be more than one point at which it might make sense to terminate a program; such a program may have more than one `return` statement. If the definition of a function promises that the function returns a value of a particular type, then every `return` statement in the function must return a value of an appropriate type.

0.7 A slightly deeper look

This program uses two additional concepts that permeate C++: expressions and scope. We will have much more to say about these concepts as this book progresses, but it is worthwhile to begin with some of the basics here.

An *expression* asks the implementation to compute something. The computation yields a *result*, and may also have *side effects*—that is, it may affect the state of the program or the implementation in ways that are not directly part of the result. For example, 3+4 is an expression that yields 7 as its result, and has no side effects, and

```
std::cout << "Hello, world!" << std::endl
```

is an expression that, as its side effect, writes Hello, world! on the standard output stream and ends the current line.

An expression contains operators and operands, both of which can take on many forms. In our Hello, world! expression, the two << symbols are operators, and std::cout, "Hello, world!" and std::endl are operands.

Every operand has a *type*. We shall have much more to say about types, but essentially, a type denotes a data structure and the meanings of operations that make sense for that data structure. The effect of an operator depends on the types of its operands.

Types often have names. For example, the core language defines int as the name of a type that represents integers, and the library defines std::ostream as the type that provides stream-based output. In our program, std::cout has type std::ostream.

The << operator takes two operands, and yet we have written two << operators and three operands. How can this be? The answer is that << is *left-associative*, which, loosely speaking, means that when << appears twice or more in the same expression, each << will use as much of the expression as it can for its left operand, and as little of it as it can for its right operand. In our example, the first << operator has "Hello, world!" as its right operand and std::cout as its left operand, and the second << operator has std::endl as its right operand and std::cout << "Hello, world!" as its left operand. If we use parentheses to clarify the relationship between operands and operators, we see that our output expression is equivalent to

```
(std::cout << "Hello, world!") << std::endl
```

Each << behaves in a way that depends on the types of its operands. The first << has std::cout, which has type std::ostream, as its left operand. Its right operand is a string literal, which has a mysterious type that we shall not even discuss until §10.2/176. With those operand types, << writes its right operand's characters onto the stream that its left operand denotes, and its result is its left operand.

The left operand of the second << is therefore an expression that yields std::cout, which has type std::ostream; the right operand is std::endl, which is a *manipulator*. The key property of manipulators is that writing a manipulator on a stream manipulates the stream, by doing something other than just writing characters to it. When the left operand of << has type std::ostream and the right operand is a manipulator, << does whatever the manipulator says to do to the given stream, and returns the stream as its result. In the case of std::endl, that action is to end the current line of output.

The entire expression therefore yields `std::cout` as its value, and, as a side effect, it writes `Hello, world!` on the standard output stream and ends the output line. When we follow the expression by a semicolon, we are asking the implementation to discard the value—which action is appropriate, because we are interested only in the side effects.

The *scope* of a name is the part of a program in which that name has its meaning. C++ has several different kinds of scopes, two of which we have seen in this program.

The first scope that we used is a namespace, which, as we've just seen, is a collection of related names. The standard library defines all of its names in a namespace named `std`, so that it can avoid conflicts with names that we might define for ourselves—as long as we are not so foolish as to try to define `std`. When we use a name from the standard library, we must specify that the name we want is the one from the library; for example, `std::cout` means `cout` as defined in the namespace named `std`.

The name `std::cout` is a *qualified name*, which uses the `::` operator. This operator is also known as the *scope operator*. To the left of the `::` is the (possibly qualified) name of a scope, which in the case of `std::cout` is the namespace named `std`. To the right of the `::` is a name that is defined in the scope named on the left. Thus, `std::cout` means "the name `cout` that is in the (namespace) scope `std`."

Curly braces form another kind of scope. The body of `main`—and the body of every function—is itself a scope. This fact is not too interesting in such a small program, but it will be relevant to almost every other function we write.

0.8 Details

Although the program we've written is simple, we've covered a lot of ground in this chapter. We intend to build on what we've introduced here, so it is important for you to be sure that you understand this chapter fully before you continue.

To help you do so, this chapter—and every chapter except Chapter 16—ends with a section called *Details* and a set of exercises. The *Details* sections summarize and occasionally expand on the information in the text. It is worth looking at each *Details* section as a reminder of the ideas that the chapter introduced.

Program structure: C++ programs are usually in *free form*, meaning that spaces are required only when they keep adjacent symbols from running together. In particular, newlines (i.e., the way in which the implementation represents the change from one line of the program to the next) are just another kind of space, and usually have no additional special meaning. Where you choose to put spaces in a program can make it much easier—or harder—to read. Programs are normally indented to improve readability.

There are three entities that are not free-form:

string literals	characters enclosed in double quotes; may not span lines
`#include` *name*	must appear on a line by themselves (except for comments)
`//` *comments*	`//` followed by anything; ends at the end of the current line

A comment that begins with `/*` is free-form; it ends with the first subsequent `*/` and can span multiple lines.

Types define data structures and operations on those data structures. C++ has two kinds of types: those built into the core language, such as `int`, and those that are defined outside the core language, such as `std::ostream`.

Namespaces are a mechanism for grouping related names. Names from the standard library are defined in the namespace called `std`.

String literals begin and end with double quotes (`"`); each string literal must appear entirely on one line of the program. Some characters in string literals have special meaning when preceded by a backslash (`\`):

`\n`	newline character
`\t`	tab character
`\b`	backspace character
`\"`	treats this symbol as part of the string rather than as the string terminator
`\'`	same meaning as `'` in string literals, for consistency with character literals (§1.2/14)
`\\`	includes a `\` in the string, treating the next character as an ordinary character

We'll see more about string literals in §10.2/176 and §A.2.1.3/302.

Definitions and headers: Every name that a C++ program uses must have a corresponding definition. The standard library defines its names in headers, which programs access through `#include`. Names must be defined before they are used; hence, a `#include` must precede the use of any name from that header. The `<iostream>` header defines the library's input–output facilities.

The `main` function: Every C++ program must define exactly one function, named `main`, that returns an `int`. The implementation runs the program by calling `main`. A zero return from `main` indicates success; a nonzero return indicates failure. In general, functions must include at least one `return` statement and are not permitted to fall off the end of the function. The `main` function is special: It may omit the return; if it does so, the implementation will assume a zero return value. However, explicitly including a return from `main` is good practice.

Braces and semicolons: These inconspicuous symbols are important in C++ programs. They are easy to overlook because they are small, and they are important because forgetting one typically evokes compiler diagnostic messages that may be hard to understand.

A sequence of zero or more statements enclosed in braces is a statement, called a *block*, which is a request to execute the constituent statements in the order in which they appear. The body of a function must be enclosed in braces, even if it is only a single statement. The statements between a pair of matching braces constitute a scope.

An expression followed by a semicolon is a statement, called an *expression statement*, which is a request to execute the expression for its side effects and discard its result. The expression is optional; omitting it results in a *null statement*, which has no effect.

Output: Evaluating `std::cout << e` writes the value of `e` on the standard-output stream, and yields `std::cout`, which has type `ostream`, as its value in order to allow chained output operations.

Exercises

0-0. Compile and run the `Hello, world!` program.

0-1. What does the following statement do?

```
3 + 4;
```

0-2. Write a program that, when run, writes

```
This (") is a quote, and this (\) is a backslash.
```

0-3. The string literal `"\t"` represents a tab character; different C++ implementations display tabs in different ways. Experiment with your implementation to learn how it treats tabs.

0-4. Write a program that, when run, writes the `Hello, world!` program as its output.

0-5. Is this a valid program? Why or why not?

```
#include <iostream>

int main()    std::cout << "Hello, world!" << std::endl;
```

0-6. Is this a valid program? Why or why not?

```
#include <iostream>

int main()    {{{{{{ std::cout << "Hello, world!" << std::endl; }}}}}}
```

0-7. What about this one?

```
#include <iostream>

int main()
{
    /* This is a comment that extends over several lines
       because it uses /* and */ as its starting and ending delimiters */
    std::cout << "Does this work?" << std::endl;
    return 0;
}
```

0-8. ...and this one?

```
#include <iostream>

int main()
{
    // This is a comment that extends over several lines
    // by using // at the beginning of each line instead of using /*
    // or */ to delimit comments.
    std::cout << "Does this work?" << std::endl;
    return 0;
}
```

0-9. What is the shortest valid program?

0-10. Rewrite the `Hello, world!` program so that a newline occurs everywhere that whitespace is allowed in the program.

Working with strings

Chapter 0 looked closely at a tiny program, which we used to introduce surprisingly many fundamental C++ ideas: comments, standard headers, scopes, namespaces, expressions, statements, string literals, and output. This chapter continues our overview of the fundamentals by writing similarly simple programs that use character strings. In the process, we'll learn about declarations, variables, and initialization, as well as something about input and the C++ `string` library. The programs in this chapter are so simple that they do not even require any control structures, which we will cover in Chapter 2.

1.1 Input

Once we can write text, the logical next step is to read it. For example, we can modify the `Hello, world!` program to say hello to a specific person:

```cpp
// ask for a person's name, and greet the person
#include <iostream>
#include <string>

int main()
{
    // ask for the person's name
    std::cout << "Please enter your first name: ";

    // read the name
    std::string name;        // define name
    std::cin >> name;        // read into name

    // write a greeting
    std::cout << "Hello, " << name  << "!" << std::endl;
    return 0;
}
```

When we execute this program, it will write

```
Please enter your first name:
```

on the standard output. If we respond, for example,

```
Vladimir
```

then the program will write

```
Hello, Vladimir!
```

Let's look at what's going on. In order to read input, we must have a place to put it. Such a place is called a **variable**. A variable is an **object** that has a name. An object, in turn, is a part of the computer's memory that has a type. The distinction between objects and variables is important because, as we'll see in §3.2.2/45, §4.2.3/65, and §10.6.1/183, it is possible to have objects that do not have names.

If we wish to use a variable, we must tell the implementation what name to give it and what type we want it to have. The requirement to supply both a name and a type makes it easier for the implementation to generate efficient machine code for our programs. The requirement also lets the compiler detect misspelled variable names—unless the misspelling happens to match one of the names that our program said it intended to use.

In this example, our variable is named name, and its type is std::string. As we saw in §0.5/3 and §0.7/5, the use of std:: implies that the name, string, that follows it is part of the standard library, not part of the core language or of a nonstandard library. As with every part of the standard library, std::string has an associated header, namely <string>, so we've added an appropriate #include directive to our program.

The first statement,

```
std::cout << "Please enter your first name: ";
```

should be familiar by now: It writes a message that asks for the user's name. An important part of this statement is what isn't there, namely the std::endl manipulator. Because we did not use std::endl, the output does not begin a new line after the program has written its message. Instead, as soon as it has written the prompt, the computer waits—on the same line—for input.

The next statement,

```
std::string name;      // define name
```

is a **definition**, which defines our variable named name that has type std::string. Because this definition appears within a function body, name is a **local variable**, which exists only while the part of the program within the braces is executing. As soon as the computer reaches the }, it **destroys** the variable name, and returns any memory that the variable occupied to the system for other uses. The limited lifetime of local variables is one reason that it is important to distinguish between variables and other objects.

Implicit in the type of an object is its **interface**—the collection of operations that are possible on an object of that type. By defining name as a variable (a named object) of type string, we are implicitly saying that we want to be able to do with name whatever the library says that we can do with strings.

One of those operations is to **initialize** the string. Defining a string variable implicitly initializes it, because the standard library says that every string object starts out with a value. We shall see shortly that we can supply a value of our own when we create a string. If we do not do so, then the string starts out containing no characters at all. We call such a string an **empty** or **null** string.

Once we have defined `name`, we execute

```
std::cin >> name;      // read into name
```

which is a statement that reads from `std::cin` into `name`. Analogous with its use of the
`<<` operator and `std::cout` for output, the library uses the **>> operator** and `std::cin`
for input. In this example, `>>` reads a `string` from the standard input and stores what it
read in the object named `name`. When we ask the library to read a `string`, it begins by
discarding *whitespace* characters (space, tab, backspace, or the end of the line) from the
input, then reads characters into `name` until it encounters another whitespace character or
end-of-file. Therefore, the result of executing `std::cin >> name` is to read a word from
the standard input, storing in `name` the characters that constitute the word.

The input operation has another side effect: It causes our prompt, which asks for the
user's name, to appear on the computer's output device. In general, the input–output
library saves its output in an internal data structure called a ***buffer***, which it uses to optimize output operations. Most systems take a significant amount of time to write characters to an output device, regardless of how many characters there are to write. To avoid
the overhead of writing in response to each output request, the library uses the buffer to
accumulate the characters to be written, and ***flushes*** the buffer, by writing its contents to
the output device, only when necessary. By doing so, it can combine several output operations into a single write.

There are three events that cause the system to flush the buffer. First, the buffer might
be full, in which case the library will flush it automatically. Second, the library might be
asked to read from the standard input stream. In that case, the library immediately
flushes the output buffer without waiting for the buffer to become full. The third occasion
for flushing the buffer is when we explicitly say to do so.

When our program writes its prompt to `cout`, that output goes into the buffer associated with the standard output stream. Next, we attempt to read from `cin`. This read
flushes the `cout` buffer, so we are assured that our user will see the prompt.

Our next statement, which generates the output, explicitly instructs the library to flush
the buffer. That statement is only slightly more complicated than the one that wrote the
prompt. Here we write the string literal `"Hello, "` followed by the value of the `string`
variable `name`, and finally by `std::endl`. Writing the value of `std::endl` ends the line
of output, and then flushes the buffer, which forces the system to write to the output
stream immediately.

Flushing output buffers at opportune moments is an important habit when you are
writing programs that might take a long time to run. Otherwise, some of the program's
output might languish in the system's buffers for a long time between when your program writes it and when you see it.

1.2 Framing a name

So far, our program has been restrained in its greetings. We'd like to change that by writing a more elaborate greeting, so that the input and output look like this:

```
Please enter your first name: Estragon

* * * * * * * * * * * * * * * * * * *
*                                   *
*  Hello, Estragon!  *
*                                   *
* * * * * * * * * * * * * * * * * * *
```

Our program will produce five lines of output. The first line begins the frame. It is a sequence of * characters as long as the person's name, plus some characters to match the salutation ("Hello,   "), plus a space and an * at each end. The line after that will be an appropriate number of spaces with an * at each end. The third line is an *, a space, the message, a space, and an *. The last two lines will be the same as the second and first lines, respectively.

A sensible strategy is to build up the output a piece at a time. First we'll read the name, then we'll use it to construct the greeting, and then we'll use the greeting to build each line of the output. Here is a program that uses that strategy to solve our problem:

```
// ask for a person's name, and generate a framed greeting
#include <iostream>
#include <string>

int main()
{
    std::cout << "Please enter your first name: ";
    std::string name;
    std::cin >> name;

    // build the message that we intend to write
    const std::string greeting = "Hello, " + name + "!";

    // build the second and fourth lines of the output
    const std::string spaces(greeting.size(), ' ');
    const std::string second = "* " + spaces + " *";

    // build the first and fifth lines of the output
    const std::string first(second.size(), '*');

    // write it all
    std::cout << std::endl;
    std::cout << first << std::endl;
    std::cout << second << std::endl;
    std::cout << "* " << greeting << " *" << std::endl;
    std::cout << second << std::endl;
    std::cout << first << std::endl;

    return 0;
}
```

First, our program asks for the user's name, and reads that name into a variable named name. Then, it defines a variable named greeting that contains the message that it intends to write. Next, it defines a variable named spaces, which contains as many spaces as the number of characters in greeting. It uses the spaces variable to define a variable named second, which will contain the second line of the output, and then the program constructs `first` as a variable that contains as many * characters as the number of characters in `second`. Finally, it writes the output, a line at a time.

The `#include` directives and the first three statements in this program should be familiar. The definition of `greeting`, on the other hand, introduces three new ideas.

One idea is that we can give a variable a value as we define it. We do so by placing, between the variable's name and the semicolon that follows it, an = symbol followed by the value that we wish the variable to have. If the variable and value have different types—as §10.2/176 shows that `strings` and string literals do—the implementation will *convert* the initial value to the type of the variable.

The second new idea is that we can use + to *concatenate* a `string` and a string literal—or, for that matter, two `strings` (but not two string literals). We noted in passing in Chapter 0 that `3+4` is `7`. Here we have an example in which + means something completely different. In each case, we can determine what the + operator does by examining the types of its operands. When an operator has different meanings for operands of different types, we say that the operator is *overloaded*.

The third idea is that of saying **const** as part of a variable's definition. Doing so promises that we are not going to change the value of the variable for the rest of its lifetime. Strictly speaking, this program gains nothing by using `const`. However, pointing out which variables will not change can make a program much easier to understand.

Note that if we say that a variable is `const`, we must initialize it then and there, because we won't have the opportunity later. Note also that the value that we use to initialize the `const` variable need not itself be a constant. In this example, we won't know the value of `greeting` until after we have read a value into `name`, which obviously can't happen until we run the program. For this reason, we cannot say that `name` is `const`, because we change its value by reading into it.

One property of an operator that never changes is its associativity. We learned in Chapter 0 that `<<` is left-associative, so that `std::cout << s << t` means the same as `(std::cout << s) << t`. Similarly, the + operator (and, for that matter, the `>>` operator) is also left-associative. Accordingly, the value of `"Hello, " + name + "!"` is the result of concatenating `"Hello, "` with `name`, and concatenating the result of that concatenation with `"!"`. So, for example, if the variable `name` contains `Estragon`, then the value of `"Hello, " + name + "!"` is `Hello, Estragon!`

At this point, we have figured out what we are going to say, and saved that information in the variable named `greeting`. Our next job is to build the frame that will enclose our greeting. In order to do so, we introduce three more ideas in a single statement:

```
std::string spaces(greeting.size(), ' ');
```

When we defined `greeting`, we used an = symbol to initialize it. Here, we are following `spaces` by two expressions, which are separated by a comma and enclosed in parentheses. When we use the = symbol, we are saying explicitly what value we would like the variable to have. By using parentheses in a definition, as we do here, we tell the implementation to *construct* the variable—in this case, `spaces`—from the expressions, in a way that depends on the type of the variable. In other words, in order to understand this definition, we must understand what it means to construct a `string` from two expressions.

How a variable is constructed depends entirely on its type. In this particular case, we are constructing a `string` from—well, from what? Both expressions are of forms that we haven't seen before. What do they mean?

The first expression, `greeting.size()`, is an example of calling a ***member function***. In effect, the object named `greeting` has a component named `size`, which turns out to be a function, and which we can therefore call to obtain a value. The variable `greeting` has type `std::string`, which is defined so that evaluating `greeting.size()` yields an integer that represents the number of characters in `greeting`.

The second expression, `' '`, is a ***character literal***. Character literals are completely distinct from string literals. A character literal is always enclosed in single quotes; a string literal is always enclosed in double quotes. The type of a character literal is the built-in type **char**; the type of a string literal is much more complicated, and we shall not explain it until §10.2/176. A character literal represents a single character. The characters that have special meaning inside a string literal have the same special meaning in a character literal. Thus, if we want `'` or `\`, we must precede it by `\`. For that matter, `'\n'`, `'\t'`, `'\"'`, and related forms work analogously to the way we saw in Chapter 0 that they work for string literals.

To complete our understanding of `spaces`, we need to know that when we construct a `string` from an integer value and a `char` value, the result has as many copies of the `char` value as the value of the integer. So, for example, if we were to define

```
std::string stars(10, '*');
```

then `stars.size()` would be 10, and `stars` itself would contain `**********`.

Thus, `spaces` contains the same number of characters as `greeting`, but all of those characters are blanks.

Understanding the definition of `second` requires no new knowledge: We concatenate `"* "`, our string of spaces, and `" *"` to obtain the second line of our framed message. The definition of `first` requires no new knowledge either; it gives `first` a value that contains as many `*` characters as the number of characters in `second`.

The rest of the program should be familiar; all it does is write strings in the same way we did in §1.1/9.

1.3 Details

Types:

char   Built-in type that holds ordinary characters as defined by the implementation.

wchar_t Built-in type intended to hold "wide characters," which are big enough to hold characters for languages such as Japanese.

The string type is defined in the standard header `<string>`. An object of type `string` contains a sequence of zero or more characters. If `n` is an integer, `c` is a `char`, `is` is an input stream, and `os` is an output stream, then the `string` operations include

```
std::string s;
```
            Defines `s` as a variable of type `std::string` that is initially empty.

```
std::string t = s;
```
> Defines t as a variable of type std::string that initially contains a copy of the characters in s, where s can be either a string or a string literal.

```
std::string z(n, c);
```
> Defines z as a variable of type std::string that initially contains n copies of the character c. Here, c must be a char, not a string or a string literal.

os << s
> Writes the characters contained in s, without any formatting changes, on the output stream denoted by os. The result of the expression is os.

is >> s
> Reads and discards characters from the stream denoted by is until encountering a character that is not whitespace. Then reads successive characters from is into s, overwriting whatever value s might have had, until the next character read would be whitespace. The result is is.

s + t
> The result of this expression is an std::string that contains a copy of the characters in s followed by a copy of the characters in t. Either s or t, but not both, may be a string literal or a value of type char.

s.size()
> The number of characters in s.

Variables can be defined in one of three ways:

```
std::string hello = "Hello";        // define the variable with an explicit initial value

std::string stars(100, '*');        // construct the variable
                                    // according to its type and the given expressions

std::string name;                   // define the variable with an implicit initialization,
                                    // which depends on its type
```

Variables defined inside a pair of curly braces are local variables, which exist only while executing the part of the program within the braces. When the implementation reaches the }, it destroys the variables, and returns any memory that they occupied to the system.

Defining a variable as const promises that the variable's value will not change during its lifetime. Such a variable must be initialized as part of its definition, because there is no way to do so later.

Input: Executing std::cin >> v discards any whitespace characters in the standard input stream, then reads from the standard input into variable v. It returns std::cin, which has type istream, in order to allow chained input operations.

Exercises

1-0. Compile, execute, and test the programs in this chapter.

1-1. Are the following definitions valid? Why or why not?

```
const std::string hello = "Hello";
const std::string message = hello + ", world" + "!";
```

1-2. Are the following definitions valid? Why or why not?

```
const std::string exclam = "!";
const std::string message = "Hello" + ", world" + exclam;
```

1-3. Is the following program valid? If so, what does it do? If not, why not?

```
#include <iostream>
#include <string>

int main()
{
    { const std::string s = "a string";
      std::cout << s << std::endl; }

    { const std::string s = "another string";
      std::cout << s << std::endl; }
    return 0;
}
```

1-4. What about this one? What if we change } } to } ; } in the third line from the end?

```
#include <iostream>
#include <string>

int main()
{
    { const std::string s = "a string";
      std::cout << s << std::endl;
    { const std::string s = "another string";
      std::cout << s << std::endl; }}
    return 0;
}
```

1-5. Is this program valid? If so, what does it do? If not, say why not, and rewrite it to be valid.

```
#include <iostream>
#include <string>

int main()
{
    { std::string s = "a string";
    { std::string x = s + ", really";
      std::cout << s << std::endl; }
      std::cout << x << std::endl;
    }
    return 0;
}
```

1-6. What does the following program do if, when it asks you for input, you type two names (for example, Samuel Beckett)? Predict the behavior before running the program, then try it.

```
#include <iostream>
#include <string>

int main()
{
    std::cout << "What is your name? ";
    std::string name;
    std::cin >> name;
    std::cout << "Hello, " << name
              << std::endl << "And what is yours? ";
    std::cin >> name;
    std::cout << "Hello, " << name
              << "; nice to meet you too!" << std::endl;
    return 0;
}
```

2

Looping and counting

In §1.2/11, we developed a program that writes a formatted frame around a greeting. In this chapter, we're going to make the program more flexible so that we can change the size of the frame without rewriting the program.

Along the way, we'll start learning about arithmetic in C++, and how C++ supports loops and conditions, and we'll explore the related idea of loop invariants.

2.1 The problem

The program in §1.2/12 wrote a greeting with a frame around it. For example, if our user gave us the name `Estragon`, our program would write

```
*********************
*                   *
* Hello, Estragon!  *
*                   *
*********************
```

The program built up the output a line at a time. It defined variables named `first` and `second` to contain the first and second lines of the output, and wrote the greeting itself, surrounded by some characters, as the third line. We didn't need separate variables for the fourth or fifth output lines, because those were the same as the second and first lines respectively.

This approach has a major shortcoming: Each line of the output has a part of the program—and a variable—that corresponds to it. Therefore, even a simple change to the output format, such as removing the spaces between the greeting and the frame, would require rewriting the program. We would like to produce a more flexible form of output without having to store each line in a local variable.

We will approach this problem by generating each character of the output separately, except for the greeting itself, which we already have available as a `string`. What we shall discover is that there is no need to store the output characters in variables, because once we have written a character, we don't need it any more.

2.2 Overall structure

We'll begin by reviewing the part of the program that we don't have to rewrite:

```
#include <iostream>
#include <string>

int main()
{
    // ask for the person's name
    std::cout << "Please enter your first name: ";

    // read the name
    std::string name;
    std::cin >> name;

    // build the message that we intend to write
    const std::string greeting = "Hello, " + name + "!";

    // we have to rewrite this part...

    return 0;
}
```

As we rewrite the part of the program that the *we have to rewrite this part...* comment represents, we shall already be in a context that defines `name`, `greeting`, and the relevant names from the standard library. We will build up the new version of the program a piece at a time, and then, in §2.5.4/29, we'll put all the pieces together.

2.3 Writing an unknown number of rows

We can think of our output as a rectangular array of characters, which we must write one row at a time. Although we don't know how many rows it has, we do know how to compute the number of rows.

The greeting takes up one row, as do the top and bottom rows of the frame. We've accounted for three rows so far. If we know how many blank rows we intend to leave between the greeting and the frame, we can double that number and add three to obtain the total number of rows in the output:

```
// the number of blanks surrounding the greeting
const int pad = 1;
// total number of rows to write
const int rows = pad * 2 + 3;
```

We want to make it easy to find the part of our program that defines the number of blanks, so we give that number a name. The variable called `pad` represents the amount of padding around the frame. Having defined `pad`, we use it in computing `rows`, which will control how many rows we write.

The built-in type `int` is the most natural type to use for integers, so we've chosen that type for `pad` and `rows`. We also said that both variables are `const`, which we know from §1.2/13 is a promise that we will not change the value of either `pad` or `rows`.

Looking ahead, we intend to use the same number of blanks on the left and right sides as on the top and bottom, so one variable will serve for all four sides. If we are careful to use this variable every time we want to refer to the number of blanks, changing the size of the frame will require only changing the program to give the variable a different value.

We have computed how many rows we need to write; our next problem is to do so:

```
// separate the output from the input
std::cout << std::endl;

// write rows rows of output
int r = 0;

// invariant: we have written r rows so far
while (r != rows) {
    // write a row of output (as we will describe in §2.4/22)
    std::cout << std::endl;
    ++r;
}
```

We start, as we did in §1.2/12, by writing a blank line, so that there will be some space between the input and the output. The rest of this fragment contains so many new ideas that we need to look at it closely. Once we've understood how it works, we'll think about how to write each individual row.

2.3.1 The `while` *statement*

Our program controls how many rows of output it writes by using a **while** *statement*, which repeatedly executes a given statement as long as a given condition is true. A `while` statement has the form

```
while (condition)
    statement
```

The *statement* is often called the **while** *body*.

The `while` statement begins by testing the value of the condition. If the condition is false, it does not execute the body at all. Otherwise, it executes the body once, after which it tests the condition again, and so on. The `while` alternates between testing the condition and executing the body until the condition is false, at which point execution continues after the end of the entire `while` statement.

Loosely speaking, we can think of the `while` statement in our example as saying, "As long as the value of r is not equal to rows, do whatever is within the { }."

It is conventional to put the `while` body on a separate line and indent it, to make programs easier to read. The implementation doesn't stop us from writing

```
while (condition) statement
```

but if we do so, we should think about whether we might be making life harder for other people who might read our program.

Note that there is no semicolon after *statement* in this description. Either the *statement* is indeed just a statement, or it is a ***block***, which is a sequence of zero or more statements enclosed in { }. If the statement is just an ordinary statement, it will end with a semi-colon of its own, so there's no need for another one. If it is a block, the block's } marks the end of the statement, so again there's no need for a semicolon. Because a block is a sequence of statements enclosed by braces, we know from §0.7/5 that a block is a scope.

The `while` begins by testing its ***condition***, which is an expression that appears in a context where a truth value is required. The expression `r != rows` is an example of a condition. This example uses the ***inequality operator***, `!=`, to compare `r` and `rows`. Such an expression has type **bool**, which is a built-in type that represents truth values. The two possible values of type `bool` are **true** and **false**, with the obvious meanings.

The other new facility in this program is the last statement in the `while` body, which is

        ++r;

The `++` is the ***increment*** operator, which has the effect of incrementing—adding 1 to—the variable `r`. We could have written

        r = r + 1;

instead, but incrementing an object is so common that a special notation for doing so is useful. Moreover, as we shall see in §5.1.2/79, the idea of transforming a value into its immediate successor, in contrast with computing an arbitrary value, is so fundamental to abstract data structures that it deserves a special notation for that reason alone.

2.3.2 Designing a `while` statement

Determining exactly what condition to write in a `while` statement is sometimes difficult. Similarly, it can be hard to understand precisely what a particular `while` statement does. It is not too hard to see that the `while` statement in §2.3/19 will write a number of output rows that depends on the value of `rows`, but how can we be confident that we know exactly how many rows the program will write? For example, how do we know whether the number will be `rows`, `rows - 1`, `rows + 1`, or something else entirely? We could trace through the `while` by hand, noting the effect of each statement's execution on the state of the program, but how do we know that we haven't made a mistake along the way?

There is a useful technique for writing and understanding `while` statements that relies on two key ideas—one about the definition of a `while` statement, and the other about the behavior of programs in general.

The first idea is that when a `while` finishes, its condition must be false—otherwise the `while` wouldn't have finished. So, for example, when the `while` in §2.3/19 finishes, we know that `r != rows` is false and, therefore, that `r` is equal to `rows`.

The second idea is that of a ***loop invariant***, which is a property that we assert will be true about a `while` each time it is about to test its condition. We choose an invariant that we can use to convince ourselves that the program behaves as we intend, and we write the program so as to make the invariant true at the proper times. Although the invariant is not part of the program text, it is a valuable intellectual tool for designing programs. Every useful `while` statement that we can imagine has an invariant associated with it. Stating the invariant in a comment can make a `while` much easier to understand.

To make this discussion concrete, we will look again at the `while` statement in §2.3/19. The comment immediately before the `while` says what the invariant is: *We have written r rows of output so far.*

To determine that this invariant is correct for this program fragment, we must verify that the invariant is true each time the `while` is about to test its condition. Doing so requires us to verify that the invariant will be true at two specific points in the program.

The first point is just before the `while` tests its condition for the first time. It is easy to verify the invariant at this point in our example: Because we have written no rows of output so far, it is obvious that setting `r` to 0 makes the invariant true.

The second point is just before we reach the end of the `while` body. If the invariant is true there, it will be true the next time the `while` tests the condition. Therefore, the invariant will be true every time.

In exchange for writing our program so that it meets these two requirements—causing the invariant to be true before the `while` starts, and again at the end of the `while` body—we can be confident that the invariant is true not only each time the `while` tests the condition, but also after the `while` finishes. Otherwise, the invariant would have had to be true at the beginning of one of the iterations of the `while` body and false afterward—and we have already arranged for that to be impossible.

Here is a summary of what we know about our program fragment:

```
// invariant: we have written r rows so far

int r = 0;
// setting r to 0 makes the invariant true

while (r != rows) {
    // we can assume that the invariant is true here

    // writing a row of output makes the invariant false
    std::cout << std::endl;

    // incrementing r makes the invariant true again
    ++r;
}
// we can conclude that the invariant is true here
```

The invariant for our `while` is that we have written `r` rows of output so far. When we define `r`, we give it an initial value of 0. At this point, we haven't written anything at all. Setting `r` to 0 obviously makes the invariant true, so we have met the first requirement.

To meet the second requirement, we must verify that whenever the invariant is true when the `while` is about to test its condition, a trip through the condition and body will leave the invariant true at the end of the body.

Writing a row of output causes the invariant to become false, because `r` is no longer the number of rows we have written. However, incrementing `r` to account for the row that was written will make the invariant true again. Doing so makes the invariant true at the end of the body, so we have met the second requirement.

Because both requirements are true, we know that after the `while` finishes, we have written `r` rows. Moreover, we have already seen that `r == rows`. Together, these two facts imply that `rows` is the total number of rows that we have written.

The strategy that we used to understand this loop will come in handy in a variety of contexts. The general idea is to find an invariant that states a relevant property of the variables that the loop involves (we have written r rows), and to use the condition to ensure that when the loop completes, those variables will have useful values (r == rows). The loop body's job is then to manipulate the relevant variables so as to arrange for the condition to be false eventually, while maintaining the truth of the invariant.

2.4 Writing a row

Now that we understand how to write a given number of rows, we can turn our attention to writing a single row. In other words, we can start filling in the part of the program represented by the *write a row of output* comment in §2.3/19.

We begin by observing that all the output lines are the same length. If we think of the output as a rectangular array, then that length is the number of columns in the array. We can compute that number by adding twice the padding to the length of the greeting, and then adding two for the asterisks at the ends:

```
const std::string::size_type cols = greeting.size() + pad * 2 + 2;
```

The easy part of reading this definition is to see that we've said that cols is const, thereby promising that the value of cols will not change after we have defined it. The harder part to understand is that we have defined cols using an unfamiliar type, namely std::string::size_type. We know that the first :: is the scope operator and that the qualified name std::string means the name string from the namespace std. The second :: similarly says that we want the name size_type from the class string. Like namespaces and blocks, classes define their own scopes. The std::string type defines size_type to be the name of the appropriate type for holding the number of characters in a string. Whenever we need a local variable to contain the size of a string, we should use std::string::size_type as the type of that variable.

The reason that we have given cols a type of std::string::size_type is to ensure that cols is capable of containing the number of characters in greeting, no matter how large that number might be. We could simply have said that cols has type int, and indeed, doing so would probably work. However, the value of cols depends on the size of the input to our program, and we have no control over how long that input might be. It is conceivable that someone might give our program a string so long that an int is insufficient to contain its length.

The int type is sufficient for rows because the number of rows depends only on the value of pad, which we control. Every C++ implementation is required to allow every int variable to take on values up to at least 32767, which is plenty. Nevertheless, whenever we define a variable that contains the size of a particular data structure, it is a good habit to use the type that the library defines as being appropriate for that specific purpose.

It is impossible for a string to contain a negative number of characters. Accordingly, std::string::size_type is an ***unsigned*** type—objects of that type are incapable of containing negative values. This property does not affect the programs in this chapter, but we shall see later on in §8.1.3/142 that it can be critically important.

Having figured out how many characters to write, we can use another `while` statement to write them:

```
std::string::size_type c = 0;

// invariant: we have written c characters so far in the current row
while (c != cols) {
        // write one or more characters
        // adjust the value of c to maintain the invariant
}
```

This `while` behaves analogously to the one in §2.3/19, except for one difference in the body: This time we have said *write one or more characters* instead of writing exactly one row as we did in §2.3/19. There is no reason that we have to write only a single character each time through the body. As long as we write at least one character, we will ensure progress. All we have to do is ensure that the total number of characters we write on this row is exactly `cols`.

2.4.1 *Writing border characters*

Our remaining problem is to figure out what characters to write. We can solve part of this problem by noting that if we are on the first or last row, or on the first or last column, then we know that we should write an asterisk. Moreover, we can use our knowledge of the loop invariants to determine whether it is time to write an asterisk.

For example, if `r` is zero, we know from the invariant that we have not yet written any rows, which means that we are writing part of the first row. Similarly, if `r` is equal to `rows - 1`, we know that we have written `rows - 1` rows already, so we must now be writing part of the last row. We can use analogous reasoning to conclude that if `c` is zero, then we are writing part of the first column, and if `c` is equal to `cols - 1`, we are writing part of the last column. Using this knowledge, we can fill in more of our program:

```
// invariant: we have written c characters so far in the current row
while (c != cols) {
        if (r == 0 || r == rows - 1 || c == 0 || c == cols - 1) {
            std::cout << "*";
            ++c;
        } else {
            // write one or more nonborder characters
            // adjust the value of c to maintain the invariant
        }
}
```

This statement introduces so many new ideas that it requires detailed explanation.

2.4.1.1 `if` *statements*

The `while` body consists of a block (§2.3.1/19) that contains an **if** *statement*, which we use to determine whether it is time to write an asterisk. An `if` statement can take either of two forms:

```
if (condition)
        statement
```

or, as used here,

```
if (condition)
        statement1
else
        statement2
```

As with the `while` statement, the *condition* is an expression that yields a truth value. If the condition is true, then the program executes the statement that follows the `if`. In the second form of the `if` statement, if the *condition* is false, then the program executes the statement that follows the `else`.

It is worth noting, just as with our description of the form of the `while` statement, that the formatting that we use to illustrate the `if` statement is merely conventional. However, readers will find it much easier if code follows formatting conventions such as the ones that we've used in the examples in this book.

2.4.1.2 Logical operators

What about the condition itself?

```
r == 0 || r == rows - 1 || c == 0 || c == cols - 1
```

This condition is true if `r` is 0 or `rows - 1`, or if `c` is 0 or `cols - 1`. The condition uses two new operators, the `==` operator and the `||` operator. C++ programs test for **equality** by using the `==` symbol, to distinguish it from the assignment operator `=`. Thus, `r == 0` yields a `bool` that indicates whether the value of `r` is equal to 0. The **logical-or** operator, written as `||`, yields `true` if either of its operands is `true`.

The relational operators have lower **precedence** than the arithmetic operators. In expressions that contain more than one operator, precedence defines how the operands group. For example,

```
r == rows - 1
```

means

```
r == (rows - 1)
```

rather than

```
(r == rows) - 1
```

because the arithmetic operator `-` has higher precedence than the relational operator `==`. In other words, we are subtracting 1 from `rows` and comparing the result with `r`, which, in this program, is what we wanted. We can override precedence by enclosing in parentheses a subexpression that we want to use as a single operand. For example, if we really wanted to execute `(r == rows) - 1`, we could do so by including the parentheses as shown. This expression would compare `r` with `rows` and subtract 1 from the result, yielding either 0 or -1 depending on whether `r` was equal to `rows`.

The logical-or operator tests whether *either* of its operands is `true`. Its form is

> *condition1* || *condition2*

where, as usual, *condition1* and *condition2* are conditions—expressions that yield truth values. The || expression yields a `bool`, which is `true` if either of the conditions is `true`.

The || operator has lower precedence than the relational operators, and, like most C++ binary operators, is left-associative. Moreover, it has a property that most other C++ operators do not share: If a program finds that the left operand of || is true, it does not evaluate the right operand at all. This property is often called **short-circuit evaluation**, and as we shall see in §5.6/89, it can have a crucial effect on how we write our programs.

Because || is left-associative, and because of the relative precedence of ||, ==, and -,

```
r == 0 || r == rows - 1 || c == 0 || c == cols - 1
```

means the same as it would if we were to place all of its subexpressions in parentheses:

```
((r == 0 || r == (rows - 1)) || c == 0) || c == (cols - 1)
```

In order to evaluate this latter expression using the short-circuit strategy, the program first evaluates the left operand of the outermost ||, which is

```
(r == 0 || r == (rows - 1)) || c == 0
```

To do so, it must first evaluate the left operand of this inner ||, which is

```
r == 0 || r == (rows - 1)
```

which, in turn, means evaluating

```
r == 0
```

If `r` is equal to `0`, then each of the expressions

```
r == 0 || r == (rows - 1)
(r == 0 || r == (rows - 1)) || c == 0
((r == 0 || r == (rows - 1)) || c == 0) || c == (cols - 1)
```

must be true. If `r` is nonzero, the next step is to compare `r` with `rows - 1`. If that test fails, then the program will compare `c` with zero, and if that fails, it will compare `c` with `cols - 1` to determine the final result.

In other words, when we write a series of conditions separated by || operators, we are asking the program to test each of these conditions in turn. If any of the inner conditions is `true`, then the whole condition is `true`; otherwise, the whole condition is `false`. Each || operator stops as soon as it can determine its result, so if any of the inner conditions is `true`, the subsequent conditions go untested. If we step back from the details, we should be able to see that these four equality tests are checking whether we are in the first row, the last row, the first column, or the last column, and, therefore, that the `if` statement writes an asterisk if we're in the top or bottom row, or if we're in the first or last column. Otherwise, it does something else, which we must now define.

2.4.2 Writing nonborder characters

It is now time to write the statements that correspond to the comments that say

> // *write one or more nonborder characters*
> // *adjust the value of* c *to maintain the invariant*

in the program fragment in §2.4.1/23. These statements must deal with the characters
that are not part of the border. It should be easy to see that each of these characters is
either a space or part of the greeting. The only problem is figuring out which one it is,
and what to do about it.

We begin by testing whether we are about to write the first character of the greeting,
which we do by finding if we're in the correct row and on the correct column within that
row. The row we seek is the one after we've written the initial row of asterisks, followed
by pad additional rows. The appropriate column comes after we have written the initial
asterisk on this row, followed by pad spaces. Our knowledge of the invariants tells us
that we're on the right row when r is equal to pad + 1, and be at the appropriate column
when c is equal to pad + 1.

In other words, to determine whether we are about to write the first character of the
greeting, we must check whether r and c are both equal to pad + 1. If we've reached the
right place to write the greeting, we'll do so; otherwise, we'll write a space instead. In
both cases, we have to remember to update c appropriately:

```
if (r == pad + 1 && c == pad + 1) {
    std::cout << greeting;
    c += greeting.size();
} else {
    std::cout << " ";
    ++c;
}
```

The condition inside the if statement uses the ***logical-and*** operator. As with the || oper-
ator, the && operator tests two conditions and yields a truth value. It is left-associative
and uses a short-circuit evaluation strategy. Unlike the || operator, the && operator
yields true only if *both* conditions are true. If either condition is false, the result of &&
is false. The second condition will be tested if and only if the first condition is true.

If the test succeeds, then it's time to write the greeting. In doing so, we falsify our
invariant, because c is no longer equal to the number of characters we have written on
this row. We make our invariant true again by adjusting the value of c to account for the
characters that we have written. The expression that updates c uses another new operator, called the ***compound-assignment*** operator, to adjust c to account for the number of
characters in the name when we wrote it. Such a compound assignment is a shorthand
way of adding the right- and left-hand sides together and storing the result in the left-
hand side. In other words, if we write c += greeting.size(), that statement has the
same effect as if we had written c = c + greeting.size().

The remaining possibility is that we're not on the border, and we're not about to write
the greeting. In that case, we need to write a space and increment c to make the invariant
true again, which we do in the else branch of the if statement.

2.5 The complete framing program

At this point, we have revised the entire program, but the code is scattered enough to be hard to find. Therefore, we shall show the whole program again. However, before we do so, we want to shorten the program in three ways.

The first abbreviation will be a kind of declaration that lets us say once and for all that a given name comes from the standard library. Doing so will allow us to avoid saying `std::` in so many places. The second abbreviation is a shorthand way of writing a particularly common kind of `while` statement. Finally, we can shorten the program slightly by incrementing c in one place instead of two.

2.5.1 Abbreviating repeated uses of `std::`

By now, you are probably tired of seeing—and writing—`std::` in front of every name from the standard library. Saying `std::` explicitly was a good way of reminding you which names came from the standard library, but you should have a pretty good idea of what they are at this point.

C++ offers a way of saying that a particular name should always be interpreted as coming from a particular namespace. For example, by writing

```
using std::cout;
```

we can say that we intend to use the name cout to mean `std::cout` exclusively, and that we do not intend to define anything named cout ourselves. Once we have done so, we can say cout instead of `std::cout`.

Logically enough, such a declaration is called a **using-declaration**. The name that it mentions behaves similarly to other names. For example, if a using-declaration appears within braces, the name that it defines has its given meaning from where it is defined to the closing brace.

From now on, we'll write using-declarations to shorten our programs.

2.5.2 Using `for` statements for compactness

Let's look again at the control structures that we used in the program in §2.3/19. If we look only at the program's outermost structure, we see

```
int r = 0;

while (r != rows) {
    //  stuff that doesn't change the value of r
    ++r;
}
```

This particular form of `while` appears frequently. Before it starts, we define and initialize a local variable, which we test in the condition. The `while` body adjusts the value of the variable so that eventually the condition will fail. Because this kind of control structure is so common, the language provides a shorthand way of writing it:

```
for (int r = 0; r != rows; ++r) {
    // stuff that doesn't change the value of r
}
```

In the body of each of these loops, r will take on a sequence of values, the first of which is 0, and the last of which is rows - 1. We can think of 0 as being the beginning of a range, and rows as being the ***off-the-end value*** for the range. Such a range is called a ***half-open range***, and is often written as [*begin*, *off-the-end*). The deliberately unbalanced brackets [ ) remind the reader that the range is asymmetric. So, for example, the range [1, 4) contains 1, 2, and 3, but not 4. Similarly, we say that r takes on the values in [0, rows).

A **for** *statement* has the following form:

```
for (init-statement    condition; expression)
        statement
```

The first line is often known as the ***for header***. It controls the statement that follows, which is often called the ***for body***. The *init-statement* must be either a definition (§1.1/10) or an expression statement (§0.8/6). Because each of these kinds of statement ends with its own semicolon, there is no additional semicolon between the *init-statement* and the *condition*.

A for statement begins by executing the *init-statement* part of the for header, which it does only once, at the beginning of the for. Typically, the *init-statement* defines and initializes the loop control variable, which will be tested as part of the *condition*. If a variable is defined in the *init-statement*, it is destroyed on exit from the for, so it is inaccessible to code that follows the for statement.

On every trip through the loop, including the first, the program evaluates the *condition*. If the condition yields true, then it executes the for body. Having done so, it executes the *expression*. It then repeats the test, continuing to execute the for body followed by the *expression* in the for header until the test condition fails.

More generally, the meaning of a for statement is

```
{
    init-statement
    while (condition) {
        statement
        expression;
    }
}
```

where we have been careful to enclose the *init-statement* and the while in extra braces, thereby limiting the lifetime of any variables declared in the *init-statement*. Note particularly the presence and absence of semicolons. We do not write a semicolon after the *init-statement* or *statement* because they are statements, with their own semicolons if they need them. We do include a semicolon after *expression* in order to turn it into a statement.

2.5.3 Collapsing tests

We can divide the code associated with the *write one or more characters* comment in §2.4/23 into three cases: We are writing a single asterisk, a space, or the entire greeting. As our program stands, we adjust c to maintain our invariant after we write an asterisk, and we adjust it again after we write a space. There's nothing wrong with doing so, but it is often possible to change the order of tests in a program so as to make it possible to merge two or more identical statements into one.

Because our three cases are mutually exclusive, we can test them in any order. If we begin by first testing whether we are about to write the greeting, then we know that in the other two cases, incrementing c suffices to maintain the invariant, so we can collapse the two increments into one:

```
if (we are about to write the greeting) {
    cout << greeting;
    c += greeting.size();
} else {
    if (we are in the border)
        cout << "*";
    else
        cout << " ";
    ++c;
}
```

After collapsing the increments, we also find that two of our blocks are just single statements, so we can drop two pairs of braces. Notice how the different indentation of ++c; draws attention to the fact that it is executed regardless of whether we are in the border.

2.5.4 *The complete framing program*

If we put all the pieces together and use these three abbreviation techniques, we get the following program:

```
#include <iostream>
#include <string>

// say what standard-library names we use
using std::cin;          using std::endl;
using std::cout;         using std::string;

int main()
{
    // ask for the person's name
    cout << "Please enter your first name: ";

    // read the name
    string name;
    cin >> name;

    // build the message that we intend to write
    const string greeting = "Hello, " + name + "!";

    // the number of blanks surrounding the greeting
    const int pad = 1;

    // the number of rows and columns to write
    const int rows = pad * 2 + 3;
    const string::size_type cols = greeting.size() + pad * 2 + 2;
```

```
//  write a blank line to separate the output from the input
cout << endl;

//  write rows rows of output
//  invariant: we have written r rows so far
for (int r = 0;  r != rows;  ++r) {

        string::size_type c = 0;

        //  invariant: we have written c characters so far in the current row
        while (c != cols) {

                //  is it time to write the greeting?
                if (r == pad + 1 && c == pad + 1) {
                    cout << greeting;
                    c += greeting.size();
                } else {

                        //  are we on the border?
                        if (r == 0 || r == rows - 1 ||
                            c == 0 || c == cols - 1)
                            cout << "*";
                        else
                            cout << " ";
                        ++c;

                }
        }

        cout << endl;
}

return 0;
}
```

2.6 Counting

Most experienced C++ programmers have a habit that may seem weird at first: Their programs invariably begin counting from 0 rather than from 1. For example, if we reduce the outer for loop of the program above to its essentials, we get

```
for (int r = 0;  r != rows;  ++r) {
    //  write a row
}
```

We could have written this loop as

```
for (int r = 1;  r <= rows;  ++r) {
    //  write a row
}
```

One version counts from 0 and uses != as its comparison; the other counts from 1 and uses <= as its comparison. The number of iterations is the same in each case. Is there any reason to prefer one form over the other?

One reason to count from 0 is that doing so encourages us to use asymmetric ranges to express intervals. For example, it is natural to use the range [0, rows) to describe the first for statement, as it is to use the range [1, rows] to describe the second one.

Asymmetric ranges are usually easier to use than symmetric ones because of an important property: A range of the form [m, n) has n - m elements, and a range of the form [m, n] has n - m + 1 elements. So, for example, the number of elements in [0, rows) is obvious (i.e., rows - 0, or rows) but the number in [1, rows] is less so.

This behavioral difference between asymmetric and symmetric ranges is particularly evident in the case of empty ranges: If we use asymmetric ranges, we can express an empty range as [n, n), in contrast to [n, n-1] for symmetric ranges. The possibility that the end of a range could ever be less than the beginning can cause no end of trouble in designing programs.

Another reason to count from 0 is that doing so makes loop invariants easier to express. In our example, counting from 0 makes the invariant straightforward: We have written r rows of output so far. What would be the invariant if we counted from 1?

One would be tempted to say that the invariant is that we are about to write the rth row, but that statement does not qualify as an invariant. The reason is that the last time the while tests its condition, r is equal to rows + 1, and we intend to write only rows rows. Therefore, we are *not* about to write the rth row, so the invariant is not true!

Our invariant could be that we have written r - 1 rows so far. However, if that's our invariant, why not simplify it by starting r at 0?

Another reason to count from 0 is that we have the option of using != as our comparison instead of <=. This distinction may seem trivial, but it affects what we know about the state of the program when a loop finishes. For example, if the condition is r != rows, then when the loop finishes, we know that r == rows. Because the invariant says that we have written r rows of output, we know that we have written exactly rows rows all told. On the other hand, if the condition is r <= rows, then all we can prove is that we have written *at least* rows rows of output. For all we know, we might have written more.

If we count from 0, then we can use r != rows as a condition when we want to ensure that there are exactly rows iterations, or we can use r < rows if we care only that the number of iterations is rows or more. If we count from 1, we can use r <= rows if we want at least rows iterations—but what if we want to ensure that rows is the exact number? Then we must test a more complicated condition, such as r == rows + 1. This extra complexity offers no compensating advantage.

2.7 Details

Expressions: C++ inherits a rich set of operators from C, several of which we have already used. In addition, as we've already seen with the input and output operators, C++ programs can extend the core language by defining what it means to apply built-in operators to objects of class type. Correctly understanding complicated expressions is a fundamental prerequisite to effective programming in C++. Understanding such expressions requires understanding

- How the operands group, which is controlled by the precedence and associativity of the operators used in the expression
- How the operands will be converted to other types, if at all
- The order in which the operands are evaluated

Different operators have different precedence. Most operators are left-associative, but the assignment operators, and the operators that take a single argument, are right-associative. We list the most common operators here—regardless of whether we've used them in this chapter. We've ordered them by precedence from highest to lowest, with a double line separating groupings with the same precedence.

`x.y`	The member y of object x
`x[y]`	The element in object x indexed by y
`x++`	Increments x, returning the original value of x
`x--`	Decrements x, returning the original value of x
`++x`	Increments x, returning the incremented value
`--x`	Decrements x, returning the decremented value
`!x`	Logical negation. If x is `true` then `!x` is `false`.
`x * y`	Product of x and y
`x / y`	Quotient of x and y. If both operands are integers, the implementation chooses whether to round toward zero or $-\infty$.
`x % y`	Remainder of x divided by y, equivalent to x - ((x / y) * y)
`x + y`	Sum of x and y
`x - y`	Result of subtracting y from x
`x >> y`	For integral x and y, x shifted right by y bits; y must be non-negative. If x is an `istream`, reads from x into y.
`x << y`	For integral x and y, x shifted left by y bits; y must be non-negative. If x is an `ostream`, writes y onto x.
`x relop y`	Relational operators yield a `bool` indicating the truth of the relation. The operators (<, >, <=, and >=) have their obvious meanings.
`x == y`	Yields a `bool` indicating whether x equals y
`x != y`	Yields a `bool` indicating whether x is not equal to y
`x && y`	Yields a `bool` indicating whether both x and y are `true`. Evaluates y only if x is `true`.
`x || y`	Yields a `bool` indicating whether either x or y is `true`. Evaluates y only if x is `false`.
`x = y`	Assign the value of y to x, yielding x as its result.
`x op= y`	Compound assignment operators; equivalent to x = x op y, where op is an arithmetic or shift operator.
`x ? y : z`	Yields y if x is `true`; z otherwise. Evaluates only one of y and z.

There is usually no guarantee as to the order in which an expression's operands are evaluated. Accordingly, it is important to avoid writing a single expression in which one operand depends on the value of another operand. We'll see an example in §4.1.5/60.

Operands will be converted to the appropriate type when possible. Numeric operands in expressions or relational expressions are converted by the ***usual arithmetic conversions*** described in detail in §A.2.4.4/304. Basically, the usual arithmetic conversions attempt to preserve precision. Smaller types are converted to larger types, and signed types are converted to unsigned. Arithmetic values may be converted to `bool`: A value of 0 is considered `false`; any other value is `true`. Operands of class type are converted as specified by the type. We'll see in Chapter 12 how to control such conversions.

Types:

`bool`	Built-in type representing truth values; may be either `true` or `false`
`unsigned`	Integral type that contains only non-negative values
`short`	Integral type that must hold at least 16 bits
`long`	Integral type that must hold at least 32 bits
`size_t`	Unsigned integral type (from `<cstddef>`) that can hold any object's size
`string::size_type`	
	Unsigned integral type that can hold the size of any `string`

Half-open ranges include one but not both of their endpoints. For example, `[1, 3)` includes `1` and `2`, but not `3`.

Condition: An expression that yields a truth value. Arithmetic values used in conditions are converted to `bool`: Nonzero values convert to `true`; zero values convert to `false`.

Statements:

`using` *namespace-name* `::` *name* `;`
> Defines *name* as a synonym for *namespace-name* `::` *name*.

type-name name `;`
> Defines *name* with type *type-name*.

type-name name `=` *value* `;`
> Defines *name* with type *type-name* initialized as a copy of *value*.

type-name name `(` *args* `)` `;`
> Defines *name* with type *type-name* constructed as appropriate for the given arguments in *args*.

expression `;`
> Executes *expression* for its side effects.

`{` *statement(s)* `}`
> Called a block. Executes the sequence of zero or more *statement(s)* in order. May be used wherever a *statement* is expected. Variables defined inside the braces have scope limited to the block.

`while` `(`*condition*`)` *statement*
> If *condition* is `false`, do nothing; otherwise, execute *statement* and then repeat the entire `while`.

`for` `(`*init-statement condition* `;` *expression*`)` *statement*
> Equivalent to `{` *init-statement* `while` `(`*condition*`)` `{` *statement expression* `;` `}` `}` (unless the *statement* contains—or is—a `continue` statement (§A.4/309)).

```
if (condition) statement
```
  Executes *statement* if *condition* is `true`.
```
if (condition) statement else statement2
```
  Executes *statement* if *condition* is `true`, otherwise executes *statement2*.
  Each `else` is associated with the nearest matching `if`.
```
return val;
```
  Exits the function and returns `val` to its caller.

Exercises

2-0.   Compile and run the program presented in this chapter.

2-1.   Change the framing program so that it writes its greeting with no separation from the frame.

2-2.   Change the framing program so that it uses a different amount of space to separate the sides from the greeting than it uses to separate the top and bottom borders from the greeting.

2-3.   Rewrite the framing program to ask the user to supply the amount of spacing to leave between the frame and the greeting.

2-4.   The framing program writes the mostly blank lines that separate the borders from the greeting one character at a time. Change the program so that it writes all the spaces needed in a single output expression.

2-5.   Write a set of ''*'' characters so that they form a square, a rectangle, and a triangle.

2-6.   What does the following code do?

```
int i = 0;
while (i < 10) {
    i += 1;
    std::cout << i << std::endl;
}
```

2-7.   Write a program to count down from 10 to −5.

2-8.   Write a program to generate the product of the numbers in the range [1, 10).

2-9.   Write a program that asks the user to enter two numbers and tells the user which number is larger than the other.

2-10. Explain each of the uses of `std::` in the following program:

```
int main()
{
    int k = 0;
    while (k != n) {              // invariant: we have written k asterisks so far
        using std::cout;
        cout << "*";
        ++k;
    }
    std::cout << std::endl;       // std:: is required here
    return 0;
}
```

3

Working with batches of data

The programs that we explored in Chapters 1 and 2 did little more than read a single string and write it again, sometimes with decoration. Most problems are more complicated than such simple programs can solve. Among the most common sources of complexity in programs is the need to handle multiple pieces of similar data.

Our programs have already started doing so, in the sense that a `string` comprises multiple characters. Indeed, it is exactly the ability to put an unknown number of characters into a single object—a `string`—that makes these programs easy to write.

In this chapter, we'll look at more ways of dealing with batches of data, by writing a program that reads a student's exam and homework grades and computes a final grade. Along the way, we'll learn how to store all the grades, even if we don't know in advance how many grades there are.

3.1 Computing student grades

Imagine a course in which each student's final exam counts for 40% of the final grade, the midterm exam counts for 20%, and the average homework grade makes up the remaining 40%. Here is our first try at a program that helps students compute their final grades:

```cpp
#include <iomanip>
#include <ios>
#include <iostream>
#include <string>

using std::cin;                      using std::setprecision;
using std::cout;                     using std::string;
using std::endl;                     using std::streamsize;

int main()
{
    // ask for and read the student's name
    cout << "Please enter your first name: ";
    string name;
    cin >> name;
    cout << "Hello, " << name << "!" << endl;
```

```
// ask for and read the midterm and final grades
cout << "Please enter your midterm and final exam grades: ";
double midterm, final;
cin >> midterm >> final;

// ask for the homework grades
cout << "Enter all your homework grades, "
        "followed by end-of-file: ";

// the number and sum of grades read so far
int count = 0;
double sum = 0;

// a variable into which to read
double x;

// invariant:
//    we have read count grades so far, and
//    sum is the sum of the first count grades
while (cin >> x) {
    ++count;
    sum += x;
}

// write the result
streamsize prec = cout.precision();
cout << "Your final grade is " << setprecision(3)
        << 0.2 * midterm + 0.4 * final + 0.4 * sum / count
        << setprecision(prec) << endl;

    return 0;
}
```

As usual, we begin with #include directives and using-declarations for the library facilities that we intend to use. These facilities include <iomanip> and <ios>, which we have not yet seen. The <ios> header defines streamsize, which is the type that the input–output library uses to represent sizes. The <iomanip> header defines the manipulator setprecision, which lets us say how many significant digits we want our output to contain.

When we used endl, which is also a manipulator, we did not have to include the <iomanip> header. The endl manipulator is used so often that its definition appears in <iostream>, rather than in <iomanip>.

The program begins by asking for and reading the student's name, and the midterm and final grades. Next, it asks for the student's homework grades, which it continues to read until it encounters an end-of-file signal. Different C++ implementations offer their users different ways of sending such a signal to a program, the most common way being to begin a new line of input, hold down the *control* key, and press z (for computers running Microsoft Windows) or d (for computers running the Unix or Linux systems).

While reading the grades, the program uses count to keep track of how many grades were entered, and stores in sum a running total of the grades. Once the program has read all the grades, it writes a greeting message, and reports the student's final grade. In doing so, it uses count and sum to compute the average homework grade.

Much of this program should already be familiar, but there are several new usages, which we will explain.

The first new idea occurs in the section that reads the student's exam grades:

```
cout << "Enter your midterm and final exam grades: ";
double midterm, final;
cin >> midterm >> final;
```

The first of these statements should be familiar: It writes a message, which, in this case, tells the student what to do next. The next statement defines `midterm` and `final` as having type `double`, which is the built-in type for double-precision floating-point numbers. There is also a single-precision floating-point type, called `float`. Even though it might seem that `float` is the appropriate type, it is almost always right to use `double` for floating-point computations.

These types' names date back to when memory was much more expensive than it is today. The shorter floating-point type, called `float`, is permitted to offer as little precision as six significant (decimal) digits or so, which is not even enough to represent the price of a house to the nearest penny. The `double` type is guaranteed to offer at least ten significant digits, and we know of no implementation that does not offer at least 15 significant digits. On modern computers, `double` is usually much more accurate than `float`, and not much slower. Sometimes, `double` is even faster.

Now that we have defined the `midterm` and `final` variables, we read values into them. Like the output operator (§0.7/4), the input operator returns its left operand as its result. So, we can chain input operations just as we chain output operations, so

```
cin >> midterm >> final;
```

has the same effect as

```
cin >> midterm;
cin >> final;
```

Either form reads a number from the standard input into `midterm`, and the next number into `final`.

The next statement asks the student to enter homework grades:

```
cout << "Enter all your homework grades, "
        "followed by end-of-file: ";
```

A careful reading will reveal that this statement contains only a single <<, even though it seems to be writing two string literals. We can get away with this because two or more string literals in a program, separated only by whitespace, are automatically concatenated. Therefore, this statement has exactly the same effect as

```
cout << "Enter all your homework grades, followed by end-of-file: ";
```

By breaking the string literal in two, we avoid lines in our programs that are too long to read conveniently.

The next section of the code defines the variables that we'll use to hold the information that we intend to read. Of these, the interesting part is

```
int count = 0;
double sum = 0;
```

Note that we give the initial value 0 to both sum and count. The value 0 has type int, which means that the implementation must convert it to type double in order to use it to initialize sum. We could have avoided this conversion by initializing sum to 0.0 instead of 0, but it makes no practical difference in this context: Any competent implementation will do the conversion during compilation, so there is no run-time overhead, and the result will be exactly the same.

In this case, what's more important than the conversion is that we give these variables an initial value at all. When we do not specify an initial value for a variable we are implicitly relying on *default-initialization*. The initialization that happens by default depends on the type of the variable. For objects of class type, the class itself says what initializer to use if there is not one specified. For example, we noted in §1.1/10 that if we do not explicitly initialize a string, then the string is implicitly initialized to be empty. No such implicit initialization happens for local variables of built-in type.

Local variables of built-in type that are not explicitly initialized are **undefined**, which means that the variable's value consists of whatever random garbage already happens to occupy the memory in which the variable is created. It is illegal to do anything to an undefined value except to overwrite it with a valid value. Many implementations do not detect the violations of this rule, and allow access to undefined values. The result is almost always a crash or a wrong result, because whatever is in memory by happenstance is almost never a correct value; often it is a value that is invalid for the type.

Had we not given either sum or count an initial value, our program most likely would have failed. The reason is that the first thing the program does with these variables is to use their values: The program reads count in order to increment it, and it reads sum in order to add its value to the one we just read. By the same token, we do not bother to give an initial value to x, because the first thing we do with it is read into it, thereby obliterating any value we might have given it.

The only new aspect of the while statement is the form of its condition:

```
//  invariant:
//      we have read count grades so far, and
//      sum is the sum of the first count grades
while (cin >> x) {
    ++count;
    sum += x;
}
```

We already know that the while loop executes so long as the condition cin >> x succeeds. We'll explore the details of what it means to treat cin >> x as a condition in §3.1.1/39, but for now, what's important to know is that this condition succeeds if the most recent input request (i.e., cin >> x) succeeded.

Inside the while, we use the increment and compound-assignment operators, both of which we used in Chapter 2. From the discussion there we know that ++count adds 1 to count, and that sum += x adds x to sum.

All that is left to explain is how the program does its output:

```
streamsize prec = cout.precision();
cout << "Your final grade is " << setprecision(3)
        << 0.2 * midterm + 0.4 * final + 0.4 * sum / count
        << setprecision(prec) << endl;
```

Our goal is to write the final grade with three significant digits, which we do by using
setprecision. Like endl, setprecision is a manipulator. It manipulates the stream
by causing subsequent output on that stream to appear with the given number of significant digits. By writing setprecision(3), we ask the implementation to write grades
with three significant digits, generally two before the decimal point and one after.

By using setprecision, we change the precision of any subsequent output that
might appear on cout. Because this statement is at the end of the program, we know that
there is no such output. Nevertheless, we believe that it is wise to reset cout's precision
to what it was before we changed it. We do so by calling a member function (§1.2/14) of
cout named precision. This function tells us the precision that a stream uses for
floating-point output. We use setprecision to set the precision to 3, write the final
grade, and then set the precision back to the value that precision gave us. The expression that computes the grade uses several of the arithmetic operators: * for multiplication,
/ for division, and + for addition, each of which has the obvious meaning.

We could have used the precision member function to set the precision, by writing

```
// set precision to 3, return previous value
streamsize prec = cout.precision(3);

cout << "Your final grade is "
        << 0.2 * midterm + 0.4 * final + 0.4 * sum / count << endl;

// reset precision to its original value
cout.precision(prec);
```

However, we prefer to use the setprecision manipulator, because by doing so, we can
minimize the part of the program in which the precision is set to an unusual value.

3.1.1 Testing for end of input

Conceptually, the only really new part of this program is the condition in the while statement. That condition implicitly uses an istream as the subject of the while condition:

```
while (cin >> x) { /* ... */ }
```

The effect of this statement is to attempt to read from cin. If the read succeeds, x will
hold the value that we just read, and the while test also succeeds. If the read fails (either
because we have run out of input or because we encountered input that was invalid for
the type of x), then the while test fails, and we should not rely on the value of x.

Understanding how this code works is a bit subtle. We can start by remembering that
the >> operator returns its left operand, so that asking for the value of cin >> x is equivalent to executing cin >> x and then asking for the value of cin. For example, we can
read a single value into x, and test whether we were successful in doing so, by executing

```
if (cin >> x) { /* ... */ }
```

This statement has the same meaning as

```
cin >> x;
if (cin) { /* ... */ }
```

When we use `cin >> x` as a condition, we aren't just testing the condition; we are also reading a value into x as a side effect. Now, all we need to do is figure out what it means to use `cin` as a condition in a `while` statement.

Because `cin` has type `istream`, which is part of the standard library, we must look to the definition of `istream` for the meaning of `if (cin)` or `while (cin)`. The details of that definition turn out to be complicated enough that we won't discuss it in detail until §12.5/222. However, even without these details, we can already understand a useful amount of what is happening.

The conditions that we used in Chapter 2 all involved relational operators that directly yield values of type `bool`. In addition, we can use expressions that yield values of arithmetic type as conditions. When used in a condition, the arithmetic value is converted to a `bool`: Nonzero values convert to `true`; zero values convert to `false`. For now, what we need to know is that similarly, the `istream` class provides a conversion that can be used to convert `cin` into a value that can be used in a condition. We don't yet know what type that value has, but we do know that the value can be converted to `bool`. Accordingly, we know that the value can be used in a condition. The value that this conversion yields depends on the internal state of the `istream` object, which will remember whether the last attempt to read worked. Thus, using `cin` as a condition is equivalent to testing whether the last attempt to read from `cin` was successful.

There are several ways in which trying to read from a stream can be unsuccessful:
- We might have reached the end of the input file.
- We might have encountered input that is incompatible with the type of the variable that we are trying to read, such as might happen if we try to read an `int` and find something that isn't a number.
- The system might have detected a hardware failure on the input device.

In any of these cases, the effect is the same: Using this input stream as a condition will indicate that the condition is false. Moreover, once we have failed to read from a stream, all further attempts to read from that stream will fail until we reset the stream, which we'll learn how to do in §4.1.3/57.

3.1.2 The loop invariant

Understanding the invariant (§2.3.2/20) for this loop requires special care, because the condition in the `while` has side effects. Those side effects affect the truth of the invariant: Successfully executing `cin >> x` makes the first part of the invariant—the part that says that we have read `count` grades—false. Accordingly, we must change our analysis to account for the effect that the condition itself might have on the invariant.

We know that the invariant was true before evaluating the condition, so we know that we have already read `count` grades. If `cin >> x` succeeds, then we have now read `count + 1` grades. We can make this part of the invariant true again by incrementing `count`. However, doing so falsifies the second part of the invariant—the part that says that `sum` is the sum of the first `count` grades—because after we have incremented `count`, `sum` is now the sum of the first `count - 1` grades, not the first `count` grades. Fortunately, we can make the second part of the invariant true by executing `sum += x;` so that the entire invariant will be true on subsequent trips through the `while`.

If the condition is false, it means that our attempt at input failed, so we didn't get any more data, and so the invariant is still true. As a result, we do not have to account for the condition's side effects after the `while` finishes.

3.2 Using medians instead of averages

The program that we've written so far has a design shortcoming: It throws away each homework grade as soon as it has read it. Doing so is fine for computing averages, but what if we wanted to use the median homework grade instead of the average?

The most straightforward way to find the median of a collection of values is to sort the values into increasing (or decreasing) order and pick the middle one—or, if the number of values is even, take the average of the two values nearest the middle. Medians are often more useful than averages, because although they still account correctly for consistent performance, they won't cause a few lousy grades to blow the whole course.

A bit of thinking should convince us that to compute medians, we must change our program fundamentally. In order to find the median of an unknown number of values, we must store every value until we have read them all. To find the average, we were able to store only the count and running total of the items we'd read. The average was just the total divided by the count.

3.2.1 Storing a collection of data in a `vector`

To compute the median, we must read and store all the homework grades, then sort them, and finally pick the middle one (or two). To do this computation conveniently and efficiently, we need a way to

- Store a number of values that we will read one at a time, without knowing in advance how many values there are
- Sort the values after we have read them all
- Get at the middle value(s) efficiently

The standard library provides a type, named **vector**, that we can use to solve all these problems easily. A `vector` holds a sequence of values of a given type, grows as needed to accommodate additional values, and lets us get at each individual value efficiently.

Let's start rewriting our grading program by making it put the grades into a `vector`, instead of computing the sum and throwing the grades away. The original version of that code looked like

```
// original program (excerpt):
int count = 0;
double sum = 0;
double x;
```

```
//  invariant:
//      we have read count grades so far, and
//      sum is the sum of the first count grades
while (cin >> x) {
    ++count;
    sum += x;
}
```

This loop kept track of how many grades it read, and kept a running total of their value. The need to keep both these variables in step with the values as we read them made the loop invariant relatively complicated. In contrast, using a `vector` to store values as we read them is much simpler:

```
//  revised version of the excerpt:
double x;
vector<double> homework;

//  invariant: homework contains all the homework grades read so far
while (cin >> x)
    homework.push_back(x);
```

We haven't changed the basic structure of our code: It still reads values one at a time into x until it encounters end-of-file or invalid input. What's different is what we do with those values.

Let's start with `homework`, which we define as having type `vector<double>`. A vector is a ***container*** that holds a collection of values. All of the values in an individual vector are the same type, but different `vectors` can hold objects of different types. Whenever we define a `vector`, we must specify the type of the values that the `vector` will hold. Our definition of `homework` says that it is a `vector`, which will hold values of type `double`.

The `vector` type is defined using a language feature called ***template classes***. We'll see how to define a template class in Chapter 11. For now, what's important is to realize that we can separate what it means to be a `vector` from the particular type of the objects that the `vector` holds. We specify the type of the objects inside angle brackets. For example, objects of type `vector<double>` are `vectors` that hold objects of type `double`, objects of type `vector<string>` hold `strings`, and so on.

The `while` loop operates by reading values from the standard input and storing them in the `vector`. As before, we read into x until we hit end-of-file or encounter input that is not a `double`. What is new is

```
homework.push_back(x);
```

As with `greeting.size()` in §1.2/14, we can see that `push_back` is a member function, which is defined as part of the `vector` type, and that we are asking that function to act on behalf of the object named `homework`. We call that function, passing it x. What `push_back` does is append a new element to the end of the `vector`. It gives that new element the value that we passed as the argument to `push_back`. Thus, `push_back` *pushes* its argument onto the *back* of a `vector`. As a side effect, it increases the size of the vector by one.

Because the push_back function is such a good match for what we're trying to do, it is trivial to see that calling it will maintain our loop invariant. Therefore, it is clear that when we drop out of the while, we will have read all the homework grades and stored them in homework, which is what we wanted.

Next, we have to think about the output.

3.2.2 Generating the output

In the original version of the program from §3.1/35, we calculated the student's grade within the output expression itself:

```
streamsize prec = cout.precision();
cout << "Your final grade is " << setprecision(3)
     << 0.2 * midterm + 0.4 * final + 0.4 * sum / count
     << setprecision(prec) << endl;
```

where final and midterm held the exam grades, and sum and count contained the sum of all the homework grades and the count of how many grades were entered.

As we remarked in §3.2.1/41, the easiest way to calculate the median is to sort our data and then find the middle value, or the average of the two middle values if we have an even number of elements. We can make the computation easier to understand if we separate the computation of the median from the code that writes the output.

In order to find the median, we begin by noting that we are going to need to know the size of the homework vector at least twice: once to check whether the size is zero, and again to compute the location of the middle element(s). To avoid having to ask for the size twice, we will store the size in a local variable:

```
typedef vector<double>::size_type vec_sz;
vec_sz size = homework.size();
```

The vector type defines a type named vector<double>::size_type, and a function named size. These members operate analogously to the ones in string: The type defined by size_type is an unsigned type guaranteed sufficient to hold the size of the largest possible vector, and size() returns a size_type value that represents the number of elements in the vector.

Because we need to know the size in two places, we will remember the value in a local variable. Different implementations use different types to represent sizes, so we cannot write the appropriate type directly and remain implementation-independent. For that reason, it is good programming practice to use the size_type that the library defines to represent container sizes, which we do in naming the type of size.

In this example, that type is unwieldy to write—and to read. To simplify our program, we have used a language facility that we haven't encountered before, called a **typedef**. When we include the word typedef as part of a definition, we are saying that we want the name that we define to be a synonym for the given type, rather than a variable of that type. Thus, because our definition includes typedef, it defines the name vec_sz as a synonym for vector<double>::size_type. Names defined via typedef have the same scope as any other names. That is, we can use the name vec_sz as a synonym for the size_type until the end of the current scope.

Once we know how to name the type of the value that homework.size() returns, we can store that value in a local variable, named size, of the same type. It is worth noting that even though we are using the name size for two different purposes, there is no conflict or ambiguity. The only way to ask for the size of a vector is by putting a call to the size function on the right-hand side of a dot, with a vector on the left-hand side. In other words, the size that is defined as a local variable is in a different scope than the one that is an operation on vectors. Because these names are in different scopes, the compiler (and the programmer) can know which size is intended.

Because it is meaningless to find the median of an empty dataset, our next job is to verify that we have some data:

```
if (size == 0) {
    cout << endl << "You must enter your grades.  "
                    "Please try again." << endl;
    return 1;
}
```

We can detect this state of affairs by checking whether size is zero. If it is, the most sensible action is to complain and stop the program. We do so by returning 1 to indicate failure. As discussed in Chapter 0, the system presumes that if main returns 0, the program succeeded. Returning anything else has an implementation-defined meaning, but most implementations treat any nonzero value as failure.

Now that we have verified that we have data, we can begin computing the median. The first part of doing so is to sort the data, which we do by calling a library function:

```
sort(homework.begin(), homework.end());
```

The sort function, defined in the <algorithm> header, rearranges the values in a container so that they are in nondecreasing order. We say nondecreasing instead of increasing because some elements might be equal to one another.

The arguments to sort specify the elements to be sorted. The vector class has member functions named begin and end for this purpose, so that homework.begin() denotes the first element in the vector named homework, and homework.end() denotes (one past) the last element in homework. We'll have much more to say in §5.2.2/81 about begin and end, and in §8.2.7/149 about the importance of "(one past)."

The sort function does its work in place: It moves the values of the container's elements around rather than creating a new container to hold the results.

Once we have sorted homework, we need to find the middle element or elements:

```
vec_sz mid = size/2;
double median;
median = size % 2 == 0 ? (homework[mid] + homework[mid-1]) / 2
                       : homework[mid];
```

We begin by dividing size by 2 in order to locate the middle of the vector. If the number of elements is even, this division is exact. If the number is odd, then the result is the next lower integer.

Exactly how we compute the median depends on whether the number of elements is even or odd. If it is even, the median is the average of the two elements closest to the middle. Otherwise, there is an element in the middle, the value of which is the median.

The expression that assigns a value to `median` uses two new operators: the **remainder** operator, `%`, and the **conditional** operator, often called the `?` `:` operator.

The remainder operator, `%`, returns the remainder that results from dividing its left operand by its right operand. If the remainder after dividing by 2 is 0, then the program has read an even number of elements.

The conditional operator is shorthand for a simple if-then-else expression. First, it evaluates the expression, `size % 2 == 0`, that precedes the `?` part of the operator as a condition to obtain a `bool` value. If the condition yields `true`, then the result is the value of the expression between the `?` and the `:` that follows; otherwise, the result is the value of the expression after the `:`. So, if we read an even number of elements, we'll set `median` to the average of the two middle elements. If we read an odd number, then we'll set `median` to `homework[mid]`. Analogous to `&&` and `||`, the `?` `:` operator first evaluates its leftmost operand. Based on the resulting value, it then evaluates exactly one of its other operands.

The references to `homework[mid]` and `homework[mid-1]` show one way to access an element of a `vector`. Every element of every `vector` has an integer, called its **index**, associated with it. So, for example, `homework[mid]` is the element of `homework` with index `mid`. As you might suspect from §2.6/30, the first element of the `vector` named `homework` is `homework[0]`, and the last element is `homework[size - 1]`.

Each element is itself an (unnamed) object of the type stored in the container. So, `homework[mid]` is an object of type `double`, on which we can invoke any of the operations that type `double` supports. In particular, we can add two elements, and we can divide the resulting sum by 2 to get the average value of the two objects.

Once we know how to access the elements of `homework`, we can see how the median computation works. Assume first that `size` is even, so that `mid` is `size / 2`. Then there must be exactly `mid` elements of `homework` on each side of the middle:

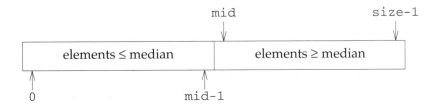

Because we know that each half of `homework` has exactly `mid` elements, it should be easy to see that the indices of the two elements nearest the middle are `mid - 1` and `mid`; the median is the average of these elements.

If the number of elements is odd, then `mid` is really `(size - 1) / 2`, because of truncation. In that case, we can think of our sorted `homework` vector as two segments with `mid` elements each, separated by a single element in the middle. That element is the median:

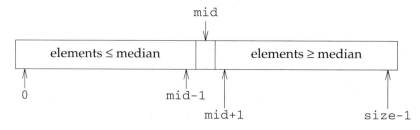

In either case, our median computation relies on the ability to access a `vector` element knowing only its index.

Once we have computed the median, we need only compute and write the final grade:

```
streamsize prec = cout.precision();
cout << "Your final grade is " << setprecision(3)
     << 0.2 * midterm + 0.4 * final + 0.4 * median
     << setprecision(prec) << endl;
```

The final program isn't much more complicated than the program in §3.1/35, even though it does much more work. In particular, even though our homework vector will grow as needed to accommodate grades for as many homework assignments as our students can tolerate, our program doesn't need to worry about obtaining the memory to store all those grades. The standard library does all that work for us.

Here is the entire program. The only parts that we have not already mentioned are the `#include` directives, the corresponding using-declarations, and a few more comments:

```
#include <algorithm>
#include <iomanip>
#include <ios>
#include <iostream>
#include <string>
#include <vector>

using std::cin;              using std::sort;
using std::cout;             using std::streamsize;
using std::endl;             using std::string;
using std::setprecision;     using std::vector;

int main()
{
    // ask for and read the student's name
    cout << "Please enter your first name: ";
    string name;
    cin >> name;
    cout << "Hello, " << name << "!" << endl;

    // ask for and read the midterm and final grades
    cout << "Please enter your midterm and final exam grades: ";
    double midterm, final;
    cin >> midterm >> final;

    // ask for and read the homework grades
    cout << "Enter all your homework grades, "
            "followed by end-of-file: ";
```

```
vector<double> homework;
double x;
// invariant: homework contains all the homework grades read so far
while (cin >> x)
    homework.push_back(x);

// check that the student entered some homework grades
typedef vector<double>::size_type vec_sz;
vec_sz size = homework.size();
if (size == 0) {
    cout << endl << "You must enter your grades.   "
                    "Please try again." << endl;
    return 1;
}

// sort the grades
sort(homework.begin(), homework.end());

// compute the median homework grade
vec_sz mid = size/2;
double median;
median = size % 2 == 0 ? (homework[mid] + homework[mid-1]) / 2
                       : homework[mid];

// compute and write the final grade
streamsize prec = cout.precision();
cout << "Your final grade is " << setprecision(3)
        << 0.2 * midterm + 0.4 * final + 0.4 * median
        << setprecision(prec) << endl;

    return 0;
}
```

3.2.3 Some additional observations

This code contains some points that deserve particular attention. First, there's a bit more to know about why we exit the program if homework is empty. Logically, taking the median of an empty collection of values is undefined—we have no idea what it might mean. Therefore, exiting does the right thing: If we don't know what to do, we might as well quit. But it is important to know what would happen if we had continued execution. If the input were empty, and we neglected to test that we had read at least one number, the code to compute the median would fail. Why?

If we had read no elements, then homework.size(), and therefore size, would be 0. Likewise, mid would be 0. When we executed homework[mid], we would be looking at the first element (the one indexed by 0) in homework. But there are no elements in homework! When we execute homework[0], all bets are off as to what we get. vectors do not check whether the index is in range. Such checking is up to the user.

The next important observation is that vector<double>::size_type, like all standard-library size types, is an **unsigned integral type**. Such types are incapable of storing negative values at all; instead, they store values modulo 2^n, where n depends on the implementation. So, for example, there would never be any point in checking whether homework.size() < 0, because that comparison would always yield false.

Moreover, whenever ordinary integers and unsigned integers combine in an expression, the ordinary integer is converted to unsigned. In consequence, expressions such as `homework.size() - 100` yield unsigned results, which means that they, too, cannot be less than zero—even if `homework.size() < 100`.

Finally, it is also worth noting that the execution performance of our program is actually quite good, even though the `vector<double>` object grows as needed to accommodate its input, rather than being allocated with the right size immediately.

We can be confident about the program's performance because the C++ standard imposes performance requirements on the library's implementation. Not only must the library meet the specifications for behavior, but it must also achieve well-specified performance goals. Every standard-conforming C++ implementation must

- Implement `vector` so that appending a large number of elements to a `vector` is no worse than proportional to the number of elements
- Implement `sort` to be no slower on average than $n\log(n)$, where n is the number of elements being sorted

Therefore, the whole program will normally run in $n\log(n)$ time or better on any standard-conforming implementation. In fact, the standard library was designed with a ruthless attention to performance. C++ is designed for use in performance-critical applications, and the emphasis on speed pervades the library as well.

3.3 Details

Local variables are default-initialized if they are defined without an explicit initializer. Default-initialization of a built-in type means that the value is undefined. Undefined values may be used only as the left-hand side of an assignment.

Type definitions:
`typedef` *type name*;   Defines *name* as a synonym for *type*.

The vector type, defined in `<vector>`, is a library type that is a container that holds a sequence of values of a specified type. `vector`s grow dynamically. Some important operations are:

`vector<T>::size_type`	
	A type guaranteed to be able to hold the number of elements in the largest possible `vector`.
`v.begin()`	Returns a value that denotes the first element in `v`.
`v.end()`	Returns a value that denotes (one past) the last element in `v`.
`vector<T> v;`	Creates an empty `vector` that can hold elements of type `T`.
`v.push_back(e)`	Grows the `vector` by one element initialized to `e`.
`v[i]`	Returns the value stored in position `i`.
`v.size()`	Returns the number of elements in `v`.

Other library facilities

`sort(b, e)`	Rearranges the elements defined by the range `[b, e)` into nondecreasing order. Defined in `<algorithm>`.
`max(e1, e2)`	Returns the larger of the expressions `e1` and `e2`; `e1` and `e2` must have exactly the same type. Defined in `<algorithm>`.
`while (cin >> x)`	Reads a value of an appropriate type into `x` and tests the state of the stream. If the stream is in an error state, the test fails; otherwise, the test succeeds, and the body of the `while` is executed.
`s.precision(n)`	Sets the precision of stream `s` to `n` for future output (or leaves it unchanged if `n` is omitted). Returns the previous precision.
`setprecision(n)`	Returns a value that, when written on an output stream `s`, has the effect of calling `s.precision(n)`. Defined in `<iomanip>`.
`streamsize`	The type of the value expected by `setprecision` and returned by `precision`. Defined in `<ios>`.

Exercises

3-0. Compile, execute, and test the programs in this chapter.

3-1. Suppose we wish to find the median of a collection of values. Assume that we have read some of the values so far, and that we have no idea how many values remain to be read. Prove that we cannot afford to discard any of the values that we have read. *Hint:* One proof strategy is to assume that we can discard a value, and then find values for the unread—and therefore unknown—part of our collection that would cause the median to be the value that we discarded.

3-2. Write a program to compute and print the quartiles (that is, the quarter of the numbers with the largest values, the next highest quarter, and so on) of a set of integers.

3-3. Write a program to count how many times each distinct word appears in its input.

3-4. Write a program to report the length of the longest and shortest `string` in its input.

3-5. Write a program that will keep track of grades for several students at once. The program could keep two `vector`s in sync: The first should hold the student's names, and the second the final grades that can be computed as input is read. For now, you should assume a fixed number of homework grades. We'll see in §4.1.3/56 how to handle a variable number of grades intermixed with student names.

3-6. The average-grade computation in §3.1/36 might divide by zero if the student didn't enter any grades. Division by zero is undefined in C++, which means that the implementation is permitted to do anything it likes. What does your C++ implementation do in this case? Rewrite the program so that its behavior does not depend on how the implementation treats division by zero.

4

Organizing programs and data

Although the program in §3.2.2/46 is larger than we would like, it would have been larger still without `vector`, `string`, and `sort`. These library facilities, like others that we have used, share several qualities: Each one

- Solves a particular kind of problem
- Is independent of most of the others
- Has a name

Our own programs have the first of these qualities, but lack the others. This lack is fine for small programs, but as we set out to solve larger problems, we will find that our solutions will become unmanageable unless we break them into independent, named parts.

Like most programming languages, C++ offers two fundamental ways of organizing large programs: functions (sometimes called subroutines) and data structures. In addition, C++ lets programmers combine functions and data structures into a single notion called a class, which we'll explore starting in Chapter 9.

Once we have learned how to use functions and data structures to organize our computations, we also need the ability to divide our programs into files that we can compile separately and combine after compilation. The last part of this chapter will show how C++ supports separate compilation.

4.1 Organizing computations

We shall begin by writing a function to calculate a student's final grade from the midterm and final exam grades and overall homework grade. We'll assume that we've already calculated the overall homework grade from the individual homework grades, which we have been computing as the average or median. Aside from that assumption, this function will use the same policy as the one that we've been using all along: The homework and final-exam grades contribute 40% each to the total, and the midterm makes up the remaining 20%.

Whenever we do—or might do—a computation in several places, we should think about putting it in a function. An obvious reason for doing so is that then we can use the function instead of redoing the computation explicitly. Not only does using functions reduce our total programming effort, but doing so also makes it easier for us to change the computation if we wish. For example, assume we wanted to change our grading policy. If we had to hunt through every program we had ever written, looking for the parts that dealt with grading, we would probably become discouraged quickly.

There is a more subtle advantage to using functions for such computations: A function has a name. If we name a computation, we can think about it more abstractly—we can think more about what it does and less about how it works. If we can identify important parts of our problems, and create named pieces of our programs that correspond to those parts, then our programs will be easier to understand and the problems easier to solve.

Here is a function that computes grades according to our policy:

```
// compute a student's overall grade from midterm and final exam grades and homework grade
double grade(double midterm, double final, double homework)
{
    return 0.2 * midterm + 0.4 * final + 0.4 * homework;
}
```

Until now, all the functions that we've defined have been named `main`. We define most other functions similarly, by specifying the return type, followed first by the function name, next by a *parameter list* enclosed in `( )`, and, finally, by the function body, which is enclosed in `{ }`. The rules are more complicated for functions that return values that denote other functions; see §A.1.2/297 for the full story.

In this example, the parameters are `midterm`, `final`, and `homework`, each of which has type `double`. They behave like variables that are local to the function, which means that calling the function creates them and returning from the function destroys them.

As with any other variables, we must define the parameters before using them. Unlike other variables, defining them does not create them immediately; only calling the function creates them. Therefore, whenever we call the function, we must supply corresponding *arguments*, which are used to initialize the parameters when the function begins execution. For example, in §3.1/36 we computed a grade by writing

```
cout << "Your final grade is " << setprecision(3)
     << 0.2 * midterm + 0.4 * final + 0.4 * sum / count
     << setprecision(prec) << endl;
```

If we had the `grade` function available, we could have written

```
cout << "Your final grade is " << setprecision(3)
     << grade(midterm, final, sum / count)
     << setprecision(prec) << endl;
```

Not only must we supply arguments that correspond to the parameters of the functions that we call, but we must supply them in the same order. Accordingly, when we call the `grade` function, the first argument must be the midterm grade, the second must be the final exam grade, and the third must be the homework grade.

Arguments can be expressions, such as `sum / count`, not just variables. In general, each argument is used to initialize the corresponding parameter, after which the parameters behave like ordinary local variables inside the function. So, for example, when we call `grade(midterm, final, sum / count)`, the `grade` function's parameters are initialized to copies of the arguments' values, and do not refer directly to the arguments themselves. This behavior is often called ***call by value***, because the parameter takes on a copy of the value of the argument.

4.1.1 Finding medians

Another problem that we solved in §3.2.2/46, and that we can imagine wanting to solve in other contexts, is finding the median of a `vector`. We'll see in §8.1.1/140 how to define a function that is so general that it works with a `vector` of any type of value. For now, we'll limit our attention to `vector<double>`.

To write our function, we'll start with the part of the program in §3.2.2/47 that computes medians, and make a few changes:

```
// compute the median of a vector<double>
// note that calling this function copies the entire argument vector
double median(vector<double> vec)
{
    typedef vector<double>::size_type vec_sz;

    vec_sz size = vec.size();
    if (size == 0)
        throw domain_error("median of an empty vector");

    sort(vec.begin(), vec.end());

    vec_sz mid = size/2;

    return size % 2 == 0 ? (vec[mid] + vec[mid-1]) / 2 : vec[mid];
}
```

One change is that we named our vector `vec`, rather than `homework`. After all, our function can compute the median of anything, not just homework grades. We also eliminated the variable `median`, because we no longer need it: We can return the median as soon as we've calculated it. We are still using `size` and `mid` as variables, but now they are local to the `median` function and, therefore, inaccessible (and irrelevant) elsewhere. Calling the `median` function will create these variables, and returning from the function will destroy them. We define `vec_sz` as a local type name, because we don't want to conflict with anyone who might want to use that name for another purpose.

The most significant change is what we do if the `vector` is empty. In §3.2.2/46, we knew that we would have to complain to whoever was running our program, and we also knew who that person would be and what kind of complaint would make sense. In this revised version, on the other hand, we don't know who is going to be using it, or for what purpose, so we need a more general way of complaining. That more general way is to **throw** an *exception* if the `vector` is empty.

When a program throws an exception, execution stops in the part of the program in which the `throw` appears, and passes to another part of the program, along with an *exception object*, which contains information that the caller can use to act on the exception.

The most important part of the information that is passed is usually the mere fact that an exception was thrown. That fact, along with the type of the exception object, is usually enough to let the caller figure out what to do. In this particular example, the exception that we throw is `domain_error`, which is a type that the standard library defines in header `<stdexcept>` for use in reporting that a function's argument is outside the set of values that the function can accept. When we create a `domain_error` object to throw, we can give it a `string` that describes what went wrong. The program that catches the exception can use this `string` in a diagnostic message, as we shall see in §4.2.3/65.

There is one more detail about how functions behave that is important to understand. When we call a function, we can think of the parameters as local variables whose initial values are the arguments. If we do so, we can see that calling a function involves copying the arguments into the parameters. In particular, when we call `median`, the `vector` that we use as an argument will be copied into `vec`.

In the case of the `median` function, it is useful to copy the argument to the parameter, even if doing so takes significant time, because the `median` function changes the value of its parameter by calling `sort`. Copying the argument prevents changes made by `sort` from propagating back to the caller. This behavior makes sense, because taking the `median` of a `vector` should not change the `vector` itself.

4.1.2 Reimplementing our grading policy

The `grade` function in §4.1/52 assumes that we already know the student's overall homework grade, and not just the individual homework assignments' grades. How we obtain that grade is part of our policy: We used the average in §3.1/36 and the median in §3.2.2/47. Accordingly, we might wish to express this part of our grading policy in a function, along the same lines as we did in §4.1/52:

```
// compute a student's overall grade from midterm and final exam grades
// and vector of homework grades.
// this function does not copy its argument, because median does so for us.
double grade(double midterm, double final, const vector<double>& hw)
{
    if (hw.size() == 0)
        throw domain_error("student has done no homework");
    return grade(midterm, final, median(hw));
}
```

This function has three points of particular interest.

The first point is the type, `const vector<double>&`, that we specify for the third argument. This type is often called "reference to `const vector` of `double`." Saying that a name is a *reference* to an object says that the name is another name for the object. So, for example, if we write

```
vector<double> homework;
vector<double>& hw = homework;        // hw is a synonym for homework
```

we are saying that `hw` is another name for `homework`. From that point on, anything we do to `hw` is equivalent to doing the same thing to `homework`, and vice versa. Adding a `const`, as in

```
// chw is a read-only synonym for homework
const vector<double>& chw = homework;
```

still says that `chw` is another name for `homework`, but the `const` promises that we will not do anything to `chw` that might change its value.

Because a reference is another name for the original, there is no such thing as a reference to a reference. Defining a reference to a reference has the same effect as defining a reference to the original object. For example, if we write

```
// hw1 and chw1 are synonyms for homework; chw1 is read-only
vector<double>& hw1 = hw;
const vector<double>& chw1 = chw;
```

then `hw1` is another name for `homework`, just as `hw` is, and `chw1`, like `chw`, is another name for `homework` that does not allow write access.

If we define a nonconst reference—a reference that allows writing—we cannot make it refer to a `const` object or reference, because doing so would require permission that the `const` denies. Therefore, we cannot write

```
vector<double>& hw2 = chw;          // error: requests write access to chw
```

because we promised not to modify `chw`.

Analogously, when we say that a parameter has type `const vector<double>&`, we are asking the implementation to give us direct access to the associated argument, without copying it, and also promising that we won't change the parameter's value (which would otherwise change the argument too). Because the parameter is a reference to `const`, we can call this function on behalf of both `const` and nonconst `vector`s. Because the parameter is a reference, we avoid the overhead of copying the argument.

The second point of particular interest about the `grade` function is that like the one in §4.1/52, it is named `grade`—even though it calls the other `grade` function. The notion that we can have several functions with the same name is called **overloading**, and figures prominently in many C++ programs. Even though we have two functions with the same name, there is no ambiguity, because whenever we call `grade`, we will supply an argument list, and the implementation will be able to tell from the type of the third argument which `grade` function we mean.

The third point is that we check whether `homework.size()` is zero, even though we know that `median` will do so for us. The reason is that if `median` discovers that we are asking for the median of an empty `vector`, it throws an exception that includes the message `median of an empty vector`. This message is not directly useful to someone who is computing student grades. Therefore, we throw our own exception, which we hope will give the user more of a clue as to what has gone wrong.

4.1.3 Reading homework grades

Another problem that we have had to solve in several contexts is reading homework grades into a `vector`.

There is a problem in designing the behavior of such a function: It needs to return two values at once. One value is, of course, the homework grades that it read. The other is an indication of whether the attempted input was successful.

There is no direct way to return more than one value from a function. One indirect way to do so is to give the function a parameter that is a reference to an object in which it is to place one of its results. This strategy is common for functions that read input, so we'll use it. Doing so will make our function look like this:

```
// read homework grades from an input stream into a vector<double>
istream& read_hw(istream& in, vector<double>& hw) {

    // we must fill in this part

    return in;
}
```

In §4.1.2/54, we saw a program with a `const vector<double>&` parameter; now we're dropping the `const`. A reference parameter without a `const` usually signals an intent to modify the object that is the function's argument. For example, when we execute

```
vector<double> homework;

read_hw(cin, homework);
```

the fact that `read_hw`'s second parameter is a reference should lead us to expect that calling `read_hw` will change the value of `homework`.

Because we expect the function to modify its argument, we cannot call the function with just any expression. Instead, we must pass an *lvalue* argument to a reference parameter. An lvalue is a value that denotes a nontemporary object. For example, a variable is an lvalue, as is a reference, or the result of calling a function that returns a reference. An expression that generates an arithmetic value, such as `sum / count`, is not an lvalue.

Both of the parameters to `read_hw` are references, because we expect the function to change the state of both arguments. We don't know the details of how `cin` works, but presumably the library defines it as a data structure that stores everything the library needs to know about the state of our input file. Reading input from the standard input file changes the state of the file, so it should logically change the value of `cin` as well.

Notice that `read_hw` returns `in`. Moreover, it does so as a reference. In effect, we are saying that we were given an object, which we are not going to copy, and we will return that same object, again without copying it. Returning the stream allows our caller to write

```
if (read_hw(cin, homework)) { /* ... */ }
```

as an abbreviation for

```
read_hw(cin, homework);
if (cin) { /* ... */ }
```

We can now think about how to read the homework grades. Obviously, we want to read as many grades as exist, so it would seem as if we could just write

```
// first try—not quite right
double x;
while (in >> x)
    hw.push_back(x);
```

This strategy doesn't quite work, for two reasons.

The first reason is that we haven't defined hw—our caller defined it for us. Because we didn't define it, we don't know what data might be there already. For all we know, our caller might be using our function to process homework for lots of students, in which case hw might contain the previous student's grades. We can solve this problem by calling hw.clear() before we begin our work.

The second reason that our strategy fails is that we don't quite know when to stop. We can keep reading grades until we can no longer do so, but at that point we have a problem. There are two reasons why we might no longer be able to read a grade: We might have reached end-of-file, or we might have encountered something that is not a grade.

In the first case, our caller will think that we have reached end-of-file. This thought will be true but misleading, because the end-of-file indication will have occurred only after we have successfully read all the data. Normally, an end-of-file indication means that an input attempt failed.

In the second case, when we have encountered something that isn't a grade, the library will mark the input stream as being in *failure state*, which means that future input requests will fail, just as if we had reached end-of file. Therefore, our caller will think that something is wrong with the input data, when the only problem was that the last homework grade was followed by something that was not a homework grade.

In either case, then, we would like to pretend that we never saw whatever followed the last homework grade. Such pretense turns out to be easy: If we reached end-of-file, there was no additional input to read; if we encountered something that wasn't a grade, the library will have left it unread for the next input attempt. Therefore, all we must do is tell the library to disregard whatever condition caused the input attempt to fail, be it end-of-file or invalid input. We do so by calling in.clear() to reset the error state inside in, which tells the library that input can continue despite the failure.

There is one more detail to consider: Perhaps we have already run out of input, or encountered an error condition, before even trying to read the first homework grade. In that case, we must leave the input stream strictly alone, lest we inadvertently seduce our caller into trying to read nonexistent input at some point in the future.

Here is the complete read_hw function:

```
// read homework grades from an input stream into a vector<double>
istream& read_hw(istream& in, vector<double>& hw)
{
    if (in) {
        // get rid of previous contents
        hw.clear();

        // read homework grades
        double x;
        while (in >> x)
            hw.push_back(x);

        // clear the stream so that input will work for the next student
        in.clear();
    }
    return in;
}
```

Note that the `clear` member behaves completely differently for `istream` objects than it does for `vector` objects. For `istream` objects, it resets any error indications so that input can continue; for `vector` objects, it discards any contents that the vector might have had, leaving us with an empty vector again.

4.1.4 Three kinds of function parameters

We would like to pause at this point for an important observation: We have defined three functions—`median`, `grade`, and `read_hw`—that operate on homework vectors. Each of these functions treats the corresponding parameter in a fundamentally different way from the others, and each treatment has a purpose.

The `median` function (§4.1.1/53) has a parameter of type `vector<double>`. Therefore, calling that function causes the argument to be copied, even though that argument might be a huge `vector`. Despite the inefficiency, `vector<double>` is the right parameter type for `median`, because this type ensures that taking the median of a `vector` doesn't change the `vector`. The `median` function `sort`s its parameter. If it did not copy its argument, then calling `median(homework)` would change the value of `homework`.

The `grade` function that takes a homework `vector` (§4.1.2/54) has a parameter of type `const vector<double>&`. In this type, the `&` asks the implementation not to copy the argument, and the `const` promises that the program will not change the parameter. Such parameters are an important technique for making programs more efficient. They are a good idea whenever the function will not change the parameter's value, and the parameter is of a type, such as `vector` or `string`, with values that might be time-consuming to copy. It is usually not worth the bother to use `const` references for parameters of simple built-in types, such as `int` or `double`. Such small objects are usually fast enough to copy that there's little, if any, overhead in passing them by value.

The `read_hw` function has a parameter of type `vector<double>&`, without the `const`. Again, the `&` asks the implementation to bind the parameter directly to the argument, thus avoiding having to copy the argument. But here, the reason to avoid the copy is that the function *intends* to change the argument's value.

Arguments that correspond to nonconst reference parameters must be lvalues—that is, they must be nontemporary objects. Arguments that are passed by value or bound to a `const` reference can be any value. For example, suppose we have a function that returns an empty `vector`:

```
vector<double> emptyvec()
{
    vector<double> v;                    // no elements
    return v;
}
```

We could call this function, and use the result as an argument to our second `grade` function from §4.1.2/54:

```
grade(midterm, final, emptyvec());
```

When run, the `grade` function would throw an exception immediately, because its argument is empty. However, calling `grade` this way would be syntactically legal.

When we call `read_hw`, both of its arguments must be lvalues, because both parameters are nonconst references. If we give `read_hw` a `vector` that is not an lvalue

```
read_hw(cin, emptyvec());          // error: emptyvec() is not an lvalue
```

the compiler will complain, because the unnamed `vector` that we create in the call to `emptyvec` will disappear as soon as `read_hw` returns. If we were allowed to make this call, the effect would be to store input in an object that we couldn't access!

4.1.5 Using functions to calculate a student's grade

The whole point of writing these functions is to use them in solving problems. For example, we can use them to reimplement our grading program from §3.2.2/46:

```
// include directives and using-declarations for library facilities
// code for median function from §4.1.1/53
// code for grade(double, double, double) function from §4.1/52
// code for grade(double, double, const vector<double>&) function from §4.1.2/54
// code for read_hw(istream&, vector<double>&) function from §4.1.3/57
int main()
{
    // ask for and read the student's name
    cout << "Please enter your first name: ";
    string name;
    cin >> name;
    cout << "Hello, " << name << "!" << endl;

    // ask for and read the midterm and final grades
    cout << "Please enter your midterm and final exam grades: ";
    double midterm, final;
    cin >> midterm >> final;

    // ask for the homework grades
    cout << "Enter all your homework grades, "
            "followed by end-of-file: ";

    vector<double> homework;

    // read the homework grades
    read_hw(cin, homework);

    // compute and generate the final grade, if possible
    try {
        double final_grade = grade(midterm, final, homework);
        streamsize prec = cout.precision();
        cout << "Your final grade is " << setprecision(3)
            << final_grade << setprecision(prec) << endl;
    } catch (domain_error) {
        cout << endl << "You must enter your grades.  "
            "Please try again." << endl;
        return 1;
    }

    return 0;
}
```

The changes from the earlier version are in how we read the homework grades, and in how we calculate and write the result.

After asking for our user's homework grades, we call our `read_hw` function to read the data. The `while` statement inside `read_hw` repeatedly reads homework grades until we hit end-of-file or encounter a data value that is not valid as a `double`.

The most important new idea in this example is the **try** statement. It tries to execute the statements in the `{ }` that follow the `try` keyword. If a `domain_error` exception occurs anywhere in these statements, then it stops executing them and continues with the other set of `{ }`-enclosed statements. These statements are part of a **catch** *clause*, which begins with the word `catch`, and indicates the type of exception it is catching.

If the statements between `try` and `catch` complete without throwing an exception, then the program skips the `catch` clause entirely and continues with the next statement, which is `return 0;` in this example.

Whenever we write a `try` statement, we must think carefully about side effects and when they occur. We must assume that anything between `try` and `catch` might throw an exception. If it does so, then any computation that would have been executed after the exception is skipped. What is important to realize is that a computation that might have followed an exception in time does not necessarily follow it in the program text.

For example, suppose that we had written the output block more succinctly as

```
// this example doesn't work
try {
    streamsize prec = cout.precision();
    cout << "Your final grade is " << setprecision(3)
        << grade(midterm, final, homework) << setprecision(prec);
} ...
```

The problem with this rewrite is that although the implementation is required to execute the `<<` operators from left to right, it is not required to evaluate the operands in any specific order. In particular, it might call `grade` after it writes `Your final grade is`. If `grade` throws an exception, then the output might contain that spurious phrase. Moreover, the first call to `setprecision` might set the output stream's precision to 3 without giving the second call the opportunity to reset the precision to its previous value. Alternatively, the implementation might call `grade` before writing any output; whether it does so depends entirely on the implementation.

This analysis explains why we separated the output block into two statements: The first statement ensures that the call to `grade` happens before any output is generated.

A good rule of thumb is to avoid more than one side effect in a single statement. Throwing an exception is a side effect, so a statement that might throw an exception should not cause any other side effects, particularly including input and output.

Of course, we cannot run our `main` function as written. We need the `include` directives and `using`-declarations for the library facilities that the program uses. We also use the names `read_hw` and the `grade` function that takes a `const vector<double>&` third argument. The definitions of these functions, in turn, use the `median` function and the `grade` function that takes three `double`s.

In order to execute this program, we have to ensure that those functions are defined (in the proper order) before our `main` function. Doing so yields an inconveniently large program. Rather than write it out directly here, we'll see in §4.3/65 how we can partition such programs more succinctly into files. Before we do so, let's look at better ways to structure our data.

4.2 Organizing data

Computing one student's grades may be useful to that student, but the computation is simple enough that a pocket calculator could handle it almost as well as our program. On the other hand, if we are teaching a course, we will want to compute grades for a class full of students. Let's revise our program to make it useful for an instructor.

Instead of interactively reporting one student's grade, we'll assume that we are given a file that contains many students' names and grades. Each name is followed by a midterm grade and a final exam grade, and then by one or more homework assignment grades. Such a file might look like

```
Smith 93 91 47 90 92 73 100 87
Carpenter 75 90 87 92 93 60 0 98
. . .
```

Our program should calculate each student's overall grade using medians: The median homework grade counts 40%; the final, 40%; and the midterm, 20%.

For this input, the output would be

```
Carpenter               86.8
Smith                   90.4
. . .
```

In the output, we want the report to be organized alphabetically by student, and we want the final grades to line up vertically so that they are easier to read. These requirements imply that we'll need a place to store the records for all the students, so that we can alphabetize them. We'll also need to find the length of the longest name, so that we know how many spaces to put between each name and its corresponding grade.

Assuming that we have a place to store the data about a single student, we can use a `vector` to hold all the student data. Once the `vector` contains data for all the students, we can `sort` it, and then calculate and write each student's grades. We'll start by creating a data structure to hold the student data, and by writing some auxiliary functions to read and process those data. After we have developed these abstractions, we'll use them to solve the overall problem.

4.2.1 Keeping all of a student's data together

We know that we need to read each student's data and then arrange the students in alphabetical order. When we do so, we want to keep the students' names and grades together. Therefore, we need a way to store in one place all the information that pertains to one student. That place should be a data structure that holds the student's name, midterm and final exam grades, and all the homework grades.

In C++, we define such a data structure as follows:

```
struct Student_info {
    string name;
    double midterm, final;
    vector<double> homework;
};    // note the semicolon—it's required
```

This **struct** definition says that Student_info is a type, which has four data members. Because Student_info is a type, we can define objects of that type, each of which will contain an instance of these four data members.

The first member, named name, is of type string; the second and third are doubles named midterm and final; and the last is a vector of doubles named homework.

Each object of Student_info type holds information about one student. Because Student_info is a type, we can use a vector<Student_info> object to hold information about an arbitrary number of students, just as we used a vector<double> object to hold an arbitrary number of homework grades.

4.2.2 Managing the student records

If we break our problem into manageable components, we'll see that there are three separable steps, which we can represent by separate functions: We need to read data into a Student_info object, we need to generate the overall grade for a Student_info object, and we need to be able to sort a vector of Student_info objects.

The function that reads one of our records is a lot like the read_hw function that we wrote in §4.1.3/57. In fact, we can use that function to read the homework grades. In addition, we'll need to read the student's name and exam grades:

```
istream& read(istream& is, Student_info& s)
{
    // read and store the student's name and midterm and final exam grades
    is >> s.name >> s.midterm >> s.final;

    read_hw(is, s.homework);    // read and store all the student's homework grades
    return is;
}
```

There is no ambiguity in naming this function read, because the type of its second parameter will tell us what we're reading. Overloading will distinguish it from any other function called read that might read into another kind of structure. Like read_hw, this function takes two references: one to the istream from which to read, and another to the object in which to store what it reads. When we use the parameter s inside the function, we will affect the state of the argument that we were passed.

This function works by reading values into the name, midterm, and final members of the object s, and then calling read_hw to read the homework grades. We might reach end-of-file, or encounter input failure, at any point during this process. If so, the subsequent input attempts will do nothing, and when we return, is will be in the appropriate error state. Note that this behavior relies on the fact that the read_hw function (§4.1.3/57) carefully leaves the input stream in an error state if it was already in such a state when we called read_hw.

The other function that we need computes a final grade for a Student_info object. We already solved most of this problem when we defined the grade function in §4.1.2/54. We will continue that work just a little further by overloading the grade function with a version that determines the overall grade for a Student_info object:

```
double grade(const Student_info& s)
{
    return grade(s.midterm, s.final, s.homework);
}
```

This function operates on an object of type Student_info, and returns a double that represents the overall grade. Note that the parameter has type const Student_info&, rather than just plain Student_info, so that when we call it, we do not incur the overhead of copying an entire Student_info object.

Note also that this function does not protect against an exception being thrown by the grade function that it calls. The reason is that there isn't anything that our grade function can do to handle the exception beyond what the grade function that it calls has already done. Because our grade function doesn't catch the exception, any exception that occurs will be passed back to our caller, which presumably will be in a better position than we are to decide what to do about students who did no homework.

Our last task, before writing the whole program, is to decide how we will sort our vector of Student_info objects. In the median function (§4.1.1/53), we sorted a vector<double> parameter, named vec, by using the library sort function:

```
sort(vec.begin(), vec.end());
```

However, assuming our data is in a vector called students, we can't just say

```
sort(students.begin(), students.end());    // not quite right
```

Why not? We'll have much more to say about sort and other library algorithms in Chapter 6, but it is worth thinking a bit abstractly about how the sort function might operate. In particular, how does sort know how to arrange the values in the vector?

The sort function must compare elements of the vector in order to put them in sequence. It does so by using the < operator for the element type of whatever vector it is asked to sort. We can call sort on a vector<double>, because the < operator will compare two doubles and give us an appropriate result. What will happen when sort tries to compare the values of type Student_info? The < operator does not have an obvious meaning when applied to Student_info objects. Indeed, when sort tries to compare two such objects, the compiler will complain.

Fortunately, the sort function takes an optional third argument that is a **_predicate_**. A predicate is a function that yields a truth value, typically of type bool. If this third argument is present, the sort function will use it to compare elements instead of using the < operator. Therefore, we need to define a function that takes two Student_infos, and that says whether the first is less than the second. Because we want to order the students alphabetically by name, we'll write our comparison function to compare only the names:

```
bool compare(const Student_info& x, const Student_info& y)
{
    return x.name < y.name;
}
```

This function simply delegates the work of comparing Student_infos to the string class, which provides a < operator for comparing strings. That operator compares strings by applying normal dictionary ordering. That is, it considers the left-hand operand to be less than the right-hand operand if it is alphabetically ahead of the right-hand operand. This behavior is exactly what we need.

Having defined compare, we can sort the vector by passing the compare function as a third argument to the sort library function:

```
sort(students.begin(), students.end(), compare);
```

When sort compares elements, it will call our compare function to do so.

4.2.3 Generating the report

Now that we have functions to process student records, we can generate our report:

```
int main()
{
    vector<Student_info> students;
    Student_info record;
    string::size_type maxlen = 0;

    // read and store all the records, and find the length of the longest name
    while (read(cin, record)) {
        maxlen = max(maxlen, record.name.size());
        students.push_back(record);
    }

    // alphabetize the records
    sort(students.begin(), students.end(), compare);

    for (vector<Student_info>::size_type i = 0;
         i != students.size(); ++i) {

        // write the name, padded on the right to maxlen + 1 characters
        cout << students[i].name
             << string(maxlen + 1 - students[i].name.size(), ' ');

        // compute and write the grade
        try {
            double final_grade = grade(students[i]);
            streamsize prec = cout.precision();
            cout << setprecision(3) << final_grade
                 << setprecision(prec);
        } catch (domain_error e) {
            cout << e.what();
        }
```

```
        cout << endl;
    }

    return 0;
}
```

We have already seen most of this code, but a couple of points are new.

The first novelty is the call to the library function `max`, which is defined in the header `<algorithm>`. On the surface, `max`'s behavior is obvious. However, one aspect of its behavior is not obvious: Its arguments must both have the same type, for complicated reasons that we shall explore in §8.1.3/142. This requirement makes it essential for us to define `maxlen` to be a variable of type `string::size_type`; it won't do merely to define it as an `int`.

The second novelty is the expression

```
string(maxlen + 1 - students[i].name.size(), ' ')
```

This expression constructs a nameless object (§1.1/10) of type `string`. The object contains `maxlen + 1 - students[i].name.size()` characters, all of which are blank. This expression is similar to the definition of `spaces` in §1.2/13, but it omits the name of the variable. This omission effectively turns the definition into an expression. Writing `students[i].name` followed by this expression yields output that contains the characters in `students[i].name`, padded on the right to exactly `maxlen + 1` characters.

The `for` statement uses the index `i` to walk through `students` one element at a time. We get the name to write by indexing into `students` to get the current `Student_info` element. We then write the `name` member from that object, using an appropriately constructed `string` of blanks to pad the output.

Next we write the final grade for each student. If the student didn't do any homework, the grade computation will throw an exception. In that case, we `catch` the exception, and instead of writing a numeric grade, we write the message that was thrown as part of the exception object. Every one of the standard-library exceptions, such as `domain_error`, remembers the (optional) argument used to describe the problem that caused the exception to be thrown. Each of these types makes a copy of the contents of that argument available through a member function named `what`. The `catch` in this program gives a name to the exception object that it gets from `grade` (§4.1.2/54), so that it can write as output the message that it obtains from `what()`. In this case, that message will tell the user that the `student` has done no homework. If there is no exception, we use the `setprecision` manipulator to specify that we'll write three significant digits, and then write the result from `grade`.

4.3 Putting it all together

So far we have defined a number of abstractions (functions and a data structure) that are useful in solving our various grading problems. The only way we have seen of using these abstractions is to put all their definitions in a single file and compile that file. Obviously, this approach becomes complicated very quickly. To reduce that complexity, C++, like many languages, supports the notion of ***separate compilation***, which allows us to put our program into separate files and to compile each of these files independently.

We'll start by understanding how to package the `median` function so that others can use it. We begin by putting the definition of the `median` function into a file by itself so that we can compile it separately. That file must include declarations for all the names that the `median` function uses. From the library, `median` uses the `vector` type, the `sort` function, and the `domain_error` exception, so we will have to include the appropriate headers for these facilities:

```
//  source file for the median function
#include <algorithm>        //  to get the declaration of sort
#include <stdexcept>        //  to get the declaration of domain_error
#include <vector>           //  to get the declaration of vector

using std::domain_error;   using std::sort;    using std::vector;

//  compute the median of a vector<double>
double median(vector<double> vec)
{
      //  function body as defined in §4.1.1/53
}
```

As with any file, we must give our source file a name. The C++ standard does not tell us how to name source files, but in general, a source file's name should suggest its contents. Moreover, most implementations constrain source-file names, usually requiring the last few characters of the name to have a specific form. Implementations use these file suffixes to determine whether a file is a C++ source file. Most implementations require the names of C++ source files to end in `.cpp`, `.C`, or `.c`, so we might put the `median` function in a file named `median.cpp`, `median.C`, or `median.c`, depending on the implementation.

The next step is to make the `median` function available to other users. Analogous with the standard library, which puts the names it defines into headers, we can write our own ***header file*** that will allow users to access names that we define. For example, we could note in a file named `median.h` that our `median` function exists. If we did so, users could use it by writing:

```
//  a much better way to use median
#include "median.h"
#include <vector>

int main() { /* ... */  }
```

When we use a `#include` directive with double quotes rather than angle brackets, surrounding the header name, we are saying that we want the compiler to copy the entire contents of the header file that corresponds to that name into our program in place of the `#include` directive. Each implementation decides where to look for header files, and what the relationship is between the string between the quotes and the name of the file. We shall talk about "the header file `median.h`" as shorthand for "the file that the implementation decides is the one that corresponds to the name `median.h`."

It is worth noting that although we refer to our own headers as header files, we refer to the implementation-supplied headers as standard headers rather than standard header

files. The reason is that header files are genuine files in every C++ implementation, but
system headers need not be implemented as files. Even though the #include directive is
used to access both header files and system headers, there is no requirement that they be
implemented in the same way.

Now that we know we must supply a header file, the obvious question is what should
be in it. The simple answer is that we must write a ***declaration*** for the median function,
which we do by replacing the function body with a semicolon. We can also eliminate the
names of the parameters, because they are irrelevant without the function body:

```
double median(vector<double>);
```

Our median.h header cannot contain just this declaration; we must also include any
names that the declaration itself uses. This declaration uses vector, so we must make
sure that that name is available before the compiler sees our declaration:

```
// median.h
#include <vector>
double median(std::vector<double>);
```

We include the vector header so that we can use the name std::vector in declaring
the argument to median. The reason that we mention std::vector explicitly, rather
than writing a using-declaration, is more subtle.

In general, header files should declare only the names that are necessary. By restrict-
ing the names contained in a header file, we can preserve maximum flexibility for our
users. For example, we use the qualified name for std::vector because we have no
way of knowing how the user of our median function wants to refer to std::vector.
Users of our code might not want a using-declaration for vector. If we write one in
our header, then all programs that include our header get a using std::vector declaration, regardless of whether they wanted it. Header files should use fully qualified
names rather than using-declarations.

There is one last detail to cover: Header files should ensure that it is safe to include the
file more than once as part of compiling the program. As it happens, our header file is
already safe as it stands, because it contains only declarations. However, we consider it
good practice to cater to multiple inclusion in every header file, not just the ones that need
it. We do so by adding some preprocessor magic to the file:

```
#ifndef GUARD_median_h
#define GUARD_median_h

// median.h—final version
#include <vector>
double median(std::vector<double>);

#endif
```

The **#ifndef** *directive* checks whether GUARD_median_h is defined. This is the name of
a ***preprocessor variable***, which is one of a variety of ways of controlling how a program is
compiled. A full discussion of the preprocessor is beyond the scope of this book.

In this context, the #ifndef directive asks the preprocessor to process everything
between it and the next matching #endif if the given name is *not* defined. We must

choose a name that is unique in the entire program, so we make one from the name of our file and a string, such as GUARD_, that we hope will not be duplicated elsewhere.

The first time median.h is included in a program, GUARD_median_h will be undefined, so the preprocessor will look at the rest of the file. The first thing it does is to define GUARD_median_h, so that subsequent attempts to include median.h will have no effect.

The only other subtlety is that it is a good idea for the #ifndef to be the very first line of the file, without even a comment before it:

```
#ifndef variable
...
#endif
```

The reason is that some C++ implementations detect files that have this form and, if the *variable* is defined, do not even bother to read the file the second time around.

4.4 Partitioning the grading program

Now that we know how to arrange to compile the median function separately, the next step is to package our Student_info structure and associated functions:

```
#ifndef GUARD_Student_info
#define GUARD_Student_info

// Student_info.h header file
#include <iostream>
#include <string>
#include <vector>

struct Student_info {
    std::string name;
    double midterm, final;
    std::vector<double> homework;
};

bool compare(const Student_info&, const Student_info&);
std::istream& read(std::istream&, Student_info&);
std::istream& read_hw(std::istream&, std::vector<double>&);
#endif
```

Notice that we explicitly use std:: to qualify names from the standard library, rather than including using-declarations, and that Student_info.h declares the compare, read, and read_hw functions, which are closely associated with the Student_info structure. We will use these functions only if we are also using this structure, so it makes sense to package these functions with the structure definition.

The functions should be defined in a source file that will look something like:

```
// source file for Student_info-related functions
#include "Student_info.h"

using std::istream;   using std::vector;
```

```
bool compare(const Student_info& x, const Student_info& y)
{
    return x.name < y.name;
}

istream& read(istream& is, Student_info& s)
{
    // as defined in §4.2.2/62
}

istream& read_hw(istream& in, vector<double>& hw)
{
    // as defined in §4.1.3/57
}
```

Note that because we include the `Student_info.h` file, this file contains both declarations and definitions of our functions. This redundancy is harmless, and is actually a good idea. It gives the compiler the opportunity to check for consistency between the declarations and the definitions. These checks are not exhaustive in most implementations, because complete checking requires seeing the entire program, but they are useful enough to make it worthwhile for source files to include the corresponding header files.

The checking and its incompleteness stem from a common source: The language requires function declarations and definitions to match exactly in their result type, and in the number and types of parameters. This rule explains the implementation's ability to check—but why the incompleteness? The reason is that if a declaration and definition differ enough, the implementation can only assume that they describe two different versions of an overloaded function, and that the missing definition will appear elsewhere. For example, suppose we defined `median` as in §4.1.1/53, and we declared it incorrectly as

```
int median(std::vector<double>);  // return type should be double
```

If the compiler sees this declaration when it compiles the definition, it will complain, because it knows that the return type of `median(vector<double>)` cannot simultaneously be `double` and `int`. Suppose, however, that instead we had declared

```
double median(double);            // argument type should be vector<double>
```

Now the compiler can't complain, because `median(double)` could be defined elsewhere. If we call the function, then the implementation must eventually look for its definition. If it doesn't find the definition, it will complain at that point.

Note, too, that in the source file, there is no problem with `using`-declarations. Unlike a header file, a source file has no effect on the programs that use these functions. Hence reliance on `using`-declarations in a source file is purely a local decision.

What's left is to write a header file to declare the various overloaded `grade` functions:

```
#ifndef GUARD_grade_h
#define GUARD_grade_h

// grade.h
#include <vector>
#include "Student_info.h"
```

```
double grade(double, double, double);
double grade(double, double, const std::vector<double>&);
double grade(const Student_info&);

#endif
```

Notice how bringing the declarations of these overloaded functions together makes it easier to see all the alternatives. We will define all three functions in a single file, because they are closely related. Again, the name of the file will depend on the implementation, but will probably be grade.cpp, grade.C, or grade.c:

```
#include <stdexcept>
#include <vector>
#include "grade.h"
#include "median.h"
#include "Student_info.h"

using std::domain_error;  using std::vector;
```

    // *definitions for the* grade *functions from §4.1/52, §4.1.2/54 and §4.2.2/63*

4.5 The revised grading program

Finally we can write our complete program:

```
#include <algorithm>
#include <iomanip>
#include <ios>
#include <iostream>
#include <stdexcept>
#include <string>
#include <vector>
#include "grade.h"
#include "Student_info.h"

using std::cin;                    using std::setprecision;
using std::cout;                   using std::sort;
using std::domain_error;           using std::streamsize;
using std::endl;                   using std::string;
using std::max;                    using std::vector;

int main()
{
    vector<Student_info> students;
    Student_info record;
    string::size_type maxlen = 0;           // the length of the longest name

    // read and store all the students' data.
    // Invariant:    students contains all the student records read so far
    //               max contains the length of the longest name in students
    while (read(cin, record)) {
        // find length of longest name
        maxlen = max(maxlen, record.name.size());
        students.push_back(record);
    }
```

```
// alphabetize the student records
sort(students.begin(), students.end(), compare);

// write the names and grades
for (vector<Student_info>::size_type i = 0;
        i != students.size(); ++i) {

    // write the name, padded on the right to maxlen + 1 characters
    cout << students[i].name
            << string(maxlen + 1 - students[i].name.size(), ' ');

    // compute and write the grade
    try {
        double final_grade = grade(students[i]);
        streamsize prec = cout.precision();
        cout << setprecision(3) << final_grade
                << setprecision(prec);
    } catch (domain_error e) {
        cout << e.what();
    }
    cout << endl;
}
return 0;
}
```

This program should be fairly straightforward to understand. As usual, we start with the necessary `includes` and `using`-declarations. Of course, we need mention only those headers and declarations that we use in this source file. In this program, we have our own headers to include as well as library headers. Those headers make available the definition of the `Student_info` type, and declarations for the functions that we use to manipulate `Student_info` objects and generate grades. The `main` function itself is the same as the one that we presented in §4.2.3/64.

4.6 Details

Program structure:

`#include <`*system-header*`>`

> Angle brackets, < >, enclose system headers. System headers may or may not be implemented as files.

`#include "`*user-defined-header-file-name*`"`

> User-defined header files are `included` by enclosing the name in quotes. Typically, user-defined headers have a suffix of `.h`.

Header files should be guarded against multiple inclusion by wrapping the file in an `#ifndef GUARD_`*header_name* directive. Headers should avoid declaring names that they do not use. In particular, they should not include `using`-declarations, but instead should prefix standard-library names with `std::` explicitly.

Types:

`T&`

> Denotes a reference to the type `T`. Most commonly used to pass a parameter that a function may change. Arguments to such parameters must be lvalues.

`const T&`   Denotes a reference to the type `T` that may not be used to change the value to which the reference is bound. Usually used to avoid cost of copying a parameter to a function.

Structures: A structure is a type that contains zero or more members. Each object of the structure type contains its own instance of each of its members.

Every structure must have a corresponding definition:

```
struct type-name {
        type-specifier member-name;
        . . .
};      // note the semicolon
```

Like all definitions, a structure definition may appear only once per source file, so it should normally appear in a properly guarded header file.

Functions: A function must be declared in every source file that uses it, and defined only once. The declarations and definitions have similar forms:

```
ret-type function-name (parm-decls) ;              // function declaration

[ inline ] ret-type function-name (parm-decls)  {    // function definition
        // function body goes here
}
```

Here, *ret-type* is the type that the function returns, *parm-decls* is a comma-separated list of the types for the parameters of the function. Functions must be declared before they are called. Each argument's type must be compatible with the corresponding parameter. A different syntax is necessary to declare or define functions with sufficiently complicated return types; see §A.1.2/297 for the full story.

Function names may be overloaded: The same *function-name* may define multiple functions so long as the functions differ in the number or types of the parameters. The implementation can distinguish between a reference and a `const` reference to the same type.

We can optionally qualify a function definition with **inline**, which asks the compiler to expand calls to the function inline when appropriate—that is, to avoid function-call overhead by replacing each call to the function by a copy of the function body, modified as necessary. To do so, the compiler needs to be able to see the function definition, so `inline`s are usually defined in header files, rather than in source files.

Exception handling:

`try { // code`   Initiates a block that might `throw` an exception.
`} catch(t) { /* code */ }`
                    Concludes the `try` block and handles exceptions that match the type `t`. The code following the `catch` performs whatever action is appropriate to handle the exception reported in `t`.
`throw e;`   Terminates the current function; `throws` the value `e` back to the caller.

Exception classes: The library defines several exception classes whose names suggest the kinds of problems they might be used to report:

```
logic_error     domain_error    invalid_argument
length_error    out_of_range    runtime_error
range_error     overflow_error  underflow_error
```

e.what()   Returns a value that reports on what happened to cause the error.

Library facilities:

s1 < s2   Compares strings s1 and s2 by applying dictionary ordering.

s.width(n)   Sets the width of stream s to n for the next output operation (or leaves it unchanged if n is omitted). The output is padded on the left to the given width. Returns the previous width. The standard output operators use the existing width value and then call width(0) to reset the width.

setw(n)   Returns a value of type streamsize (§3.1/36) that, when written on an output stream s, has the effect of calling s.width(n).

Exercises

4-0. Compile, execute, and test the programs in this chapter.

4-1. We noted in §4.2.3/65 that it is essential that the argument types in a call to max match exactly. Will the following code work? If there is a problem, how would you fix it?

```
int maxlen;
Student_info s;
max(s.name.size(), maxlen);
```

4-2. Write a program to calculate the squares of int values up to 100. The program should write two columns: The first lists the value; the second contains the square of that value. Use setw (described above) to manage the output so that the values line up in columns.

4-3. What happens if we rewrite the previous program to allow values up to but not including 1000 but neglect to change the arguments to setw? Rewrite the program to be more robust in the face of changes that allow i to grow without adjusting the setw arguments.

4-4. Now change your squares program to use double values instead of ints. Use manipulators to manage the output so that the values line up in columns.

4-5. Write a function that reads words from an input stream and stores them in a vector. Use that function both to write programs that count the number of words in the input, and to count how many times each word occurred.

4-6. Rewrite the Student_info structure, and the read and grade functions, so that they calculate each student's grades as part of reading the input, and store only the final grade.

4-7. Write a program to calculate the average of the numbers stored in a vector<double>.

4-8. If the following code is legal, what can we infer about the return type of f?

```
double d = f()[n];
```

5

Using sequential containers and analyzing strings

We've made a fair start on the core C++ language, and we've learned something about the `string` and `vector` classes as well. We can solve a lot of problems with just these tools.

In this chapter, we'll expand our focus beyond these facilities, and start to understand in more depth how to use the library. As we'll see, the facilities that the library provides can help us solve messier problems than the ones that we've confronted so far.

Not only does the standard library provide useful data structures and functions, but it also reflects a consistent architecture: Once we have learned how one kind of container behaves, we are well on our way to understanding how to use all the library containers.

For example, as we'll see in the second half of this chapter, we can often use a `string` as if it were a `vector`. Many useful operations on one library type are logically the same as the operations on another. The library is constructed so that such equivalent operations work the same way on different types.

5.1 Separating students into categories

Let's revisit our student-grading problem from §4.2/61, supposing this time that not only do we wish to calculate all the students' grades, but we would also like to know which students failed the course. The idea is that if we have a `vector` of `Student_info` records, we would like to extract the ones for students who failed the course, and store those records in another `vector`. We also want to remove the data for failing students from the original `vector`, so that it will contain only records for students who passed.

We'll start by writing a simple function to test whether a student failed:

```
//  predicate to determine whether a student failed
bool fgrade(const Student_info& s)
{
    return grade(s) < 60;
}
```

We use the `grade` function from §4.2.2/63 to calculate the grade, and we arbitrarily define a failing grade as one that is less than 60.

The most straightforward approach to solving our overall problem is to examine each student record and push it onto one of two `vectors`, one for students with passing grades and the other for students with failing grades:

```
// separate passing and failing student records: first try
vector<Student_info> extract_fails(vector<Student_info>& students)
{
    vector<Student_info> pass, fail;

    for (vector<Student_info>::size_type i = 0;
         i != students.size(); ++i)
        if (fgrade(students[i]))
            fail.push_back(students[i]);
        else
            pass.push_back(students[i]);

    students = pass;
    return fail;
}
```

Of course, before we can compile this code, we must add `#include` directives and `using`-declarations for the names that we are using. In general, we will no longer show these statements in code that we present. When we use a new header, though, we will continue to mention it.

Like the `read_hw` and `read` functions from Chapter 4, this function effectively has two outputs: One is the `vector<Student_info>` that we return, which contains the records for students who failed; the other is created as a side effect of calling `extract_fails`. The function's parameter is a reference, so changes to the parameter are reflected in the argument. When the function finishes, the `vector` that was passed as an argument will contain records only for students who passed the course.

The function works by creating two `vectors`, which hold the data for passing and failing students respectively. The function looks at each record in `students`, and appends a copy of that record to `pass` or `fail` depending on the student's grade.

After the `for` statement is finished, we copy the passing records back into `students`, obliterating the previous contents of `students`, and return the failing records.

5.1.1 Erasing elements in place

Our `extract_fails` function does what we want, and is reasonably efficient, but it has a subtle flaw: It requires enough memory to hold two copies of each student record. The reason is that as it builds up `pass` and `fail`, the original records are still around. When the function is done with its `for` statement, and is ready to copy the results and return, there are two copies of each student record.

We would like to avoid keeping multiple copies of data around any longer than necessary. One way to do so is to eliminate `pass` entirely. Instead of creating two `vectors`, we will create a single local variable, named `fail`, to hold the value that we intend to return. For each record in `students`, we will compute the grade. If it is a passing grade, we'll leave the record alone; if it's a failing grade, we'll append a copy of it to `fail` and remove it from `students`.

To use this strategy, we need a way to remove an element from a `vector`. The good news is that such a facility exists; the bad news is that removing elements from `vector`s is slow enough to argue against using this approach for large amounts of input data. If the data we process get really big, performance degrades to an astonishing extent.

For example, if all of our students were to fail, the execution time of the function that we are about to see would grow proportionally to the square of the number of students. That means that for a class of 100 students, the program would take 10,000 times as long to run as it would for one student. The problem is that our input records are stored in a `vector`, which is optimized for fast random access. One price of that optimization is that it can be expensive to insert or delete elements other than at the end of the `vector`.

We shall see two ways to solve the performance problem: We can use a data structure that is better suited to our algorithm, or we can use a smarter algorithm that avoids the overhead of our initial design. From here through §5.5.2/87, we'll develop a solution that uses a more appropriate data structure. We'll show an algorithmic solution in §6.3/116.

Before we can understand why these solutions are improvements, we must have something to improve. Therefore, we'll begin by looking at the slow but direct solution:

```
// second try: correct but potentially slow
vector<Student_info> extract_fails(vector<Student_info>& students)
{
    vector<Student_info> fail;
    vector<Student_info>::size_type i = 0;

    // invariant: elements [0, i) of students represent passing grades
    while (i != students.size()) {
        if (fgrade(students[i])) {
            fail.push_back(students[i]);
            students.erase(students.begin() + i);
        } else
            ++i;
    }
    return fail;
}
```

We begin this version by creating `fail`, which is the `vector` into which we'll copy the records for students with failing grades. We next define `i`, which we'll use as an index into `students`. We'll process each record, iterating through `students` until we've seen all the entries in `students`.

For each record in `students`, we determine whether it represents a failing grade. If so, then we need to copy that record into `fail` and remove it from `students`. The `push_back` call to append a copy of `students[i]` to `fail` is nothing new. What is new is the way we remove the element from `students`:

```
students.erase(students.begin() + i);
```

The `vector` type includes a member named `erase`, which removes an element from the `vector`. The argument to `erase` indicates which element to remove. As it happens, there is no version of the `erase` function that operates on indices, because, as we shall see in §5.5/85, not all containers support indices, and it is more useful for the library to offer a form of `erase` that will work the same way with all containers. Instead, the `erase` function takes a type that we shall discuss in §5.2.1/80. What's important to understand now is that we can indicate which element to erase by adding our index to the value returned by `students.begin()`. Recall that `students.begin()` returns a value that denotes the `vector`'s initial element—the one with index `0`. If we add an integer, such as `i`, to that value, the result denotes the element with index `i`. We can now see that this call to `erase` removes the `i`th element from `students`.

Once we have removed an element from the `vector`, the `vector` now has one fewer element than it did before:

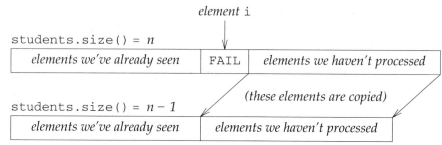

In addition to changing the size of the `vector`, `erase` removes the element with index `i`, thereby causing `i` to denote the next element in the sequence. Each element after position `i` is copied to the preceding position. Thus, although `i` does not change, `erase` has the effect of adjusting the index to denote the next element in the `vector`, which means that we must not increment it for the next iteration.

If the record we're looking at does not contain a failing grade, then we want to leave it in `students`. In that case, we must increment `i`, so that `i` will refer to the next record on the next trip through the `while`.

We determine whether we have seen all the records in `students` by comparing `i` with `students.size()`. When we erase an element from the `vector`, the `vector` has one fewer element than it did before. Therefore, it is essential that we call `students.size` on each trip through the condition. If, instead, we precomputed and stored the result of `size`

```
//  this code will fail because of misguided optimization
vector<Student_info>::size_type size = students.size();
while (i != size) {
    if (fgrade(students[i])) {
        fail.push_back(students[i]);
        students.erase(students.begin() + i);
    } else
        ++i;
}
```

our program would fail, because calling `erase` would have changed the number of elements in `students`. If we precomputed the `size` and actually `erased` any records for failing students, then we would make too many trips through `students`, and the references to `students[i]` would be to nonexistent elements! Fortunately, calls to `size()` are usually fast, so the expected overhead from calling `size` each time is negligible.

5.1.2 Sequential versus random access

Both versions of our `extract_fails` function share a property with many programs that work with containers, which property is not immediately obvious from the code: Each of these functions accesses container elements only sequentially. That is, each version of the function looks at each student record in turn, decides what to do with it, and then proceeds to the next record.

The reason that this property is not obvious from the code is that the function uses an integer, `i`, to access each element of `students`. It is possible to compute the value of an integer in arbitrary ways, which means that in order for us to determine whether we are accessing the container sequentially, we must look at every operation that might affect the value of `i`, and determine that operation's effect. Another way to view the problem is that when we write `students[i]` to access an element of `students`, we are implicitly saying that we might access `students`'s elements in any order, not just sequentially.

The reason we care about the sequence in which we access container elements is that different types of containers have different performance characteristics and support different operations. If we know that our program uses only those operations that a particular type of container supports efficiently, then we can make our program more efficient by using that kind of container.

In other words, because our function requires only sequential access, we do not need to use indices, which provide the ability to access any element randomly. Instead, we'd like to rewrite the function so as to restrict access to the container elements to operations that support only sequential access. To that end, the C++ library supplies an assortment of types called iterators, which allow access to data structures in ways that the library can control. This control lets the library ensure efficient implementation.

5.2 Iterators

To make our discussion more concrete, let us look at the container operations that `extract_fails` actually uses.

The first such operation is using the index i to fetch values from the `Student_info` structure. For example, `fgrade(students[i])` fetches the ith element of the `vector` named `students`, and passes that element to the `fgrade` function. We know that we access the elements of `students` sequentially, because we access those elements only by using i as an index, and the only operations we ever perform on i are to read it in order to compare it with the size of the `vector`, and to increment it:

```
while (i != students.size()) {
    // work gets done here; but doesn't change the value of i
    ++i;
}
```

From this usage, it is clear that we use i only sequentially.

Unfortunately, even though we know this fact, the library has no way to know it. By using iterators instead of indices, we can make that knowledge available to the library. An *iterator* is a value that

- Identifies a container and an element in the container
- Lets us examine the value stored in that element
- Provides operations for moving between elements in the container
- Restricts the available operations in ways that correspond to what the container can handle efficiently

Because iterators behave analogously to indices, we can often rewrite programs that use indices to make them use iterators instead. As an example, suppose that students is a vector<Student_info> that contains records for some students. Let's look at how we could write those students' names onto cout. One way uses an index for the iteration:

```
for (vector<Student_info>::size_type i = 0;
     i != students.size(); ++i)
   cout << students[i].name << endl;
```

Another way uses iterators:

```
for (vector<Student_info>::const_iterator iter = students.begin();
     iter != students.end(); ++iter) {
   cout << (*iter).name << endl;
}
```

There's quite a lot going on in this rewrite, so let's pick it apart a bit at a time.

5.2.1 Iterator types

Every standard container, such as vector, defines two associated iterator types:

```
container-type::const_iterator
container-type::iterator
```

where *container-type* is the container type, such as vector<Student_info>, that includes the type of the container elements. When we want to use an iterator to change the values stored in the container, we use the iterator type. If we need only read access, then we use the const_iterator type.

Abstraction is selective ignorance. The details of what particular type an iterator has may be complicated, but we don't need to understand these details. All we need to know is how to refer to the iterator type, and what operations the iterator allows. We need to know the type so that we can create variables that are iterators. We don't need to know anything about that type's implementation. For example, our definition of iter

```
vector<Student_info>::const_iterator iter = students.begin();
```

says that iter is of type vector<Student_info>::const_iterator. We don't know the *actual* type of iter—that's an implementation detail of vector—nor do we need to know. All that we need to know is that vector<Student_info> has a member named `const_iterator` that defines a type that we can use to obtain read-only access to elements of the `vector`.

The other thing we need to know is that there is an automatic conversion from type `iterator` to type `const_iterator`. As we're about to learn, `students.begin()` returns an `iterator`, but we said that `iter` is a `const_iterator`. In order to initialize `iter` with the value of `students.begin()`, the implementation converts the `iterator` value into the corresponding `const_iterator`. This conversion is one way, meaning that we can convert an `iterator` to a `const_iterator` but not vice versa.

5.2.2 Iterator operations

Having defined `iter`, we set it to the value of `students.begin()`. We have used the `begin` and `end` functions before, so we should know what these functions do: They return a value that denotes the beginning or (one past) the end of a container. We'll explain our repeated emphasis on "(one past)" in §8.2.7/149. What's useful to know now is that `begin` and `end` functions return a value of the iterator type for the container. Thus, `begin` returns a `vector<Student_info>::iterator` positioned at the initial element of the container, so `iter` initially refers to the first element in `students`.

The condition in the `for` statement,

```
iter != students.end()
```

checks whether we've reached the end of the container. Recall that `end` returns a value that denotes (one past) the end of the container. As with `begin`, the type of this value is `vector<Student_info>::iterator`. We can compare two iterators, `const` or not, for inequality (or equality). If `iter` is equal to the value returned by `students.end()`, then we're through.

The last expression in the `for` header, `++iter`, increments the iterator so that it refers to the next element in `students` on the next trip through the `for`. The expression `++iter` uses the increment operator, overloaded for the iterator type. The increment operator has the effect of advancing the iterator to the next element in the container. We don't know, and shouldn't care, how the increment operator works. All that we need to know is that afterward, the iterator denotes the next element in the container.

In the body of the `for`, `iter` is positioned on an element in `students`, which element we need to write. We access that element by calling the *dereference* operator, `*`. When applied to an iterator, the `*` operator returns an lvalue (§4.1.3/56) that is the element to which the iterator refers. Therefore, the output operation

```
cout << (*iter).name
```

has the effect of writing the current element's `name` member on the standard output.

In order to execute correctly, this expression requires parentheses that override the normal operator precedence. The expression `*iter` returns the value that the iterator `iter` denotes. The precedence of `.` is higher than the precedence of `*`, which means that if we want the `*` operation to apply only to the left operand of the `.`, we must enclose `*iter` in parentheses to get `(*iter)`. If we wrote `*iter.name`, the compiler would treat it as `*(iter.name)`, which would be a request to fetch the `name` member from object `iter`, and apply the dereference operator to that object. The compiler would complain because `iter` does not have a member named `name`. By writing `(*iter).name`, we say that we want to refer to the `name` member of the `*iter` object.

5.2.3 Some syntactic sugar

In the code we just saw, we dereferenced an iterator, and then fetched an element from the value returned. This combination of operations is so common that there is an abbreviation for it: Instead of

```
(*iter).name
```

we can write

```
iter->name
```

We can use this syntactic sugar to rewrite the last example in §5.2/80:

```
for (vector<Student_info>::const_iterator iter = students.begin();
        iter != students.end(); ++iter) {
    cout << iter->name << endl;
}
```

5.2.4 The meaning of `students.erase(students.begin() + i)`

Now that we understand more about iterators, we can see the real point of

```
students.erase(students.begin() + i);
```

in the program in §5.1.1/77. We've already seen that `students.begin()` is an iterator that refers to the initial element of `students`, and that `students.begin() + i` refers to the `i`th element of `students`. What is important to realize is that this latter expression gets its meaning from the definition of + on the types of `students.begin()` and `i`. In other words, the iterator and index types determine the meaning of + in this expression.

If `students` were a container that did not support random-access indexing, it is likely that `students.begin()` would be of a type that did not have + defined—in which case the expression `students.begin() + i` would not compile. In effect, such a container would be able to shut off random access to its elements, while still allowing sequential access through iterators.

5.3 Using iterators instead of indices

Using what we have learned about iterators, and one more new fact, we can reimplement the `extract_fails` function in a way that does not use indexing at all:

```
// version 3: iterators but no indexing; still potentially slow
vector<Student_info> extract_fails(vector<Student_info>& students)
{
    vector<Student_info> fail;
    vector<Student_info>::iterator iter = students.begin();
```

```
        while (iter != students.end()) {
            if (fgrade(*iter)) {
                fail.push_back(*iter);
                iter = students.erase(iter);
            } else
                ++iter;
        }
        return fail;
    }
```

We start by defining `fail` as we did before. Next, we define the iterator, named `iter`, that we'll use—in place of an index—to look at the elements in `students`. Note that we give it type `iterator` instead of `const_iterator`:

```
vector<Student_info>::iterator iter = students.begin();
```

because we intend to use it to modify `students`, which we do in the call to `erase`. We initialize `iter` to denote the first element in `students`.

We continue with a `while` statement that will look at every element of `students`. Remember that `iter` is an iterator that denotes an element in the container, so `*iter` is the value of that element. To decide whether a student passed or failed, we pass that value to `fgrade`. Similarly, we changed the code that copies the failing records into `fail` by writing

```
fail.push_back(*iter);          // dereference the iterator to get the element
```

instead of

```
fail.push_back(students[i]);   // index into the vector to get the element
```

The `erase` has gotten simpler, because we now have an iterator to pass directly:

```
iter = students.erase(iter);
```

We no longer have to calculate an iterator by adding the index `i` to `students.begin()`.

The new fact that we used here is easy to overlook, but crucially important: We now assign to `iter` the value that `erase` returns. Why?

A bit of thinking should convince us that removing the element that `iter` denoted must *invalidate* that iterator. After we have called `students.erase(iter)`, we know that `iter` can no longer refer to the same element because that element is gone. In fact, calling `erase` on a `vector` invalidates all iterators that refer to elements after the one that was just `erase`d. If you look back at the diagram in §5.1.1/78, it should be obvious that after we `erase` the element marked `FAIL`, that element is gone, and each of the elements after it has moved. If the elements have moved, any iterators referring to them must be meaningless as well.

Fortunately, `erase` returns an iterator that is positioned on the element that follows the one that we just erased. Therefore, executing

```
iter = students.erase(iter);
```

makes `iter` refer to the element after the erasure, which is exactly what we need.

If we're dealing with an element that did not represent a failing grade, then we still need to increment `iter` so that we'll be positioned on the next element for the next trip through the loop. We do so by incrementing `iter` in the `else` branch.

Incidentally, as in §5.1.1/78, we might be tempted to optimize the loop by saving the value of `students.end()` to avoid evaluating it each time through the `while`. In other words, we might be tempted to change

```
while (iter != students.end())
```

to

```
// this code will fail because of misguided optimization
vector<Student_info>::iterator iter = students.begin(),
                            end_iter = students.end();
while (iter != end_iter) {
    // ...
}
```

This loop will almost surely fail at run time. Why?

The reason is that if we ever execute `students.erase`, doing so will invalidate every iterator after the point erased, including `end_iter`! Therefore, it is essential that we call `students.end` each time through the loop, just as it was essential in §5.1.1/78 to call `students.size` each time through the loop.

5.4 Rethinking our data structure for better performance

For small inputs, our implementation works fine. However, as we said in §5.1.1/77, as our input grows, the performance degrades substantially. Why?

Let's think again about using `erase` to remove an element from a `vector`. The library optimizes the `vector` data structure for fast access to arbitrary elements. Moreover, we saw in §3.2.3/48 that `vector`s perform well when growing a `vector` one element at a time, as long as elements are added at the *end* of the `vector`.

Inserting or removing elements from the interior of a `vector` is another story. Doing so requires that all elements after the one inserted or removed be moved in order to preserve fast random access. Moving elements means that the run time of our new code might be as slow as quadratic in the number of elements in the `vector`. For small inputs, we might not notice, but each time the size of our input doubles, the execution time can quadruple. If we ask our program to deal with all the students in a school rather than just the students in a class, even a fast computer will take too long to execute the program.

If we want to do better, we need a data structure that lets us insert and delete elements efficiently anywhere in the container. Such a container is unlikely to support random access through indices. Even if it did so, integer indices would be less than useful, because inserting and deleting elements would have to change the indices of other elements. Now that we know how to use iterators, we have a way of dealing with such a data structure that does not provide index operations.

5.5 The list type

By rewriting the code to use iterators, we have removed our reliance on indices. We now need to reimplement our program using a data structure that will let us delete elements efficiently from within the container.

The need to insert or delete elements inside a data structure is pretty common. Not surprisingly, the library provides a type, named list and defined in the <list> header, that is optimized for this kind of access.

Just as vectors are optimized for fast random access, lists are optimized for fast insertion and deletion anywhere within the container. Because lists have to maintain a more complicated structure, they are slower than vectors if the container is accessed only sequentially. That is, if the container grows and shrinks only or primarily from the end, a vector will outperform a list. However, if a program deletes many elements from the middle of the container—as our program does—then lists will be faster for large inputs, becoming much faster as the inputs grow.

Like a vector, a list is a container that can hold objects of most any type. As we'll see, lists and vectors share many operations. As a result, we can often translate programs that operate on vectors into programs that operate on lists, and vice versa. Often, all that changes is our variables' types.

One key operation that vectors support, but lists do not, is indexing. As we just saw, we can write a version of extract_fails that uses vectors to extract records that correspond to failing students, but that uses iterators instead of indices. It turns out that we can transform that version of extract_fails to use lists instead of vectors merely by changing the appropriate types:

```
// version 4: use list instead of vector
list<Student_info> extract_fails(list<Student_info>& students)
{
    list<Student_info> fail;
    list<Student_info>::iterator iter = students.begin();

    while (iter != students.end()) {
        if (fgrade(*iter)) {
            fail.push_back(*iter);
            iter = students.erase(iter);
        } else
            ++iter;
    }
    return fail;
}
```

If we compare this code with the version from §5.3/82, we see that the only change is to replace vector by list in the first four lines. So, for example, the return type and the parameter to the function are now list<Student_info>, as is the local container fail, into which we put the failing grades. Similarly, the type of the iterator is the one defined by the list class. Hence, we define iter as the iterator type that is a member of list<Student_info>. The list type is a template, so we must say what kind of object the `list` holds by naming that type inside angle brackets, just as we do when we define a `vector`.

There are no changes in the program's logic. Of course, our caller will now have to provide us with a `list`, and will get a `list` in return. Moreover, the details of how the library implements the operations are quite different, because this version operates on `lists` and the other ones operate on `vectors`. When we execute `++iter`, we are doing whatever it means to advance the iterator to the next element in the `list`. Similarly,

```
iter = students.erase(iter);
```

calls the `list` version of `erase` and assigns the `list` iterator returned from `erase` into `iter`. The implementations of the increment and `erase` operations will surely differ from their `vector` counterparts.

5.5.1 Some important differences

One important way in which the operations on `lists` differ from those on `vectors` is the effect of some of the operations on iterators. For example, when we `erase` an element from a `vector`, all iterators that refer to the element erased, or subsequent elements, are invalidated. Using `push_back` to append an element to a `vector` invalidates all iterators referring to that `vector`. This behavior follows from the fact that erasing an element moves the following elements, and appending to a `vector` might reallocate the entire `vector` to make room for the new element. Loops that use these operations must be especially careful to ensure that they have not saved copies of any iterators that may be invalidated. Inappropriately saving the value of `students.end()` is a particularly rich source of bugs.

For `lists`, on the other hand, the `erase` and `push_back` operations do not invalidate iterators to other elements. Only iterators that refer to the element actually `erased` are invalidated, because that element no longer exists.

We have already mentioned that `list` class iterators do not support full random-access properties. We'll have much more to say about iterator properties in §8.2.1/144. For now, what's important to know is that, because of this lack of support, we cannot use the standard-library `sort` function to sort values that are stored in a `list`. Because of this restriction, the `list` class provides its own `sort` member function, which uses an algorithm that is optimized for sorting data stored in a `list`. Thus, to sort elements in a `list`, we must call the `sort` member

```
list<Student_info> students;
students.sort(compare);
```

rather than the global `sort` function

```
vector<Student_info> students;
sort(students.begin(), students.end(), compare);
```

as we do for `vectors`. It is worth noting that because the `compare` function operates on `Student_info` objects, we can use the same `compare` function to `sort` a `list` of `Student_info` records that we used to sort a `vector` of them.

5.5.2 Why bother?

The code that extracts records for failing students is a good example of the effect of data structure choices on performance. The code accesses elements sequentially, which generally implies that a `vector` is the best choice. On the other hand, we also delete elements from the interior of the container, thus favoring `list`s.

As with any performance-related question, the data structure that is "best" depends on whether performance even matters. Performance is a tricky subject that is generally outside the scope of this book, but it is worth noting that the choice of data structure can have a profound effect on a program's performance. For small inputs, `list`s are slower than `vector`s. For large inputs, a program that uses `vector`s in an inappropriate way can run much more slowly than it would if it were to use `list`s. It can be surprising how quickly performance degrades as the input grows.

To test our programs' performance, we used three files of student records. The first file had 735 records. The second file was ten times as big, and the third, ten times bigger than that, or 73,500 records. The following table records the time, in seconds, that it took to execute the programs on each file size:

File size	list	vector
735	0.1	0.1
7,350	0.8	6.7
73,500	8.8	597.1

For the file with 73,500 records, the `list` version of the program took less than nine seconds to run, whereas the `vector` version took nearly ten minutes. The discrepancy would have been even greater had there been more failing students.

5.6 Taking `strings` apart

Now that we've seen some of what we can do with containers, we're going to turn our attention back to `strings`. Until now, we've done only a few things with `strings`: We've created them, read them, concatenated them, written them, and looked at their size. In each of these uses, we have dealt with the `string` as a single entity. Often, this kind of abstract usage is what we want: We want to ignore the detailed contents of a `string`. Sometimes, though, we need to look at the specific characters in a `string`.

As it turns out, we can think of a `string` as a special kind of container: It contains only characters, and it supports some, but not all, of the container operations. The operations that it does support include indexing, and the `string` type provides an iterator that is similar to a `vector` iterator. Thus, many of the techniques that we can apply to `vectors` apply also to `strings`.

For example, we might want to break a line of input into words, separated from each other by whitespace (space, tab, backspace, or the end of the line). If we can read the input directly, we can get the words from the input trivially. After all, that's exactly how the `string` input operator executes: It reads characters up to the whitespace character.

However, there are times when we want to read an entire line of input and examine the words within that line. We'll see examples in §7.3/126 and §7.4.2/131.

Because such an operation might be generally useful, we'll write a function to do it. The function will take a string and return a vector<string>, which will contain an entry for each whitespace-separated word in that string. In order to understand this function, you need to know that strings support indexing much the same way as vectors do. So, for example, if s is a string that contains at least one character, the first character of s is s[0], and the last character of s is s[s.size() - 1].

Our function will define two indices, i and j, that will delimit each word in turn. The idea is that we will locate a word by computing values for i and j such that the word will be the characters in the range [i, j). For example,

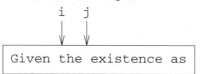

Once we have these indices, we'll use the characters that they delimit to create a new string, which we will copy into our vector. When we are done, we will return the vector to our caller:

```
vector<string> split(const string& s)
{
    vector<string> ret;
    typedef string::size_type string_size;
    string_size i = 0;

    // invariant: we have processed characters [original value of i, i)
    while (i != s.size()) {
        // ignore leading blanks
        // invariant: characters in range [original i, current i) are all spaces
        while (i != s.size() && isspace(s[i]))
            ++i;

        // find end of next word
        string_size j = i;
        // invariant: none of the characters in range [original j, current j) is a space
        while (j != s.size() && !isspace(s[j]))
            ++j;

        // if we found some nonwhitespace characters
        if (i != j) {
            // copy from s starting at i and taking j − i chars
            ret.push_back(s.substr(i, j - i));
            i = j;
        }

    }
    return ret;
}
```

In addition to the system headers that we have already encountered, this code needs the `<cctype>` header, which defines `isspace`. More generally, this header defines useful functions for processing individual characters. The c at the beginning of `cctype` is a reminder that the `ctype` facility is part of C++'s inheritance from C.

The `split` function has a single parameter, which is a reference to a `const string` that we'll name `s`. Because we will be copying words from `s`, `split` does not need to change the `string`. As in §4.1.2/54, we can pass a `const` reference to avoid the cost of copying the `string`, while still ensuring that `split` will not change its argument.

We start off by defining `ret`, which will hold the words from the input `string`. The next two statements define and initialize our first index, `i`. As we saw in §2.4/22, `string::size_type` is the name for the appropriate type to index a `string`. Because we need to use this type more than once, we start by defining a shorter synonym for this type, as we did in §3.2.2/43, to simplify the subsequent declarations. We will use `i` as the index that finds the start of each word, advancing `i` through the input `string` one word at a time.

The test in the outermost `while` ensures that once we've processed the last word in the input, we'll stop.

Inside the `while`, we start by positioning our two indices. First, we find the first non-space character in `s` that is at or after the position currently indicated by `i`. Because there might be multiple whitespace characters in the input, we increment `i` until it denotes a character that is not whitespace.

There is a lot going on in this statement:

```
while (i != s.size() && isspace(s[i]))
    ++i;
```

The `isspace` function is a predicate that takes a `char` and returns a value that indicates whether that `char` is whitespace. The `&&` operator tests whether both its operands are `true`, failing if either of them is `false`. In this expression, the operation will succeed if `i` is not equal to the size of `s` (meaning that we have not reached the end of the `string`), and `s[i]` is a whitespace character. In that case, we will increment `i` and check again.

As we described in §2.4.2.2/26, the logical `&&` operation uses a short-circuit strategy for evaluating its operands. Unlike our earlier examples, this one relies on the short-circuit property of `&&`. The binary logical operations (operators `&&` and `||`) execute by testing their left-hand operands first. If that test suffices to determine the overall result, then the right-hand operand is not evaluated. In the case of the `&&`, the second condition is evaluated if and only if the first condition is `true`. Thus, the condition in the `while` executes by first checking whether `i != s.size()`. Only if this test succeeds does it use `i` to look at a character in `s`. Of course, if `i` is equal to `s.size()`, then there are no more characters left to examine, and so we drop out of the loop.

Once we fall out of this `while`, we know either that `i` denotes a character that is not whitespace, or that we've run out of input without finding such a character.

Assuming that `i` is still a valid index, the next `while` will find the space that terminates the current word in `s`. We start by creating our other index, `j`, and initializing it to the value of `i`. The next `while`,

```
while (j != s.size() && !isspace(s[j]))
    ++j;
```

executes similarly to the previous one, but this time the `while` stops when it encounters a whitespace character. As before, we start by ensuring that `j` is still in range. If so, we again call `isspace` on the character indexed by `j`. This time, we negate the return from `isspace` using the *logical negation* operator, `!`. In other words, we want the condition to be true if `isspace(s[j])` is *not* true.

Having completed the two inner `while` loops, we know that we have either found another word or run out of input while looking for a word. If we have run out of input, then both `i` and `j` will be equal to `s.size()`. Otherwise, we have found a word, which we must push onto `ret`:

```
//  if we found some nonwhitespace characters
if (i != j) {
    //  copy from s starting at i and taking j − i chars
    ret.push_back(s.substr(i, j - i));
    i = j;
}
```

The call to `push_back` uses a member of the `string` class, named `substr`, that we have not previously seen. It takes an index and a length, and creates a new `string` that contains a copy of characters from the initial `string`, starting at the index given by the first argument, and copying as many characters as indicated by its second argument. The substring that we extract starts at `i`, which is the first character in the word that we just found. We copy characters from s starting with the one indexed by `i`, and continuing until we have copied the characters in the (half-open) range `[i, j)`. Remembering from §2.6/31 that the number of elements in a half-open range is the difference between the bounds, we see that we will copy exactly `j - i` characters.

5.7 Testing our `split` function

Having written our function, we'd like to test it. The easiest way to do so is to write a program that reads a line of input and passes that line to the `split` function. We can then write the contents of the `vector` that `split` returns. Such a test program will make it easy to inspect the output, and to verify that the `split` function generates the words that we expect.

More usefully, this test function should produce the same results as a program that just reads words from the standard input and writes the words one per output line. We can write this latter program, run it and our test program on the same input files, and verify that our programs generate identical output. If so, we can be fairly confident in our `split` function.

Let's start by writing the test program for `split`:

```
int main()
{
    string s;
```

```
// read and split each line of input
while (getline(cin, s)) {
    vector<string> v = split(s);

    // write each word in v
    for (vector<string>::size_type i = 0; i != v.size(); ++i)
        cout << v[i] << endl;
}
return 0;
}
```

This program needs to read the input an entire line at a time. Fortunately, the string library provides what we need in the getline function, which reads input until it reaches the end of the line. The getline function takes two arguments. The first is the istream from which to read; the second is a reference to the string into which to store what is read. As usual, the getline function returns a reference to the istream from which we read, so that we can test that istream in a condition. If we hit end-of-file or encounter invalid input, then the return from getline will indicate failure and we'll break out of the while.

As long as we can read a line of input, we store that line in s and pass it to split, storing the return value from split in v. Next, we loop through v, writing each string in that vector on a separate line.

Assuming that we added the proper #includes, including one for our own header that contained a declaration for split, we could run this function and visually verify that it and split work as expected. We can do even better, though, by comparing the output of this program with a program that lets the library do all the work:

```
int main()
{
    string s;
    while (cin >> s)
        cout << s << endl;
    return 0;
}
```

This program and the previous one should generate identical output. Here, we let the string input operator separate the input stream into a series of words, which we write one to a line. By running both programs on the same, complex input, we can have a good idea that our split function works.

5.8 Putting strings together

In §1.2/12 and §2.5.4/29, we wrote a program to write someone's name centered in a box of asterisks. However, we never actually created a string to hold our program's output. Instead, we wrote the various parts of our output, one at a time, and let the output file combine those fragments into a picture.

We will now revisit this problem, with the aim of building a single data structure that represents the entire framed string. This program is a simplified version of one of our favorite examples, called *character pictures*. A character picture is a rectangular array of characters that can be displayed. It is a simplification of what happens in a real application—in this case, applications based on bitmap graphics. The simplifications are to use characters instead of bits, and to write onto ordinary files instead of displaying on graphical hardware. The problem builds on an exercise originally presented in the first edition of Stroustrup's *The C++ Programming Language* (Addison-Wesley, 1986), and that we explored in some depth in *Ruminations on C++* (Addison-Wesley, 1997).

5.8.1 Framing a picture

The particular variation of the character-picture problem that we'd like to explore in this section writes all the words stored in a `vector<string>`, one to a line, and surrounds these `strings` with a border. We'll line the `strings` up along the left-hand border, and leave a single space between the edge of asterisks and the words we are writing.

Assume that `p` is a `vector<string>` that contains the `strings` `"this is an"`, `"example"`, `"to"`, `"illustrate"`, and `"framing"`. Then we would like to have a function named `frame`, which behaves in such a way that calling `frame(p)` yields a value of type `vector<string>` with elements that, when written, are

```
* * * * * * * * * * * * *
*  this is an  *
*  example       *
*  to               *
*  illustrate   *
*  framing       *
* * * * * * * * * * * * *
```

Note that the border is rectangular, not ragged, even though the `strings` themselves are of different lengths. This fact implies that we'll need a function to find the length of the longest `string` in the `vector`. Let's start there:

```
string::size_type width(const vector<string>& v)
{
    string::size_type maxlen = 0;
    for(vector<string>::size_type i = 0; i != v.size(); ++i)
        maxlen = max(maxlen, v[i].size());
    return maxlen;
}
```

This function will iterate through the `vector`, setting `maxlen` to the largest size that we've seen so far. When we fall out of the loop, `maxlen` will hold the length of the longest `string` in `v`.

The only tricky aspect of the `frame` function is its interface. We know that it will operate on a `vector<string>`, but what about the return type? It will be convenient if the function creates a new picture rather than change the picture it was given:

```
vector<string> frame(const vector<string>& v)
{
    vector<string> ret;
    string::size_type maxlen = width(v);
    string border(maxlen + 4, '*');


    // write the top border
    ret.push_back(border);


    // write each interior row, bordered by an asterisk and a space
    for (vector<string>::size_type i = 0; i != v.size(); ++i) {
        ret.push_back("* " + v[i] +
                        string(maxlen - v[i].size(), ' ') + " *");
    }


    // write the bottom border
    ret.push_back(border);
    return ret;
}
```

We said that the function will not change the picture that it is passed, so we declare the parameter as a reference to const. The function will return a vector<string>, which we'll build in ret. We begin by figuring out how long each output string will be; then we create a string with that many asterisks, which we'll use to create the top and bottom border.

These borders are four characters longer than the longest string: one each for the right- and left-hand borders, and another two for the spaces that separate the borders from the strings. Taking a syntactic cue from the definition of spaces in §1.2/12 that we explained in §1.2/13, we define border to be a string that contains maxlen + 4 asterisks. We call push_back to append a copy of border to ret, thereby forming the top border.

Next, we copy the picture that we are framing. We define the index i, which we will use to walk through v until we've copied each element. In the call to push_back, we use the + operator from string, which, as we learned in §1.2/13, concatenates its arguments.

To form the output line, we concatenate the right- and left-hand borders with the string that we want to display, which is stored in v[i]. The third string in our concatenation, string(maxlen − v[i].size(), ' '), constructs an unnamed, temporary string that holds the right number of blanks. We construct this string in the same way that we initialized border. We obtain the number of blanks by subtracting the size of the current string from maxlen.

With this knowledge, we can see that the argument to push_back is a new string that consists of an asterisk, followed by a space, followed by the current string, followed by enough spaces to make the string as long as the longest string, followed by another space and another asterisk.

All that's left is to append the bottom border and return.

5.8.2 Vertical concatenation

What makes character pictures a fun example is that, once we have them, we can do things with them. We just saw one operation—framing a picture. Another operation is concatenation, which we can do both vertically and horizontally. We'll look at vertical concatenation here, and at horizontal concatenation in the next section.

Pictures are naturally organized by rows, in the sense that we represent a picture by a vector<string>, each element of which is a row. Therefore, concatenating two pictures vertically is simple: We merely concatenate the vectors that represent them. Doing so will cause the two pictures to line up along their left margins, which is a reasonable way to define vertical concatenation.

The only problem is that although there is a string concatenation operation, there is no vector concatenation operation. As a result, we have to do the work ourselves:

```
vector<string> vcat(const vector<string>& top,
                    const vector<string>& bottom)
{
    // copy the top picture
    vector<string> ret = top;

    // copy entire bottom picture
    for (vector<string>::const_iterator it = bottom.begin();
         it != bottom.end(); ++it)
        ret.push_back(*it);

    return ret;
}
```

This function uses only facilities that we have already seen: We define ret as a copy of top, append each element of bottom to ret, and return ret as its result.

The loop in this function implements one form of a common idea, namely, that of inserting a copy of elements from one container into another. In this particular case, we are appending the elements, which we can think of as inserting them at the end.

Because this operation is so common, the library offers a way of doing it without writing a loop. Instead of

```
for (vector<string>::const_iterator it = bottom.begin();
     it != bottom.end(); ++it)
    ret.push_back(*it);
```

we can write

```
ret.insert(ret.end(), bottom.begin(), bottom.end());
```

with the same effect.

5.8.3 Horizontal concatenation

By horizontal concatenation, we mean taking two pictures, and making a new picture in which one of the input pictures forms the left part of the new picture, and the other forms the right part. Before we start, we need to think about what we want to do when the pictures to concatenate are different sizes. We'll arbitrarily decide that we'll align them

along their top edges. Thus, each row of the output picture will be the result of concatenating the corresponding rows of the two input pictures. We'll have to pad the left-hand
picture's rows to make them take up the right amount of space in the output picture.

In addition to padding the left-hand picture, we also have to worry about what to do
when the pictures have a different number of rows. For example, if p holds our initial picture, we might want to concatenate the original value of p horizontally with the result of
framing p. That is, we'd like hcat(p, frame(p)) to produce

```
this is an **************
example      * this is an *
to           * example    *
illustrate * to           *
framing      * illustrate *
             * framing     *
             **************
```

Note that the left-hand picture has fewer rows than the right-hand picture. This fact
implies that we will have to pad the output on the left-hand side to account for these missing rows. If the left-hand picture is longer, we'll just copy the strings from it into the
new picture; we won't bother to pad the (empty) right side with blanks.

With this analysis complete, we can write our function:

```
vector<string>
hcat(const vector<string>& left, const vector<string>& right)
{
    vector<string> ret;

    // add 1 to leave a space between pictures
    string::size_type width1 = width(left) + 1;

    // indices to look at elements from left and right respectively
    vector<string>::size_type i = 0, j = 0;

    // continue until we've seen all rows from both pictures
    while (i != left.size() || j != right.size()) {
        // construct new string to hold characters from both pictures
        string s;

        // copy a row from the left-hand side, if there is one
        if (i != left.size())
            s = left[i++];

        // pad to full width
        s += string(width1 - s.size(), ' ');

        // copy a row from the right-hand side, if there is one
        if (j != right.size())
            s += right[j++];

        // add s to the picture we're creating
        ret.push_back(s);
    }

    return ret;
}
```

We start, as we did for `frame` and `vcat`, by defining the picture that we'll return. Our next step is to compute the width to which we must pad the left-hand picture. That width will be one more than the width of the picture itself, to leave a space between the pictures when we concatenate them. Next, we iterate through both pictures, copying an element from the first, padded as necessary, followed by an element from the second.

The only tricky part is taking care of what to do if we run out of elements in one picture before we run out of elements in the other. Our iteration continues until we have copied all the elements for each input `vector`. Hence, the `while` loop continues until both indices reach the end of their respective pictures.

If we have not yet exhausted `left`, we copy its current element into s. Regardless of whether we copied anything from `left`, we next call the `string` compound assignment operator, `+=`, to pad the output to the appropriate width. The compound assignment operator defined by the `string` library operates as you might expect: It adds the right-hand operand to its left-hand operand and stores the result in the left-hand side. Of course, "add" here means string concatenation.

We determine how much to pad by subtracting `s.size()` from `width1`. We know that either `s.size()` is the size of the `string` that we copied from `left`, or it is zero because there was no entry to copy. In the first case, `s.size()` will be greater than zero and less than `width1`, because we added one to the length of the longest `string` to account for a space between the two pictures. Thus, in this case, we'll append one or more blanks to s. If `s.size()` is zero , then we'll pad the entire output line.

Having copied and padded the `string` for the left-hand picture, we need only append the `string` from the right-hand picture, assuming that there still is an element from `right` to copy. Regardless of whether we added a value from `right`, we push s onto the output `vector`, and continue until we've processed both input `vectors`— remembering to return to our caller the picture that we've created.

It is important to note that the correct behavior of our program depends on the fact that s is local to the `while` loop. Because s is declared inside the `while`, it is created, with a null value, and destroyed on each trip through the loop.

5.9 Details

Containers and iterators: The standard library is designed so that similar operations on different containers have the same interface and the same semantics. The containers we have used so far are all *sequential* containers. We'll see in Chapter 7 that the library also provides associative containers. All the sequential containers and the `string` type provide the following operations:

container<T>`::iterator`
container<T>`::const_iterator`
        The name of the type of the iterator on this container.
container<T>`::size_type`
        The name of the appropriate type to hold the size of the largest possible instance of this container.

```
c.begin()
c.end()        Iterators referring to the first and (one past) the last element in the container.
c.rbegin()
c.rend()       Iterators referring to the last and (one beyond) the first element in the con-
               tainer that grant access to the container's elements in reverse order.
container<T>  c;
container<T>  c(c2);
               Defines c as a container that is empty or a copy of c2 if given.
container<T>  c(n);
               Defines c as a container with n elements that are value-initialized (§7.2/125)
               according to the type of T. If T is a class type, that type will control how to
               initialize the elements. If T is a built-in arithmetic type, then the elements
               will be initialized to 0.
container<T>  c(n, t);
               Defines c as a container with n elements that are copies of t.
container<T>  c(b, e);
               Creates a container that holds a copy of the elements denoted by iterators in
               the range [b, e).
c = c2         Replaces the contents of container c with a copy of the container c2.
c.size()       Returns the number of elements in c as a size_type.
c.empty()      Predicate that indicates whether c has no elements.
c.insert(d, b, e)
               Copies elements denoted by iterators in the range [b, e) and inserts them
               into c immediately before d.
c.erase(it)
c.erase(b, e)
               Removes the element denoted by it or the range of elements denoted by
               [b, e) from the container c. Returns an iterator referring to the position
               immediately after the erasure. This operation is fast for list, but can be
               slow for vector and string, because for these types it involves copying
               all the elements after the one(s) removed. Invalidates any iterators referring
               to the element(s) that are erased, and, if the container is vector or string,
               also invalidates all iterators referring to elements after the erasure.
c.push_back(t)
               Appends an element with the value t to the end of c.
```

Containers that support random access, and the string type, also provide the following:

```
c[n]           The container element (which is a single character if c is a string) at posi-
               tion n in the container c. The initial element is at position 0.
```

Iterator operations:

```
*it            Dereferences the iterator it to obtain the value stored in the container at the
               position that it denotes. This operation is often combined with . to obtain a
               member of a class object, as in (*it).x, which yields the member x of the
```

object denoted by the iterator `it`. `*` has lower precedence than `.` and the same precedence as `++` and `--`.

`it->x`	Equivalent to `(*it).x`, which returns the member `x` denoted by the object obtained by dereferencing the iterator `it`. Same precedence as the `.` operator.
`++it`	
`it++`	Increments the iterator so that it denotes the next element in the container.
`b == e`	
`b != e`	Compares two iterators for equality or inequality.

The `string` type offers iterators that support the same operations as do iterators on `vectors`. In particular, `string` supports full random access, about which we'll learn more in Chapter 8. In addition to the operations on containers, `string` also provides:

`s.substr(i, j)`	Creates a new `string` that holds a copy of the characters in `s` with indices in the range `[i, i + j)`.
`getline(is, s)`	Reads a line of input from `is` and stores it in `s`.
`s += s2`	Replaces the value of `s` by `s + s2`.

The `vector` type offers the most powerful iterators, called random-access iterators, of any of the library containers. We'll learn more about these in Chapter 8.

Although all the functions we've written have relied on dynamically allocating our `vector` elements, there are also mechanisms for preallocating elements, and an operation to direct the `vector` to allocate, but not to use, additional memory in order to avoid the overhead of repeated memory allocations.

`v.reserve(n)`	Reserves space to hold `n` elements, but does not initialize them. This operation does not change the size of the container. It affects only the frequency with which `vector` may have to allocate memory in response to repeated calls to `insert` or `push_back`.
`v.resize(n)`	Gives `v` a new size equal to `n`. If `n` is smaller than the current size of `v`, elements beyond `n` are removed from the `vector`. If `n` is greater than the current size, then new elements are added to `v` and initialized as appropriate to the type in `v`.

The `list` type is optimized for efficiently inserting and deleting elements at any point in the container. The operations on `list`s and `list` iterators include those described in §5.9/96. In addition,

`l.sort()`	
`l.sort(cmp)`	Sorts the elements in `l` using the `<` operator for the type in the `list`, or the predicate `cmp`.

The `<cctype>` header provides useful functions for manipulating character data:

`isspace(c)`	true if `c` is a whitespace character.
`isalpha(c)`	true if `c` is an alphabetic character.
`isdigit(c)`	true if `c` is a digit character.
`isalnum(c)`	true if `c` is a letter or a digit.

`ispunct(c)`	true if c is a punctuation character.
`isupper(c)`	true if c is an uppercase letter.
`islower(c)`	true if c is a lowercase letter.
`toupper(c)`	Yields the uppercase equivalent to c
`tolower(c)`	Yields the lowercase equivalent to c

Exercises

5-0. Compile, execute, and test the programs in this chapter.

5-1. Design and implement a program to produce a permuted index. A permuted index is one in which each phrase is indexed by every word in the phrase. So, given the following input,

```
The quick brown fox
jumped over the fence
```

the output would be

```
       The quick      brown fox
jumped over the        fence
The quick brown        fox
                       jumped over the fence
          jumped       over the fence
             The       quick brown fox
   jumped over         the fence
                       The quick brown fox
```

A good algorithm is suggested in *The AWK Programming Language* by Aho, Kernighan, and Weinberger (Addison-Wesley, 1988). That solution divides the problem into three steps:

1. Read each line of the input and generate a set of rotations of that line. Each rotation puts the next word of the input in the first position and rotates the previous first word to the end of the phrase. So the output of this phase for the first line of our input would be

```
The quick brown fox
quick brown fox The
brown fox The quick
fox The quick brown
```

Of course, it will be important to know where the original phrase ends and where the rotated beginning begins.

2. Sort the rotations.
3. Unrotate and write the permuted index, which involves finding the separator, putting the phrase back together, and writing it properly formatted.

5-2. Write the complete new version of the student-grading program, which extracts records for failing students, using `vectors`. Write another that uses `lists`. Measure the performance difference on input files of ten lines, 1,000 lines, and 10,000 lines.

5-3. By using a `typedef`, we can write one version of the program that implements either a `vector`-based solution or a `list`-based one. Write and test this version of the program.

5-4. Look again at the driver functions you wrote in the previous exercise. Note that it is possible to write a driver that differs only in the declaration of the type for the data structure that holds the input file. If your `vector` and `list` test drivers differ in any other way, rewrite them so that they differ only in this declaration.

5-5. Write a function named `center(const vector<string>&)` that returns a picture in which all the lines of the original picture are padded out to their full width, and the padding is as evenly divided as possible between the left and right sides of the picture. What are the properties of pictures for which such a function is useful? How can you tell whether a given picture has those properties?

5-6. Rewrite the `extract_fails` function from §5.1.1/77 so that instead of erasing each failing student from the input vector `students`, it copies the records for the passing students to the beginning of `students`, and then uses the `resize` function to remove the extra elements from the end of `students`. How does the performance of this version compare with the one in §5.1.1/77?

5-7. Given the implementation of `frame` in §5.8.1/93, and the following code fragment

```
vector<string> v;
frame(v);
```

describe what happens in this call. In particular, trace through how both the `width` function and the `frame` function operate. Now, run this code. If the results differ from your expectations, first understand why your expectations and the program differ, and then change one to match the other.

5-8. In the `hcat` function from §5.8.3/95, what would happen if we defined s outside the scope of the `while`? Rewrite and execute the program to confirm your hypothesis.

5-9. Write a program to write the lowercase words in the input followed by the uppercase words.

5-10. Palindromes are words that are spelled the same right to left as left to right. Write a program to find all the palindromes in a dictionary. Next, find the longest palindrome.

5-11. In text processing it is sometimes useful to know whether a word has any ascenders or descenders. Ascenders are the parts of lowercase letters that extend above the text line; in the English alphabet, the letters b, d, f, h, k, l, and t have ascenders. Similarly, the descenders are the parts of lowercase letters that descend below the line; In English, the letters g, j, p, q, and y have descenders. Write a program to determine whether a word has any ascenders or descenders. Extend that program to find the longest word in the dictionary that has neither ascenders nor descenders.

6

Using library algorithms

As we saw in Chapter 5, many container operations apply to more than one type of container. For example, `vector`, `string`, and `list` allow us to insert elements by calling `insert` and remove elements by calling `erase`. These operations have the same interface for each type that supports them. For that matter, many container operations also apply to the `string` class.

Every container—as well as the `string` class—provides companion iterator types, which let us navigate through a container and examine its elements. Again, the library ensures that every iterator that supplies an operation does so through the same interface. For example, we can use the ++ operator to advance any type of iterator from one element to the next; we can use the * operator to access the element associated with any type of iterator; and so on.

In this chapter, we'll see how the library exploits these common interfaces to provide a collection of standard algorithms. By using these algorithms, we can avoid writing (and rewriting) the same code over and over again. More important, we can write programs that are smaller and simpler than we would write otherwise—sometimes astonishingly so.

Like containers and iterators, algorithms also use consistent interface conventions. This consistency lets us learn a few of the algorithms and then apply that knowledge to others as the need arises. In this chapter, we'll use several of the library algorithms to solve problems related to processing `strings` and student grades. Along the way, we'll cover most of the core concepts in the algorithm library.

Unless we say otherwise, the <algorithm> header defines all the algorithms that we introduce in this chapter.

6.1 Analyzing strings

In §5.8.2/94, we used a loop to concatenate two character pictures:

```
for (vector<string>::const_iterator it = bottom.begin();
     it != bottom.end(); ++it)
    ret.push_back(*it);
```

We noted that this loop was equivalent to inserting a copy of the elements of `bottom` at the end of `ret`, an operation that `vectors` provided directly:

```
ret.insert(ret.end(), bottom.begin(), bottom.end());
```

This problem has an even more general solution: We can separate the notion of copying elements from that of inserting elements at the end of a container, as follows:

```
copy(bottom.begin(), bottom.end(), back_inserter(ret));
```

Here, `copy` is an example of a generic algorithm, and `back_inserter` is an example of an iterator adaptor.

A **generic algorithm** is an algorithm that is not part of any particular kind of container, but instead takes a cue from its arguments' types about how to access the data it uses. The standard library's generic algorithms usually take iterators among their arguments, which they use to manipulate the elements of the underlying containers. So, for example, the `copy` algorithm takes three iterators, which we'll call `begin`, `end`, and `out`, and copies all the elements in the range [`begin`, `end`) to a sequence of elements starting at `out` and extending as far as necessary. In other words,

```
copy(begin, end, out);
```

has the same effect as

```
while (begin != end)
    *out++ = *begin++;
```

except that the `while` body changes the values of the iterators, and `copy` doesn't.

Before we describe iterator adaptors, we should note that this loop depends on the use of the **postfix** version of the increment operators. These operators differ from the prefix versions, which we have used up to now, in that `begin++` returns a copy of the original value of `begin`, incrementing the stored value of `begin` as a side effect. In other words,

```
it = begin++;
```

is equivalent to

```
it = begin;
++begin;
```

The increment operators have the same precedence as `*`, and they are both right-associative, which means that `*out++` has the same meaning as `*(out++)`. Thus,

```
*out++ = *begin++;
```

is equivalent to the more verbose

```
{ *out = *begin; ++out; ++begin; }
```

Let's return to **iterator adaptors**, which are functions that yield iterators with properties that are related to their arguments in useful ways. The iterator adaptors are defined in `<iterator>`. The most common iterator adaptor is `back_inserter`, which takes a container as its argument and yields an iterator that, when used as a destination, appends values to the container. For example, `back_inserter(ret)` is an iterator that, when used as a destination, appends elements to `ret`. Therefore,

```
copy(bottom.begin(), bottom.end(), back_inserter(ret));
```

copies all of the elements of `bottom` and appends them to the end of `ret`. After this function completes, the size of `ret` will have increased by `bottom.size()`.

Notice that we could not call

```
// error—ret is not an iterator
copy(bottom.begin(), bottom.end(), ret);
```

because `copy`'s third parameter is required to be an iterator, and we supplied a container as the corresponding argument. Nor could we call

```
// error—no element at ret.end()
copy(bottom.begin(), bottom.end(), ret.end());
```

This latter mistake is particularly insidious, because the program will compile. What it does when you try to run it is another story entirely. The first thing `copy` will try to do is assign a value to the element at `ret.end()`. There's no element there, so what the implementation will do is anybody's guess.

Why is `copy` designed this way? Because separating the notions of copying elements and expanding a container allows programmers to choose which operations to use. For example, we might want to copy elements on top of elements that already exist in a container, without changing the container's size. As another example, which we shall see in §6.2.2/112, we might want to use `back_inserter` to append elements to a container that are not merely copies of another container's elements.

6.1.1 Another way to `split`

Another function that we can write more directly using the standard algorithms is `split`, which we saw in §5.6/88. The hard part of writing that function was dealing with the indices that delimited each word in the input line. We can replace the indices by iterators, and use standard-library algorithms to do much of the work for us:

```
// true if the argument is whitespace, false otherwise
bool space(char c)
{
    return isspace(c);
}
// false if the argument is whitespace, true otherwise
bool not_space(char c)
{
    return !isspace(c);
}
vector<string> split(const string& str)
{
    typedef string::const_iterator iter;
    vector<string> ret;

    iter i = str.begin();
    while (i != str.end()) {

        // ignore leading blanks
        i = find_if(i, str.end(), not_space);
```

```
        // find end of next word
        iter j = find_if(i, str.end(), space);

        // copy the characters in [i, j)
        if (i != str.end())
            ret.push_back(string(i, j));
        i = j;
    }
    return ret;
}
```

This code uses a lot of new functions, so it will take a bit of explanation. The key idea to keep in mind is that it implements the same algorithm as the original, using i and j to delimit each word in str, along the lines of the illustration in §5.6/88. Once we've found a word, we copy it from str, and push the copy onto the back of ret.

This time, i and j are iterators, not indices. We use typedef to abbreviate the iterator type, so that we can use iter instead of the longer string::const_iterator. Although the string type does not support all of the container operations, it does support iterators. Therefore, we can use the standard-library algorithms on the characters of a string, just as we can use them on the elements of a vector.

The algorithm that we use in this example is find_if. Its first two arguments are iterators that denote a sequence; the third is a predicate, which tests its argument and returns true or false. The find_if function calls the predicate on each element in the sequence, stopping when it finds an element for which the predicate yields true.

The standard library provides an isspace function to test whether a character is a space. However, that function is overloaded, so that it will work with languages, such as Japanese, that use other character types, such as wchar_t (§1.3/14). It's not easy to pass an overloaded function directly as an argument to a template function. The trouble is that the compiler doesn't know which version of the overloaded function we mean, because we haven't supplied any arguments that the compiler might use to select a version. Accordingly, we'll write our own predicates, called space and not_space, that make clear which version of isspace we intend.

The first call to find_if seeks the first nonspace character, which begins a word. Remember that one or more spaces might begin a line or might separate adjacent words in the input. We don't want to include these spaces in the output.

After the first call to find_if, i will denote the first nonspace, if any, in str. We use i in the next call to find_if, which looks for the first space in [i, str.end()). If find_if fails to find a value that satisfies the predicate, it returns its second argument, which, in this case, is str.end(). Therefore, j will be initialized to denote the blank that separates the next word in str from the rest of the line, or, if we are on the last word in the line, j will be equal to str.end().

At this point, i and j delimit a word in str. All that's left is to use these iterators to copy the data from str into ret. In the earlier version of split, we used string::substr to create the copy. However, that version of split operated on indices, not iterators, and there isn't a version of substr that operates on iterators. Instead, we construct a new string directly from the iterators that we have. We do so by using an expression, string(i, j), that is somewhat similar to the definition of spaces that we explained in §1.2/13. Our present example constructs a string that is a copy of the characters in the range [i, j). We push this new string onto the back of ret.

It is worth pointing out that this version of the program omits the tests of the index i against str.size(). Nor are there the obvious equivalent tests of the iterator against str.end(). The reason is that the library algorithms are written to handle gracefully calls that pass an empty range. For example, at some point the first call to find_if will set i to the value returned by str.end(), but there is no need to check i before passing it to the second call to find_if. The reason is that find_if will look in the empty range [i, str.end()) and will return str.end() to indicate that there is no match.

6.1.2 Palindromes

Another character-manipulation problem that we can use the library to solve succinctly is determining whether a word is a palindrome. Palindromes are words that are spelled the same way front to back as back to front. For example, "civic," "eye," "level," "madam," and "rotor" are all palindromes.

Here is a compact solution that uses the library:

```
bool is_palindrome(const string& s)
{
    return equal(s.begin(), s.end(), s.rbegin());
}
```

The return statement in this function's body calls the equal function and the rbegin member function, both of which we have not yet seen.

Like begin, rbegin returns an iterator, but this time it is an iterator that starts with the last element in the container and marches backward through the container.

The equal function compares two sequences to determine whether they contain equal values. As usual, the first two iterators passed to equal specify the first sequence. The third argument is the starting point for the second sequence. The equal function assumes that the second sequence is the same size as the first, so it does not need an ending iterator. Because we pass s.rbegin() as the starting point for the second sequence, the effect of this call is to compare values from the back of s to values in the front. The equal function will compare the first character in s with the last. Then it will compare the second to the next to last, and so on. This behavior is precisely what we want.

6.1.3 Finding URLs

As the last of our examples of character manipulation, let's write a function that finds Web addresses, called uniform resource locators (URLs), that are embedded in a string. We might use such a function by creating a single string that holds the entire contents of a document. The function would then scan the document and find all the URLs in it.

A URL is a sequence of characters of the form

protocol-name : / / *resource-name*

where *protocol-name* contains only letters, and *resource-name* may consist of letters, digits, and certain punctuation characters. Our function will take a `string` argument and will look for instances of `://` in that `string`. Each time we find such an instance, we'll look for the *protocol-name* that precedes it, and the *resource-name* that follows it.

Because we want our function to find *all* the URLs in its input, we'll want it to return a `vector<string>`, with one element for each URL. The function executes by moving the iterator b through the `string`, looking for the characters `://` that might be a part of a URL. If we find these characters, it looks backward to find the *protocol-name*, and it looks forward to find the *resource-name*:

```
vector<string> find_urls(const string& s)
{
    vector<string> ret;
    typedef string::const_iterator iter;
    iter b = s.begin(), e = s.end();

    // look through the entire input
    while (b != e) {

        // look for one or more letters followed by ://
        b = url_beg(b, e);

        // if we found it
        if (b != e) {
            // get the rest of the URL
            iter after = url_end(b, e);

            // remember the URL
            ret.push_back(string(b, after));

            // advance b and check for more URLs on this line
            b = after;
        }
    }
    return ret;
}
```

We start by declaring `ret`, which is the `vector` into which we will put the URLs as we find them, and by obtaining iterators that delimit the `string`. We will have to write the `url_beg` and `url_end` functions, which will find the beginning and end of any URL in the input. The `url_beg` function will be responsible for identifying whether a valid URL is present and, if so, for returning an iterator that refers to the first character of the *protocol-name*. If it does not identify a URL in the input, then it will return its second argument (e in this case) to indicate failure.

If `url_beg` finds a URL, the next task is to find the end of the URL by calling `url_end`. That function will search from the given position until it reaches either the end of the input or a character that cannot be part of a URL. It will return an iterator positioned one past the last character in the URL.

Thus, after the calls to `url_beg` and `url_end`, the iterator b denotes the beginning of a URL, and the iterator `after` denotes the position one past the last character in the URL:

$$b = \text{url\_beg(b, e)}\qquad\qquad \text{after} = \text{url\_end(b, e)}$$

We construct a new `string` from the characters in this range, and push that `string` onto the back of `ret`.

All that remains is to increment the value of `b` and to look for the next URL. Because URLs cannot overlap one another, we set `b` to (one past) the end of the URL that we just found, and continue the `while` loop until we've looked at all the input. Once that loop exits, we return the `vector` that contains the URLs to our caller.

Now we have to think about `url_beg` and `url_end`. The `url_end` function is simpler, so we'll start there:

```
string::const_iterator
url_end(string::const_iterator b, string::const_iterator e)
{
    return find_if(b, e, not_url_char);
}
```

This function just forwards its work to the library `find_if` function, which we used in §6.1.1/103. The predicate that we pass to `find_if` is one that we will write, named `not_url_char`. It will return `true` when passed a character that cannot be in a URL:

```
bool not_url_char(char c)
{
    // characters, in addition to alphanumerics, that can appear in a URL
    static const string url_ch = "~;/?:@=&$-_.+!*'(),";

    // see whether c can appear in a URL and return the negative
    return !(isalnum(c) ||
            find(url_ch.begin(), url_ch.end(), c) != url_ch.end());
}
```

Despite being small, this function uses a fair bit of new material. First is the use of the `static` *storage class specifier*. Local variables that are declared to be `static` are preserved across invocations of the function. Thus, we will construct and initialize the `string url_ch` only on the first call to `not_url_char`. Subsequent calls will use the object that the first call constructed. Because `url_ch` is a `const string`, its value will not change once we have initialized it.

The `not_url_char` function also uses the `isalnum` function, which the `<cctype>` header defines. This function tests whether its argument is an alphanumeric character (a letter or a digit).

Finally, `find` is another algorithm that we haven't used yet. It is similar to `find_if`, except that instead of calling a predicate, it looks for the specific value given as its third argument. As with `find_if`, if the value that we want is present, the function returns an iterator denoting the first occurrence of the value in the given sequence. If the value is not found, then `find` returns its second argument.

With this information in hand, we can now understand the `not_url_char` function. Because we negate the value of the entire expression before we return it, `not_url_char` will yield `false` if `c` is a letter, a digit, or any of the characters in `url_ch`. If `c` is any other value, the function returns `true`.

Now the hard part begins: implementing `url_beg`. This function is messy, because it must deal with the possibility that the input might contain `://` in a context that cannot be a valid URL. In practice, we'd probably have a list of acceptable *protocol-names* and look only for those. For simplicity, though, we'll limit ourselves to being sure that one or more letters precede the `://` separator, and at least one character follows it:

```
string::const_iterator
url_beg(string::const_iterator b, string::const_iterator e)
{
    static const string sep = "://";

    typedef string::const_iterator iter;

    // i marks where the separator was found
    iter i = b;

    while ((i = search(i, e, sep.begin(), sep.end())) != e) {

        // make sure the separator isn't at the beginning or end of the line
        if (i != b && i + sep.size() != e) {

            // beg marks the beginning of the protocol-name
            iter beg = i;
            while (beg != b && isalpha(beg[-1]))
                --beg;

            // is there at least one appropriate character before and after the separator?
            if (beg != i && !not_url_char(i[sep.size()]))
                return beg;
        }

        // the separator we found wasn't part of a URL; advance i past this separator
        i += sep.size();
    }
    return e;
}
```

The easy part is to write the function header. We know that we'll be passed two iterators denoting the range in which to look, and that we'll return an iterator that denotes the beginning of the first URL in that range, if one exists. We also declare and initialize a local `string`, which will hold the characters that make up the separator that identifies a potential URL. Like `url_ch` in the `not_url_char` function (§6.1.3/107), this `string` is `static` and `const`. Thus, we will not be able to change the `string`, and its value will be created only on the first invocation of `url_beg`.

The function executes by placing two iterators into the `string` delimited by `b` and `e`:

The iterator i will denote the beginning of the URL separator, if any, and beg will indicate the beginning of the *protocol-name*, if any.

The function first looks for the separator, by calling search, a library function that we haven't used before. This function takes two pairs of iterators: The first pair denotes the sequence in which we are looking, and the second pair denotes the sequence that we wish to locate. As with other library functions, if search fails, it returns the second iterator. Therefore, after the call to search, either i denotes (one past) the end of the input string, or it denotes a : that is followed by //.

If we found a separator, the next task is to get the letters (if any) that make up the *protocol-name*. We first check whether the separator is at the beginning or end of the input. If the separator is in either of those places, we know that we don't have a URL, because a URL has at least one character on each side of its separator. Otherwise, we need to try to position the iterator beg. The inner while loop moves beg backward through the input until it hits either a nonalphabetic character or the beginning of the string. It uses two new ideas: The first is the notion that if a container supports indexing, so do its iterators. In other words, beg[-1] is the character at the position immediately before the one that beg denotes. We can think of beg[-1] as an abbreviation for *(beg - 1). We'll learn more about such iterators in §8.2.6/148. The second new idea is the isalpha function, defined in <cctype>, which tests whether its argument is a letter.

If we were able to advance the iterator over as much as a single character, we assume that we've found a *protocol-name*. Before returning beg, we still have to check that there's at least one valid character following the separator. This test is more complicated. We know that there is at least one more character in the input, because we're inside the body of an if that compares the value of i + sep.size() with e. We can access the first such character as i[sep.size()], which is an abbreviation for *(i + sep.size()). We test whether that character can appear in a URL by passing the character to not_url_char. This function returns true if the character is not valid, so we negate the return to check whether the character is valid.

If the separator is not part of a URL, then the function advances i past the separator and keeps looking.

This code uses the ***decrement operator***, which we mentioned in the operator table in §2.7/32, but which we have not previously used. It works like the increment operator, but it decrements its operand instead. As with the increment operator, it comes in prefix and postfix versions. The prefix version, which we use here, decrements its operand and returns the new value.

6.2 Comparing grading schemes

In §4.2/61, we presented a grading scheme that based students' final grades, in part, on their median homework scores. Devious students can exploit this scheme by deliberately not turning in all their homework assignments. After all, the bottom half of their homework grades has no effect on their final grade. If they've done enough homework to ensure a good grade, why not stop doing homework altogether?

In our experience, most students do not exploit this particular loophole. However, we did have occasion to teach one class that gleefully and openly did so. We wondered whether the students who skipped homework had, on average, different final grades than those who did all the homework. While we were thinking about how to answer that question, we decided that it might be interesting to see what the answer would be if we used one of two alternative grading schemes:

- Using the average instead of the median, and treating those assignments that the student failed to turn in as zero
- Using the median of only the assignments that the student actually submitted

For each of these grading schemes, we wanted to compare the median grade of the students who turned in all their homework with the median grade of the students who missed one or more assignments. We wound up with a program that had to solve two distinct subproblems:

1. Read all the student records, separating the students who did all the homework from the others.
2. Apply each of the grading schemes to all the students in each group, and report the median grade of each group.

6.2.1 Working with student records

Our first subproblem is to read and classify the student records. Fortunately, we already have some code we can use in solving this part of the problem: We can use the `Student_info` type from §4.2.1/61 and the associated `read` function from §4.2.2/62 to read the student data records. What we don't have yet is a function that checks whether a student has done all the homework. Writing such a function is easy:

```
bool did_all_hw(const Student_info& s)
{
    return ((find(s.homework.begin(), s.homework.end(), 0))
        == s.homework.end());
}
```

This function looks in `s.homework` to see whether any of the values stored there is 0. Because we give at least partial credit for any assignment that is turned in, a 0 grade means that the assignment was not submitted. We compare the return from `find` with `homework.end()`. As usual, `find` returns its second argument if it fails to find the value that it seeks.

With these two functions, writing code to read and separate the student records is simplicity itself. We'll read each student record, check whether the student did all the homework, and append the record to one of two `vectors`, which, for want of a better idea, we'll name did and didnt. While we're at it, we'll check that neither vector is empty, so that we'll know that our analysis will actually tell us something useful:

```
vector<Student_info> did, didnt;
Student_info student;

// read all the records, separating them based on whether all homework was done
while (read(cin, student)) {
    if (did_all_hw(student))
        did.push_back(student);
    else
        didnt.push_back(student);
}

// check that both groups contain data
if (did.empty()) {
    cout << "No student did all the homework!" << endl;
    return 1;
}
if (didnt.empty()) {
    cout << "Every student did all the homework!" << endl;
    return 1;
}
```

The only new idea here is the empty member function, which yields true if the container is empty and false otherwise. It is a better idea to use this function to check for an empty container than it is to compare the size with 0, because for some kinds of containers, it might be more efficient to check whether the container has any elements than to figure out exactly how many elements there are.

6.2.2 Analyzing the grades

We now know how to read and classify student records into the did and didnt vectors. The next step is to analyze them, which means we need to think a little about how to structure the analysis.

We know that we have three analyses to perform, and each analysis has two parts, which analyze separately the students who did and who didn't do all the homework. Because we will do each analysis on two sets of data, we certainly want to make each analysis its own function. However, there are some operations, such as reporting in a common format, that we are going to want to do on pairs of analyses, rather than on individual analyses. Evidently, we'll want to make writing the results of each pair of analyses into a function as well.

The tricky part is that we want to call the function that writes the analysis results three times, once for each kind of analysis. We want that function to call the appropriate analysis function twice, once each for the did and didn't objects. However, we want the function that generates the reports to call a different analysis function each time we call it! How do we arrange that?

The easiest solution is to define three analysis functions and pass each one as an argument to the reporting function. Remember that we've used such arguments already, such as when we passed the `compare` function to the library `sort` routine in §4.2.2/64. In this case, we want our output routine to take five arguments:

• The stream on which to write the output
• A `string` that represents the name of the analysis
• The function to use for the analysis
• Two arguments, each of which is one of the `vectors` that we want to analyze

For example, let's assume that the first analysis, which looks at the medians, is done by a function called `median_analysis`. Then, we'd like to report the results for each group of students by executing

```
write_analysis(cout, "median", median_analysis, did, didnt);
```

Before we define `write_analysis`, let's define `median_analysis`. We would like to give that function a `vector` of student records, and we would like it to compute the students' grades according to the normal grading scheme and to return the median of those grades. We can define that function as follows:

```
//  this function doesn't quite work
double median_analysis(const vector<Student_info>& students)
{
    vector<double> grades;

    transform(students.begin(), students.end(),
            back_inserter(grades), grade);
    return median(grades);
}
```

Although this function might appear difficult at first glance, it introduces only one new idea, namely the `transform` function. This function takes three iterators and a function. The first two iterators specify a range of elements to transform; the third iterator is the destination into which to put the result of running the function.

When we call `transform`, we are responsible for ensuring that the destination has room for the values from the input sequence. In this case, there is no problem, because we obtain the destination by calling `back_inserter` (§6.1/102), thereby arranging that `transform`'s results will be appended to `grades`, which will automatically grow as necessary to accommodate the results.

The fourth argument to `transform` is a function that `transform` applies to each element of the input sequence to obtain the corresponding element of the output sequence. Therefore, when we call `transform` in this example, the effect is to apply the `grade` function to each element of `students`, and to append each grade to the `vector` named `grades`. When we have all these students' grades, we call `median`, which we defined in §4.1.1/53, to compute their median.

There's only one problem: As the comment notes, this function doesn't quite work.

One reason that it doesn't work is that there are several overloaded versions of the `grade` function. The compiler doesn't know which version to call, because we haven't given `grade` any arguments. We know that we want to call the version from §4.2.2/63, but we need a way to tell the compiler to do so.

The other reason is that the `grade` function will `throw` an exception if any student did no homework at all, and the `transform` function does nothing about exceptions. If an exception occurs, the `transform` function will be stopped at the point of the exception, and control will return to `median_analysis`. Because `median_analysis` doesn't handle the exception either, the exception will continue to propagate outward. The effect will be that this function will also exit prematurely, passing control to its caller, and so on, until control reaches an appropriate `catch`. If there is no such `catch`, as would be likely in this case, the program itself is terminated, and the message that was thrown is printed (or not, depending on the implementation).

We can solve both problems by writing an auxiliary function that will `try` the `grade` function and handle the exception. Because we are calling the `grade` function explicitly, rather than passing it as an argument, the compiler will be able to figure out which version we mean:

```
double grade_aux(const Student_info& s)
{
    try {
        return grade(s);
    } catch (domain_error) {
        return grade(s.midterm, s.final, 0);
    }
}
```

This function will call the version of `grade` from §4.2.2/63. If an exception occurs, we will `catch` it and call the version of `grade`, from §4.1/52, that takes three `double`s that represent the exam scores and overall homework grade. Thus, we'll assume that students who did no homework at all got a 0 grade on their homework, but their exams still count.

Now, we can rewrite the analysis function to use `grade_aux`:

```
// this version works fine
double median_analysis(const vector<Student_info>& students)
{
    vector<double> grades;

    transform(students.begin(), students.end(),
              back_inserter(grades), grade_aux);
    return median(grades);
}
```

Having seen what an analysis routine looks like, we are now in a position to define `write_analysis`, which uses an analysis routine to compare two sets of students:

```
void write_analysis(ostream& out, const string& name,
                    double analysis(const vector<Student_info>&),
                    const vector<Student_info>& did,
                    const vector<Student_info>& didnt)
{
    out << name << ": median(did) = " << analysis(did) <<
           ", median(didnt) = " << analysis(didnt) << endl;
}
```

Again, this function is surprisingly small, although it does introduce two new ideas. The first is how to define a parameter that represents a function. The parameter definition for `analysis` looks just like the function declaration that we wrote in §4.3/67. (Actually, as we shall learn in §10.1.2/172, there is slightly more going on here than meets the eye. The additional detail doesn't affect the current discussion directly.)

The other new idea is the return type, **void**. The built-in type void can be used only in a few restricted ways, one of which is to name a return type. When we say a function "returns" a void, we're really saying that it has no return value. We can exit from such a function by executing a `return` statement with no value, such as

```
return;
```

or, as we do here, by falling off the end of the function. Ordinarily, we cannot just fall off the end of a function, but the language allows functions that return void to do so.

At this point, we can write the rest of our program:

```
int main()
{
    // students who did and didn't do all their homework
    vector<Student_info> did, didnt;

    // read the student records and partition them
    Student_info student;
    while (read(cin, student)) {
        if (did_all_hw(student))
            did.push_back(student);
        else
            didnt.push_back(student);
    }

    // verify that the analyses will show us something
    if (did.empty()) {
        cout << "No student did all the homework!" << endl;
        return 1;
    }
    if (didnt.empty()) {
        cout << "Every student did all the homework!" << endl;
        return 1;
    }

    // do the analyses
    write_analysis(cout, "median", median_analysis, did, didnt);
    write_analysis(cout, "average", average_analysis, did, didnt);
    write_analysis(cout, "median of homework turned in",
                   optimistic_median_analysis, did, didnt);

    return 0;
}
```

All that remains is to write `average_analysis` and `optimistic_median_analysis`.

6.2.3 Grading based on average homework grade

We would like the `average_analysis` function to compute the students' grades by using the average homework grade, rather than the median. Therefore, the logical first step is to write a function to compute the average of a `vector`, with the aim of using it instead of `median` for grade computation:

```
double average(const vector<double>& v)
{
    return accumulate(v.begin(), v.end(), 0.0) / v.size();
}
```

This function uses `accumulate`, which, unlike the other library algorithms we've used, is declared in `<numeric>`. As this header's name implies, it offers tools for numeric computation. The `accumulate` function adds the values in the range denoted by its first two arguments, starting the summation with the value given by its third argument.

The type of the sum is the type of the third argument, so it is crucially important for us to use `0.0`, as we did here, instead of `0`. Otherwise, the result would be an `int`, and any fractional part would be lost.

Having used `accumulate` to generate the sum of all the elements in the range, we divide that sum by `v.size()`, which is the number of elements in the range. The result of that division, of course, is the average, which we return to our caller.

Once we have the `average` function, we can use it to implement the `average_grade` function to reflect this alternative grading policy:

```
double average_grade(const Student_info& s)
{
    return grade(s.midterm, s.final, average(s.homework));
}
```

This function uses the `average` function to compute an overall homework grade, which it then gives to the `grade` function from §4.1/52 to use in computing the final grade.

With this infrastructure in place, the `average_analysis` function is simplicity itself:

```
double average_analysis(const vector<Student_info>& students)
{
    vector<double> grades;

    transform(students.begin(), students.end(),
              back_inserter(grades), average_grade);
    return median(grades);
}
```

The only difference between this function and `median_analysis` (§6.2.2/113) is its name and its use of `average_grade` instead of `grade_aux`.

6.2.4 Median of the completed homework

The last analysis scheme, `optimistic_median_analysis`, gets its name from the optimistic assumption that the students' grades on the homework that they didn't turn in would have been the same as the homework that they did turn in. With that assumption, we would like to compute the median of just the homework that each student submitted. We'll call this computation an *optimistic* median, and we'll begin by writing a function to compute it. Of course, we have to contend with the possibility that a student did no homework at all, in which case we'll use 0 as the overall homework grade:

```
// median of the nonzero elements of s.homework, or 0 if no such elements exist
double optimistic_median(const Student_info& s)
{
    vector<double> nonzero;
    remove_copy(s.homework.begin(), s.homework.end(),
                back_inserter(nonzero), 0);

    if (nonzero.empty())
        return grade(s.midterm, s.final, 0);
    else
        return grade(s.midterm, s.final, median(nonzero));
}
```

This function works by extracting the nonzero elements from the homework vector and putting them into a new vector, called nonzero. Once we have the nonzero homework grades, we call the version of grade defined in §4.1/52 to compute the final score based on the median of the homework assignments that were actually submitted.

The only new idea in this function is how we get values into nonzero, which we do by calling the remove_copy algorithm. To understand the call to remove_copy, you may find it useful to know that the library provides "copying" versions of many of the algorithms. So, for example, remove_copy does what remove does, but copies its results to an indicated destination.

The remove function finds all values that match a given value and "removes" those values from the container. All the values in the input sequence that are not "removed" will be copied into the destination. We'll have more to say shortly about what "remove" means in this context.

The remove_copy function takes three iterators and a value. As with most algorithms, the first two iterators denote the input sequence. The third denotes the beginning of the destination for the copy. As with copy, the remove_copy algorithm assumes that there is enough space in the destination to hold all the elements that are copied. We call back_inserter to grow nonzero as needed.

We should now be able to see that the effect of the remove_copy call is to copy into nonzero all the nonzero elements in s.homework. We then check whether nonzero is empty, and if not, we do the normal grade calculation based on the median of the nonzero grades. If nonzero is empty, then we use 0 as the homework grade.

Of course, to complete our analysis, we need to write an analysis function to call our optimistic_median function. We leave doing so as an exercise.

6.3 Classifying students, revisited

In Chapter 5, we looked at the problem of copying records with failing grades into a separate vector and then removing those records from the existing vector. The obvious, easy approach to this problem proved to have abysmal performance as the input size grew. We went on to show how to solve the performance problem by using a `list` instead of a `vector`, but we also promised to revisit the problem and show an algorithmic solution that would perform similarly to the revised data structure.

We can use the algorithm library to demonstrate two other solutions. The first is slightly slower because it uses a pair of library algorithms and visits every element twice. We can do better by using a more specialized library algorithm that will let us solve the problem in a single pass.

6.3.1 A two-pass solution

Our first approach will use a strategy similar to the one that we used in §6.2.4/115, when we wanted only the nonzero homework grades. In that case, we didn't want to change `homework` itself, so we used `remove_copy` to put copies of the nonzero homework grades into a separate `vector`. In our current problem, we need both to copy and remove the nonzero elements:

```
vector<Student_info>
extract_fails(vector<Student_info>& students) {
    vector<Student_info> fail;
    remove_copy_if(students.begin(), students.end(),
                   back_inserter(fail), pgrade);
    students.erase(remove_if(students.begin(), students.end(),
                             fgrade), students.end());
    return fail;
}
```

The interface to the program is identical to that from §5.3/82, which presented the obvious `vector`-based solution that used iterators instead of indices. As in that solution, we'll use the `vector` that we were passed to hold grades for students who passed, and define `fail` to hold the failing grades. There the similarities end.

In the original program, we used an iterator named `iter` to march through the container, copying the records with failing grades into `fail`, and using the `erase` member to erase them from `students`. This time, we use the `remove_copy_if` function to copy the failing grades into `fail`. That function operates as did the `remove_copy` function that we used in §6.2.4/116, except that it uses a predicate as its test, rather than a value. We give it a predicate that inverts the result of calling `fgrade` (§5.1/75):

```
bool pgrade(const Student_info& s)
{
    return !fgrade(s);
}
```

When we pass a predicate to `remove_copy_if`, we are asking it "remove" each element that satisfies the predicate. In this context, "removing" an element means not copying it, so we copy only those elements that *do not* satisfy the predicate. Therefore, passing `pgrade` to `remove_copy_if` copies only the student records with failing grades.

The next statement is somewhat complicated. First, we call `remove_if` to "remove" the elements that correspond to failing grades. Again, the quotes around "remove" are because nothing is actually removed. Instead, `remove_if` copies all the elements that *do not* satisfy the predicate—in this case, all the student records with passing grades.

This call is tricky to understand because `remove_if` uses the same sequence as its source and destination. What it really does is copy to the beginning of the sequence the elements that don't meet the predicate. For example, suppose we started with seven students with grades as follows:

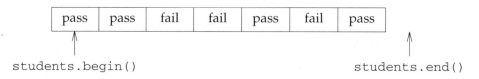

Then the call to `remove_if` would leave the first two records untouched, because they're already in the right places. It would "remove" the next two records by treating them as free space to be overwritten by the next records that should be kept. So, when it sees the fifth record, which represents a student who passed, it would copy that record into the now free position that used to hold the first of the "removed" failing records, and so on:

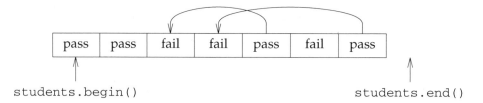

The result in this case would be to copy the four passing records to the beginning of the sequence, leaving the remaining three records untouched. So that we can know how much of the sequence is still relevant, `remove_if` returns an iterator that refers to one past the last element that it did not "remove":

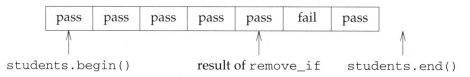

Next, we need to `erase` these unneeded records from `students`. We have not used this version of `erase` before. It takes two iterators, and erases all the elements in the range delimited by those iterators. If we `erase` the elements between the iterator returned from the call to `remove_if` and `students.end()`, we are left with just the passing records:

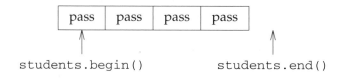

6.3.2 A single-pass solution

Our first algorithmic solution performs pretty well, but we should be able to do slightly better. The reason is that the solution in §6.3.1/117 calculates the grade for every element in students twice: once from remove_copy_if and a second time from remove_if.

Although there is no library algorithm that does exactly what we want, there is one that approaches our problem from a different angle: It takes a sequence and rearranges its elements so that the ones that satisfy a predicate precede the ones that do not satisfy it.

There are really two versions of this algorithm, which are named partition and stable_partition. The difference is that partition might rearrange the elements within each category, and stable_partition keeps them in the same order aside from the partitioning. So, for example, if the student names were already in alphabetical order, and we wanted to keep them that way within each category, we would need to use stable_partition rather than partition.

Each of these algorithms returns an iterator that represents the first element of the second section. Therefore, we can extract the failing grades this way:

```
vector<Student_info>
extract_fails(vector<Student_info>& students)
{
    vector<Student_info>::iterator iter =
        stable_partition(students.begin(), students.end(), pgrade);
    vector<Student_info> fail(iter, students.end());
    students.erase(iter, students.end());

    return fail;
}
```

To understand what is going on here, let's start with our hypothetical input data again:

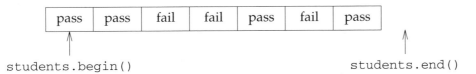

After calling stable_partition, we would have

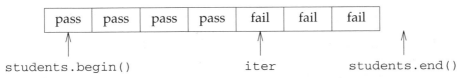

We construct fail from a copy of the failing records, which are the ones in the range [iter, students.end()), and then erase those elements from students.

When we ran our algorithm-based solutions, they had roughly the same overall performance as the list-based solution. As expected, once the input was large enough, the algorithm and list-based solutions were substantially better than the vector solution that used erase. The two algorithmic solutions are good enough that the time consumed by the input library dominated the timings for input files up to about 75,000 records. To compare the effects of the two strategies in `extract_fails`, we separately analyzed the performance of just this portion of the program. Our timings confirmed that the one-pass algorithm ran about twice as fast as the two-pass solution.

6.4 Algorithms, containers, and iterators

There is a fact that is crucial to understand in using algorithms, iterators, and containers:

> *Algorithms act on container elements—they do not act on containers.*

The `sort`, `remove_if`, and `partition` functions all move elements to new positions in the underlying container, but they do not change the properties of the container itself. For example, `remove_if` does not change the size of the container on which it operates; it merely copies elements around within the container.

This distinction is especially important in understanding how algorithms interact with the containers that they use for output. Let's look in more detail at our use of `remove_if` in §6.3.1/117. As we've seen, the call

```
remove_if(students.begin(), students.end(), fgrade)
```

did not change the size of `students`. Rather, it copied each element for which the predicate was `false` to the beginning of `students`, and left the rest of the elements alone. When we need to shorten the vector to discard those elements, we must do so ourselves.

In our example, we said

```
students.erase(remove_if(students.begin(), students.end(), fgrade),
               students.end());
```

Here, `erase` changes the `vector` by removing the sequence indicated by its arguments. This call to `erase` shortens `students` so that it contains only the elements we want. Note that `erase` must be a member of `vector`, because it acts directly on the container, not just on its elements.

Similarly, it is important to be aware of the interaction between iterators and algorithms, and between iterators and container operations. We've already seen, in §5.3/83 and §5.5.1/86, that container operations such as `erase` and `insert` invalidate the iterator for the element erased. More important, in the case of `vector`s and `string`s, operations such as `erase` or `insert` also invalidate any iterator denoting elements *after* the one `erase`d or `insert`ed. Because these operations can invalidate iterators, we must be careful about saving iterator values if we are using these operations.

Similarly, functions such as `partition` or `remove_if`, which can move elements around within the container, will change which element is denoted by particular iterators. After running one of these functions, we cannot rely on an iterator continuing to denote a specific element.

6.5 Details

Type modifiers:

static *type variable*;

> For local declarations, declares *variable* with static storage class. The value of *variable* persists across executions of this scope and is guaranteed to be initialized before the variable is used for the first time. When the program exits from the scope, the variable keeps its value until the next time the program enters that scope. We'll see in §13.4/244 that the meaning of static varies with context.

Types: The built-in type void can be used in a restricted number of ways, one of which is to indicate that a function yields no return value. Such functions can be exited through a return; that has no value or by falling off the end of the function.

Iterator adaptors are functions that yield iterators. The most common are the adaptors that generate insert_iterators, which are iterators that grow the associated container dynamically. Such iterators can be used safely as the destination of a copying algorithm. They are defined in header <iterator>:

back_inserter(c)

> Yields an iterator on the container c that appends elements to c. The container must support push_back, which the list, vector, and the string types all do.

front_inserter(c)

> Like back_inserter, but inserts at the front of the container. The container must support push_front, which list does, but string and vector do not.

inserter(c, it)

> Like back_inserter, but inserts elements before the iterator it.

Algorithms: Unless otherwise indicated, <algorithm> defines these algorithms:

accumulate(b, e, t)

> Creates a local variable and initializes it to a copy of t (with the same type as t, which means that the type of t is crucially important to the behavior of accumulate), adds each element in the range [b, e) to the variable, and returns a copy of the variable as its result. Defined in <numeric>.

find(b, e, t)

find_if(b, e, p)

search(b, e, b2, e2)

> Algorithms to look for a given value in the sequence [b, e). The find algorithm looks for the value t; the find_if algorithm tests each element against the predicate p; the search algorithm looks for the sequence denoted by [b2, e2).

copy(b, e, d)

remove_copy(b, e, d, t)

remove_copy_if(b, e, d, p)

> Algorithms to copy the sequence from [b, e) to the destination denoted by d. The copy algorithm copies the entire sequence; remove_copy copies all elements not equal to t; and remove_copy_if copies all elements for which the predicate p fails.

`remove_if(b, e, p)`

  Arranges the container so that the elements in the range `[b, e)` for which the predicate `p` is false are at the front of the range. Returns an iterator denoting one past the range of these "unremoved" elements.

`remove(b, e, t)`

  Like `remove_if`, but tests which elements to keep against the value `t`.

`transform(b, e, d, f)`

  Runs the function `f` on the elements in the range `[b, e)`, storing the result of `f` in `d`.

`partition(b, e, p)`
`stable_partition(b, e, p)`

  Partitions the elements in the range `[b, e)`, based on the predicate `p`, so that elements for which the predicate is `true` are at the front of the container. Returns an iterator to the first element for which the predicate is `false`, or `e` if the predicate is `true` for all elements. The `stable_partition` function maintains the input order among the elements in each partition.

Exercises

6-0. Compile, execute, and test the programs in this chapter.

6-1. Reimplement the `frame` and `hcat` operations from §5.8.1/93 and §5.8.3/94 to use iterators.

6-2. Write a program to test the `find_urls` function.

6-3. What does this program fragment do?

```
vector<int> u(10, 100);
vector<int> v;
copy(u.begin(), u.end(), v.begin());
```

  Write a program that contains this fragment, and compile and execute it.

6-4. Correct the program you wrote in the previous exercise to copy from u into v. There are at least two possible ways to correct the program. Implement both, and describe the relative advantages and disadvantages of each approach.

6-5. Write an analysis function to call `optimistic_median`.

6-6. Note that the function from the previous exercise and the functions from §6.2.2/113 and §6.2.3/115 do the same task. Merge these three analysis functions into a single function.

6-7. The portion of the grading analysis program from §6.2.1/110 that read and classified student records depending on whether they did (or did not) do all the homework is similar to the problem we solved in `extract_fails`. Write a function to handle this subproblem.

6-8. Write a single function that can be used to classify students based on criteria of your choice. Test this function by using it in place of the `extract_fails` program, and use it in the program to analyze student grades.

6-9. Use a library algorithm to concatenate all the elements of a `vector<string>`.

7

Using associative containers

All the containers that we have used until now have been sequential containers, whose elements remain in the sequence that we choose for them. When we use push_back or insert to add elements to a sequential container, each element will stay where we put it until we do something to the container that reorders the elements.

Some kinds of programs are hard to write efficiently if we restrict ourselves to sequential containers. For example, if we have a container of integers, and we wish to write a program that determines whether any element of the container has the value 42, we have two plausible strategies—neither of which is ideal. One alternative is to inspect every element of the container until we find 42 or run out of elements. This approach is straightforward, but potentially slow—especially if the container has many elements. The other alternative is for us to keep the container in an appropriate order and devise an efficient algorithm to find the element we seek. This approach can yield fast searches, but such algorithms are not easy to devise. In other words, we must live with a slow program, or come up with our own sophisticated algorithm. Fortunately, as we'll see in this chapter, the library offers a third alternative.

7.1 Containers that support efficient look-up

Instead of storing data in a sequential container, we can use an *associative container*. Such containers automatically arrange their elements into a sequence that depends on the values of the elements themselves, rather than the sequence in which we inserted them. Moreover, associative containers exploit this ordering to let us locate particular elements much more quickly than do the sequential containers, without our having to keep the container ordered by ourselves.

Associative containers offer efficient ways to find an element that contains a particular value, and might contain additional information as well. The part of each container element that we can use for these efficient searches is called a *key*. For example, if we were keeping track of information about students, we might use the student's name as the key, so that we could find students efficiently by name.

In the sequential containers, the closest that we have seen to a key is the integer index that accompanies every element of a vector. However, even these indices are not really keys, because every time we insert or delete a `vector` element, we implicitly change the index of every element *after* the one that we touched.

The most common kind of associative data structure is one that stores key–value pairs, associating a value with each key, and that lets us insert and retrieve elements quickly based on their keys. When we put a particular key–value pair into the data structure, that key will continue to be associated with the same value until we delete the pair. Such a data structure is called an ***associative array***. Many languages, such as AWK, Perl, and Snobol, have associative arrays built in. In C++, associative arrays are part of the library. The most common kind of associative array in C++ is called a **map**, and, analogous with other containers, it is defined in the <map> header.

In many ways, maps behave like `vectors`. One fundamental difference is that the index of a `map` need not be an integer; it can be a `string`, or any other type with values that we can compare so as to keep them ordered.

Another important difference between associative and sequential containers is that, because associative containers are self-ordering, our own programs must not do anything that changes the order of the elements. For that reason, algorithms that change the contents of containers often don't work for associative containers. In exchange for that restriction, associative containers offer a variety of useful operations that are impossible to implement efficiently for sequential containers.

This chapter presents several programming examples that use `maps` to write compact and efficient look-up–intensive programs.

7.2 Counting words

As a simple example, think about how we might count the number of times that each distinct word occurs in our input. With associative arrays, the solution is almost trivial:

```
int main()
{
    string s;
    map<string, int> counters;  // store each word and an associated counter

    // read the input, keeping track of each word and how often we see it
    while (cin >> s)
        ++counters[s];

    // write the words and associated counts
    for (map<string, int>::const_iterator it = counters.begin();
            it != counters.end(); ++it) {
        cout << it->first << "\t" << it->second << endl;
    }
    return 0;
}
```

As with other containers, we must specify the type of the objects that the `map` will hold. Because a `map` holds key–value pairs, we need to mention not only the type of the values, but also the type of the keys. So,

```
map<string, int> counters;
```

defines `counters` as a `map` that holds values of type `int` that are associated with keys of type `string`. We often speak of such a container as "a `map` from `string` to `int`," because we can use the `map` by giving it a `string` as a key, and getting back the associated `int` data.

The way we define `counters` captures our intent to associate each word that we read with an integer counter that records how many times we have seen that word. The input loop reads the standard input, a word at a time, into `s`. The interesting part is

```
++counters[s];
```

What happens here is that we look in `counters`, using the word that we just read as the key. The result of `counters[s]` is the integer that is associated with the `string` stored in `s`. We then use `++` to increment that integer, which indicates that we have seen the word once more.

What happens when we encounter a word for the first time? In that case, `counters` will not yet contain an element with that key. When we index a `map` with a key that has not yet been seen, the `map` automatically creates a new element with that key. That element is **value-initialized**, which, for simple types such as `int`, is equivalent to setting the value to zero. Thus, when we read a new word for the first time and execute `++counters[s]` with that new word, we are guaranteed that the value of `counters[s]` will be zero before we increment it. Incrementing `counters[s]` will, therefore, correctly indicate that we have seen that word once so far.

Once we have read the entire input, we must write the counters and the associated words. We do so in much the same way as we would write the contents of a `list` or a `vector`: We iterate through the container in a `for` loop, which uses a variable of the iterator type defined by the `map` class. The only real difference is in how we write the data in the body of the `for` statement:

```
cout << it->first << "\t" << it->second << endl;
```

Recall that an associative array stores a collection of key–value pairs. Using `[]` to access a `map` element conceals this fact, because we put the key inside the `[]` and get back the associated value. So, for example, `counters[s]` is an `int`. However, when we iterate over a `map`, we must have a way to get at both the key and the associated value. The `map` container lets us do so by using a companion library type called `pair`.

A **pair** is a simple data structure that holds two elements, which are named `first` and `second`. Each element in a `map` is really a `pair`, with a `first` member that contains the key and a `second` member that contains the associated value. When we dereference a `map` iterator, we obtain a value that is of the `pair` type associated with the `map`.

The `pair` class can hold values of various types, so when we create a `pair`, we say what the types of the `first` and `second` data members should be. For a `map` that has a key of type `K` and a value of type `V`, the associated `pair` type is `pair<const K, V>`.

Note that the `pair` associated with a `map` has a key type that is `const`. Because the `pair` key is `const`, we are prevented from changing the value of an element's key. If the key were not `const`, we might implicitly change the element's position within the `map`. Accordingly, the key is always `const`, so that if we dereference a `map<string, int>`

iterator, we get a `pair<const string, int>`. Thus, `it->first` is the current element's key, and `it->second` is the associated value. Because `it` is an iterator, `*it` is an lvalue (§4.1.3/56), and therefore `it->first` and `it->second` are also lvalues. However, the type of `it->first` includes `const`, which prevents us from changing it.

With this knowledge, we can see that the output statement writes each key (that is, each distinct word from the input), followed by a tab and the corresponding count.

7.3 Generating a cross-reference table

Once we know how to count how often words occur in the input, a logical next step is to write a program to generate a cross-reference table that indicates where each word occurs in the input. This extension requires several changes to our basic program.

First, instead of reading a word at a time, we'll need to read a line at a time, so that we can associate line numbers with words. Once we're reading lines instead of words, we'll need a way to break each line into its constituent words. Fortunately, we already wrote such a function, named `split`, in §6.1.1/103. We can use this function to turn each input line into a `vector<string>`, from which we can extract each word.

Rather than using `split` directly, we're going to make it a parameter to the cross-reference function. That way, we leave open the possibility of changing the way we find the words on a line. For example, we could pass the `find_urls` function from §6.1.3/105, and use the cross-reference function to see where URLs appear in the input.

As before, we will use a `map` with keys that are the distinct words from the input. This time, however, we will have to associate a more complicated value with each key. Instead of keeping track of how often the word occurs, we want to know all the line numbers on which the word occurred. Because any given word may occur on many lines, we will need to store the line numbers in a container.

When we get a new line number, all we will need to do is append that number to those that we already have for that word. Sequential access to the container elements will suffice, so we can use a `vector` to keep track of line numbers. Therefore, we will need a map from `string` to `vector<int>`.

With these preliminaries out of the way, let's look at the code:

```
// find all the lines that refer to each word in the input
map<string, vector<int> >
    xref(istream& in,
        vector<string> find_words(const string&) = split)
{
    string line;
    int line_number = 0;
    map<string, vector<int> > ret;

    // read the next line
    while (getline(in, line)) {
        ++line_number;

        // break the input line into words
        vector<string> words = find_words(line);
```

```
                   // remember that each word occurs on the current line
               for (vector<string>::const_iterator it = words.begin();
                       it != words.end(); ++it)
                   ret[*it].push_back(line_number);
       }
       return ret;
   }
```

Both the return type and the argument list of this function deserve attention. If you look at the declaration of our return type and the local variable `ret`, you will see that we carefully wrote > > instead of >>. The compiler needs that space, because if it sees >> without intervening spaces, it will assume that it is looking at an >> operator, rather than at two separate > symbols.

In the argument list, notice that `find_words` defines a function parameter, which captures our intent to pass to `xref` the function to use to split the input into words. The other interesting thing is that we say = `split` after the definition of `find_words`, which indicates that this parameter has a ***default argument***. When we give a parameter a default argument, we're saying that callers can omit that argument if they wish. If they supply an argument, the function will use it. If they omit the argument, the compiler will substitute the default. Thus, users can call this function in either of two ways:

```
   xref(cin);              // uses split to find words in the input stream
   xref(cin, find_urls);   // uses the function named find_urls to find words
```

The function body starts by defining a `string` variable, named `line`, which will hold each line of input as we read it, and an `int` variable, named `line_number`, to hold the line number of the line that we are currently processing. The input loop calls `getline` (§5.7/91) to read a line at a time into `line`. As long as there is input, we increment the line counter and then process each word in the line.

We begin that processing by declaring a local variable named `words`, which will hold all the words from `line`, and initialize it by calling `find_words`. That function will be either our `split` function (§6.1.1/103), which splits `line` into its component words, or another function that takes a `string` argument and returns a `vector<string>` result. We continue with a `for` statement that visits each element in `words`, updating the `map` each time through `words`.

The `for` header should be familiar: It defines an iterator, and marches that iterator sequentially through `words`. The statement that forms the body of the `for` may be hard to understand on first reading,

```
   ret[*it].push_back(line_number);
```

so we'll pick it apart a bit at a time. The iterator `it` denotes an element of `words`, and so `*it` is one of the words in the input line. We use that word to index our `map`. The expression `ret[*it]` returns the value stored in the `map` at the position indexed by `*it`. That value is a `vector<int>`, which holds the line numbers on which this word has appeared so far. We call that `vector`'s `push_back` member to append the current line number to the `vector`.

As we saw in §7.2/125, if this is the first time we've seen this word, then the associated `vector<int>` will be value-initialized. Value-initialization of class types is a bit compli- cated, as we'll see in §9.5/164; what we need to know is that `vectors` are value- initialized the same way that variables of type `vector` are created when we don't give them an initial value explicitly. In both cases, the `vector` is created without any ele- ments. Thus, when we insert a new `string` key into the `map`, it will be associated with an empty `vector<int>`. The call to `push_back` will append the current line number to this initially empty `vector`.

Having written the `xref` function, we can use it to generate a cross-reference table:

```
int main()
{
    // call xref using split by default
    map<string, vector<int> > ret = xref(cin);

    // write the results
    for (map<string, vector<int> >::const_iterator it = ret.begin();
            it != ret.end(); ++it) {
        // write the word
        cout << it->first << " occurs on line(s): ";

        // followed by one or more line numbers
        vector<int>::const_iterator line_it = it->second.begin();
        cout << *line_it;     // write the first line number

        ++line_it;
        // write the rest of the line numbers, if any
        while (line_it != it->second.end()) {
            cout << ", " << *line_it;
            ++line_it;
        }
        // write a new line to separate each word from the next
        cout << endl;
    }

    return 0;
}
```

We expect that this code will look as unfamiliar as the code that updated the `map`. Never- theless, it uses only operations that we've already seen.

We begin by calling `xref` to build a data structure that contains the numbers of the lines on which each word appears. We use the default value for the function parameter, so this call to `xref` will use `split` to break the input into words. The rest of the program writes the contents of the data structure that `split` returns.

Most of the program is the `for` statement, the form of which should be familiar from §7.2/124. It starts at the first element in `ret` and looks at all the elements in sequence.

As you read the body of the `for` loop, remember that dereferencing a `map` iterator yields a value of type `pair`. The `first` element of the `pair` holds the (`const`) key, and the `second` element is the value associated with that key.

We begin the `for` loop by writing the word that we're processing and a message:

```
cout << it->first << " occurs on line(s): ";
```

That word is the key at the position in the `map` associated with the iterator `it`. We get at the key by dereferencing the iterator and fetching the `first` element from the `pair`.

We are justified in writing the message at this point because the only way an element could have gotten into `ret` is if it represents a word with one or more references. In this case, we know for certain that at least one line number will follow the message. We don't know if there will be more than one, so we are ambiguous about the plural.

Just as `it->first` is the key, `it->second` is the associated value, which in this case is a `vector<int>` that holds the current word's line numbers. We define `line_it` as an iterator that we will use to access the elements of `it->second`.

We want commas to separate those numbers, but we don't want a stray comma at the end. Therefore, we must treat either the first or the last element specially. We choose to treat the first one specially, by writing that element explicitly. It is safe to do so because every element of `ret` represents a word with at least one reference to it. Having written an element, we increment the iterator to indicate that we've done so. Then the `while` loop iterates through the remaining elements (if any) of the `vector<int>`. For each element, it writes a comma, followed by the value of the element.

7.4 Generating sentences

We'll wrap up this chapter with a slightly more complicated example: We can use a `map` to write a program that takes a description of a sentence structure—a grammar—and generates random sentences that meet that description. For example, we might describe an English sentence as a noun and a verb, or as a noun, a verb, and an object, and so on.

The sentences that we can construct will be more interesting if we can handle complicated rules. For example, rather than saying merely that a sentence is a noun followed by a verb, we might allow noun phrases, where a noun phrase is either simply a noun or an adjective followed by a noun phrase. As a concrete example, given the following input

Categories	Rules
`<noun>`	`cat`
`<noun>`	`dog`
`<noun>`	`table`
`<noun-phrase>`	`<noun>`
`<noun-phrase>`	`<adjective> <noun-phrase>`
`<adjective>`	`large`
`<adjective>`	`brown`
`<adjective>`	`absurd`
`<verb>`	`jumps`
`<verb>`	`sits`
`<location>`	`on the stairs`
`<location>`	`under the sky`
`<location>`	`wherever it wants`
`<sentence>`	`the <noun-phrase> <verb> <location>`

our program might generate

```
the table jumps wherever it wants
```

The program should always start by finding a rule for how to make a sentence. In this input, there is only one such rule—the last one in our table:

```
<sentence>    the <noun-phrase> <verb> <location>
```

This rule says that to make a sentence, we write the word the, a noun-phrase, a verb, and finally a location. The program begins by randomly selecting a rule that matches <noun-phrase>. Evidently the program chose the rule

```
<noun-phrase> <noun>
```

and then resolved the noun using the rule

```
<noun>    table
```

The program must still resolve verb and location, which apparently it did by selecting

```
<verb>    jumps
```

for the verb and

```
<location>  wherever it wants
```

for the location. Note that this last rule maps a category to several words that wind up in the generated sentence.

7.4.1 Representing the rules

Our table contains two kinds of entries: categories, which are enclosed in angle brackets, and ordinary words. Each category has one or more rules; each ordinary word stands for itself. When the program sees a string enclosed in angle brackets, we know that the string will represent a category, so we will have to make the program find a rule that matches the category and expand the right-hand part of that rule. If the program sees words that are unadorned by angle brackets, then we know that it will be able to place those words directly into the generated sentence.

Thinking about how our program might operate, it appears that the program will read a description of how to create sentences, and then randomly generate a sentence. So the first question is: How should we store the description? When we generate sentences, we need to be able to match each category to a rule that will expand that category. For example, we first need to find the rule for how to create a <sentence>; from that rule, we will need to find rules for <noun-phrase>, <verb>, <location>; and so on. Apparently, we'll want a map that maps categories to the corresponding rules.

But what kind of map? The categories are easy: We can store them as strings, so the key type of our map will be string.

The value type is more complicated. If we look at the table again, we can see that any given rule may be a collection of strings. For example, the category sentence is associated with a rule that has four components: the word the and three other strings, which are themselves categories. We know how to represent values of this kind: We can use a `vector<string>` to hold each rule. The problem is that each category may appear more than once in the input. For example, in our sample input description, the category `<noun>` appears three times, as do the categories `<adjective>` and `<location>`. Because these categories appear three times, each one will have three matching rules.

The easiest way to manage multiple instances of the same key will be to store each collection of rules in its own `vector`. Thus, we'll store the grammar in a `map` from `string` to `vectors`, which themselves hold `vector<string>`.

This type is quite a mouthful. Our program will be clearer if we introduce synonyms for our intermediate types. We said that each rule is a `vector<string>`, and that each category maps to a `vector` of these rules. Our analysis implies that we really want to define three types—one for the rule, one for a collection of rules, and one for the map:

```
typedef vector<string> Rule;
typedef vector<Rule> Rule_collection;
typedef map<string, Rule_collection> Grammar;
```

7.4.2 Reading the grammar

Having resolved how to represent the grammar, let's write a function to read it:

```
// read a grammar from a given input stream
Grammar read_grammar(istream& in)
{
    Grammar ret;
    string line;

    // read the input
    while (getline(in, line)) {

        // split the input into words
        vector<string> entry = split(line);

        if (!entry.empty())
            // use the category to store the associated rule
            ret[entry[0]].push_back(
                Rule(entry.begin() + 1, entry.end()));
    }
    return ret;
}
```

The function will read from an input stream and generate a `Grammar` as output. The `while` loop looks like many that we've seen before: It reads a line at a time from `in` and stores what it read in `line`. The `while` terminates when we run out of input or encounter invalid data.

The body of the `while` is astonishingly concise. We use the `split` function from §6.1.1/103 to break the input into words, and store the resulting `vector` in a variable called `entry`. If `entry` is empty, we saw a blank input line, so we disregard it. Otherwise, we know that the first element in `entry` will be the category that we are defining.

We use this element as the index into `ret`. The expression `ret[entry[0]]` yields the object of type `Rule_collection` that is associated with the category in `entry[0]`, remembering that a `Rule_collection` is a `vector`, each element of which holds a

Rule (or, equivalently, a vector<string>). Therefore, ret[entry[0]] is a vector, onto the back of which we push the rule that we just read. That rule is in entry, starting with the second element; the first element in entry is the category. We construct a new, unnamed Rule, by copying the elements from entry (except for the first element), and push that newly created Rule onto the back of the Rule_collection indexed by ret[entry[0]].

7.4.3 Generating the sentence

Having read all the input, we must next generate a random sentence. We know that our input will be a grammar, and that we want to produce a sentence. Our output will be a vector<string> that represents the output sentence.

That's the easy part. The more interesting problem is how the function should work. We know that initially we'll need to find a rule that corresponds to <sentence>. Moreover, we know that we are going to build our output in pieces, which we will assemble from various rules and parts of rules.

In principle, we could concatenate those pieces to form our result. However, because there is no built-in concatenation operation for vectors, we will start with an empty vector and call push_back repeatedly on it.

These two constraints—starting with <sentence>, and calling push_back repeatedly on an initially empty vector—suggest that we are going to want to define our sentence generator in terms of an auxiliary function, which we will call as follows:

```
vector<string> gen_sentence(const Grammar& g)
{
    vector<string> ret;
    gen_aux(g, "<sentence>", ret);
    return ret;
}
```

In effect, the call to gen_aux is a request to use the grammar g to generate a sentence according to the <sentence> rule, and to append that sentence to ret.

Our remaining task is to define gen_aux. Before we do so, we note that gen_aux will have to determine whether a word represents a category, which it will do by checking whether the word is bracketed. We shall, therefore, define a predicate to do so:

```
bool bracketed(const string& s)
{
    return s.size() > 1 && s[0] == '<' && s[s.size() - 1] == '>';
}
```

The job of gen_aux is to expand the input string that it is given as its second argument by looking up that string in the grammar that is its first parameter and placing its output into its third parameter. By "expand" we mean the process that we described in §7.4/129. If our string is bracketed, we then have to find a corresponding rule, which we'll expand in place of the bracketed category. If the input string is not bracketed, then the input itself is part of our output and can be pushed onto the output vector with no further processing:

```
void
gen_aux(const Grammar& g, const string& word, vector<string>& ret)
{
    if (!bracketed(word)) {
        ret.push_back(word);
    } else {
        // locate the rule that corresponds to word
        Grammar::const_iterator it = g.find(word);
        if (it == g.end())
            throw logic_error("empty rule");

        // fetch the set of possible rules
        const Rule_collection& c = it->second;

        // from which we select one at random
        const Rule& r = c[nrand(c.size())];

        // recursively expand the selected rule
        for (Rule::const_iterator i = r.begin(); i != r.end(); ++i)
            gen_aux(g, *i, ret);
    }
}
```

Our first job is trivial: If the word is not bracketed, it represents itself, so we can append it to `ret` and we're done. Now comes the interesting part: finding in `g` the rule that corresponds to our word. You might think that we could simply refer to `g[word]`, but doing so would give us the wrong result. Recall from §7.2/125 that when you try to index a map with a nonexistent key, it automatically creates an element with that key. That will never do in this case, because we don't want to litter our grammar with spurious rules. Moreover, `g` is a `const map`, so even if we wanted to create new entries, we couldn't do so. Indeed, `[]` isn't even defined on a `const map`.

Evidently, we must use a different facility: The `find` member of the `map` class looks for the element, if any, with the given key, and returns an iterator that refers to that element if it can find one. If no such element exists in `g`, the `find` algorithm returns `g.end()`. The comparison between `it` and `g.end()`, therefore, serves to ensure that the rule exists. If it doesn't exist, that means the input was inconsistent—it used a bracketed word without a corresponding rule—so we throw an exception.

At this point, `it` is an iterator that refers to an element of `g`, which is a `map`. Dereferencing this iterator yields a `pair`, the `second` member of which is the value of the `map` element. Therefore, `it->second` denotes the collection of rules that correspond to this category. For convenience, we define a reference named `c` as a synonym for this object.

Our next job is to select a random element from this collection, which we do in the initialization of `r`. This code

```
const Rule& r = c[nrand(c.size())];
```

is unfamiliar, and is, therefore, worth a close look. First, recall that we defined `c` to be a `Rule_collection`, which is a kind of `vector`. We call a function named `nrand`, which we will define in §7.4.4/135, to select a random element of this `vector`. When we give

nrand an argument n, it returns a random integer in the range [0, n). Finally, we
define r as a synonym for that element.

Our final task in gen_aux is to examine every element of r. If the element is bracketed, we have to expand it into a sequence of words; otherwise, we append it to ret.
What may seem like magic on first reading is that this processing is exactly what we are
doing in gen_aux—and therefore, we can call gen_aux to do it!

Such a call is called **recursive**, and it is one of those techniques that looks like it can't
possibly work—until you've tried it a few times. To convince yourself that this function
works, begin by noting that the function obviously works if word is not bracketed.

Next, assume that word is bracketed, but its rule's right-hand side has no bracketed
words of its own. It should still be easy to see that the program will work in this case,
because when it makes each recursive call, the gen_aux that it calls will immediately see
that the word is not bracketed. Therefore, it will append the word to ret and return.

The next step is to assume that word refers to a slightly more complicated rule—one
that uses bracketed words in its right-hand side, but only words that refer to rules with no
bracketed words of their own. When you encounter a recursive call to gen_aux, do not
try to figure out what it does. Instead, remember that you have already convinced yourself that it works in this case, because you know that at worst, its argument is a category
that does not lead to any further bracketed words. Eventually, you will see that the function works in all cases, because each recursive call simplifies the argument.

We do not know any sure way to explain recursion. Our experience is that people
stare at recursive programs for a long time without understanding how they work. Then,
one day, they suddenly get it—and they don't understand why they ever thought it was
difficult. Evidently, the key to understanding recursion is to begin by understanding
recursion. The rest is easy.

Having written gen_sentence, read_grammar, and the associated auxiliary functions, we'll want to use them:

```
int main()
{
    // generate the sentence
    vector<string> sentence = gen_sentence(read_grammar(cin));

    // write the first word, if any
    vector<string>::const_iterator it = sentence.begin();
    if (!sentence.empty()) {
        cout << *it;
        ++it;
    }

    // write the rest of the words, each preceded by a space
    while (it != sentence.end()) {
        cout << " " << *it;
        ++it;
    }

    cout << endl;
    return 0;
}
```

We read the grammar, generate a sentence from it, and then write the sentence a word at a time. The only even minor complexity is that we put a space in front of the second and subsequent words of the sentence.

7.4.4 Selecting a random element

It is now time to write `nrand`. We begin by noting that the standard library includes a function named `rand` (defined in `<cstdlib>`). That function takes no arguments, and returns a random integer in the range `[0, RAND_MAX]`, where `RAND_MAX` is a large integer that is also defined in `<cstdlib>`. Our job is to reduce the range `[0, RAND_MAX]`, which includes both 0 and `RAND_MAX`, to `[0, n)`, which includes 0 but not n, with the understanding that `n <= RAND_MAX`.

You might think that it would suffice to compute `rand() % n`, which is the remainder when dividing the random integer by n. In practice, this technique fails for two reasons.

The most important reason is pragmatic: `rand()` really returns only pseudo-random numbers. Many C++ implementations' pseudo-random-number generators give remainders that aren't very random when the quotients are small integers. For example, it is not uncommon for successive results of `rand()` to be alternately even and odd. In that case, if n is 2, successive results of `rand() % n` will alternate between 0 and 1.

There is another, more subtle reason to avoid using `rand() % n`: If the value of n is large, and `RAND_MAX` is not evenly divisible by n, some remainders will appear more often than others. For example, suppose that `RAND_MAX` is 32767 (the smallest permissible value of `RAND_MAX` for any implementation) and n is 20000. In that case, there would be two distinct values of `rand()` that would cause `rand() % n` to be 10000 (namely, 10000 and 30000), but only one value of `rand()` that would cause `rand() % n` to be 15000 (namely, 15000). Therefore, the naive implementation of `nrand` would yield 10000 as a value of `nrand(20000)` twice as often as it would yield 15000.

To avoid these pitfalls, we'll use a different strategy. We'll partition the available random numbers into n equal-sized buckets, perhaps with some numbers left over. Then we can compute a random number, figure out into which bucket it falls, and return that bucket's number. If the random number isn't in any bucket, we will ignore it, and keep asking for random numbers until we get one that lands in a bucket.

The function is easier to write than to describe:

```
// return a random integer in the range [0, n)
int nrand(int n)
{
    if (n <= 0 || n > RAND_MAX)
        throw domain_error("Argument to nrand is out of range");

    const int bucket_size = RAND_MAX / n;
    int r;

    do r = rand() / bucket_size;
    while (r >= n);

    return r;
}
```

The definition of bucket_size relies on the fact that integer division truncates its result. This property implies that RAND_MAX / n is the largest integer that is less than or equal to the exact quotient. As a consequence, bucket_size is the largest integer with the property that n * bucket_size ≤ RAND_MAX.

The next statement is a **do while** statement. A do while is like a while statement, except that it always executes the body at least once, and tests the condition at the end. If that condition yields true, then the loop repeats, executing the body until the while fails. In this case, the body of the loop sets r to a bucket number. Bucket 0 will correspond to values of rand() in the range [0, bucket_size), bucket 1 will correspond to values in the range [bucket_size, bucket_size * 2), and so on. If the value of rand() is so large that r ≥ n, the program will continue trying random numbers until it finds one that it likes, at which point it returns the corresponding value of r.

For example, let's assume that RAND_MAX is 32767 and n is 20000. Then bucket_size will be 1, and nrand will work by discarding random numbers until it finds one less than 20000. As another example, assume that n is 3. Then bucket_size will be 10922. In this case, values of rand() in the range [0, 10922) will yield 0, values in the range [10922, 21844) will yield 1, values in the range [21844, 32766) will yield 2, and values of 32766 or 32767 will be discarded.

7.5 A note on performance

If you have used associative arrays in other languages, those arrays were probably implemented in terms of a data structure called a *hash table*. Hash tables can be very fast, but they have compensating disadvantages:

- For each key type, someone must supply a hash function, which computes an appropriate integer value from the value of the key.
- A hash table's performance is exquisitely sensitive to the details of the hash function.
- There is usually no easy way to retrieve the elements of a hash table in a useful order.

C++ associative containers are hard to implement in terms of hash tables:

- The key type needs only the < operator or equivalent comparison function.
- The time to access an associative-container element with a given key is logarithmic in the total number of elements in that container, regardless of the keys' values.
- Associative-container elements are always kept sorted by key.

In other words, although C++ associative containers will typically be slightly slower than the best hash-table data structures, they perform much better than naive data structures, their performance does not require their users to design good hash functions, and they are more convenient than hash tables because of their automatic ordering. If you're generally familiar with associative data structures, you might want to know that C++ libraries typically use a balanced self-adjusting tree structure to implement associative containers.

If you really want hash tables, they are available as parts of many C++ implementations. However, because they are not part of standard C++, they are beyond the scope of this book. Although no standard can be ideal for every purpose, the standard associative containers are more than adequate for most applications.

7.6 Details

The do while statement is similar to the `while` statement (§2.3.1/19), except that the test is at the end. The general form of the statement is

```
do statement
while (condition);
```

The *statement* is executed first, after which the *condition* and *statement* are executed alternately until the *condition* is `false`.

Value-initialization: Accessing a `map` element that doesn't yet exist creates an element with a value of `V()`, where `V` is the type of the values stored in the `map`. Such an expression is said to be value-initialized. §9.5/164 explains the details of value-initialization; the most important aspect is that built-in types are initialized to `0`.

rand() is a function that yields a random integer in the range `[0, RAND_MAX]`. Both `rand` and `RAND_MAX` are defined in `<cstdlib>`.

pair<K, V> is a simple type whose objects hold pairs of values. Access to these data values is through their names, `first` and `second` respectively.

map<K, V> is an associative array with key type `K` and value type `V`. The elements of a map are key–value pairs, which are maintained in key order to allow efficient access of elements by key. The iterators on `maps` are bidirectional (§8.2.5/148). Dereferencing a map iterator yields a value of type `pair<const K, V>`. The map operations include:

`map<K, V> m;`	Creates a new empty `map`, with keys of type `const K` and values of type `V`.
`map<K, V> m(cmp);`	Creates a new empty `map` with keys of type `const K` and values of type `V`, that uses the predicate `cmp` to determine the order of the elements.
`m[k]`	Indexes the `map` using a key, `k`, of type `K`, and returns an lvalue of type `V`. If there is no entry for the given key, a new value-initialized element is created and inserted into the `map` with this key. Because using `[]` to access a map might create a new element, `[]` is not allowed on a `const map`.
`m.begin()`	
`m.end()`	Return iterators that can be used to access the elements of a `map`. Note that dereferencing one of these iterators yields a key–value pair, not just a value.
`m.find(k)`	Returns an iterator referring to the element with key `k`, or `m.end()` if no such element exists.

For a `map<K, V>` and an associated iterator `p`, the following apply:

`p->first`	Yields an lvalue of type `const K` that is the key for the element `p` denotes.
`p->second`	Yields an lvalue of type `V` that is the value part of the element that `p` denotes.

Exercises

7-0.   Compile, execute, and test the programs in this chapter.

7-1.   Extend the program from §7.2/124 to produce its output sorted by occurrence count. That is, the output should group all the words that occur once, followed by those that occur twice, and so on.

7-2.   Extend the program in §4.2.3/64 to assign letter grades by ranges:

> A   90–100
> B   80–89.99 . . .
> C   70–79.99 . . .
> D   60–69.99 . . .
> F   < 60

The output should list how many students fall into each category.

7-3.   The cross-reference program from §7.3/126 could be improved: As it stands, if a word occurs more than once on the same input line, the program will report that line multiple times. Change the code so that it detects multiple occurrences of the same line number and inserts the line number only once.

7-4.   The output produced by the cross-reference program will be ungainly if the input file is large. Rewrite the program to break up the output if the lines get too long.

7-5.   Reimplement the grammar program using a `list` as the data structure in which we build the sentence.

7-6.   Reimplement the `gen_sentence` program using two `vector`s: One will hold the fully unwound, generated sentence, and the other will hold the rules and will be used as a stack. Do not use any recursive calls.

7-7.   Change the driver for the cross-reference program so that it writes `line` if there is only one line and `lines` otherwise.

7-8.   Change the cross-reference program to find all the URLs in a file, and write all the lines on which each distinct URL occurs.

7-9.   (difficult) The implementation of `nrand` in §7.4.4/135 will not work for arguments greater than `RAND_MAX`. Usually, this restriction is no problem, because `RAND_MAX` is often the largest possible integer anyway. Nevertheless, there are implementations under which `RAND_MAX` is much smaller than the largest possible integer. For example, it is not uncommon for `RAND_MAX` to be 32767 ($2^{15} - 1$) and the largest possible integer to be 2147483647 ($2^{31} - 1$). Reimplement `nrand` so that it works well for all values of n.

8

Writing generic functions

The first part of this book concentrated on writing programs that use the fundamentals of the C++ language, and the abstractions that the standard library provides, to solve concrete problems. Starting with this chapter, we'll turn our attention to learning how to write our own abstractions.

These abstractions take several forms. This chapter discusses generic functions, which are functions with parameter types that we do not know until we call the functions. Chapters 9 through 12 show how to implement abstract data types. Finally, starting in Chapter 13, we will learn about object-oriented programming (OOP).

8.1 What is a generic function?

Whenever we have written a function so far, we've known the types of the function's parameters and return value. This knowledge may seem at first like an integral part of any function's description. Nonetheless, a closer look will reveal that we have already used—but not written—functions with argument and return types that we do not know until we use the functions.

For example, in §6.1.3/107, we used a library function named find, which takes two iterators and a value as arguments. We can use the same find function to find values of any appropriate type in any kind of container. This usage implies that we do not know what find's argument or result types will be until we use it. Such a function is called a *generic function*, and the ability to use and create generic functions is a key feature of the C++ language.

The language support for generic functions is not hard to understand. What is difficult is understanding exactly what we mean when we say that find can accept arguments of "any appropriate type." For example, how can we describe how find behaves in a way that will enable someone who wishes to use it to know whether it will work with particular arguments? The answer to this question lies partly within the C++ language and partly outside it.

The part that is inside the language is the idea that the ways in which a function uses a parameter of unknown type constrain that parameter's type. For example, if a function has parameters x and y, and computes x + y, then the mere existence of that computation implicitly requires that x and y have types for which x + y is defined. Whenever you call such a function, the implementation checks that your arguments' types meet the constraints implied by the ways in which the function uses its parameters.

The part of the answer that lies outside the C++ language is the way in which the standard library organizes the constraints on its functions' parameters. We have already shown you one example of this organization—namely, the notion of an iterator. Some types are iterators; others aren't. The find function takes three arguments, of which the first two are required to be iterators.

When we say that a particular type is an iterator, we are really saying something about the operations that the type supports: A type is an iterator if and only if it supports a particular collection of operations in a particular way. If we were to set out to write the find function ourselves, we would do so in a way that relies only on the operations that every iterator must support. If we were to write our own container—as we shall do in Chapter 11—then we would have to supply iterators that support all the appropriate operations.

The notion of an iterator is not part of the C++ language proper. However, it is a fundamental part of the standard library's organization, and it is that part that makes generic functions as useful as they are. This chapter shows some examples of how the library might implement generic functions. Along the way, it explains just what an iterator is—or, more precisely, what iterators are, because they come in five different varieties.

This chapter is more abstract than the ones we've seen so far, because it is in the very nature of generic functions to be abstract. If we wrote functions that solved specific problems, those functions wouldn't be generic. Nevertheless, you will find that most of the functions that we describe are familiar, because we have used them in earlier examples. Moreover, it shouldn't be hard to imagine how you might use even the unfamiliar ones.

8.1.1 Medians of unknown type

The language feature that implements generic functions is called *template functions*. Templates let us write a single definition for a family of functions—or types—that behave similarly, except for differences that we can attribute to the types of their *template parameters*. We'll explore template functions in this chapter, and template classes in Chapter 11.

The key idea behind templates is that objects of different types may nevertheless share common behavior. Template parameters let us write programs in terms of that common behavior, even though we do not know the specific types that correspond to the template parameters when we define the template. We do know the types when we use a template, and that knowledge is available when we compile and link our programs. For generic parameters, the implementation doesn't need to worry about what to do about objects with types that might vary during execution—only during compilation.

Although templates are a cornerstone of the standard library, we can use them for our own programs as well. For example, we wrote a function in §4.1.1/53 to calculate the median of a vector<double>. That function relied on the ability to sort a vector, and then to fetch a specific element given its index, so we cannot easily make that function work on arbitrary sequences of values. Even so, there is no reason to restrict the function to `vector<double>`; we can take the median of `vector`s of other types as well. Template functions allow us to do so:

```
template<class T>
T median(vector<T> v)
{
    typedef typename vector<T>::size_type vec_sz;

    vec_sz size = v.size();
    if (size == 0)
        throw domain_error("median of an empty vector");

    sort(v.begin(), v.end());

    vec_sz mid = size/2;

    return size % 2 == 0 ? (v[mid] + v[mid-1]) / 2 : v[mid];
}
```

The first novelties here are the template header,

```
template<class T>
```

and the use of `T` in the parameter list and return type. The template header tells the implementation that we are defining a template function, and that the function will take a *type parameter*. Type parameters operate much like function parameters: They define names that can be used within the scope of the function. However, type parameters refer to types, not to variables. Thus, wherever `T` appears in the function, the implementation will assume that `T` names a type. In the `median` function, we use the type parameter explicitly to say what type of objects the `vector` named `v` holds, and to specify the return type of the function.

When we call this `median` function, the implementation will bind `T` to a type that it determines at that point, during compilation. For example, we might take the `median` of a `vector<int>` object named `vi` by calling `median(vi)`. From this call, the implementation can infer that `T` is `int`. Wherever we use `T` in this function, the implementation generates code as if we had written `int`. In effect, the implementation *instantiates* our code as if we had written a specific version of `median` that took a `vector<int>` and returned an `int`. We'll have more to say about instantiation shortly.

The next novelty is the use of **typename** in the definition of `vec_sz`. It is there to tell the implementation that `vector<T>::size_type` is the name of a type, even though the implementation doesn't yet know what type `T` represents. Whenever you have a type, such as `vector<T>`, that depends on a template parameter, and you want to use a member of that type, such as `size_type`, that is itself a type, you must precede the entire name by `typename` to let the implementation know to treat the name as a type. Although the standard library ensures that `vector<T>::size_type` is the name of a type for any `T`, the implementation, having no special knowledge of the standard-library types, has no way of knowing this fact.

As you read a template, you will usually see that the type parameters pervade its definition, even if many of the type dependencies are implicit. In our `median` function, we use the type parameters explicitly only in the function return type and parameter list, and in the definition of vec_sz. However, because v has type vector<T>, any operation involving v implicitly involves this type. For example, in the expression

```
(v[mid] + v[mid-1]) / 2
```

we have to know the type of v's elements in order to know the types of v[mid] and v[mid-1]. These types, in turn, determine the type of the + and / operators. If we call median on a vector<int>, then we can see that + and / take int operands and return int results. Calling median for a vector<double> does the arithmetic on double values. We can't call median for a vector<string>, because the median function uses division, and the string type does not have a division operator. This behavior is what we want. After all, what would it mean to find the median of a vector<string>?

8.1.2   Template instantiation

When we call median on behalf of a vector<int>, the implementation will effectively create and compile an instance of the function that replaces every use of T by int. If we also call median for a vector<double>, then the implementation will again infer the types from the call. In this case, T will be bound to double, and the implementation will generate another version of median using double in place of T.

The C++ standard says nothing about how implementations should manage template instantiation, so every implementation handles instantiation in its own particular way. While we cannot say exactly how your compiler will handle instantiation, there are two important points to keep in mind: The first is that for C++ implementations that follow the traditional edit–compile–link model, instantiation often happens not at compile time, but at link time. It is not until the implementation gets around to instantiating the templates that it can check the types that the programmer specified against the types that the templates expect. Hence, it is possible to get what seem like compile-time errors at link time.

The second point matters if you write your own templates: Most current implementations require that in order to instantiate a template, the definition of the template, not just the declaration, has to be accessible to the implementation. Generally, this requirement implies access to the source files that define the template, as well as the header file. How the implementation locates the source file differs from one implementation to another. Many implementations expect the header file for the template to include the source file, either directly or via a #include. The most certain way to know what your implementation expects is to check its documentation.

8.1.3   Generic functions and types

We said in §8.1/139 that the difficult part of designing and using templates is understanding precisely the interaction between a template and the "appropriate types" that can be used with the template. We saw one obvious type dependency in our definition of the template version of median: The types stored in the vectors that are passed to the median function must support addition and division, and these operations had better map to their normal arithmetic meanings. Fortunately, most types that define division are arithmetic types, so such dependencies are unlikely to create problems in practice.

More subtle type issues arise in the interactions between templates and type conversions. For example, when we called `find` to check whether students had done all their homework, we wrote

```
find(s.homework.begin(), s.homework.end(), 0);
```

In this case, `homework` is a `vector<double>`, but we told `find` to look for an `int`. This particular type mismatch is of no consequence: We can compare an `int` value with a `double` value with no loss of meaning.

However, when we called `accumulate`

```
accumulate(v.begin(), v.end(), 0.0)
```

we noted that the correctness of our program depended on our using the `double` form of zero, rather than the `int`. The reason is that the `accumulate` function uses the type of its third argument as the type of its accumulator. If that type is `int`—even if we're adding a sequence of `double`s—the addition will be truncated to just the integer part. In this case, the implementation would let us pass an `int`, but the sum that we obtained would lack precision.

Finally, when we called `max`

```
string::size_type maxlen = 0;
maxlen = max(maxlen, name.size());
```

we noted that it was essential that the type of `maxlen` match exactly the type returned by `name.size()`. If the types don't match, the call will not compile. Now that we know that template parameter types are inferred from the argument types, we can understand why this behavior exists. Consider a plausible implementation of the `max` function:

```
template<class T>
T max(const T& left, const T& right)
{
    return left > right ? left : right;
}
```

If we pass an `int` and a `double` to this function, the implementation has no way to infer which argument to convert to the other argument's type. Should it resolve the call as comparing the values as `int`s, and so return an `int`, or should it treat both arguments as `double` and return a `double`? There's no way for the implementation to make this determination, so the call fails at compile time.

8.2 Data-structure independence

The `median` function that we just implemented used templates to generalize across types that a `vector` might contain. We can call this function to find the median of a `vector` of values of any kind of arithmetic type.

More generally, we would like to be able to write a simple function that deals with values stored in any kind of data structure, such as a `list`, a `vector`, or a `string`. For that matter, we would like to be able to act on part of a container, rather than having to use the entire container.

For example, the standard library uses iterators to allow us to call `find` on any contiguous part of any container. If c is a container, and `val` is a value of the type stored in the container, we use `find` by writing expressions such as

```
find(c.begin(), c.end(), val)
```

Why did we have to mention c twice? Why doesn't the library let us say

```
c.find(val)
```

by analogy with `c.size()`, or even

```
find(c, val)
```

passing the container directly to `find` as an argument? Both questions turn out to have the same answer: By using iterators, and thereby requiring us to mention c twice, the library makes it possible to write a single `find` function that can find a value in any contiguous part of any container. Neither of these other approaches allows us to do so.

Let's look first at `c.find(val)`. If the library let us use `c.find(val)`, we would be calling `find` as a member of whatever type c has—which means that whoever defined the type of c would have to define `find` as a member. Also, if the library used the `c.find(val)` style for the algorithms, then we would be unable to use these functions for built-in arrays, about which we shall learn in Chapter 10.

Why does the library require us to give `c.begin()` and `c.end()` as arguments to `find` instead of letting us pass c directly? The reason to pass two values is that doing so delimits a range, which makes it possible to look in part of a container instead of insisting on looking through the whole thing. For example, think about how you would write the `split` function in §6.1.1/103 if `find_if` were restricted to searching an entire container.

There is a more subtle reason for generic functions to take iterator arguments instead of container arguments directly: It is possible for iterators to access elements that aren't in containers at all in the ordinary sense. For example, in §6.1.2/105, we used the `rbegin` function, which yields an iterator that grants access to its container's elements in reverse order. Passing such an iterator as an argument to `find` or `find_if` lets us search the container's elements in reverse order, which would be impossible if these functions insisted on taking a container as an argument directly.

Of course, it would be possible to overload the library functions, so that one could call them with either a container or a pair of iterators as an argument. However, it is far from clear that the extra convenience would outweigh the extra complexity in the library.

8.2.1 Algorithms and iterators

The easiest way to understand how templates let us write data-structure–independent programs is to look at implementations of some of the more popular standard-library functions. These functions all include iterators among their arguments, which identify the container elements on which the functions will act. All standard-library containers, and some other types, such as `string`, supply iterators that allow these functions to act on the containers' elements.

Some containers support operations that others do not. This support, or lack thereof, translates into operations that some iterators support and others do not. For example, it is possible to access an element with a given index directly in a `vector`, but not in a `list`. Accordingly, if we have an iterator that refers to an element of a `vector`, the design of that iterator makes it possible to obtain an iterator that refers to another element of that same `vector` by adding the difference between the elements' indices to the iterator. Iterators that refer to `list` elements offer no analogous facility.

Because different kinds of iterators offer different kinds of operations, it is important to understand the requirements that various algorithms place on the iterators that they use, and the operations that various kinds of iterators support. Whenever two iterators support the same operation, they give it the same name. For example, all iterators use ++ to cause an iterator to refer to the next element of its container.

Not all algorithms need all the iterator operations. Some algorithms, such as `find`, use very few iterator operations. We can `find` values using any of the container iterators that we've seen. Other algorithms, such as `sort`, use the most powerful operations, including arithmetic, on iterators. Of the types we've seen in the library, only `vectors` and `strings` are compatible with `sort`. (Sorting a `string` arranges its individual characters in nondecreasing order.)

The library defines five *iterator categories*, each one of which corresponds to a specific collection of iterator operations. These iterator categories classify the kind of iterator that each of the library containers provides. Each standard-library algorithm says what category it expects for each iterator argument. Thus, the iterator categories give us a way to understand which containers can use which algorithms.

Each iterator category corresponds to a strategy for accessing container elements. Because iterator categories correspond to access strategies, they also correspond to particular kinds of algorithms. For example, some algorithms make only a single pass over their input, so they don't need iterators that can make multiple passes. Others require the ability to access arbitrary elements efficiently given only their indices, and, therefore, require the ability to add indices and integers.

We will now describe each access strategy, show an algorithm that uses it, and describe the corresponding iterator category.

8.2.2 Sequential read-only access

One straightforward way to access a sequence is to read its elements sequentially. Among the library functions that does so is `find`, which we can implement as

```
template <class In, class X> In find(In begin, In end, const X& x)
{
    while (begin != end && *begin != x)
        ++begin;
    return begin;
}
```

If we call `find(begin, end, x)`, the result is either the first iterator `iter` in the range `[begin, end)` such that `*iter == x`, or `end` if no such iterator exists.

We know that this function accesses the elements in the range `[begin, end)` sequentially, because the only operation it ever uses to change the value of `begin` is `++`. In addition to using `++` to change the value of `begin`, it uses `!=` to compare `begin` and `end`, and `*` to access the container element to which `begin` refers. These operations are sufficient to read sequentially the elements to which a range of iterator values refers.

Although the operations are sufficient, they are not the only operations that we might want to use. For example, we might have implemented `find` this way:

```
template <class In, class X> In find(In begin, In end, const X& x)
{
    if (begin == end || *begin == x)
        return begin;
    begin++;
    return find(begin, end, x);
}
```

Although most C++ programmers would find this recursive programming style unusual, programmers accustomed to languages such as Lisp or ML will feel right at home. This version of `find` uses `begin++` instead of `++begin`, and `==` instead of `!=`. From these two examples, we can conclude that an iterator that offers sequential read-only access to elements of a sequence should support `++` (both prefix and postfix), `==`, `!=`, and unary `*`.

There is one other operator that such an iterator ought to support, and that is the equivalence between `iter->member` and `(*iter).member` that we used, for example, in §7.2/124. There we used `it->first` as an abbreviation for `(*it).first`, and we would certainly like to be able to do so in general.

If a type provides all of these operations, we call it an *input iterator*. Every container iterator that we've seen supports all these operations, so they are all input iterators. Of course, they support other operations as well, but that additional support does not affect the fact that they are input iterators.

When we say that `find` requires input iterators as its first and second arguments, we are saying that we can give `find` arguments of any type that meets the input-iterator requirements, including iterators that support additional operations.

8.2.3 Sequential write-only access

Input iterators can be used only for reading elements of a sequence. Obviously, there are contexts in which we would like to be able to use iterators to write elements of a sequence. For example, consider the `copy` function

```
template<class In, class Out>
Out copy(In begin, In end, Out dest)
{
    while (begin != end)
        *dest++ = *begin++;
    return dest;
}
```

This function takes three iterators; the first two denote the sequence from which to copy, and the third denotes the beginning of the destination sequence. We saw this same `while` loop in §6.1/102: The function operates by advancing `begin` through the container until it reaches `end`, copying each element into `dest` as it goes.

As the name `In` suggests, `begin` and `end` are input iterators. We use them only for reading elements, just as we did in `find`. What about `Out`, the type of the parameter `dest`? Looking at the operations on `dest`, we see that in this function, we need only be able to evaluate `*dest = value` and `dest++`. As with `find`, logical completeness argues that we should also be able to evaluate `++dest`.

There is one other requirement that is less evident. Suppose `it` is an iterator that we wish to use for output only, and we execute

```
*it = x;
++it;
++it;
*it = y;
```

By incrementing `it` twice between assignments to `*it`, we have left a gap in our output sequence. Therefore, if we wish to use an iterator exclusively for output, there is an implicit requirement that we not execute `++it` more than once between assignments to `*it`, or assign a value to `*it` more than once without incrementing `it`.

If a function uses a type in a way that meets these requirements, we call that type an **output iterator**. All the standard containers provide iterators that meet these requirements, as does `back_inserter`. It is worth noting that the "write-once" property is a requirement on programs that use iterators, not on iterators themselves. That is, iterators that satisfy only the output-iterator requirements are required to support only programs that maintain that property. The iterator generated by `back_inserter` is an output iterator, so programs that use it must obey the "write-once" requirement. The container iterators all offer additional operations, so programs that use them are not restricted in this way.

8.2.4 Sequential read-write access

Suppose we want to be able to read and write the elements of a sequence, but only sequentially: We intend to advance iterators forward but never backward. An example of a library function that does so is `replace`, from the `<algorithm>` header:

```
template<class For, class X>
void replace(For beg, For end, const X& x, const X& y)
{
    while (beg != end) {
        if (*beg == x)
            *beg = y;
        ++beg;
    }
}
```

This function examines the elements in the range `[beg, end)` and replaces every element that is equal to x by y. It should be clear that the type `For` needs to support all the operations supported by an input iterator, as well as all the operations supported by an output iterator. Moreover, it should not need to meet the single-assignment requirement of output iterators, because it now makes sense to read the element value after assigning it, and perhaps to change it. Such a type is a *forward iterator*, and it is required to support

> `*it` (for both reading and writing)
> `++it` and `it++` (but not `--it` or `it--`)
> `it == j` and `it != j` (where `j` has the same type as `it`)
> `it->member` (as a synonym for `(*it).member`)

All the standard-library containers meet the forward-iterator requirements.

8.2.5 *Reversible access*

Some functions need to get at a container's elements in reverse order. The most straightforward example of such a function is `reverse`, which the standard library defines in the `<algorithm>` header

```
template<class Bi> void reverse(Bi begin, Bi end)
{
    while (begin != end) {
        --end;
        if (begin != end)
            swap(*begin++, *end);
    }
}
```

In this algorithm, we march `end` backward from the end of the `vector` and `beg` forward from the beginning, exchanging the elements that they reference as we go.

   This function uses the iterators `begin` and `end` as if they were forward iterators, except that it also uses `--`, which is obviously the key to being able to traverse a sequence backward. If a type meets all the requirements of a forward iterator, and also supports `--` (both prefix and postfix), we call it a *bidirectional iterator*.

   The standard-library container classes all support bidirectional iterators.

8.2.6 *Random access*

Some functions need to be able to jump around in a container. One good example of such a function is the classical binary-search algorithm. The standard library implements this algorithm in several forms, the most straightforward of which is called—you guessed it—`binary_search`. The standard-library implementation actually uses some clever techniques (well beyond the scope of this book) that allow it to do binary searches on sequences defined by forward iterators. A simpler version, which requires random-access iterators, looks like this:

```
template<class Ran, class X>
bool binary_search(Ran begin, Ran end, const X& x)
{
    while (begin < end) {
        // find the midpoint of the range
        Ran mid = begin + (end - begin) / 2;
```

```
            // see which part of the range contains x; keep looking only in that part
            if (x < *mid)
                end = mid;
            else if (*mid < x)
                begin = mid + 1;
            // if we got here, then *mid == x so we're done
            else return true;
        }
        return false;
    }
```

In addition to relying on the other usual iterator properties, this function relies on the ability to do arithmetic on iterators. For example, it subtracts one iterator from another to obtain an integer, and adds an iterator and an integer to obtain another iterator. Again, the notion of logical completeness adds requirements to random-access iterators. If p and q are such iterators, and n is an integer, then the complete list of additional requirements, beyond those for bidirectional iterators, is

$p + n, p - n$, and $n + p$
$p - q$
p[n] (equivalent to * (p + n))
$p < q, p > q, p <= q$, and $p >= q$

Subtracting two iterators yields the distance between the iterators as an integral type that we will discuss in §10.1.4/175. We did not include == and != in the requirements because random-access iterators also support the requirements on bidirectional iterators.

The only algorithm that we have used that requires random-access iterators is the sort function. The vector and string iterators are random-access iterators. However, the list iterator is not; it supports only bidirectional iterators. Why?

The essential reason is that lists are optimized for fast insertion and deletion. Hence, there is no quick way to navigate to an arbitrary element of the list. The only way to navigate through a list is to look at each element in sequence.

8.2.7 Iterator ranges and off-the-end values

As we've seen, the convention that algorithms take two arguments to specify ranges is nearly universal in the library. The first argument refers to the first element of the range; the second argument refers to *one past* the last element of the range. Why do we specify one past the end of the range? When is it even valid to do so?

In §2.6/30, we saw one reason to use an upper bound for a range that is one past the last value in the range—namely, that if we specified the end of a range by a value equal to the last element, then we would be saying implicitly that the last element was special somehow. If the end value is treated specially, it is easy to write programs that mistakenly stop one iteration before the end. As far as iterators are concerned, there are at least three more reasons to mark the end of a range by an iterator that is one past the last element, instead of one that refers to the last element directly.

One reason is that if the range had no elements at all, there would be no last element to mark the end. We would then be in the curious position of having to designate an empty range by an iterator that refers to where the element before the beginning of the range would be. With that strategy, we would have to handle empty ranges differently from all others, which would make our programs harder to understand and less reliable. We saw in §6.1.1/103 that treating empty ranges the same as any others simplified our program.

The second reason is that marking the end of a range by an iterator that is one past the end lets us get away with comparing iterators only for equality and inequality, and makes it unnecessary to define what it means for one iterator to be less than another. The point is that we can tell immediately if the range is empty by comparing the two iterators; the range is empty if and only if the iterators are equal. If they are unequal, then we know that the beginning iterator refers to an element, so we can do something and then increment that iterator to reduce the size of the range. In other words, marking ranges by the beginning and one past the end allows us to use loops of the form

```
// invariant: we must still process the elements in the range [begin, end)
while (begin != end) {
    // do something with the element to which begin refers
    ++begin;
}
```

and we need only to be able to do (in)equality comparisons on iterators.

The third reason is that defining a range by the beginning and one past the end gives us a natural way to indicate "out of range." Many standard-library algorithms—and algorithms that we ourselves write—take advantage of this out-of-range value by returning the second iterator of a range to indicate failure. For example, our `url_beg` function in §6.1.3/108 used this convention to signal its inability to find a URL. If the algorithms did not have this value available, they would have to invent one, which would complicate both the algorithms and the programs that use them.

In short, although it may seem odd to indicate the end of a range by an iterator that refers to one element past the end, doing so makes most programs simpler and more reliable than they would be otherwise. To this end, every container type is required to support an off-the-end value for its iterators. Each container's `end` member returns such a value, and that value can be the result of other iterator operations as well. For example, if `c` is a container, copying `c.begin()` and incrementing that copy a number of times equal to `c.size()` will yield an iterator that is equal to `c.end()`. The effect of dereferencing an off-the-end iterator is undefined, as is that of computing an iterator value that is before the beginning of a container, or more than one past the end.

8.3 Input and output iterators

Why are input and output iterators separate categories from forward iterators if no standard container requires the distinction? One reason is that not all iterators are associated with containers. For example, if `c` is a container that supports `push_back`, then `back_inserter(c)` is an output iterator that meets no other iterator requirements.

As another example, the standard library provides iterators that can be bound to input and output streams. Not surprisingly, the iterators for `istream` meet the requirements for input iterators, and those for `ostreams` meet the requirements for output iterators. Using the appropriate stream iterator, we can use the normal iterator operations to manipulate an `istream` or an `ostream`. For example, `++` will advance the iterator to the next value in the stream. For input streams, `*` will yield the value at the current position in the input, and for output streams, `*` will let us write to the corresponding `ostream`. The stream iterators are defined in the `<iterator>` header.

The input stream iterator is an input-iterator type named `istream_iterator`:

```
vector<int> v;

// read ints from the standard input and append them to v
copy(istream_iterator<int>(cin), istream_iterator<int>(),
    back_inserter(v));
```

As usual, the first two arguments to `copy` specify a range from which to copy. The first argument constructs a new `istream_iterator`, bound to `cin`, that expects to read values of type `int`. Remember that C++ input and output are typed operations: When we read from a stream, we always say the type of value that we expect to read, although those types are often implicit in the operations that do the read. For example,

```
getline(cin, s);                    // read data into a string
cin >> s.name >> s.midterm >> s.final;   // read a string and two doubles
```

Similarly, when we define a stream iterator, we must have a way to tell it what type it should read from or write to the stream. Accordingly, the stream iterators are templates.

The second argument to `copy` creates a default (empty) `istream_iterator<int>`, which is not bound to any file. The `istream_iterator` type has a default value with the property that any `istream_iterator` that has reached end-of-file or is in an error state will appear to be equal to the default value. Therefore, we can use the default value to indicate the "one-past-the-end" convention for `copy`.

We can now see that the call to `copy` will read values from the standard input until we hit end-of-file or an input that is not valid as an `int`.

We cannot use an `istream_iterator` for writing. If we wish to write, we need an `ostream_iterator`, which is the iterator type whose objects we use for output:

```
// write the elements of v each separated from the other by a space
copy(v.begin(), v.end(), ostream_iterator<int>(cout, " "));
```

Here we copy the entire `vector` onto the standard output. The third argument constructs a new iterator bound to `cout`, which expects to write values of type `int`.

The second argument used to construct the `ostream_iterator<int>` object specifies a value to be written after each element. Typically, this value is a string literal, and may not be a `string`; we'll discuss the exact requirements on such values in §10.2/176 and §B.1/312. If we do not supply such a value, the `ostream_iterator` will write values without any separation. Therefore, if we omit the separator, a call to `copy` will run all the values together into one unreadable mess:

```
// no separation between elements!
copy(v.begin(), v.end(), ostream_iterator<int>(cout));
```

8.4 Using iterators for flexibility

We can make a slight improvement in the `split` function that we presented in §6.1.1/103. As written, the `split` function returns a `vector<string>`, which is limiting: Instead of a `vector`, our users might want a `list<string>` or another kind of container. Nothing about the `split` algorithm requires that we produce a `vector`.

We can be more flexible by rewriting `split` to take an output iterator instead of returning a value. In this version of the function, we'll use that iterator to write the words that we find. Our caller will have bound the iterator to the output location where the values should be placed:

```
template <class Out>                                    // changed
void split(const string& str, Out os) {                 // changed

    typedef string::const_iterator iter;

    iter i = str.begin();
    while (i != str.end()) {
        // ignore leading blanks
        i = find_if(i, str.end(), not_space);

        // find end of next word
        iter j = find_if(i, str.end(), space);

        // copy the characters in [i, j)
        if (i != str.end())
            *os++ = string(i, j);    // changed

        i = j;
    }
}
```

Like the `write_analysis` function that we wrote in §6.2.2/113, our new version of `split` has nothing to return, so we say that its return type is `void`. We have now made `split` a template function that takes a single type parameter `Out`, the name of which suggests an output iterator. Recall that because forward, bidirectional, and random-access iterators meet all the output-iterator requirements, we can use our `split` with any kind of iterator except a pure input iterator such as `istream_iterator`.

The parameter `os` is of type `Out`. We will use it to write the values of the words as we find them. We do so near the end of the function

```
*os++ = string(i, j);    // changed
```

which writes the word that we just found. The subexpression `*os` denotes the current position in the container to which `os` is bound, so we assign the value of `string(i, j)` to the element at that position. Having done the assignment, we increment `os` so that we meet the output-iterator requirements, and so that the next trip through the loop will assign a value to the next container element.

Programmers who wish to use this revised `split` function will have to change their programs, but now we can write the words into almost any container. For example, if s is the `string` whose words we want to append to a `list` called `word_list`, then we could call `split` as follows:

```
        split(s, back_inserter(word_list));
```

Similarly, we can write a trivial program to test our `split` program:

```
int main()
{
    string s;
    while (getline(cin, s))
        split(s, ostream_iterator<string>(cout, "\n"));
    return 0;
}
```

Like the driver function that we wrote in §5.7/90, this function calls `split` to separate the input line into separate words, and writes those words onto the standard output. We write to `cout` by passing to `split` an `ostream_iterator<string>` that we bind to `cout`. When `split` assigns to `*os`, it will be writing to `cout`.

8.5 Details

Template functions that return simple types have the form

```
template<class type-parameter [, class type-parameter ] ... >
ret-type function-name (parameter-list)
```

Each *type-parameter* is a name that may be used inside the function definition wherever a type is required. Each of these names should be used in the function *parameter-list* to name the type of one or more parameters.

If the types do not all appear in the argument list, then the caller must qualify the *function-name* with the actual types that cannot be inferred. For example,

```
template<class T> T zero() { return 0; }
```

defines `zero` to be a template function with a single type parameter, which is used to name the return type. In calling this function, we must supply the return type explicitly:

```
double x = zero<double>();
```

The `typename` keyword must be used to qualify declarations that use types that are defined by the template type parameters. For example,

```
typename T::size_type name;
```

declares *name* to have type `size_type`, which must be defined as a type inside `T`.

The implementation automatically instantiates a separate instance of the template function for each set of types used in a call to the function.

Iterators: A key contribution of the C++ standard library is the idea that algorithms can achieve data-structure independence by using iterators as the glue between algorithms and containers. Furthermore, the realization that algorithms can be factored based on the operations that are required for the iterators that they use means that it is easy to match a container with the algorithms that can be used on it.

There are five iterator categories. In general, the later categories subsume the operations in the earlier ones:

Input iterator:	Sequential access in one direction, input only
Output iterator:	Sequential access in one direction, output only
Forward iterator:	Sequential access in one direction, input and output
Bidirectional iterator:	Sequential access in both directions, input and output
Random-access iterator:	Efficient access to any element, input and output

Exercises

8-0. Compile, execute, and test the programs in this chapter.

8-1. Note that the various `analysis` functions we wrote in §6.2/110 share the same behavior; they differ only in terms of the functions they call to calculate the final grade. Write a template function, parameterized by the type of the grading function, and use that function to evaluate the grading schemes.

8-2. Implement the following library algorithms, which we used in Chapter 6 and described in §6.5/121. Specify what kinds of iterators they require. Try to minimize the number of distinct iterator operations that each function requires. After you have finished your implementation, see §B.3/321 to see how well you did.

```
equal(b, e, b2)              search(b, e, b2, e2)
find(b, e, t)                find_if(b, e, p)
copy(b, e, d)                remove_copy(b, e, d, t)
remove_copy_if(b, e, d, p)   remove(b, e, t)
transform(b, e, d, f)        partition(b, e, p)
accumulate(b, e, t)
```

8-3. As we learned in §4.1.4/58, it can be expensive to return (or pass) a container by value. Yet the `median` function that we wrote in §8.1.1/140 passes the `vector` by value. Could we rewrite the `median` function to operate on iterators instead of passing the `vector`? If we did so, what would you expect the performance impact to be?

8-4. Implement the `swap` function that we used in §8.2.5/148. Why did we call `swap` rather than exchange the values of `*beg` and `*end` directly? *Hint:* Try it and see.

8-5. Reimplement the `gen_sentence` and `xref` functions from Chapter 7 to use output iterators rather than putting their entire output in one data structure. Test these new versions by writing programs that attach the output iterator directly to the standard output, and by storing the results in a `list<string>` and a `map<string, vector<int> >`, respectively.

8-6. Suppose that `m` has type `map<int, string>`, and that we encounter a call to `copy(m.begin(), m.end(), back_inserter(x))`. What can we say about the type of `x`? What if the call were `copy(x.begin() x.end(), back_inserter(m))` instead?

8-7. Why doesn't the `max` function use two template parameters, one for each argument type?

8-8. In the `binary_search` function in §8.2.6/148, why didn't we write `(begin + end)/2` instead of the more complicated `begin + (end - begin)/2`?

9

Defining new types

C++ has two kinds of types: built-in types and class types. Built-in types, so called because they are defined as part of the core language, include char, int, and double. The types that we've used from the library, such as string, vector, and istream, are all class types. Except for some of the low-level, system-specific routines in the input–output library, the library classes rely only on the same language facilities that any programmer can use to define application-specific types.

Much of the design of C++ rests on the idea of letting programmers create types that are as easy to use as are the built-in types. As we shall see, the ability to create types with straightforward, intuitive interfaces requires substantial language support, as well as taste and judgment in class design. We'll start by using the grading problem from Chapter 4 as a way of exploring the most fundamental class-definition facilities. Starting in Chapter 11, we will build on these basic concepts by looking at how we can build types that are as complete as the ones that the library offers.

9.1 Student_info revisited

In §4.2.1/61, we wrote a simple data structure called Student_info and a handful of functions, which made it easy to write programs to deal with students' course grades. However, the data structure and functions that we wrote were not well suited for other programmers to use.

Whether we were aware of it or not, programmers who wanted to use our functions had to follow certain conventions. For example, we assumed that anyone who used a newly created Student_info object would first read data into it. Failure to do so would result in an object that had an empty homework vector and undefined values (§3.1/38) for midterm and final. Any use of these values would yield unpredictable behavior— either incorrect results or an outright crash. Moreover, if a user wanted to check whether a Student_info contained valid data, the only way to do so would be to look at the actual data members, which would require detailed knowledge of how we had implemented the Student_info class.

A related problem is that someone who used our programs would probably assume that once a record for a student has been read from a file, that student's data will not change in the future. Unfortunately, our code offers no basis for that assumption.

A third problem is that the "interface" to our original `Student_info` structure is scattered. By convention, we might put the functions, such as `read`, that change the state of a `Student_info` object into a single header file. Doing so would help subsequent users of our code—if we decide to do so—but there is no requirement for such grouping.

As we'll see in this chapter, we can extend the `Student_info` structure to solve each of these problems.

9.2 Class types

At its most fundamental level, a class type is a mechanism for combining related data values into a data structure, so that we can treat that data structure as a single entity. For example, the `Student_info` structure that we built in §4.2.1/61,

```
struct Student_info {
    std::string name;
    double midterm, final;
    std::vector<double> homework;
};
```

let us define and manipulate objects of type `Student_info`. Each object of this type has four data elements: a `std::string` named `name`, a `std::vector<double>` named `homework`, and two `double`s named `midterm` and `final`.

As it stands, programmers who use the `Student_info` type may—and must—manipulate these data elements directly. They may manipulate the data directly because the definition of `Student_info` has not restricted access to the data elements. They must do so because no other operations are available on `Student_info`.

Rather than letting users access the data directly, we would like to hide the implementation details of how `Student_info`s are stored. In particular, we want to require the type's users to access objects only through functions. To do so, we first need to provide the users with convenient operations for manipulating `Student_info` objects. These operations will form the interface to our class.

Before looking at these functions, it is worth reviewing why we are using the fully qualified names for `std::string` and `std::vector`, rather than assuming that a using-declaration that allowed us to access the names directly had been made. Code that wants to use our `Student_info` structure must have access to the class definition, so we will put the definition in a header file. As we pointed out in §4.3/67, code that is intended for use by others should contain the minimal number of declarations necessary. Obviously, we must define the name `Student_info`, because that is the name we want users to use. The fact that `string` and `vector` are used by `Student_info` is an implementation artifact. There is no reason to force using-declarations on users of `Student_info` just because we use these types in the implementation.

In our programming examples, and as a matter of good practice, we use the qualified names in code that goes into header files, but we will continue to assume that the corresponding source files contain appropriate using-declarations. Therefore, when we write program text that we intend to appear outside a header file, we will generally not use fully qualified names.

9.2.1 Member functions

In order to control access to Student_info objects, we need to define an interface that programmers can use. Let's start by defining operations to read a record and to calculate the overall grade:

```
struct Student_info {
    std::string name;
    double midterm, final;
    std::vector<double> homework;

    std::istream& read(std::istream&);    // added
    double grade() const;                 // added
};
```

We still say that each Student_info object has four data elements, but we've also given Student_info two member functions. These member functions will let us read a record from an input stream and calculate the final grade for any Student_info object. The const on the declaration of grade is a promise that calling the grade function will not change any of the data members of the Student_info object.

We first discussed member functions in §1.2/14 when we talked about using the size member of class string. Essentially, a member function is a function that is a member of a class object. In order to call a member function, our users must nominate the object of which the function to be called is a member. So, analogous to calling greeting.size() for a string object named greeting, our users will call s.read(cin) or s.grade() on behalf of a Student_info object named s. The call s.read(cin) will read values from the standard input and set the state of s appropriately. The call s.grade() will calculate and return the final grade for s.

The definition of the first of our member functions looks a lot like the original version of read in §4.2.2/62:

```
istream& Student_info::read(istream& in)
{
    in >> name >> midterm >> final;
    read_hw(in, homework);
    return in;
}
```

As we did originally, we would put these functions in a common source file named Student_info.cpp, Student_info.C, or Student_info.c. The important point is that the declarations for these functions are now part of our Student_info structure, so they must be available to all users of the Student_info class.

There are three important comparison points between this code and the original:

1. The name of the function is `Student_info::read` instead of plain `read`.
2. Because this function is a member of a `Student_info` object, we do not need to pass a `Student_info` object as an argument, or to define a `Student_info` object at all.
3. We access the data elements of our object directly. For example, in §4.2.2/62, we referred to `s.midterm`; here we refer to just `midterm`.

We will explain each of these differences in turn.

The `::` in the function name is the same scope operator that we have already used, as far back as §0.7/5, to access names that the standard library defines. For example, we wrote `string::size_type` to get the name `size_type` that is a member of class `string`. Similarly, by writing `Student_info::read`, we are defining the function, named `read`, that is a member of the `Student_info` type.

This member function requires only an `istream&` parameter, because the `Student_info&` parameter will be implicit in any call. Remember that when we call a function that is a member of a `vector` or `string` object, we must say which `vector` or `string` we want. For example, if `s` is a `string`, then we write `s.size()` to call the `size` member of object `s`. There is no way to call the `size` function from class `string` without nominating a `string` object. In the same way, when we call the `read` function, we will have to say explicitly into which `Student_info` object we're reading. That object is implicitly used in the `read` function.

The references to the members inside `read` are unqualified because they are references to members of the object on which we are operating. In other words, if we call `s.read(cin)` for a `Student_info` object named `s`, then we are operating on object `s`. When `read` uses `midterm`, `final`, and `homework`, it will be using `s.midterm`, `s.final`, and `s.homework` respectively.

Now let's look at the `grade` member:

```
double Student_info::grade() const
{
    return ::grade(midterm, final, homework);
}
```

This version resembles the version in §4.2.2/63, and differs from it in ways analogous to the differences in `read`: We define `grade` as a member of `Student_info`, the function takes an implicit rather than an explicit reference to a `Student_info` object, and it accesses the members of that object without any qualification.

This code contains two more important differences. First, note the call to `::grade`. Putting `::` in front of a name insists on using a version of that name that is not a member of anything. In this case, we need the `::` so that the call will reach the version of `grade` that takes two `double`s and a `vector<double>`, which we defined in §4.1.2/54. Without it, the compiler would think that we were referring to `Student_info::grade`, and would complain because we tried to call it with too many arguments.

The other important difference is the use of `const` immediately after `grade`'s parameter list. We can understand this usage by comparing our new function declaration with the original:

```
double Student_info::grade() const { ... }    // member-function version
double grade(const Student_info&) { ... }      // original from §4.2.2/63
```

In the original function, we passed the `Student_info` as a reference to `const`. By doing so, we ensured that we could ask for the `grade` of a `const Student_info` object, and that the compiler would complain if the `grade` function tried to change its parameter.

When we call a member function, the object of which it is a member is not an argument. Therefore, there is no entry in the parameter list in which we might be able to say that the object is `const`. Instead, we qualify the function itself, thereby making it a **const *member function***. Member functions that are `const` may not change the internal state of the object on which they are executing: We are guaranteed that if we call `s.grade()` on behalf of a `Student_info` object named `s`, doing so will not change the data members of `s`.

Because the function guarantees that it will not change the values in the object, we can call it for `const` objects. By the same token, we cannot call nonconst functions on `const` objects, so, for example, we cannot call the `read` member on behalf of a `const Student_info` object. After all, a function such as `read` says that it can change the object's state. Calling such a function on a `const` object could violate our `const` promise.

It is important to note that even if a program never creates any `const` objects directly, it may create lots of references to `const` objects through function calls. When we pass a nonconst object to a function that takes a `const` reference, then the function treats that object as if it were `const`, and the compiler will permit it to call only `const` members of such objects.

Note that we included the `const` qualifier in both the declaration of the function inside the class definition and in the definition of the function. As always, argument types must be identical between the function declaration and definition (§4.4/69).

9.2.2 Nonmember functions

Our new design made `read` and `grade` into member functions. What about `compare`? Should it also be a member of the class?

As we'll see in §9.5/164, §11.2.4/193, §11.3.2/196, §12.5/222, and §13.2.1/234, the C++ language requires certain kinds of functions to be defined as members. It turns out that `compare` is not one of these, so we have the option to do it either way. There is a general rule that helps us decide what to do in such cases: If the function changes the state of an object, then it ought to be a member of that object. Unfortunately, even this rule says nothing about functions that do not change the state of the object, so we still must decide what to do about `compare`.

To do so, we should think a bit about what the function does and how users might want to call it. The `compare` function decides which of its `Student_info` arguments is "less than" the other, based on inspecting the arguments' name members. We'll see in §12.2/213 that there is sometimes an advantage to defining operations such as `compare` outside the class body. Therefore, we shall leave `compare` as a global function, which we will implement shortly.

9.3 Protection

By defining the `grade` and `read` functions as members, we have fixed half of our problem: Users of type `Student_info` no longer *have* to manipulate the internal state of the object directly. However, they still *can* do so. We would like to hide the data, and allow users to access the data only through our member functions.

C++ supports data hiding by allowing authors of types to say which members of those types are **public**, and hence accessible to all users of the type, and which parts are **private**, and inaccessible to users of the type:

```
class Student_info {
public:
     // interface goes here
     double grade() const;
     std::istream& read(std::istream&);

private:
     // implementation goes here
     std::string name;
     double midterm, final;
     std::vector<double> homework;
};
```

We've made a couple of changes to our definition of `Student_info`: We've said **class** instead of `struct`, and we've added two *protection labels*. Each protection label defines the accessibility of all the members that follow the label. Labels can occur in any order within the class, and can occur multiple times.

By putting `name`, `homework`, `midterm`, and `final` after a `private` label, we have made these data elements inaccessible to users of the `Student_info` type. References to these members from nonmember functions are now illegal, and the compiler will generate a diagnostic message to the effect that the member is private or inaccessible. The members in the `public` section are fully available; any user may call `read` or `grade`.

What about the use of `class` instead of `struct`? We can use either keyword to define a new type. The *only* difference between saying `struct` and `class` is the default protection, which applies to every member defined before the first protection label. If we say `class Student_info`, then every member between the first { and the first protection label is `private`. If, instead, we write `struct Student_info`, then every member declared between the { and the first protection label is `public`. For example,

```
class Student_info {
public:
     double grade() const;
     // etc.
};
```

is equivalent to

```
struct Student_info {
     double grade() const;   // public by default
     // etc.
};
```

and

```
class Student_info {
    std::string name;          // private by default
    // other private members
public:
    double grade() const;
    // other public members
};
```

is equivalent to

```
struct Student_info {
private:
    std::string name;
    // other private members
public:
    double grade() const;
    // other public members
};
```

In each of these definitions, we're saying that we'll allow users to get at the member functions of `Student_info` objects, but we will not allow them to access the data members.

There is no difference between what we can do with a `struct` or a `class`. In fact, there is no way, short of reading the code, for our users to distinguish whether we used `struct` or `class` to define our class type. Our choice of `struct` or `class` can have a useful documentation role. In general, our programming style is to reserve `struct` to denote simple types whose data structure we intend to expose. For that reason, we used `struct` to define our original `Student_info` data type in Chapter 4. Now that we intend to build a type that will control access to its members, we use `class` to define our `Student_info` type.

9.3.1 Accessor functions

At this point, we've hidden our data members, so that users can no longer modify the data in a `Student_info` object. Instead, they must use the `read` operation to set the data members, and the `grade` function to find out the final grade for a given `Student_info`. There's one more operation that we must still provide: We must give users a way to get at the student's name. For example, think a bit about the program in §4.5/70, in which we wrote a formatted report of student grades. That program needs to access the student's name in order to generate the report. Although we want to allow read access, we do not want to allow write access. Doing so is straightforward:

```
class Student_info {
public:
    double grade() const;
    std::istream& read(std::istream&);        // must change definition
    std::string name() const { return n; }    // added
```

```
    private:
        std::string n;                                    // changed
        double midterm, final;
        std::vector<double> homework;
};
```

Instead of giving our users access to the name data member, we've added a member function, also named name, that will give (read-only) access to the corresponding data value. Of course, we have to change the data member's name to avoid confusing it with the name of the function.

The name function is a const member function, which takes no arguments and which returns a string that is a copy of n. By copying n, rather than returning a reference to it, we ensure that users can read but not change the value of n. Because we need only read access to the data, we declare the member function as const.

When we defined grade and read, we did so outside the class definition. When we define a member function as part of the class definition, as we have done here with the name function, we are hinting to the compiler that it should avoid function-call overhead and expand calls to the function inline (§4.6/72) if possible.

Functions such as name are often called *accessor functions*. This nomenclature is potentially misleading, because it implies that we are granting access to a part of our data structure. Indeed, historically, such functions were often introduced to allow easy access to hidden data, thus breaking the encapsulation that we were trying to achieve. Accessors should be provided only when they are part of the abstract interface of the class. In the case of Student_info, our abstraction is that of a student and a corresponding final grade. Therefore, the notion of a student name is part of our abstraction, and it is fitting to provide a name function. On the other hand, we do not provide accessors to the other grades—midterm, final, or homework. These grades are an essential part of our implementation, but they are not part of our interface.

Having added the name member function, we can now write the compare function:

```
bool compare(const Student_info& x, const Student_info& y)
{
    return x.name() < y.name();
}
```

This function looks a lot like the version from §4.2.2/64. The only difference is how we get at the student's name. In the original version, we could access the data member directly; here, we must invoke the name function, which returns the student's name. Because compare is part of our interface, we should include a declaration for this function in the same header that defines Student_info and we should include this definition in the associated source file that contains the definitions of the member functions.

9.3.2 Testing for empty

Having hidden our members and provided the appropriate accessor function, we have one remaining problem: There is still a reason that a user might want to look directly at an object's data. For example, consider what happens if we call grade on an object for which read has not been called:

```
Student_info s;
cout << s.grade() << endl;      // exception: s has no data
```

Because we haven't called read to give s any values, the homework member of s will be empty, and the call to grade will throw an exception. Although our users can catch the exception, they have no way to detect the problem in advance, so that they can avoid making the call at all.

Using the original Student_info structure from Chapter 4, users could test the homework member to determine whether a call to grade would succeed. If homework turned out to be empty, then they knew not to call grade. This approach worked, but at the cost of forcing users to know about the structure of the object in order to perform the test. We can do better, by offering the same test in a more abstract form:

```
class Student_info {
public:
     bool valid() const { return !homework.empty(); }
     // as before
};
```

The valid function will tell the user whether the object contains valid data, with a value of true indicating that the student did at least one homework assignment, and therefore that it is possible to compute the student's grade. Our users can call valid to determine whether subsequent operations will succeed. For example, before calling grade, a user can check whether the object is valid, thereby avoiding a potential exception.

9.4 The Student_info class

At this point we have resolved most of our objections to the original Student_info structure, so it is worth reviewing what we've done:

```
class Student_info {
public:
     std::string name() const { return n; }
     bool valid() const { return !homework.empty(); }
     // as defined in §9.2.1/157, and changed to read into n instead of name
     std::istream& read(std::istream&);
     double grade() const;      // as defined in §9.2.1/158
private:
     std::string n;
     double midterm, final;
     std::vector<double> homework;
};
bool compare(const Student_info&, const Student_info&);
```

Users can change the state of a Student_info object only by calling the read member function. They cannot reach inside an object and directly change any of the data members. Instead, we provide operations that hide our implementation. Finally, all the operations on Student_info objects are logically gathered together.

9.5 Constructors

Although our class is reasonably complete and usable as it stands, there is one more thing to think about: We have not said anything about what happens when objects are created.

We know that the library guarantees that when we create an object of a library class, the object starts with an appropriate value. For example, when we define a `string` or a `vector` without an initial value, we get an empty `string` or `vector`. Both `string` and `vector` also allow us to give a new object an initial value, such as specifying a size or a count and a fill character.

Constructors are special member functions that define how objects are initialized. There is no way to call a constructor explicitly. Instead, creating an object of class type calls the appropriate constructor automatically as a side effect.

If we do not define any constructors, the compiler will synthesize one for us. We'll have more to say about synthesized operations in §11.3.5/201. What we need to know now is what happens if we do not define any constructors. In this case, our users will be able to define `Student_info` objects, but will not be able to initialize them explicitly, except as copies of other `Student_info` objects.

The synthesized constructor will initialize the data members to a value that depends on how the object is being created. If the object is a local variable, then the data members will be default-initialized (§3.1/38). If the object is used to initialize a container element, either as a side effect of adding a new element to a `map`, or as the elements of a container defined to have a given size, then the members will be value-initialized (§7.2/125). These rules are slightly complicated, but their essentials are:

• If an object is of a class type that defines one or more constructors, then the appropriate constructor completely controls initialization of the objects of that class.
• If an object is of built-in type, then value-initializing it sets it to zero, and default-initializing it gives it an undefined value.
• Otherwise, the object can be only of a class type that does not define any constructors. In that case, value- or default-initializing the object value- or default-initializes each of its data members. This initialization process will be recursive if any of the data members is of a class type with its own constructor.

As it stands, our `Student_info` class is in this third category: It is a class type, but we do not explicitly say how to construct `Student_info` objects. So, if we define a local `Student_info` variable, then the `n` and `homework` members will be automatically initialized to the empty `string` and `vector` respectively, because they are class objects with constructors. In contrast, default-initializing `midterm` and `final` will give them undefined values, meaning they will hold whatever garbage happens to be in memory when the object is created.

Given our simple operations, this behavior may appear harmless: None of our operations uses the value of `midterm` or `final` without first initializing the object by calling `read`, which assigns values to these members. However, it is normally good practice to ensure that every data member has a sensible value at all times. For example, it is possible that later we (or a subsequent maintainer of our code) will add operations that examine these data members. If we don't initialize them in the constructor, then these new operations might cause future failures. Moreover, as we'll see in §11.3.5/201, even though we do not explicitly use `midterm` or `final`, there are synthesized operations on the class that could do so. Any use other than writing to an undefined value is illegal (§3.1/38), and so, strictly speaking, we must initialize these values.

In practice, we'll want to define two constructors: The first constructor takes no arguments and creates an empty `Student_info` object; the second takes a reference to an input stream and initializes the object by reading a student record from that stream. This strategy allows our users to write code such as

```
Student_info s;          // an empty Student_info
Student_info s2(cin);    // initialize s2 by reading from cin
```

Constructors are distinguished from other member functions in two ways: They have the same name as the name of the class itself, and they have no return type. Constructors are similar to other functions in that we can define multiple versions of constructors that differ in terms of the number or type of their arguments. With this knowledge, we might update our class to add our two constructors:

```
class Student_info {
public:
      Student_info();                    // construct an empty Student_info object
      Student_info(std::istream&);       // construct one by reading a stream
      // as before
};
```

9.5.1 The default constructor

The constructor that takes no arguments is known as the *default constructor*. Its job is normally to ensure that its object's data members are properly initialized. In the case of `Student_info` objects, we want to initialize the data to indicate that we haven't yet read a record: We'll want the `homework` member to be an empty `vector`, the n member to be an empty `string`, and the `midterm` and `final` members to be initialized to zero:

```
Student_info::Student_info(): midterm(0), final(0) { }
```

The constructor definition uses some new syntax. Between the : and the { is a sequence of *constructor initializers*, which tell the compiler to initialize the given members with the values that appear between the corresponding parentheses. Therefore, this particular default constructor works by explicitly setting the `midterm` and `final` grades to 0. Other than that, the constructor does no overt work: The body of the function is empty. As we shall see, n and `homework` are implicitly initialized.

Understanding constructor initializers is crucial to understanding how to create and initialize objects. When we create a new class object, several steps happen in sequence:

1. The implementation allocates memory to hold the object.
2. It initializes the object using initial values as specified in the initializer list.
3. It executes the constructor body.

The implementation initializes the data members in the same order as they appear within the class definition, regardless of their order in the initializer list. It initializes *all* data members, even if the initializer list does not mention the members at all. The constructor body may *change* these initial values subsequently, but the initialization happens before the constructor body begins execution. It is usually better to give a member an initial value explicitly, rather than assigning to it in the body of the constructor. By initializing rather than assigning a value, we avoid doing the same work twice.

We said that constructors exist to ensure that objects are created with their data members in a sensible state. In general, this design goal means that every constructor should initialize every data member. The need to give members a value is especially critical for members of built-in type. If the constructor fails to initialize such members, objects declared at local scope will be initialized with garbage, which is almost never correct.

We can now understand why we said that the Student_info default constructor did no other "overt" work. Although we explicitly initialized only midterm and final, the other data members are initialized implicitly. Specifically, n is initialized by the string default constructor, and homework is initialized by the vector default constructor.

9.5.2 Constructors with arguments

Our second Student_info constructor is even easier:

```
Student_info::Student_info(istream& is) { read(is); }
```

This constructor delegates the real work to the read function. The constructor has no explicit initializer, so the homework and n members will be initialized by the default constructors for vector and string respectively. The midterm and final members will have explicit initial values only if the object is being value-initialized. This lack of initialization doesn't matter, because read immediately gives these variables new values.

9.6 Using the Student_info class

Our new Student_info class is now quite different from the original Student_info structure from Chapter 4. Not surprisingly, using the class is different from using the original structure. After all, our objective was to prevent users from being able to change our data values, which we accomplished by making them private. Instead, we intend for users to write their programs in terms of the interface provided by our class. As an example, we can rewrite our original main program from §4.5/70, which wrote the final grades for the students in a formatted report, to use this version of the class:

```
int main()
{
    vector<Student_info> students;
    Student_info record;
    string::size_type maxlen = 0;

    // read and store the data
    while (record.read(cin)) {                                      // changed
        maxlen = max(maxlen, record.name().size());                 // changed
        students.push_back(record);
    }
```

```
// alphabetize the student records
sort(students.begin(), students.end(), compare);

// write the names and grades
for (vector<Student_info>::size_type i = 0;
     i != students.size(); ++i) {
    cout << students[i].name()      // this and the next line changed
        << string(maxlen + 1 - students[i].name().size(), ' ');
    try {
        double final_grade = students[i].grade();    // changed
        streamsize prec = cout.precision();
        cout << setprecision(3) << final_grade
            << setprecision(prec) << endl;
    } catch (domain_error e) {
        cout << e.what() << endl;
    }
}
return 0;
}
```

The changes here are to the calls of `name`, `read`, and `grade`. So, for example, the first `while` loop now says

```
while (record.read(cin)) {
```

instead of

```
while (read(cin, record)) {
```

Our revised version calls the member `read` of the object `record`. The earlier version called the global `read` function, passing it `record` as an explicit parameter. Both calls have the same effect: The object `record` will be assigned values read from `cin`.

9.7 Details

User-defined types can be defined as either `struct`s or `class`es. The only difference is in the default protection that applies to members defined before the first protection label: Members defined after `struct` are `public`; those defined after `class` are `private`.

Protection labels control access to members of a class type: `public` members are generally accessible; `private` members are accessible only to members of the class. Protection labels can appear in any order and multiple times within a class.

Member functions: Types may define member functions as well as data. Member functions are implicitly called on behalf of a specific object. References to member data or functions from within a member function are implicitly bound to that object.

Member functions can be defined inside or outside the class definition. Defining a member function inside the class asks the implementation to expand calls to it inline, thus avoiding function call overhead. Outside the class, the name of the function must be qualified to indicate that it is from the class scope: *class-name* `::` *member-name* refers to the member *member-name* from the class *class-name*.

Member functions can be defined as `const` by inserting the `const` keyword after the parameter list. Such members may not change the state of the object on which they are invoked. Only `const` member functions may be called for `const` objects.

Constructors are special member functions that define how objects of the type are initialized. Constructors have the same name as the class and have no return value. A class can define multiple constructors as long as they differ in the number or types of their arguments. It is good practice for every constructor to ensure that every data member has a sensible value on exit from the constructor.

Constructor initializer list: A constructor initializer is a comma-separated list of *member-name* (*value*) pairs. Each *member-name* is initialized from the associated *value*. Data members that are not explicitly initialized are implicitly initialized.

The order in which members are initialized is determined by the order of declaration in the class, so care must be taken when using one class member to initialize another. It is safer practice to avoid such interdependence by assigning values to these members inside the constructor body and not initializing them in the constructor initializer.

Exercises

9-0. Compile, execute, and test the programs in this chapter.

9-1. Reimplement the `Student_info` class so that it calculates the final grade when reading the student's record, and stores that grade in the object. Reimplement the `grade` function to use this precomputed value.

9-2. If we define the `name` function as a plain, `nonconst` member function, what other functions in our system must change and why?

9-3. Our `grade` function was written to throw an exception if a user tried to calculate a grade for a `Student_info` object whose values had not yet been read. Users who care are expected to catch this exception. Write a program that triggers the exception but does not catch it. Write a program that catches the exception.

9-4. Rewrite your program from the previous exercise to use the `valid` function, thereby avoiding the exception altogether.

9-5. Write a class and associated functions to generate grades for students who take the course for pass/fail credit. Assume that only the midterm and final grades matter, and that a student passes with an average exam score greater than 60. The report should list the students in alphabetical order, and indicate `P` or `F` as the grade.

9-6. Rewrite the grading program for the pass/fail students so that the report shows all the students who passed, followed by all the students who failed.

9-7. The `read_hw` function §4.1.3/57 solves a general problem (reading a sequence of values into a `vector`) even though its name suggests that it should be part of the implementation of `Student_info`. Of course, we could change its name—but suppose, instead, that you wanted to integrate it with the rest of the `Student_info` code, in order to clarify that it was not intended for public access despite its apparent generality? How would you do so?

10

Managing memory and low-level data structures

Until now, we have been storing data either in variables or in containers, such as `vector`, that come from the standard library. The reason for this strategy is that the standard-library facilities are usually more flexible and easier to use than the facilities that are part of the core language.

Once you know how to use the library, the logical next step is to understand how it works. The key to this understanding turns out to involve core-language programming tools and techniques that come in handy in other contexts as well. We use the term *low-level* to refer to these ideas because they underlie the standard library and because they correspond closely to the way typical computer hardware works. For these reasons, they tend to be harder to use, and are more dangerous, but they sometimes can be more efficient—provided that you understand them thoroughly—than are the related ideas in the standard library. Because no library can solve all problems, many C++ programs wind up using low-level techniques from time to time.

This chapter departs from our usual style of presenting problems before their solutions, because the tools that we are going to present work at a low enough level that it is hard to use any one tool by itself to solve useful problems. Instead, we are going to begin by presenting two related ideas: arrays and pointers. Once we have done so, we'll show how those ideas combine with `new`-expressions and `delete`-expressions to allow a form of dynamic memory allocation that programmers can control more directly than they can control the automatic memory management offered by library classes such as `vector` and `list`.

Once we understand how arrays and pointers work, we will explore, in Chapter 11, how the library uses these facilities to implement its containers.

10.1 Pointers and arrays

An array is a kind of container, similar to a `vector` but less powerful. A pointer is a kind of random-access iterator that is essential for accessing elements of arrays, and has other uses as well. Pointers and arrays are among the most primitive data structures in C and

C++. They are virtually inseparable from one another, in the sense that it is impossible to do anything useful with an array without using pointers, and pointers become much more useful in the presence of arrays.

Because these two notions are so closely intertwined, we shall explain them both before trying to solve significant problems with either. It is easier to explain pointers without understanding arrays than to explain arrays without understanding pointers, so we shall discuss pointers first.

10.1.1 Pointers

A *pointer* is a value that represents the *address* of an object. Every distinct object has a unique address, which denotes the part of the computer's memory that contains the object. If you can access an object, you can obtain its address, and vice versa. For example, if x is an object, then &x is the address of that object, and if p is the address of an object, then *p is the object itself. The & in &x is an *address operator*, and is distinct from the use of & to define reference types (§4.1.2/54). The * is a *dereference operator*, which works analogously to the way * works when applied to any other iterator (§5.2.2/81). If p contains the address of x, we also say that p is a *pointer* that *points to* x. It is common to represent such a state of affairs with a diagram such as

As with other built-in types, a local variable that is a pointer has no meaningful value until we give it one. Programmers frequently use the value 0 to initialize pointers, because converting 0 to a pointer yields a value that is guaranteed to be distinct from a pointer to any object. Moreover, the constant 0 is the only integer value that can be converted to a pointer type. The resulting value, often called a *null pointer*, is often useful in comparisons.

As with all C++ values, pointers have types. The address of an object of type T has type "pointer to T," written as T* in definitions and similar contexts.

Suppose that x is an object of type int, defined as

```
int x;
```

and we want to define p to have a type that will allow p to contain the address of x. We do so by saying that the type of p is "pointer to int," which we say implicitly by defining *p to have type int:

```
int *p;                    // *p has type int
```

Here *p is a *declarator*, which is the part of a definition that defines a single variable. Even though the * and the p are part of a single declarator, most C++ programmers write this definition as

```
int* p;                    // p has type int*
```

to emphasize the notion that p has a particular type (i.e., int*). These two usages are equivalent because spaces around the * are neutral. However, the latter usage conceals a pitfall that is so important that it deserves special attention:

```
int* p, q;                    // What does this definition mean?
```

defines p as an object of type "pointer to int" and q as an object of type int. This example is easier to understand if we view it this way:

```
int *p, q;                    // *p and q have type int
```

or, for that matter, this way:

```
int (*p), q;                  // (*p) and q have type int
```

Still better, we can make our intentions crystal clear by writing

```
int* p;                       // *p has type int
int q;                        // q has type int
```

We now know enough to write a simple program that uses pointers:

```
int main()
{
    int x = 5;

    // p points to x
    int* p = &x;
    cout << "x = " << x << endl;

    // change the value of x through p
    *p = 6;
    cout << "x = " << x << endl;
    return 0;
}
```

The output of this program will be

```
x = 5
x = 6
```

Immediately after we have defined p, the state of our variables is

It should be no surprise that x is 5 when we execute the first output expression. The next statement changes the value of x to 6 by executing *p = 6. Remember, once p contains the address of x, *p and x are two different ways of referring to the same object. Thus, the x is 6 when the second output expression is executed.

It may be useful to think of a pointer to an object as an iterator that refers to the only element of a "container" that contains that object and nothing else.

10.1.2   Pointers to functions

In §6.2.2/113, we saw a program that passed a function as an argument to another function, and noted that there was slightly more going on there than met the eye. The truth is that functions are not objects, and there is no way to copy or assign them, or to pass them as arguments directly. In particular, there is no way for a program to create or modify a function—only the compiler can do that. All that a program can ever do with a function is call it or take its address.

Nevertheless, we can call a function with another function as an argument, as we did when we passed median_analysis as an argument to write_analysis in §6.2.2/112. What happens is that the compiler quietly translates such calls so as to use pointers to functions instead of using functions directly. Pointers to functions behave similarly to any other pointers. Once you have dereferenced such a pointer, however, all you can do with the resulting function is call it—or take the function's address yet again.

Declarators for pointers to functions resemble other declarators. For example, just as we wrote

```
int *p;
```

to say that *p has type int, thereby implying that p is a pointer, we might write

```
int (*fp)(int);
```

to say that if we dereference fp, and call it with an int argument, the result has type int. By implication, fp is a pointer to a function that takes an int argument and returns an int result.

Because all that you can do with a function is to take its address or call it, any use of a function that is not a call is assumed to be taking its address, even without an explicit &. Similarly, you can call a pointer to a function without dereferencing the pointer explicitly. So, for example, if we have a function whose type matches fp, such as

```
int next(int n)
{
    return n + 1;
}
```

then we can make fp point to next by writing either of the following two statements:

```
// these two statements are equivalent
fp = &next;
fp = next;
```

Similarly, if we have an int variable named i, we can use fp to call next, and thereby increment i, by writing either

```
// these two statements are equivalent
i = (*fp)(i);
i = fp(i);
```

Finally, if we write a function that looks like it takes another function as a parameter, the compiler quietly translates the parameter to be a pointer to a function instead. So, for example, in the write_analysis function in §6.2.2/113, the parameter that we wrote as

```
double analysis(const vector<Student_info>&)
```

could equivalently have been written as

```
double (*analysis)(const vector<Student_info>&)
```

However, this automatic translation does not apply to return values from functions. If we wanted to write a function that returned a function pointer, of the same type as the parameter to `write_analysis`, then we would have to say explicitly that the function returns a pointer. One way to do so is to begin by using a `typedef` to define, say, `analysis_fp` as the name of the type of an appropriate pointer:

```
typedef double (*analysis_fp)(const vector<Student_info>&);
```

Then we can use that type to declare our function:

```
// get_analysis_ptr returns a pointer to an analysis function
analysis_fp get_analysis_ptr();
```

The alternative

```
double (*get_analysis_ptr())(const vector<Student_info>&);
```

is arcane. In effect, we are saying that if you call `get_analysis_ptr()`, and dereference the result, what you get is a function that takes a `const vector<Student_info>&` and returns a `double`. Fortunately, functions that return pointers to functions are rare! We use this syntax nowhere else in this book, but we explain it in more detail in §A.1/295.

Pointers to functions are most commonly used as arguments to other functions. As an example, here is a sample implementation of the `find_if` library function:

```
template<class In, class Pred>
In find_if(In begin, In end, Pred f)
{
    while (begin != end && !f(*begin))
        ++begin;
    return begin;
}
```

In this example, `Pred` can potentially be any type at all, as long as `f(*begin)` has a meaningful value. Suppose we have a predicate function, such as

```
bool is_negative(int n)
{
    return n < 0;
}
```

and we use `find_if` to locate the first negative element in a `vector<int>` named `v`:

```
vector<int>::iterator i = find_if(v.begin(), v.end(), is_negative);
```

We are able to write `is_negative` instead of `&is_negative` only because the name of a function turns into a pointer to the function automatically. Similarly, the implementation of `find_if` is permitted to call `f(*beg)` instead of `(*f)(*beg)` only because calling a function pointer automatically calls the function to which it points.

10.1.3 Arrays

An *array* is a kind of container that is part of the core language rather than part of the standard library. Every array contains a sequence of one or more objects of the same type. The number of elements in the array must be known at compile time, which requirement implies that arrays cannot grow or shrink dynamically the way library containers do.

Because arrays are not class types, they have no members. In particular, they do not have the `size_type` member to name an appropriate type to deal with the size of an array. Instead, the `<cstddef>` header defines **size_t**, which is a more general type. The implementation defines `size_t` as the appropriate `unsigned` type large enough to hold the size of any object. Thus, we can (and should) use `size_t` to refer to the size of an array, similarly to the way we use `size_type` to deal with the size of a container.

For example, a three-dimensional geometry program might represent a point this way:

```
double coords[3];
```

knowing that the number of dimensions in physical space is unlikely to change any time soon. A more experienced programmer might represent the point this way:

```
const size_t NDim = 3;
double coords[NDim];
```

taking advantage, for documentation purposes, of the fact that the value of `NDim` is known at compilation time (because it is a `const size_t` that is initialized from a constant). Using `NDim` instead of 3 distinguishes the 3 that represents the number of dimensions from a 3 that represents, say, the number of sides in a triangle.

No matter how we define an array, there is always a fundamental relationship between arrays and pointers: Whenever we use the name of an array as a value, that name represents a pointer to the initial element of the array. We have defined `coords` as an array, so using `coords` as a value gives us the address of the array's initial element. As with any other pointer, we can dereference it with the * operator to get the object to which it points, so that executing

```
*coords = 1.5;
```

sets the initial element of `coords` to `1.5`.

10.1.4 Pointer arithmetic

We now know how to define arrays, and how to obtain the address of the initial element of an array. What about the other elements? Recall that in §10.1/169 we said that a pointer was a kind of iterator. More specifically, a pointer is a random-access iterator. This fact gives us a second fundamental property of arrays: If p points to the mth element of an array, then p + n points to the (m + n)th element of the array and (p − n) points to the (m − n)th element—assuming, of course, that these elements exist.

Continuing our example, and noting that, as usual, the initial element of `coords` has number 0, we see that `coord + 1` is the address of element number 1 of the `coords` array (i.e., the element after the initial element), and `coords + 2` is the address of element number 2, which is also the last element because we defined `coords` to have three elements.

What about `coords + 3`? That value represents the address of where element number 3 would be in the `coords` array if the element existed—but the element doesn't exist.

Nevertheless, `coords + 3` is a valid pointer, even though it doesn't point to an element. Analogous with `vector` and `string` iterators, adding n to the address of the initial element of an n-element array yields an address that is not guaranteed to be the address of any object, but it is one that we can use for comparisons. Moreover, the rules that relate p, p + n, and p - n are valid even if one or more of those expressions yields a value that is one (but not more than one) past the end of an array.

So, for example, we can copy the contents of `coords` into a `vector` by writing

```
vector<double> v;
copy(coords, coords + NDim, back_inserter(v));
```

where, as before, `NDim` is just a fancy way of spelling 3. In this example, `coords + NDim` does not point to an element, but it is a valid off-the-end iterator, and passing it as the second argument to `copy` presents no difficulty.

As another example, because we can construct a `vector` from two iterators, we could have constructed v directly as a copy of the elements in `coords` by writing

```
vector<double> v(coords, coords + NDim);
```

In other words, suppose that a is an n-element array, that v is a `vector`, and that we want to apply standard-library algorithms to elements of a. Then, wherever we might use `v.begin()` and `v.end()` to give standard-library algorithms access to elements of v, we should use a and a + n as arguments when we wish to apply these algorithms to the elements of a.

If p and q are pointers to elements of the same array, then p - q is an integer that represents the distance in elements between p and q. More precisely, p - q is defined so that (p - q) + q is equal to p. Because p - q might be negative, it has a signed integer type. Whether that type is `int` or `long` depends on the implementation, so the library provides a synonym, named **ptrdiff_t**, to represent the appropriate type. Like `size_t`, the `ptrdiff_t` type is defined in the `<cstddef>` header.

We saw in §8.2.7/150 that there is no guarantee of being able to compute an iterator that refers to a point before the beginning of a container. Analogously, it is never legitimate to compute an address that falls before the beginning of an array. In other words, if a is an n-element array, then a+i is valid if and only if $0 \leq i \leq n$, and a+i refers to an element of a if and only if $0 \leq i < n$ (but not if i and n are equal).

10.1.5 Indexing

We said in §10.1/169 that pointers are random-access iterators for arrays. Therefore, like all random-access iterators, they support indexing. Specifically, if p points to the mth element of an array, p[n] is the m+nth element of the array—not the address of the element, but the element itself.

Recall from §10.1.3/174 that the name of an array is the address of the initial element of the array. This fact, together with the definition of p[n], implies that if a is an array, `a[n]` is the nth element of the array. More formally, if `p` is a pointer and `n` is an integer, then `p[n]` is equivalent to `*(p + n)`.

In most languages, the behavior of indexing is fundamental and obvious. In C++, this behavior is not a direct property of arrays. Rather, it is a corollary to the properties of array names and pointers, and the fact that pointers supply the operations defined for random-access iterators.

10.1.6 Array initialization

Arrays have an important property that the standard-library containers do not share: There is a convenient syntax for giving an initial value to each element of an array. Moreover, using this syntax often lets us avoid having to state the size of the array explicitly.

For example, if we were writing a program that deals with dates, we might like to know how many days are in each month. One way to do so would be the following:

```
const int month_lengths[] = {
    31, 28, 31, 30, 31, 30,    // we will deal elsewhere with leap years
    31, 31, 30, 31, 30, 31
};
```

Here, we have given an initial value to each element that corresponds to the length of a month, with January being month 0 and December being month 11. Now, we can use `month_lengths[i]` to refer to the length of month `i`.

Note that we did not say explicitly how many elements the `month_lengths` array has. Because we initialized it explicitly, the compiler will count elements for us—a task to which it is much better suited than we.

10.2 String literals revisited

We have finally learned enough to understand the true meaning of string literals: A string literal is really an array of `const char` with one more element than the number of characters in the literal. That extra character is a null character (i.e., `'\0'`) that the compiler automatically appends to the rest of the characters. In other words, if we define

```
const char hello[] = { 'H', 'e', 'l', 'l', 'o', '\0' };
```

then the variable `hello` has exactly the same meaning as the string literal `"Hello"`, except, of course, that the variable and the literal are two distinct objects and, therefore, have different addresses.

The reason that the compiler inserts the null character is to allow the programmer to locate the end of the literal given only the address of its initial character. The null character acts as an end marker, so that the programmer can know where the string ends. There is a library function in `<cstring>` called `strlen`, which tells us how many characters are in a string literal or other null-terminated array of characters, *not counting the null at the end*. The `strlen` function might be implemented as follows:

```
// Example implementation of standard-library function
size_t strlen(const char* p)
{
    size_t size = 0;
    while (*p++ != '\0')
        ++size;
    return size;
}
```

Recall from §10.1.3/174 that `size_t` is an unsigned integral type that is appropriate to contain the size of any array, which makes it the appropriate type for `size`. The `strlen` function counts characters in the array denoted by p up to but not including the null.

Because the variable `hello` has the same meaning as the string literal `"Hello"`,

```
string s(hello);
```

will define a `string` variable named s that contains a copy of the characters stored in `hello`, just as

```
string s("Hello");
```

defines a `string` variable named s that contains a copy of the characters in `"Hello"`. Moreover, because we can construct a `string` from two iterators, we can also write

```
string s(hello, hello + strlen(hello));
```

Here, using the name of the array `hello` yields a pointer to the initial character of the `hello` array, and `hello + strlen(hello)` is a pointer to the `'\0'` that is at the end of the array, which is also one character past the o of `hello`. Because pointers are iterators, we can construct a `string` from two pointers, similar to what we did in §6.1.1/103, where we created a new `string` from two iterators. In both cases, the first iterator refers to the initial character of the sequence that we wish to use to initialize the string that we are constructing, and the second iterator refers to one past the last character.

10.3 Initializing arrays of character pointers

We said in §10.2/176 that a string literal is just a convenient way of writing the address of the initial character of a null-terminated sequence of characters. We said in §10.1.6/176 that we can initialize the elements of an array by giving a sequence of appropriate values, enclosed in curly braces, as an initializer. By combining these two facts, we learn that we can initialize an array of character pointers by giving a sequence of string literals.

This claim is quite a mouthful. To make it concrete, suppose that we wish to convert numeric grades to letter grades according to the following rule:

If the grade is at least	97	94	90	87	84	80	77	74	70	60	0
then the letter grade is	A+	A	A−	B+	B	B−	C+	C	C−	D	F

Here is a program that does the conversion:

```
string letter_grade(double grade)
{
    // range posts for numeric grades
    static const double numbers[] = {
        97, 94, 90, 87, 84, 80, 77, 74, 70, 60, 0
    };

    // names for the letter grades
    static const char* const letters[] = {
        "A+", "A", "A-", "B+", "B", "B-", "C+", "C", "C-", "D", "F"
    };

    // compute the number of grades given the size of the array
    // and the size of a single element
    static const size_t ngrades = sizeof(numbers)/sizeof(*numbers);

    // given a numeric grade, find and return the associated letter grade
    for (size_t i = 0; i < ngrades; ++i) {
        if (grade >= numbers[i])
            return letters[i];
    }

    return "?\?\?";
}
```

The definition of numbers uses the keyword static, which we saw in §6.1.3/107. In the present context, it tells the compiler to initialize the letters and numbers arrays only once, no later than the first time each array is used. Without the static, the compiler would have initialized the array for each call, which would have slowed the program needlessly. We have said that the array elements are const because we do not intend to change them—which is what allows us to get away with initializing the array only once.

The letters array is an array of constant pointers to const char. In this case, each element points to the initial element of its respective letter-grade string literal.

The definition of ngrades introduces a new keyword, sizeof, which we use to determine how many elements the numbers array has without having to count the elements ourselves. If e is an expression, then sizeof(e) returns a size_t value that tells us how much memory an object of the type of e consumes. It does so without actually evaluating the expression, which is possible because it does not need to evaluate the expression in order to determine its type, and because all objects of a given type occupy the same amount of storage.

The sizeof operator reports its result in *bytes*, which are storage units whose exact nature varies from one implementation to another. The only guarantees about bytes are that a byte contains at least eight bits, every object occupies at least one byte, and that a char occupies exactly one byte.

Of course, we want to determine how many elements the numbers array has, not how many bytes it occupies. To do so, we divide the size of the entire array by the size of a single element. Recall from §10.1.3/174 that because numbers is an array, *numbers is an element of the array. It happens to be the initial element, but the particular element is irrelevant in this context because all elements are the same size. What is relevant is that `sizeof(*numbers)` is the size of a single element of the `numbers` array, so that `sizeof(numbers)/sizeof(*numbers)` is the number of elements in the array.

Once we have established our tables, determining the letter grade is simplicity itself. We look sequentially at the elements of `numbers` until we find that `grade` is greater than or equal to one of them. When we find the relevant element of `numbers`, we return the corresponding element of `letters`. This element is a pointer, but we have already seen in §10.2/176 that we can convert a character pointer to a `string`.

If we cannot find an appropriate letter grade, it means that our user gave us a negative numeric grade, in which case we return a nonsense letter grade. The \ characters are there because, as we explain in more detail in §A.2.1.4/302, C++ programs should not contain two or more consecutive question marks. We must, therefore, use `"?\?\?"` to represent `???` in a program.

10.4 Arguments to `main`

Now that we understand pointers and character arrays, we can understand how to pass arguments to the `main` function. Most operating systems provide a way to pass a sequence of character strings to `main` as an argument, if the `main` function is willing to accept them. The way the author of `main` signals such willingness is by giving `main` two parameters: an `int` and a pointer to a pointer to `char`. Like any parameters, these can have arbitrary names, but programmers often call them `argc` and `argv`. The value of `argv` is a pointer to the initial element of an array of pointers, one for each argument. The value of `argc` is the number of pointers in the array of which `argv` points to the initial element. The initial element of that array always represents the name by which the program is called, so `argc` is always at least `1`. The arguments, if any, occupy subsequent elements of the array.

As an example, this program writes its arguments, if any, with spaces between them:

```
int main(int argc, char** argv)
{
    // if there are arguments, write them
    if (argc > 1) {
        int i;        // declare i outside the for because we need it after the loop finishes
        for (i = 1; i < argc-1; ++i)      // write all but the last entry and a space
            cout << argv[i] << " ";       // argv[i] is a char*

        cout << argv[i] << endl;          // write the last entry but not a space
    }
    return 0;
}
```

If we compile this program and put the resulting executable in a file called `say`, then by asking the system to execute

```
say Hello, world
```

we will cause our program to write

```
Hello, world
```

In this case, `argc` will be `3`, and the three elements of `argv` will be pointers to the initial characters of arrays initialized with `say`, `Hello`, and `world` respectively. We can visualize the value of `argv` this way:

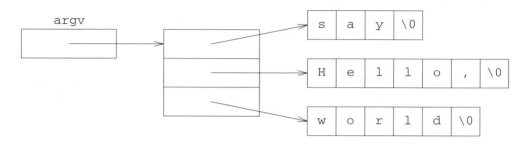

10.5 Reading and writing files

The programs in this book use only `cin` and `cout` for their input and output. Larger applications, however, often need to work with multiple files, both for input and output. C++ offers a wide variety of facilities for doing so, of which we will discuss only a few.

10.5.1 The standard error stream

It is often useful for a program to be able to comment about what it is doing in a way that is not part of its regular output. Such comments might notify the user about error conditions, or might constitute a log of events that the program considers significant.

To make such comments easy to distinguish from ordinary output, the C++ library defines a *standard error* stream, in addition to the standard input and output streams. This stream is often merged with the standard output, but most systems provide a way to separate them.

To write to the standard error stream, C++ programs can use either `cerr` or `clog`. These output streams are both attached to the same destination. The difference between them is how they handle buffering (§1.1/11).

The `clog` stream, as its name suggests, is intended for logging purposes. Accordingly, it has the same buffering properties as `cout`: It saves characters and writes them when the system decides that it is appropriate to do so. The `cerr` stream, on the other hand, always writes its output immediately. This strategy guarantees that the output will become visible as soon as possible, but it imposes what might be substantial overhead. Therefore, to write an urgent complaint, you should use `cerr`; to produce a running commentary about what the program is doing, you should use `clog`.

10.5.2 Dealing with multiple input and output files

The standard input, output, and error streams might or might not be associated with files. For example, a window system might run C++ programs with these streams connected to a window associated with the program, and might use completely different facilities to do so than it would to access disk files.

For this reason, the objects that the C++ standard library uses for file input and output have different types than the objects that it uses to denote the standard input and output streams. If you wish to work with an input or output file, you must create an object of type ifstream or ofstream respectively. This requirement may seem to cause needless difficulty. After all, we have seen that the library's input and output facilities are all defined in terms of types istream and ostream. Does the library have another set of definitions for ifstream and ofstream?

Fortunately, the answer is no. As we shall see in Chapter 13, it is possible to say that one type is similar enough to another that one can stand in for the other. The standard library says exactly that, by defining ifstream to be a kind of istream and ofstream to be a kind of ostream. As a result, it is possible to use an ifstream wherever the library expects an istream and an ofstream wherever the library expects an ostream. The definitions of both of these classes appear in header <fstream>.

When we define an ifstream or ofstream object, we might expect to have to supply, in the form of a string, the name of the file that we wish to use. In fact, we are required to supply, not a string, but rather a pointer to the initial element of a null-terminated character array. One reason for this curious requirement is to give programs the option of using the input–output library without using the string facilities. Another reason is historical: The input–output library predates the string class by several years. A third reason is that this requirement makes it easier to interface with operating-system input–output facilities, which typically use such pointers to communicate. Whatever the reasons, the fact is that programs that deal with files must ultimately express the files' names as pointers to null-terminated character arrays.

As an example, here is a program that copies a file named in to a file named out:

```
int main()
{
    ifstream infile("in");
    ofstream outfile("out");

    string s;

    while (getline(infile, s))
        outfile << s << endl;
    return 0;
}
```

This program takes advantage of the fact that a string literal is effectively a pointer to the initial character of a null-terminated array. If we don't want to have to give the name of the file as a literal, the best alternative is to store the file name in a string and then use the c_str member function that we will describe in §12.6/224. So, for example, if file is a string variable that contains the name of a file that we want to read, we can create an ifstream object that will read it by defining it as

```
ifstream infile(file.c_str());
```

As a final example, here is a program that produces, on its standard output, a copy of the contents of all the files whose names are given as arguments to `main`:

```
int main(int argc, char **argv)
{
    int fail_count = 0;
    // for each file in the input list
    for (int i = 1; i < argc; ++i) {
        ifstream in(argv[i]);

        // if it exists, write its contents, otherwise generate an error message
        if (in) {
            string s;
            while (getline(in, s))
                cout << s << endl;
        } else {
            cerr << "cannot open file " << argv[i] << endl;
            ++fail_count;
        }
    }
    return fail_count;
}
```

For each argument given to `main` (§10.4/179), the program creates an `ifstream` object to read the file by that name. If the object appears `false` when used as a condition, that means that the file does not exist, or that it cannot be read for some reason. Accordingly, the program complains on `cerr`, and keeps a count of how many failures it had. If the program created the `ifstream` object successfully, it reads the file, one line at a time, into `s`, and writes the contents of each line on the standard output.

When the program returns control to the system, it passes back the number of files that it was unable to read. As usual, a return value of zero indicates success, which in this case will indicate that we were able to read all the files.

10.6 Three kinds of memory management

So far, we have seen two distinct kinds of memory management, although we have not discussed them explicitly. The first kind is usually called **automatic** memory management, and is associated with local variables: A local variable occupies memory that the system allocates when it encounters the variable's definition during execution. The system automatically deallocates that memory at the end of the block that contains the definition.

Once a variable has been deallocated, any pointers to it become invalid. It is the programmer's responsibility to avoid using such invalid pointers. For example,

```
// this function deliberately yields an invalid pointer.
// it is intended as a negative example—don't do this!
int* invalid_pointer()
{
    int x;
    return &x;                     // instant disaster!
}
```

This function returns the address of the local variable x. Unfortunately, when the function returns, doing so ends execution of the block that contains the definition of x, which deallocates x. The pointer that &x created is now invalid, but the function tries to return it anyway. What happens at this point is anybody's guess. In particular, C++ implementations are not required to diagnose the error—you get what you get.

If we want to return the address of a variable such as x, one way to do so is to use the other kind of memory management, by asking for x to be *statically allocated*:

```
// This function is completely legitimate.
int* pointer_to_static()
{
    static int x;
    return &x;
}
```

By saying that x is static, we are saying that we want to allocate it once, and only once, at some point before the first time that pointer_to_static is ever called, and that we do not want to deallocate it as long as our program runs. There is nothing wrong with returning the address of a static variable; the pointer will be valid as long as the program runs, and it will be irrelevant afterward.

However, static allocation has the potential disadvantage that every call to pointer_to_static will return a pointer to the same object! Suppose we want to define a function such that each time we call it, we get a pointer to a brand new object, which stays around until we decide that we no longer want it. To do so, we use *dynamic allocation*, which we request by using the **new** and **delete** keywords.

10.6.1 Allocating and deallocating an object

If T is the type of an object, new T is an expression that allocates an object of type T, which is default-initialized, and yields a pointer to this (unnamed) newly allocated object. It is possible to give a specific value to use when initializing the object by executing new T(*args*). The object stays around until the program either ends or executes delete p (whichever happens first), where p is (a copy of) the pointer returned by new. In order to delete a pointer, the pointer must point to an object that was allocated by new, or be equal to zero. Deleting a zero pointer has no effect.

As an example,

```
int* p = new int(42);
```

will allocate an unnamed new object of type int, initialize the object to 42, and cause p to point to that object. We can affect the value of the object by executing statements such as

```
++*p;                        // p is now 43
```

after which the object has the value 43. When we're done with the object, we can execute

```
delete p;
```

after which the space occupied by *p is freed and p becomes an invalid pointer, with a value that we can no longer use until we have assigned a new value to it.

As another example, we might write a function that allocates an `int` object, initializes it, and returns a pointer to it:

```
int* pointer_to_dynamic()
{
    return new int(0);
}
```

which imposes on its caller the responsibility of freeing the object at an appropriate time.

10.6.2 Allocating and deallocating an array

If `T` is a type and `n` is a non-negative integral value, `new T[n]` allocates an array of n objects of type `T` and returns a pointer (which has type `T*`) to the initial element of the array. Each object is default-initialized, meaning that if `T` is a built-in type and the array is allocated at local scope, then the objects are uninitialized. If `T` is a class type, then each element is initialized by running its default constructor.

When `T` is a class type, there are two important implications of this initialization process: First, if the class doesn't allow default-initialization, then the compiler will reject the program. Second, each of the n elements in the array is initialized, which can be a substantial execution overhead. In Chapter 11, we'll see that the standard library provides a more flexible mechanism for dynamically allocating arrays. It is often preferable to use that mechanism, rather than `new`, when dynamically allocating an array.

Although every ordinary array is required to have at least one element, it is possible to allocate an "array" with no elements by executing `new T[n]` with n equal to zero. In this case, `new` has a little trouble returning a pointer to the initial element—because there isn't one. What it does instead is return a valid off-the-end pointer (§8.2.7/149), which we can later use as an argument to `delete[]`, and which we can think of as being a pointer to where the initial element would be if it existed.

The point of this curious behavior is to permit programs such as

```
T* p = new T[n];
vector<T> v(p, p + n);
delete[] p;
```

to work even if n is zero. The fact that `p` doesn't point to an element when n is zero is irrelevant; all that matters is that `p` and `p + n` are pointers that can legitimately be compared with each other and found to be equal. In all cases, the `vector` will have n elements. It is a great convenience for such programs to work properly even when n is zero.

Note the use of `delete[]` in this example. The brackets are necessary to tell the system to deallocate an entire array, rather than a single element. An array allocated by `new[]` stays around until the program ends or until the program executes `delete[] p`, where p is (a copy of) the pointer that `new[]` yielded. Before deallocating the array, the system destroys each element, in reverse order.

As an example, here is a function that takes a pointer to the initial character of a null-terminated character array such as a string literal, copies all the characters in the array (including the null character at the end) into a newly allocated array, and returns a pointer to the initial element of the new array:

```
char* duplicate_chars(const char* p)
{
    //  allocate enough space; remember to add one for the null
    size_t length = strlen(p) + 1;
    char* result = new char[length];

    //  copy into our newly allocated space and return pointer to first element
    copy(p, p + length, result);
    return result;
}
```

Recall from §10.2/176 that `strlen` returns the number of characters in a null-terminated array, excluding the null character at the end. We therefore add 1 to the result of `strlen` to account for the null, and allocate that many characters. Because pointers are iterators, we can use the `copy` algorithm to copy characters from the array denoted by p into the array denoted by `result`. Because `length` includes the null character at the end of the array, the call to `copy` copies that character as well as the ones before it.

As before, this function imposes on its caller the obligation to free the memory that it allocated. In general, finding an opportune time to free dynamically allocated memory is far from easy. We shall discuss techniques for automating this task in §11.3.4/200.

10.7 Details

Pointers are random-access iterators that hold the addresses of objects. For example:

`p = &s`   Makes p point to s.

`*p = s2`   Dereferences p and assigns a new value to the object to which p points.

`vector<string> (*sp)(const string&) = split;`

Defines sp as a function pointer that points to the `split` function.

`int nums[100];`

Defines nums as an array of 100 ints.

`int* bn = nums;`

Defines bn as a pointer to the first element of the array nums.

`int* en = nums + 100;`

Defines en as a pointer to (one past) the last element of the array nums.

Pointers can point at single objects, arrays of objects, or functions. When a pointer refers to a function, its value may be used only to call the function.

Arrays are fixed-size, built-in containers whose iterators are pointers. Uses of the name of an array are automatically converted to a pointer to the initial element of the array. A string literal is a null-terminated array of characters. Indexing an array is defined in terms of pointer operations: For every array a and an index n, a[n] is the same as *(a + n). If a is an array with n elements, then the range [a, a + n) represents all the elements of a.

Arrays can be initialized when they are defined:

```
string days[] = { "Mon", "Tues", "Wed", "Thu", "Fri", "Sat", "Sun" };
```

The implementation infers the size of days from the number of initializers.

The main function may (optionally) take two arguments. The first argument, an int, says how many character arrays are stored in the second argument, which is a char**. The second argument to main is sometimes written as

```
char* argv[]
```

which is equivalent to char**. This syntax is legal only in parameter lists.

Input–Output:

cerr	Standard error stream. Output is not buffered.
clog	Standard error intended for logging. Output is buffered.
ifstream(cp)	Input stream bound to the file named by the char* cp. Supports the operations on istreams.
ofstream(cp)	Output stream bound to the file named by the char* cp. Supports the operations on ostreams.

Input and output file streams are defined in <fstream>.

Memory management:

new T	Allocates and default-initializes a new object of type T and returns a pointer to the object.
new T(*args*)	Allocates and initializes a new object of type T using *args* to initialize the object. Returns a pointer to the object.
delete p	Destroys the object to which p points and frees the memory used to hold *p. The pointer must point at an object that was dynamically allocated.
new T[n]	Allocates and default-initializes an array of n new objects of type T. Returns a pointer to the initial element in the array.
delete[] p	Destroys the objects in the array to which p points and frees the memory used to hold the array. The pointer must point to the initial element of an array that was dynamically allocated.

Exercises

10-0. Compile, execute, and test the programs in this chapter.

10-1. Rewrite the student-grading program from §9.6/166 to generate letter grades.

10-2. Rewrite the median function from §8.1.1/140 so that we can call it with either a vector or a built-in array. The function should allow containers of any arithmetic type.

10-3. Write a test program to verify that the median function operates correctly. Ensure that calling median does not change the order of the elements in the container.

10-4. Write a class that implements a list that holds strings.

10-5. Write a bidirectional iterator for your String_list class.

10-6. Test the class by rewriting the split function to put its output into a String_list.

11

Defining abstract data types

In Chapter 9, we learned something about the basic language features required to define new types. However, the `Student_info` type that we defined in that chapter did not specify what should happen when objects of type `Student_info` are copied, assigned, or destroyed. As we'll see in this chapter, the class author also controls all these aspects of an object's behavior. What may be surprising is how essential the correct definition of these operations is for creating a type that is intuitive and easy to use.

Because we've used `vectors` extensively, we'll build a similar class to further our understanding of how to design and implement classes. The implementation that we present will be greatly simplified in terms of which operations we provide and our attention to efficiency. Because it is a stripped-down version of the standard-library `vector` class, we'll call our class `Vec` to avoid confusing it with the library class. Although we are largely concerned with how to copy, assign, and destroy objects of class `Vec`, we will find it useful to start by implementing some simpler member functions. Once we have completed these other functions, we will come back and look at how we can control copying, assigning, and destroying class objects.

11.1 The `Vec` class

When we design a class, we normally start by specifying the interface that we want to provide. One way to determine the right interface is to look at the kind of programs we want our users to be able to write. Because we want to implement a useful subset of the standard `vector` class, a good place to start is to look at how we've used `vectors`:

```
// construct a vector
vector<Student_info> vs;          // empty vector
vector<double> v(100);            // vector with 100 elements

// obtain the names of the types used by the vector
vector<Student_info>::const_iterator b, e;
vector<Student_info>::size_type i = 0;

// use size and the index operator to look at each element in the vector
for (i = 0; i != vs.size(); ++i)
    cout << vs[i].name();
```

```
// return iterators positioned on the first and one past the last element
b = vs.begin(); e = vs.end();
```

Of course, this list of operations is but a subset of what the standard `vector` class provides—but by implementing this subset, we can understand the language facilities necessary to support much of the `vector` interface.

11.2 Implementing the Vec class

Having determined our operations, we next need to think about how to represent a `Vec`.

The easiest implementation decision is that we need to define a ***template class***. We want to allow users to use `Vec`s to hold a variety of types. The template facility that we described in §8.1.1/140 for functions also applies to classes. That facility let us write one definition of a template function, and use that template to create versions that could be run on a variety of types. Similarly, we can define a template class, and then use that class to create a family of types that differ only with respect to the types used in the template parameter list. We've already used such types, including `vector`, `list`, and `map`.

As with template functions, when we define a template class, we have to signal that the class is a template, and list the type parameters that will be used in the class definition:

```
template <class T> class Vec {
public:
        // interface
private:
        // implementation
};
```

This code says that `Vec` is a template class, with one type parameter named `T`. As with other class types, we can assume that there will be `public` and `private` parts that define the interface and implementation respectively.

The next question we must resolve is what data we will store. Presumably we'll need some storage to hold the elements in the `Vec`, and we'll want to keep track of the number of elements that the `Vec` contains. The most obvious choice is to hold the elements in a dynamically allocated array.

What information about the array do we need to store? We intend to implement the `begin`, `end`, and `size` functions. This intention suggests that we might store the address of the initial element, one past the address of the last element, and the number of elements. However, we do not need to store all three of these items, because we can compute any of them from the other two. Therefore, we'll make the arbitrary decision to store only pointers to the first and (one past) the last element of the array, and to compute the size as needed. We envision a data structure that looks like this:

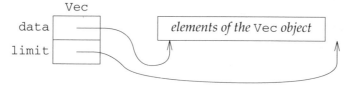

With these implementation decisions made, we can update our Vec class:

```
template <class T> class Vec {
public:
    // interface
private:
    T* data;      // first element in the Vec
    T* limit;     // one past the last element in the Vec
};
```

This class definition says that Vec is a template type, and that it takes a single type parameter. In the body of the class definition, we'll call that type T. Whenever we use T, the compiler will replace it with whatever type the user names when creating a Vec. So for example, if we write

```
Vec<int> v;
```

this definition will cause the compiler to instantiate (§8.1.2/142) a version of the Vec class in which it replaces each reference to T by int. The code that the compiler generates for that class will resolve expressions that involve T as if they had been written using int. Thus, because we used the type parameter T in the declaration of data and limit, the type of these pointers depends on the type of the objects that the Vec will hold.

This type is not known until the definition of a Vec is instantiated. Once we say that we want a Vec<int>, the types of data and limit are known: They will be int* for this instance of Vec. Similarly, if we also used Vec<string>, then the compiler would generate a second, different instantiation of Vec that bound T to string, thereby giving data and limit the type string* in that instantiation.

11.2.1 Memory allocation

Because our class will allocate its array dynamically (§10.6.2/184), we might expect that we should allocate space for our Vec by using new T[n], where n is the number of elements we want to allocate. However, remember that not only does new T[n] allocate space, but it also initializes the elements by running the default constructor for T. If we were to use new T[n], then we would be imposing a requirement on T: Users could create a Vec<T> only if T has a default constructor. The standard vector class imposes no such restriction. Because we want to emulate standard vectors, we don't want to impose this restriction either.

It turns out that the library provides a memory allocation class that offers more detailed control over memory allocation. This class will suit our needs exactly, if we use it instead of new and delete. The class lets us allocate raw memory, and then—in a separate step—build objects in that memory. Rather than diving right into the details of that class, we will assume that eventually we shall have to write some utility functions that will manage the memory for us. For now, we'll assume that these functions exist, and we'll use them in completing the Vec class. As we use them, we'll get a better picture of just what we would like them to do, so that when it's time to implement them, we will know just what it is that we need to implement.

These new utility members will be part of the `private` implementation of our class. They will be responsible for allocating and deallocating the memory that we need, and for initializing and destroying the elements stored in the `Vec`. Thus, these functions will manage our pointers—data and `limit`. Only these memory management functions will give new values to these data members. The `public` members of `Vec` will read `data` and `limit`, but will not change them.

When the `public` members need to do something, such as constructing a new `Vec` that needs to change the value of `data` or `limit`, they will call an appropriate memory-management function to do so. This strategy will let us partition our work: One set of members will provide the interface to our user, and another set will deal with the implementation details.

We'll come back to fill in the details of these utility functions in §11.5/203.

11.2.2 Constructors

We know that we must define two constructors:

```
Vec<Student_info> vs;          // uses the default constructor
Vec<double> vs(100);           // uses the constructor that takes a size
```

The standard `vector` also provides a closely related third constructor, which takes a size and an initial value to use to initialize the elements of the `vector`, and initializes all the elements to copies of that value. This constructor is similar to the one that takes a size alone, so we may as well implement this third constructor too.

The role of any constructor is to ensure that the object is correctly initialized. For `Vec` objects, we need to initialize `data` and `limit`. Doing so involves allocating space to hold the elements of the `Vec` and initializing those elements to an appropriate value. In the case of the default constructor, we want to create an empty `Vec`, so we need not allocate any space. For the constructors that take a size, we will allocate the given amount of storage. If the user gives us an initial value as well as a size, we'll use that value to initialize all the elements that we allocated. If the user gives us just a size, then we'll use the default constructor for `T` to obtain a value to use in initializing the elements. For now, we'll forward to our as yet unwritten memory-management functions the job of initializing `data` and `limit`, and the related work of allocating and initializing the elements:

```
template <class T> class Vec {
public:
    Vec() { create(); }
    explicit Vec(size_type n, const T& val = T()) { create(n, val); }
    // remaining interface

private:
    T* data;
    T* limit;
};
```

The default constructor, which is the one that takes no arguments, needs to indicate that the `Vec` is empty (i.e., that it has no elements). It does so by calling a member named create, which we'll have to write. When we return from create, we intend for both data and limit to be set to zero.

Our second constructor uses a keyword that we have not yet seen, **explicit**, which we will explain shortly. First, let's understand what the constructor does. Note that it uses a default argument (§7.3/127) for the second parameter. Thus, the constructor effectively defines two constructors: One takes a single argument of type size_type; the other takes a size_type and a const T&. In both cases we call a version of create that takes a size and a value. We'll assume that this function, which we'll write in §11.5/203, will allocate enough memory to hold n objects of type T, and will give those elements the initial value specified by val. Our users will have supplied that value explicitly, or else the default constructor for T will have generated it using the rules outlined in §9.5/164 for value-initialization.

Now let's understand a bit about the use of explicit. This keyword makes sense only in the definition of a constructor that takes a single argument. When we say that a constructor is explicit, we're saying that the compiler will use the constructor only in contexts in which the user expressly invokes the constructor, and not otherwise:

```
Vec<int> vi(100);    //  ok, explicitly construct the Vec from an int
Vec<int> vi = 100;   //  error: implicitly construct the Vec (§11.3.3/199) and copy it to vi
```

Use of explicit can be crucial in other contexts in which a constructor might be used, so we will discuss it further in §12.2/213. For consistency with the standard vector class, we have made this constructor explicit even though none of our subsequent examples in this chapter relies on this fact.

11.2.3 Type definitions

Following the convention used by the standard template classes, we want to provide type names that our users can use, and that will hide the implementation details of how we implement our class. Specifically, we need to provide typedefs for the const and nonconst iterator types, and for the type that we use to denote the size of a Vec.

It turns out that the library containers also define three other types. The first, named value_type, is a synonym for type of each object that the container stores. The other two types, named reference and const_reference, are synonyms for references to value_type and const value_type, respectively. We will want to add push_back to class Vec, so that users can dynamically grow their Vec objects. If we also define these three types, then users will be able to use back_inserter (which uses push_back and the three types) to generate an output iterator that can grow the Vec.

The only hard part of defining these types is deciding what types to choose. As we've seen, iterators are objects that navigate among the objects in a container and let us examine their values. Often iterators are themselves of class type. For example, consider a class that implements a linked list. A logical strategy for such a class would be to model a list as a set of nodes, where each node contains a value and a pointer to the next node in the list. The iterator for such a class would contain a pointer to one of these nodes and would implement the ++ operator to follow the pointer to the next node in the list. Such an iterator would have to be implemented as a class type.

Because we used an array to hold the elements of a Vec, we can use plain pointers as our Vec iterator type. Each such pointer will point into the underlying data array. As we learned in §10.1/169, pointers support all the random-access-iterator operations. By using a pointer as our underlying iterator type, we will provide full random-access properties, which is consistent with the standard vector class.

What about the other types? The type of value_type is obvious: It must be T. But, what about the type that represents the size? We know that size_t is big enough to hold the number of elements in any array. Because we are storing Vecs in an array, we can use size_t as the underlying type for Vec::size_type. These decisions give us a class that now looks like

```
template <class T> class Vec {
public:
    typedef T* iterator;                    // added
    typedef const T* const_iterator;        // added
    typedef size_t size_type;               // added
    typedef T value_type;                   // added
    typedef T& reference;                   // added
    typedef const T& const_reference;       // added

    Vec() { create(); }
    explicit Vec(size_type n, const T& val = T()) { create(n, val); }
    // remaining interface

private:
    iterator data;                          // changed
    iterator limit;                         // changed
};
```

In addition to adding the appropriate typedefs, we've also updated the class to use our new types. By using the same names inside the class that we defined with our typedef declarations, we make our code more readable and ensure the code will not get out of sync if we subsequently change one of these types.

11.2.4 Index and size

We said that our users should be able to call size to find out how many elements are in the Vec and to use the index operator to access the elements in the Vec. For example,

```
for (i = 0; i != vs.size(); ++i)
    cout << vs[i].name();
```

From this usage we can see that the size function should be a member of class Vec, and that we'll need to define what it means to use the subscript operator, [], on a Vec. The size function is easiest: It takes no argument and should return the number of elements in the Vec as a Vec::size_type. Before we define the index operation, we need to know a bit more about how overloaded operators work.

We define an overloaded operator much as we define any other function: It has a name, takes arguments, and specifies a return type.

We form the name of an overloaded operator by appending the operator symbol to the word `operator`. Thus, the function we need to define will be called `operator[]`.

The kind of operator—whether it is a unary or binary operator—is part of what determines how many parameters the corresponding function has. If the operator is a function that is not a member, then the function has as many arguments as the operator has operands. The first argument is bound to the left operand; the second is bound to the right operand. If the operator is defined as a member function, then its left operand is implicitly bound to the object on which the operator is invoked. Member operator functions, therefore, take one less argument than the operator indicates.

In general, operator functions may be member or nonmember functions. However, the index operator is one of a handful of operations that *must* be member functions. When our user writes an expression such as `vs[i]`, that expression will call the member named `operator[]` of `vs`, passing `i` as its argument.

We know that the operand must be an integral type large enough to denote the last element in the largest possible `Vec`, and that this type is `Vec::size_type`. What remains is to decide what type the index operator should return.

If we give it a bit of thought, we'll conclude that we should return a reference to the element stored in the `Vec`. Doing so will allow users to write through the index as well as read from it. Although our sample program uses the index only to read a value from `vs`, it is reasonable to expect that users will also want write access to the elements. With this analysis complete, we can update our class appropriately:

```
template <class T> class Vec {
public:
    // typedef definitions as in §11.2.3/192

    Vec() { create(); }
    explicit Vec(size_type n, const T& val = T()) { create(n, val); }

    // new operations: size and index
    size_type size() const { return limit - data; }

    T& operator[](size_type i) { return data[i]; }
    const T& operator[](size_type i) const { return data[i]; }
private:
    iterator data;
    iterator limit;
};
```

The `size` function calculates the number of elements in the `Vec` by subtracting the pointers that delimit the array that holds our values. Remember from §10.1.4/175 that subtracting two pointers yields the number of elements apart the locations are to which the pointers refer (a value of type `ptrdiff_t`). Returning that value from the `size` function converts it to `size_type`, the function's return type, which is a synonym for `size_t` (§10.1.3/174). Taking the `size` of a `Vec` doesn't change the `Vec`, so we declare `size` as a `const` member function. Doing so lets us take the `size` of a `const Vec`.

The index operator finds the corresponding position in the underlying array and returns a reference to the element. By returning a reference, we allow the user to use the index operation to change the values that are stored in the `Vec`. This ability to write to the element implies that we need two versions: one for const Vec objects, the other for nonconst objects of type Vec. Note that the const version returns a reference to const. Doing so ensures that users may use the index only to read the Vec, not to write to it. It is worth noting that we still return a reference, rather than returning a value, for consistency with the standard vector. The reason to return a reference is that if the objects stored in the container are large, it is more efficient to avoid copying them.

It may be surprising that we can overload the index operator, because it appears that both argument lists are the same; each appears to take a single parameter of type size_type. However, every member function, including each of these operators, takes an implicit parameter, which is the object on which it operates. Because the operations differ regarding whether that object is const, we can overload the operation.

11.2.5 Operations that return iterators

Next, we need to consider the functions that return iterators. Our specification called for us to implement the begin and end operations, which return an iterator positioned at the beginning and one past the end of the Vec respectively:

```
template <class T> class Vec {
public:
    // typedef definitions as in §11.2.3/192

    Vec() { create(); }
    explicit Vec(size_type n, const T& val = T()) { create(n, val); }

    T& operator[](size_type i) { return data[i]; }
    const T& operator[](size_type i) const { return data[i]; }

    size_type size() const { return limit - data; }

    // new functions to return iterators
    iterator begin() { return data; }                        // added
    const_iterator begin() const { return data; }            // added

    iterator end() { return limit; }                         // added
    const_iterator end() const { return limit; }             // added

private:
    iterator data;
    iterator limit;
};
```

We offer two versions of the begin and end operations, which are overloaded based on whether the Vec is const. The const versions return const_iterators, so our users will be able to read but not modify the Vec elements through the iterator.

At this point, our Vec class is still pretty basic, but the essentials are in place. In fact, if we add only a few more operations, such as push_back and clear, we could use this class instead of the standard vector for all the examples in this book. Unfortunately, though, our Vec class fails to meet the vector specification in some critically important ways, which we must now address.

11.3 Copy control

In the introduction to this chapter, we said that the class author controls what happens when objects are created, copied, assigned, and destroyed. We've explained how to create objects, but not how to control what happens when they are copied, assigned, or destroyed. As we'll see, if we fail to define these operations, the compiler will synthesize definitions for us. These synthesized operations are sometimes exactly what we need. The rest of the time, the synthesized operations can lead to counterintuitive behavior, and even to run-time failures.

C++ is the only language in widespread use that gives the programmer this level of control over an object's behavior. Not surprisingly, getting these operations correct is essential in building useful data types.

11.3.1 Copy constructor

Passing an object by value to a function, or returning an object by value from a function, implicitly copies the object. For example,

```
vector<int> vi;
double d;
d = median(vi);              // copy vi into the parameter in median

string line;
vector<string> words = split(line); // copy the return from split into words
```

Similarly, we can explicitly copy an object by using it to initialize another object:

```
vector<Student_info> vs;
vector<Student_info> v2 = vs;       // copy vs into v2
```

Both explicit and implicit copies are controlled by a special constructor called the *copy constructor*. Like other constructors, the copy constructor is a member function with the same name as the name of the class. Because it exists to initialize a new object as a copy of an existing object of the same type, it follows that the copy constructor takes a single argument that has the same type as the class itself. Because we are defining what it means to make a copy, including making copies of function arguments, this is one case when it is essential that the parameter be a reference type! Furthermore, copying an object should not change the original object, so the copy constructor takes a const reference to the object from which to copy:

```
template <class T> class Vec {
public:
    Vec(const Vec& v); // copy constructor
    // as before
};
```

Having declared the copy constructor, we have to figure out what it should do. In general, copy constructors "copy" each data element from an existing object into the new object. We say "copy" because sometimes copying involves more than just copying the contents of a data element. For example, in our Vec class, we have two data elements, both of which are pointers. If we copy the values of the pointers, then the original and the copy will both point to the same underlying data. For example, assume that v is a Vec, and that we want to copy v into v2. If we copied the pointers, then what we'd have is

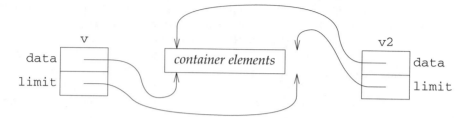

Clearly, any change made to an element of one "copy" would result in changing the value of the element of the other "copy" as well. That is, if we assigned a value to v[0], doing so would also change v2[0]. Is this behavior what we want?

As with other operations, we can answer this question by seeing what the standard vector does. Recall the discussion in §4.1.1/53, in which we noted that we needed to pass the vector to the median function by value so that the vector would be copied. Making a copy ensured that changes made inside median would not propagate out of the function. This analysis, and the behavior that we observe when we run the median function, indicates that the standard vector class does not share the same underlying storage once a copy is made. Instead, it arranges that each copy of a vector is independent, so that changes to one are not reflected in the other:

Evidently, when we copy a Vec, we'll need to allocate new space and copy the contents from the source into the newly allocated destination. As before, we'll assume that one of our utility functions will handle the allocation and copy so that the copy constructor can forward its work to that function:

```
template <class T> class Vec {
public:
    Vec(const Vec& v) { create(v.begin(), v.end()); }
    // as before
};
```

When we get around to writing it, the function will be yet another version of create— this one taking a pair of iterators (i.e., pointers) and initializing the elements being created from the elements in the range bounded by those pointers.

11.3.2 Assignment

Just as a class definition specifies what happens when objects of that class are copied, the class definition also controls the behavior of the *assignment operator*. Although a class

may define several instances of the assignment operator—overloaded, as usual, by differ-
ing types for its argument—the version that takes a `const` reference to the class itself is
special: It defines what it means to assign one value of the class type to another. This version is typically called "the assignment operator," even if the class defines several other
versions of the `operator=` function. The assignment operator, like the index operator,
must be a member of the class. As with any other operator, the assignment operator has a
return value, and so it must define a return type. For consistency with the built-in assignment operators, we return a reference to the left-hand side:

```
template <class T> class Vec {
public:
    Vec& operator=(const Vec&);
    // as before
};
```

Assignment differs from the copy constructor in that assignment always involves obliterating an existing value (the left-hand side) and replacing it with a new value (the right-
hand side). When we make a copy, we are creating a new object for the first time, so there
is no preexisting object to deallocate. Like the copy constructor, assignment usually
involves assigning each of the data values. Data members that are pointers present the
same issues for assignment as they did for copying. We'll want assignment to ensure that
each object has its own copy of the data from the right-hand side.

There's one last detail to consider before writing the code, and that is self-assignment.
It is possible that a user might wind up assigning an object to itself. As we shall see, it is
crucial that assignment operators deal correctly with self-assignment:

```
template <class T>
Vec<T>& Vec<T>::operator=(const Vec& rhs)
{
    // check for self-assignment
    if (&rhs != this) {

        // free the array in the left-hand side
        uncreate();

        // copy elements from the right-hand to the left-hand side
        create(rhs.begin(), rhs.end());
    }
    return *this;
}
```

This function uses a couple of new concepts, which we'll need to explain.

First is the syntax that we use to define a template member function outside the class
header. As with any template, we begin by signaling to the compiler that we are defining
a template, and naming the template parameters. Next comes the return type, which in
this case is `Vec<T>&`. If we compare this definition with the corresponding declaration in
the header file, we'll see that we said the function returned a `Vec&`. We did not explicitly
name the type parameter in the return type. As a bit of syntactic sugar, the language
allows us to omit the type parameters when we are within the scope of the template.
Thus, inside the header file, we need not repeat `<T>` because the template parameter is

implicit. When we name the return type, we are outside the scope of the class, so we must explicitly state the template parameters, if any. Similarly, the name of the function is `Vec<T>::operator=`, not simply `Vec::operator=`. However, once we have specified that it is a member of `Vec<T>` that we are defining, we need no longer repeat the template qualifiers. Hence, the argument is simply `const Vec&`, although we could have written the redundant `const Vec<T>&`.

The other new aspect of this function is the use of a new keyword, **this**. The `this` keyword is valid only inside a member function, where it denotes a pointer to the object on which the member function is operating. For example, inside `Vec::operator=`, the type of `this` is `Vec*`, because `this` is a pointer to the `Vec` object of which `operator=` is a member. For a binary operator, such as assignment, `this` is bound to the left-hand operand. Ordinarily, `this` is used when we need to refer to the object itself, as we do here both in the initial `if` test and in the `return`.

We use `this` to determine whether the right- and left-hand sides of the assignment refer to the same object. If they do, then they will have the same address. As we saw in §10.1.1/170, `&rhs` yields a pointer that is the address of `rhs`. We explicitly test for self-assignment by comparing that pointer and `this`, which points to the left-hand side. If the objects are the same, then there's nothing to do in the assignment operator, and we immediately fall through to the `return` statement. If the objects are different, we need to free the old space and assign new values to each data element, copying the contents from the right-hand side to the newly allocated array. Evidently, we will need to write another of our utility functions, `uncreate`, which will destroy the elements that had been in this `Vec`, and will free the storage that it had consumed. Once we call `uncreate` to obliterate the old values, we can use the version of `create` that copies from an existing `Vec` to allocate new space and copy the values from the right-hand to the left-hand side.

It is crucially important that assignment operators correctly handle self-assignment, which we did here by explicitly checking whether the left- and right-hand operands are the same object. To see the importance, consider what would happen if we were to remove this test from our assignment operator. In that case, we would always `uncreate` the existing array from the left-hand operand, destroying the elements and returning the space that had been used. However, if the two operands were the same object, then the right operand would refer to this same space. Had we used the elements from the right operand to `create` a new array for the left operand, the result would have been a disaster: When we freed the space held by the left operand, we would also have freed the space for the right-hand object. When `create` attempted to copy the elements from `rhs`, those elements would have been destroyed and the memory returned to the system.

Although it is most common to handle self-assignment through a direct check, such as we did here, it is not universal, nor is it always the best approach. The important point is to handle self-assignment correctly. How to do so is a matter of tactics.

The last interesting bit is the `return` statement, which dereferences `this` to obtain the object to which it points. We then return a reference to that object. As usual in returning a reference, it is crucial that the object to which the reference refers persist after the function has returned. Returning a reference to a local object ensures disaster: The referenced object will have gone away when the function returns, resulting in a reference to garbage.

In the case of the assignment operator, we are returning a reference to the object that is the left-hand side of the expression. That object exists outside the scope of the assignment operator and hence is guaranteed to be around even after the function returns.

11.3.3 *Assignment is not initialization*

Experience leads us to believe that the difference between assignment and initialization is one of the trickier aspects of learning C++ well. Many programming languages, C notably among them, do not expose the distinction, so programmers often are unaware of the difference. The fact that the = symbol can be involved in both initialization and assignment can make the distinction harder to grasp. When we use = to give an initial value to a variable, we are invoking the copy constructor. When we use it in an assignment expression, we're calling `operator=`. Class authors must be attuned to the difference in order to implement the right semantics.

The key difference stems from two observations: Assignment (`operator=`) always obliterates a previous value; initialization never does so. Rather, initialization involves creating a new object and giving it a value at the same time. Initialization happens

- In variable declarations
- For function parameters on entry to a function
- For the return value of a function on return from the function
- In constructor initializers

Assignment happens only when using the = operator in an expression. For example:

```
string url_ch = "~;/?:@=&$-_.+!*'(),";    // initialization
string spaces(url_ch.size(), ' ');        // initialization
string y;                                 // initialization
y = url_ch;                               // assignment
```

The first declaration creates a new object. Therefore, we know that we are initializing that object, and hence that we will be invoking a constructor. The syntax

```
string url_ch = "~;/?:@=&$-_.+!*'(),";
```

says to create a `string` from the `const char*` that represents the string literal `"~;/?:@=&$-_.+!*'(),"`. To do so, the compiler will call the `string` constructor that takes a `const char*`. That constructor can construct `url_ch` directly from the string literal, or it can construct an unnamed temporary variable from the string literal, and then call the copy constructor to construct `url_ch` as a copy of that temporary variable.

The second declaration shows another form of initialization: giving one or more constructor arguments directly. The compiler will call whichever constructor is most appropriate for the number of arguments and their types. In this example, it will use the `string` constructor that takes two arguments. The first argument says how many characters the variable `spaces` is to have; the second tells what value to give each of those characters. The effect will be to define `spaces` as having the same number of characters as `url_ch`, with all of the characters being blank.

The third declaration is easier: We're invoking the default constructor to create an empty `string`. The last statement is not a declaration at all. Instead, it is using the =

operator as part of an expression; hence, it is an assignment. That assignment will be accomplished by running the `string` assignment operator.

A slightly more complicated example involves function arguments and return values. For example, assume that `line` holds a line of input, and we call `split` from §6.1.1/103:

```
vector<string> split(const string&);     // function declaration
vector<string> v;                         // initialization

v = split(line);          // on entry, initialization of split's parameter from line;
                          // on exit, both initialization of the return value
                          // and assignment to v
```

The declaration of `split` is interesting because it defines a return type that is a class type. Assigning a class type return value from a function is a two-step process: First, the copy constructor is run to copy the return value into a temporary at the call site. Then the assignment operator is run to assign the value of that temporary to the left-hand operand.

The distinction between initialization and assignment is important because each one causes different operations to run:

- Constructors always control initialization.
- The `operator=` member function always controls assignment.

11.3.4 Destructor

We must still provide one more operation, which defines what happens when a `Vec` object is destroyed. An object that is created in a local scope is destroyed as soon as it goes out of scope; a dynamically allocated object is destroyed when we `delete` a pointer to the object. For example, consider the `split` function from §6.1.1/103:

```
vector<string> split(const string& str)
{
    vector<string> ret;
    // split str into words and store in ret
    return ret;
}
```

When we return from `split`, the local variable `ret` goes out of scope and is destroyed.

Just as with copy and assignment, it is up to the class to say what happens when objects are destroyed. Like constructors, which say how to create objects, there is a special member function, called a **destructor**, that controls what happens when objects of the type are destroyed. Destructors have the same name as the name of the class prefixed by a tilde (~). Destructors take no arguments and have no return value.

The work of the destructor is to do any cleanup that should be done whenever an object goes away. Typically, this cleanup involves releasing resources, such as memory, that the constructor has allocated:

```
template <class T> class Vec {
public:
    ~Vec() { uncreate(); }
    // as before
};
```

For `Vecs`, we allocate memory in the constructors, and so we must free it in the destructor. This job is similar to what the assignment operator does to obliterate the old left-hand side. Not surprisingly, we can call the same utility function from the destructor, with the aim of destroying the elements and freeing the space that they occupied.

11.3.5 Default operations

Some classes, such as the `Student_info` types that we defined in Chapters 4 and 9, do not explicitly define a copy constructor, assignment operator, or destructor. A logical question is: What happens when objects of such types are created, copied, assigned, and destroyed? The answer is that if the class author does not specify these operations, the compiler synthesizes default versions of the unspecified operations.

The default versions are defined to operate recursively—copying, assigning, or destroying each data element according to the appropriate rules for the type of that element. Each member that is of class type is copied, assigned, or destroyed by calling that member's copy constructor, assignment operator, or destructor, respectively. Members that are of built-in type are copied or assigned by copying or assigning their values. The destructor for built-in types has no work to do—even if the type is a pointer. In particular, destroying a pointer through the default destructor does not free the space at which the pointer points.

Now we can understand how the default `Student_info` operations execute. For example, the copy constructor copies four data elements. To do so, it invokes the `string` and `vector` copy constructors to copy the `name` and `homework` members respectively. It copies the two `double` values, `midterm` and `final`, directly.

Finally, as we saw in §9.5/164, there is a default for the default constructor. If the class defines no constructors at all, then the compiler will synthesize the default constructor, which is the constructor that has no parameters. The synthesized default constructor recursively initializes each data member in the same way as the object itself is initialized: If the context requires default-initialization, it will default-initialize the data members; if the context requires value-initialization, it will value-initialize the data members.

It is important to note that if a class defines any constructor explicitly, even a copy constructor, then the compiler will not synthesize a default constructor for that class. Default constructors are essential in several contexts: One such context is in the synthesized default constructor itself. In order to be used as a data member of a class that relies on the synthesized default constructor, the data type must itself provide a default constructor. Therefore, it is usually a good idea to give a class a default constructor, either explicitly, as we did in Chapter 9, or implicitly, as we did in Chapter 4.

11.3.6 The rule of three

Classes that manage resources such as memory require close attention to copy control. In general, the default operations will not suffice for such classes. Failure to control every copy can confuse users of the class and often will lead to run-time errors.

Consider our `Vec` class, but pretend that we did not define the copy constructor, assignment operator, or destructor. As we saw in §11.3.1/195, at best we will surprise our users. Users of Vec will almost surely expect that once they've copied one Vec into another, the two objects will be distinct. They will expect that operations on one Vec will not have any effect on the data held by the other.

Even worse, though, is that if we do not define a destructor, then the default destructor will be used. That destructor will destroy the pointer, but destroying a pointer does not free the space to which it points. The result will be a memory leak: The space consumed by Vecs will never be reclaimed.

If we fix the leak by providing a destructor, but we do not also add the copy constructor and assignment operator, then we set things up so that a crash is likely. In such a flawed implementation, it would be possible for two Vecs to share the same underlying storage, as we illustrated in the first diagram in §11.3.1/196. When one of those objects is destroyed, the destructor will destroy that shared storage. Any subsequent reference through the undestroyed copy will lead to disaster.

Classes that allocate resources in their constructors require that every copy deal correctly with those resources. Such classes almost surely need a destructor to free the resources. If the class needs a destructor, it almost surely needs a copy constructor, as well as an assignment operator. Copying or assigning objects of classes that allocate resources usually allocates those resources in the same way that creating an object from scratch does. To control how every object of class T deals with its resources, you need

`T::T()`	*one or more constructors, perhaps with arguments*
`T::~T()`	*the destructor*
`T::T(const T&)`	*the copy constructor*
`T::operator=(const T&)`	*the assignment operator*

Once we have defined these operations, the compiler will invoke them whenever an object of our type is created, copied, assigned, or destroyed. Remember that objects may be created, copied, or destroyed implicitly. Whether implicitly or explicitly, the compiler will invoke the appropriate operation.

Because the copy constructor, destructor, and assignment operator are so tightly coupled, the relationship among them has become known as the **rule of three**: If your class needs a destructor, it probably needs a copy constructor and an assignment operator too.

11.4 Dynamic Vecs

Before we implement our memory management functions, we should realize that our Vecs are inferior to standard vectors in an important way: We do not provide a push_back operation, and so our Vecs are of fixed size. Remember that push_back pushes its argument onto the back of the vector and, in the process, increases the size of the vector by one element.

We could add a push_back function that allocated new space to hold one more element than the current Vec holds. We'd have to copy the existing elements into this new space, constructing a new last element from the argument to push_back. We can see that this strategy would be expensive if our users made many calls to push_back.

There is a classic approach to solving a problem such as this one: Allocate more storage than we need. Only when we exhaust the preallocated storage will we go back for more. For simplicity, whenever `push_back` needs to get more space, we'll allocate twice as much storage as we currently use. So, if we create a `Vec` with 100 elements, and then call `push_back` for the first time, it will allocate enough space to hold 200 elements. It will copy the existing 100 elements into the first half of the newly allocated space and construct a new, last element at the end of that sequence. The next 99 calls to `push_back` will be satisfied without having to go back for more memory.

This strategy implies that we'll need to change how we keep track of the array that holds our elements. We'll still need to keep track of the first element, but now we'll need two "end" pointers. One will point (one past) the last constructed element, which, equivalently, is a pointer to the first available element. The other pointer will point (one past) the last allocated element. So, our `Vec` objects will now look like

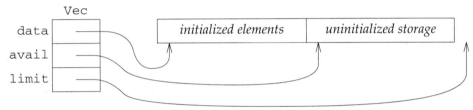

Our `size` and `end` functions must be rewritten to use the new member `avail`. In addition, `push_back`, and our as yet unwritten memory management functions will use this new member. Moreover, `push_back` itself is pretty simple; it forwards the hard work to two of our memory-management functions, named `grow` and `unchecked_append`:

```
template <class T> class Vec {
public:
    size_type size() const { return avail - data; }   // changed
    iterator end() { return avail; }                   // changed
    const_iterator end() const { return avail; }       // changed
    void push_back(const T& val) {
        if (avail == limit)      // get space if needed
            grow();
        unchecked_append(val);   // append the new element
    }
private:
    iterator data;    // as before, pointer to the first element in the Vec
    iterator avail;   // pointer to (one past) the last constructed element
    iterator limit;   // now points to (one past) the last available element
    // rest of the class interface and implementation as before
};
```

11.5 Flexible memory management

When we wrote our `Vec` class, we noted that we did not want to use the built-in `new` and `delete` operations to manage our memory. The reason is that if we relied on these operations, our `Vec` would be more restrictive than the standard `vector`. The `new` operator does too much for our purposes: It both allocates and initializes memory. When used to allocate an array of type `T`, it needs the default constructor for `T`. This approach prevents us from offering our users as much flexibility as we would like to offer.

Using `new` would also be unduly expensive. If we use `new`, it always initializes every element of a `T` array by using `T::T()`. If we wanted to initialize the `Vec` elements ourselves, we would have to initialize each element twice—once by `new`, and again to install the value that our user supplied. Even worse, consider the allocation strategy that we propose to use for `push_back`. This strategy implies that we'll double the size of the `Vec` each time we need to get more storage. We have no reason to want the extra elements initialized. They'll be used only by `push_back`, which will use the space only when we have a new element to construct in that space. If we used `new` to allocate the underlying array, these elements would be initialized regardless of whether we ever use them.

Instead of using the built-in `new` and `delete` operators, we can do better by using standard-library facilities designed to support flexible memory management. The core language itself does not have any notion of memory allocation, because the properties of memory are too variable to wire into the language itself.

For example, modern computers have many kinds of memory. There may be many different speeds of memory on the machine. There may be memory with special properties, such as graphical buffers or shared memory. There may be memory that is persistent across power failures. Because users might want to allocate any of these (or other) kinds of memory, it is best left to the library to specify how we allocate and manage memory. The standard library doesn't support all these kinds of memory; instead, it offers a facility to manage memory along with a uniform interface for memory managers. As with the decision to make input–output a library rather than a language facility, the decision to make memory management part of the library gives us greater flexibility in using these different kinds of memory.

The `<memory>` header provides a class, called `allocator<T>`, that allocates a block of uninitialized memory that is intended to contain objects of type `T`, and returns a pointer to the initial element of that memory. Such pointers are dangerous, because their type suggests that they point to objects, but the memory doesn't really contain those objects yet. The library also provides a way to construct objects in that memory, and to destroy the objects again—all without deallocating the memory itself. It is up to the programmer using the `allocator` class to keep track of which space holds constructed objects and which space is still uninitialized.

The interesting part of the `allocator` class, for our purposes, comprises four member functions and two associated nonmember functions. The member functions are:

```
template<class T> class allocator {
public:
    T* allocate(size_t);
    void deallocate(T*, size_t);
    void construct(T*, const T&);
    void destroy(T*);
    // ...
};
```

The `allocate` member allocates enough typed, uninitialized storage to hold the given number of elements. We say that this storage is typed because we will eventually use it to hold values of type `T`, and we will address it with pointers of type `T*`. However, it is uninitialized in the sense that no objects have yet been constructed in it.

The `deallocate` member frees this uninitialized storage. It takes a pointer to storage that `allocate` allocated, and a size that indicates how many elements were allocated.

The `construct` member constructs a single object in uninitialized storage. We give `construct` a pointer into storage that `allocate` allocated, and a value to copy into that storage. The `destroy` function destroys the object of type `T` to which its argument points. It runs `T`'s destructor for that object, rendering the storage uninitialized again.

The nonmember functions associated with the `allocator` class are:

```
template<class In, class For> For uninitialized_copy(In, In, For);
template<class For, class T>
    void uninitialized_fill(For, For, const T&);
```

These functions construct and initialize new objects in storage that `allocate` has previously allocated. `In` is an input-iterator type (§8.2.2/145), and `For` is a forward-iterator type (§8.2.4/147) that is typically a pointer. Constructing a new object is more than just assigning to it, so `For` must be a forward-iterator type, not just an output-iterator type.

The `uninitialized_copy` function works like the library `copy` function, in that it copies values from the sequence denoted by its first two arguments into a sequence that its third argument denotes. The `uninitialized_fill` function constructs as many copies of its third argument as needed to fill the storage given by its first two arguments.

When we use the type `allocator<T>`, the compiler will generate an appropriate `allocator` class for us, as it does with any template. In order to obtain an `allocator` that we can use to allocate and deallocate objects of type `T`, we'll add an `allocator<T>` member, named `alloc`, to our `Vec<T>` class. By adding this member, and by using its associated library functions, we can provide the same kind of efficient, flexible memory management as the standard `vector` class provides.

11.5.1 The final Vec class

Our complete `Vec` class, including declarations, but not definitions, for the functions that manage memory, now looks like this:

```
template <class T> class Vec {
public:
    typedef T* iterator;
    typedef const T* const_iterator;
    typedef size_t size_type;
    typedef T value_type;
    typedef T& reference;
    typedef const T& const_reference;

    Vec() { create(); }
    explicit Vec(size_type n, const T& t = T()) { create(n, t); }
```

```
Vec(const Vec& v) { create(v.begin(), v.end()); }
Vec& operator=(const Vec&);  // as defined in §11.3.2/196
~Vec() { uncreate(); }

T& operator[](size_type i) { return data[i]; }
const T& operator[](size_type i) const { return data[i]; }

void push_back(const T& t) {
    if (avail == limit)
        grow();
    unchecked_append(t);
}

size_type size() const { return avail - data; }   // changed

iterator begin() { return data; }
const_iterator begin() const { return data; }

iterator end() { return avail; }                   // changed
const_iterator end() const { return avail; }       // changed
private:
    iterator data;   // first element in the Vec
    iterator avail;  // (one past) the last element in the Vec
    iterator limit;  // (one past) the allocated memory

    // facilities for memory allocation
    allocator<T> alloc;  // object to handle memory allocation

    // allocate and initialize the underlying array
    void create();
    void create(size_type, const T&);
    void create(const_iterator, const_iterator);

    // destroy the elements in the array and free the memory
    void uncreate();

    // support functions for push_back
    void grow();
    void unchecked_append(const T&);
};
```

All that remains is to implement the `private` members that handle memory allocation. As we write these members, our program will be easier to understand if we remember that whenever we have a valid `Vec` object, four things are always true:

1. `data` points at our initial data element, if we have any, and is zero otherwise.
2. `data` ≤ `avail` ≤ `limit`.
3. Elements have been constructed in the range [`data`, `avail`).
4. Elements have not been constructed in the range [`avail`, `limit`).

We shall call these conditions the ***class invariant***. Much as we did with loop invariants in §2.3.2/20, we intend to establish the class invariant as soon as we construct an object of that class. If we do so, and we ensure that none of our member functions falsifies the class invariant, we can be assured that the invariant will always be true.

Note that none of the `public` members is capable of falsifying the invariant, because the only way to do so would be to change the value of `data`, `avail`, or `limit`, and none of those member functions does so.

We shall begin by looking at the various `create` functions, which are responsible for allocating memory, initializing elements in that memory, and setting the pointers appropriately. In each case, we initialize whatever memory is allocated and so, after running `create`, the pointers `limit` and `avail` are always equal: The last constructed element is the same as the last allocated element. You should verify for yourself that the class invariant is true after we have executed any of the following functions:

```
template <class T> void Vec<T>::create()
{
    data = avail = limit = 0;
}

template <class T> void Vec<T>::create(size_type n, const T& val)
{
    data = alloc.allocate(n);
    limit = avail = data + n;
    uninitialized_fill(data, limit, val);
}

template <class T>
void Vec<T>::create(const_iterator i, const_iterator j)
{
    data = alloc.allocate(j - i);
    limit = avail = uninitialized_copy(i, j, data);
}
```

The version of `create` that takes no arguments creates an empty `Vec`, so its job is to ensure that the pointers start out with zero values.

The version that takes a size and a value uses the size to allocate the appropriate amount of memory. The `allocate` member of class `allocator<T>` allocates enough memory to hold the specified number of objects of type `T`. Thus, `alloc.allocate(n)` allocates enough space to hold n objects. The `allocate` function returns a pointer to the initial element, which we store in `data`. The memory returned by `allocate` is uninitialized, so we arrange to initialize it by calling `uninitialized_fill`, which copies its third argument into the sequence of uninitialized elements specified by its first two arguments. When the function completes, it will have constructed new elements in the space obtained by `allocate` and will have initialized each of these elements to `val`.

The final version of `create` operates similarly to the other two, except that it calls `uninitialized_copy` to initialize the space obtained from `allocate`. That function copies elements from the sequence denoted by its first two arguments into a target sequence of uninitialized elements denoted by its third argument. It returns a pointer to (one past) the last element that it initialized, which is exactly the value that we need for `limit` and `avail`.

The `uncreate` member has to undo what the `create` members did: It must run the destructors on the elements, and return the space that the `Vec` used:

```
template <class T> void Vec<T>::uncreate()
{
    if (data) {
        // destroy (in reverse order) the elements that were constructed
        iterator it = avail;
        while (it != data)
            alloc.destroy(--it);

        // return all the space that was allocated
        alloc.deallocate(data, limit - data);
    }
    // reset pointers to indicate that the Vec is empty again
    data = limit = avail = 0;

}
```

If `data` is zero, there's no work to do. If we were using `delete`, we might not bother to
compare `data` to zero, knowing that executing `delete` on a zero pointer is harmless.
However, unlike `delete`, the `alloc.deallocate` function requires a nonzero pointer,
even if no memory is being freed. Therefore, we must check whether `data` is zero.

If we have work to do, we march the iterator `it` through the constructed elements of
the `Vec`, calling `destroy` to destroy each element. We go backward through the `Vec` to
match the behavior of `delete[]`, which destroys elements in reverse order. Once we've
destroyed the elements, we free all the space in the call to `deallocate`. This function
takes a pointer to the first element of the memory to free, and an integral value that indicates how many elements of type `T` are to be freed. Because we want to return all the
space that was allocated, we `deallocate` the space between `data` and `limit`.

What's left is to implement the members used by `push_back`:

```
template <class T> void Vec<T>::grow()
{
    // when growing, allocate twice as much space as currently in use
    size_type new_size = max(2 * (limit - data), ptrdiff_t(1));

    // allocate new space and copy existing elements to the new space
    iterator new_data = alloc.allocate(new_size);
    iterator new_avail = uninitialized_copy(data, avail, new_data);

    // return the old space
    uncreate();

    // reset pointers to point to the newly allocated space
    data = new_data;
    avail = new_avail;
    limit = data + new_size;
}

// assumes avail points at allocated, but uninitialized space
template <class T> void Vec<T>::unchecked_append(const T& val)
{
    alloc.construct(avail++, val);
}
```

The job of `grow` is to allocate enough space to hold at least another element. It allocates more than it needs, so that subsequent calls to `push_back` can use the excess, avoiding the overhead of frequent memory allocations. In §11.4/202, we said that our strategy would be to double the amount of space for each new allocation. Of course, the `Vec` might currently be empty, so we cater to this possibility by allocating the `max` of one element and twice the existing space. Remembering from §8.1.3/142 that the two arguments to `max` must have exactly the same type, we explicitly construct an object with value 1 of type `ptrdiff_t`, which we know from §10.1.4/175 is the type of `limit - data`.

We start by remembering in `new_size` how many elements we will allocate. We `allocate` the appropriate space, and then call `uninitialized_copy` to copy the elements from the current space into the newly allocated space. We then return the old memory, and destroy the elements there by calling `uncreate`. Finally, we reset the pointers so that `data` points to the first element in the newly allocated array, `avail` points to (one past) the last constructed element in the `Vec`, and `limit` points to (one past) the last allocated but as yet uninitialized element.

Note that it is essential that we save the values returned by `allocate` and `uninitialized_copy`. The reason is that if we used those values immediately to reset `data` and `limit`, then the subsequent calls to `uncreate` would destroy and free the memory that we just allocated, rather than getting rid of the old space!

The `unchecked_append` function builds an element in the first location after the constructed elements. It assumes that `avail` points at space that was allocated, but has not yet been used to hold a constructed element. Because we call `unchecked_append` only immediately after a previous call to `grow`, we know that this call is safe.

11.6 Details

Template classes can be formed using the template facility described in §8.1.1/140:

```
template <class type-parameter [, class type-parameter ] ... >
class class-name { ... };
```

creates a template class named *class-name* that depends on the given type parameters. These type-parameter names may be used inside the template wherever a type is required. In the scope of the class, the template class may be referred to without qualification; outside the class scope, *class-name* must be qualified with the type parameters:

```
template <class T>
Vec<T>& Vec<T>::operator=(const Vec&) { ... }
```

Users specify the actual types when creating objects of template types: `Vec<int>` causes the implementation to instantiate a version of `Vec` binding the type parameter to `int`.

Copy control: In general, classes control what happens when objects are created, copied, assigned, or destroyed. Constructors are invoked as a side effect of creating or copying objects; the assignment operator is invoked in expressions involving assignment; and the destructor is run automatically when objects are destroyed or go out of scope.

Classes that allocate resources in a constructor almost invariably must define the copy constructor, the assignment operator, and the destructor. When we write an assignment operator, it is essential for us to check for self-assignment. For consistency with the built-in assignment operators, it is good practice to return a reference to the left-hand operand.

Synthesized operations: If a class defines no constructors, the compiler will synthesize the default constructor. If the class does not explicitly define them, the compiler will synthesize the copy constructor, assignment operator, and/or destructor. The synthesized operations are defined recursively: Each synthesized operator recursively applies the appropriate operation for the data members of the class.

Overloaded operators are defined by defining a function named operator *op*, where *op* is the operator being defined. At least one parameter must be of class type. When an operator function is a member of a class, its left-hand operand (if it is a binary operator) or its only operand (if it is a unary operator) is bound to the object on which it is invoked. The index operator and the assignment operator must be class members.

Exercises

11-0.   Compile, execute, and test the programs in this chapter.

11-1.   The Student_info structure that we defined in Chapter 9 did not define a copy constructor, assignment operator, or destructor. Why not?

11-2.   That structure did define a default constructor. Why?

11-3.   What does the synthesized assignment operator for Student_info objects do?

11-4.   How many members does the synthesized Student_info destructor destroy?

11-5.   Instrument the Student_info class to count how often objects are created, copied, assigned, and destroyed. Use this instrumented class to execute the student record programs from Chapter 6. Using the instrumented Student_info class will let you see how many copies the library algorithms are doing. Comparing the number of copies will let you estimate what proportion of the cost differences we saw are accounted for by the use of each library class. Do this instrumentation and analysis.

11-6.   Add an operation to remove an element from a Vec and another to empty the entire Vec. These should behave analogously to the erase and clear operations on vectors.

11-7.   Once you've added erase and clear to Vec, you can use that class instead of vector in most of the earlier programs in this book. Rewrite the Student_info programs from Chapter 9 and the programs that work with character pictures from Chapter 5 to use Vecs instead of vectors.

11-8.   Write a simplified version of the standard list class and its associated iterator.

11-9.   The grow function in §11.5.1/208 doubles the amount of memory each time it needs more. Estimate the efficiency gains of this strategy. Once you've predicted how much of a difference it makes, change the grow function appropriately and measure the difference.

12

Making class objects
act like values

Objects of built-in types generally behave like values: Whenever we copy an object of such a type, the original and the copy have the same value but are otherwise independent. Subsequent changes to one object do not affect the other. We can create objects of these types, pass them to and from functions, copy them, or assign them to other objects.

For most of the built-in types, the language also defines a rich set of operators and provides automatic conversions between logically similar types. For example, if we add an `int` and a `double`, the compiler automatically converts the `int` into a `double`.

When we define our own classes, we control the extent to which the resulting objects behave like values. We saw in Chapters 9 and 11 that the class author controls what happens when objects are created, copied, assigned, and destroyed. By defining copying and assignment appropriately, the class author can arrange for objects of that class to act like values. That is, the class author can arrange for each object to have state that is independent of any other object. Our `Vec` and `Student_info` classes are examples of types that act like values.

In this chapter, we shall see that the class author can also control conversions and related operations on class objects, thereby providing classes whose objects behave even more similarly to objects of built-in types. The standard-library `string` class is a good example of such a type because of its rich set of operators and support for automatic conversions. Accordingly, in this chapter, we will define a simplified version of `string`, called `Str`, much as we defined a simplified version of `vector` in Chapter 11. We will focus on the operators and conversions that let us write expressions involving `string`s. In this chapter, we will not concern ourselves with efficiency. Instead, in Chapter 14, we will revisit `Str` to understand techniques for managing more efficiently the storage associated with each `Str` object.

We do not need to worry much about the implementation details of our `Str` class, because we did most of the work already when we implemented the `Vec` class. Accordingly, most of the discussion in this chapter will revolve around how to design an appropriate interface to our class.

12.1 A simple string class

Let's start by defining a `Str` class that lets us create objects that behave approximately as we would like:

```
class Str {
public:
    typedef Vec<char>::size_type size_type;

    // default constructor; create an empty Str
    Str() { }

    // create a Str containing n copies of c
    Str(size_type n, char c): data(n, c) { }

    // create a Str from a null-terminated array of char
    Str(const char* cp) {
        std::copy(cp, cp + std::strlen(cp), std::back_inserter(data));
    }

    // create a Str from the range denoted by iterators b and e
    template<class In> Str(In b, In e) {
        std::copy(b, e, std::back_inserter(data));
    }

private:
    Vec<char> data;
};
```

Our class delegates the work of managing its data to the `Vec` class that we wrote in Chapter 11. That class is almost good enough to support our `Str`; it lacks only the `clear` function that Chapter 11 had left as an exercise.

The `Str` class has four constructors, each of which arranges to create `data` as an appropriately initialized `Vec` object.

The default constructor for `Str` implicitly invokes the `Vec` default constructor to create an empty `Str`. Note that because our class has other constructors, we must explicitly define the default constructor, even though it does exactly what the synthesized default constructor would have done. The other three constructors take values, which we use to construct or initialize `data`.

The constructor that takes a size and a character uses the corresponding `Vec` constructor to construct `data`. It has no further work to do, so the constructor body is empty.

The last two constructors are similar to each other. Their constructor initializers are empty, which means that `data` is implicitly initialized as an empty `Vec`. Each constructor asks `copy` to append the supplied characters to the initially empty `data`. For example, the constructor that takes a `const char*` uses `strlen` to determine the length of the string. From this length, it computes two iterators that denote the input characters, and asks `copy` and `back_inserter` to append those characters to `data`. Thus, the constructor will cause `data` to contain copies of the characters in the array denoted by `cp`.

The most interesting constructor is the final one, which takes two iterators and creates a new `Str` that contains a copy of the characters in the given sequence. Like the previous constructor, it relies on `copy` and `back_inserter` to append the values in the range of

[b, e) to data. What's interesting about this constructor is that it is itself a template
function. Because it is a template, it effectively defines a family of constructors that can be
instantiated for different types of iterators. For example, this constructor could be used to
create a `Str` from an array of characters, or from a `Vec<char>`.

It is important to note that the class does not define a copy constructor, assignment
operator, or destructor. Why not?

The answer is that the defaults work. The `Str` class itself does no memory allocation.
It can leave the details of memory management to the synthesized operations, which call
the corresponding `Vec` operations. One way to see that the defaults work is to note that
the `Str` class does not need a destructor. Indeed, if it had one, there would be no work
for it to do. In general, a class that needs no destructor doesn't need an explicit copy constructor or assignment operator either (§11.3.6/201).

12.2 Automatic conversions

So far, we have defined a set of constructors and implicitly defined copying, assignment,
and destruction. These operations give `Str` valuelike behavior: When we copy a `Str`
object the original and the copy will be independent of each other. Our next problem is to
think about conversions. Values of built-in type can often be converted automatically
from one type to another. For example, we can initialize a `double` from an `int`, and we
can also assign an `int` to a `double`:

```
double d = 10;    // convert 10 to double and use the converted value to initialize d
double d2;
d2 = 10;          // convert 10 to double and assign the converted value to d2
```

In the case of our `Str` class, we have defined how to construct a `Str` from a `const
char*`, so we can write

```
Str s("hello");          // construct s
```

This definition constructs s by explicitly asking for the constructor that takes a `const
char*` argument. We would also like to be able to write

```
Str t = "hello";     // initialize t
s = "hello";         // assign a new value to s
```

Remember from §11.3.3/199 that the = symbol has two different meanings in this last
example. The first statement defines `t`, so the = indicates initialization. This form of initialization always requires the copy constructor, which takes a `const Str&` as its argument. The second statement is an expression statement, not a declaration, so the = is an
assignment operator. The only assignment operator that is relevant for `Str` objects is the
one that the compiler defined for us, which also expects a `const Str&` as its argument. In
other words, each statement in this second example uses a string literal, which has type
`const char*`, where a `const Str&` is expected.

We might think, therefore, that we need to give class `Str` an additional assignment
operator with a parameter of type `const char*`, and figure out how to overload the
copy constructor. Fortunately, it turns out that we do not need to do so, because there is

already a constructor that takes a `const char*`, and that constructor also acts as a ***user-defined conversion***. User-defined conversions say how to transform to and from objects of class type. As with built-in conversions, the compiler will apply user-defined conversions to convert a value into the type that is needed.

A class can define conversions in two ways: It can convert from other types to its type, or from its type to other types. We'll discuss this second form of conversion in §12.5/222. The more common conversion defines how to convert other types to the type that we are defining. We do so by defining a constructor with a single argument.

Our `Str` class already has such a constructor, namely the one that takes a `const char*`. Therefore, the compiler will use this constructor when an object of type `Str` is needed and an object of type `const char*` is available. The assignment of a `const char*` to a `Str` is exactly such a situation. When we write `s = "hello";` what really happens is that the compiler uses the `Str(const char*)` constructor to create an unnamed local temporary of type `Str` from the string literal. It then calls the (synthesized) assignment operator of class `Str` to assign this temporary to `s`.

12.3 `Str` operations

If we think about the kind of code we've written that used `strings`, we can see that we used several operators:

```
cin >> s      // use the input operator to read a string
cout << s     // use the output operator to write a string
s[i]          // use the index operator to access a character
s1 + s2       // use the addition operator to concatenate two strings
```

All these are binary operators, so that if we define them as functions, each function will have two parameters, one of which may be implicit if the function is a member. As we saw in §11.2.4/192, names for overloaded operators are formed by appending the operator symbol to the word `operator`. Hence, `operator>>` is the name of the function that overloads the input operator, `operator[]` names the index operation, and so on.

We may as well start with the index operator, because in §11.2.4/192, we've already seen how to implement this operation, and we know that it must be a member of the class:

```
class Str {
public:
    // constructors as before
    char& operator[](size_type i) { return data[i]; }
    const char& operator[](size_type i) const { return data[i]; }

private:
    Vec<char> data;
};
```

The index operators just forward their work to the corresponding `Vec` operations. It is worth noting that, as we did for class `Vec`, we define two versions of the index operator—one that can operate on `const` objects and the other that cannot. By returning a reference to the character, the nonconst version gives write access to the character that it returns. The `const` version returns a reference to a `const char`, thereby preventing the user from writing to the underlying character. We return `const char&` instead of a plain `char` for consistency with the standard `string` class.

What about the other operators? The most interesting problem in defining these functions is deciding whether these operations should be members of the `Str` class. It turns out that answering this question involves different issues for each of these kinds of operators. We will address input–output operators first; then, in §12.3.3/218, we'll look at the concatenation operator.

12.3.1 Input–output operators

In §9.2.2/159, we had to decide whether `compare` should be a member of `Student_info`. We suggested that one way to decide was to ask whether the operation affects the state of the object. The input operator certainly changes its object's state. After all, we use the input operator to read a new value into a preexisting object. Accordingly, we might think that we should make the input operator a member of the `Str` class. However, doing so won't work as we might expect.

To see why, we have to remember (§11.2.4/192) how the operands of an expression are bound to the parameters of the overloaded operator function. For a binary operation, the left operand is always bound to the first parameter, and the right operand is bound to the second. In the case of member operator functions, the first parameter (the left operand) is always the one that is passed implicitly to the member function. Thus,

```
cin >> s;
```

is equivalent to

```
cin.operator>>(s);
```

which calls the overloaded `>>` operator defined for the object `cin`. This behavior implies that the `>>` operator must be a member of class `istream`.

Of course, we do not own the definition of `istream`, so we cannot add this operation to it. If instead we make `operator>>` a member of `Str`, then our users would have to invoke the operation on behalf of a `Str`:

```
s.operator>>(cin);
```

or, equivalently,

```
s >> cin;
```

which would flout the conventions used throughout the library. Therefore, we can conclude that the input—and, by analogy, the output—operator must be a nonmember.

We can now update our `Str` class appropriately, by adding declarations for the input and output operators to `Str.h`:

```
std::istream& operator>>(std::istream&, Str&);        // added
std::ostream& operator<<(std::ostream&, const Str&);  // added
```

The output operator is easy to write: It will iterate through the `Str`, writing a single character at a time:

```
ostream& operator<<(ostream& os, const Str& s)
{
    for (Str::size_type i = 0; i != s.size(); ++i)
        os << s[i];
    return os;
}
```

The only catch is that this usage forces us to give Str a size function:

```
class Str {
public:
    size_type size() const { return data.size(); }
    // as before
};
```

Despite the simple form of the output operator, we should understand it thoroughly. Each time through the loop, we invoke the Str::operator[] to fetch a character to write. That operator, in turn, calls Vec::operator[] to obtain the actual value from the underlying vector. Similarly, each time through the loop, we determine the size of our Str object by calling s.size(), which calls the size member of the underlying Vec object to determine that object's size.

12.3.2 Friends

The input operator isn't much harder to write than the output operator. It needs to read and remember characters from the input stream. Each time we call the input operator, it should read and discard any leading whitespace, and then read and remember characters until it hits whitespace or end-of-file. Our input operator is a bit simplified—it ignores some subtleties of the input–output library that are beyond the scope of this book—but it does what we need done:

```
// this code won't compile quite yet
istream& operator>>(istream& is, Str& s)
{
    // obliterate existing value(s)
    s.data.clear();

    // read and discard leading whitespace
    char c;
    while (is.get(c) && isspace(c))
        ;    // nothing to do, except testing the condition

    // if still something to read, do so until next whitespace character
    if (is) {
        do   s.data.push_back(c);        // compile error!, data is private
        while (is.get(c) && !isspace(c));

        // if we read whitespace, then put it back on the stream
        if (is)
            is.unget();
    }

    return is;
}
```

First we'll explain this function; then we'll explain why it doesn't compile.

We start by discarding any previous value that data might have, because reading into a Str should obliterate whatever data were present. Next we need to read characters, one at a time, from the given stream, until we encounter a character that is not white-space. Because we need to be able to detect whether we just read a whitespace character, we use the get function on the input stream. Unlike the overloaded >> operators, which ignore whitespace, the get function reads and returns whatever character is next in the stream, including whitespace. Therefore, the while loop reads characters until it finds one that is not whitespace, or it runs out of input. If the character we read was white-space, then there is nothing to do but read again, so the body of the while is empty.

The if test checks whether we exited the while because we read a nonwhitespace character or because we ran out of input. If the former, we want to read characters until we hit whitespace again, appending each character that we read to data. We do so in the next statement, which is a do while loop (§7.4.4/136) that arranges to append to data the character that we had already read in the previous while loop, and then continues reading until we run out of input or hit a whitespace character. Each time it reads a non-whitespace character, it uses push_back to append that character to data.

We could fall out of the do while either because we can no longer read from is, or because we encountered a whitespace character. If the latter, we have read one character too many, which we put back onto the input stream by calling is.unget(). The unget function undoes the most recent get by backspacing the input stream by one character. After the call to unget, the stream behaves as if the previous get had never been done.

As the comments indicate, this code fails to compile. The problem is that operator>> is not a member of class Str, so it cannot access the data member of s. We faced a similar problem in §9.3.1/161, when the compare function needed access to the name member from Student_info objects. We solved that problem by adding an accessor function. In this case, giving read access to data isn't enough: The input operator needs to be able to write data, not just read it. The input operator is a part of our general Str abstraction, so giving it write access to data is fine. On the other hand, we do not want all users to have write access to data, so we cannot solve our problem by adding a public member that would let operator>> (and therefore any user) write to data.

Rather than adding a (public) access function, we can say that the input operator is a **friend** of class Str. A friend has the same access rights as a member. By making the input operator a friend, we can allow it, along with our member functions, to access the private members of class Str:

```
class Str {
    friend std::istream& operator>>(std::istream&, Str&);
    // as before
};
```

We've added a friend declaration to class Str. This declaration says that the version of operator>> that takes an istream& and a Str& may access the private members of Str. Once we have added this declaration to Str, our input operator will compile.

A friend declaration may appear at any point in the class definition: It makes no difference whether it follows a private or public label. Because a friend function has special access privileges, it is part of the interface to the class. Therefore, it makes sense to group `friend` declarations at the beginning of the class definition, near the `public` interface for the class.

12.3.3 Other binary operators

What remains of our work on the `Str` class is to implement the + operator. Before we can do so, we must make several decisions: Should the operator be a member? What are its operands' types? What type should it return? As we shall see, these questions turn out to have subtle implications.

For now, let's make some initial guesses about the answers. First, we know that we want to be able to concatenate values that are of type `Str`. Second, we can observe that concatenation does not change the value of either operand. These facts suggest that there is no particular reason to decide to make the operator a member function. Finally, we know that we want to be able to chain several concatenations into a single expression in order to allow expressions such as

```
s1 + s2 + s3
```

where `s1`, `s2`, and `s3` all have type `Str`. This usage suggests that the operator should return a `Str`.

These decisions imply that we should implement concatenation as a nonmember:

```
Str operator+(const Str&, const Str&);
```

Before we launch into implementation, a bit of thought might suggest that if we offer `operator+`, we might want to provide our users with `operator+=` as well. That is, we'd like to let our users assign to s the value obtained by concatenating s and s1 in either of these forms:

```
s = s + s1;
s += s1;
```

It turns out that the most convenient way to implement `operator+` is to implement `operator+=` first. Unlike the simple concatenation operator, the compound version changes its left operand, so we make it a member of the `Str` class. After adding definitions for the new concatenation operations, our final `Str` class looks like this:

```
class Str {
    // input operator implemented in §12.3.2/216
    friend std::istream& operator>>(std::istream&, Str&);
public:
    Str& operator+=(const Str& s) {
        std::copy(s.data.begin(), s.data.end(),
                std::back_inserter(data));
        return *this;
    }

    // as before
    typedef Vec<char>::size_type size_type;
```

```
        Str() { }
        Str(size_type n, char c): data(n, c) { }
        Str(const char* cp) {
            std::copy(cp, cp + std::strlen(cp), std::back_inserter(data));
        }
        template<class In> Str(In i, In j) {
            std::copy(i, j, std::back_inserter(data));
        }

        char& operator[](size_type i) { return data[i]; }
        const char& operator[](size_type i) const { return data[i]; }
        size_type size() const { return data.size(); }
    private:
        Vec<char> data;
    };

    // output operator implemented in §12.3.2/216
    std::ostream& operator<<(std::ostream&, const Str&);

    Str operator+(const Str&, const Str&);
```

Because we use a Vec for our underlying storage, implementing operator+= is trivial:
We call copy to append a copy of the right operand to the Vec that is the left operand. As
usual for assignment, we return a reference to the left object as our result.

Now we can implement operator+ in terms of operator+=:

```
    Str operator+(const Str& s, const Str& t)
    {
        Str r = s;
        r += t;
        return r;
    }
```

Recall that concatenation is a nonmember function that will create a new Str. We create
this new Str by initializing a local variable named r to be a copy of s. That initialization
uses the Str copy constructor. Next, we invoke the += operator on r to concatenate t,
and then we return r (again through an implicit call to the copy constructor) as the result.

12.3.4 Mixed-type expressions

We have defined the concatenation operator to take operands of type const Str&. What
about expressions that involve character pointers? For example, what if we wanted to use
our Str class to implement the program from §1.2/12? That program contained code that
looked like

```
    const std::string greeting = "Hello, " + name + "!";
```

where name is a string. Analogously, we'd like to be able to write

```
    const Str greeting = "Hello, " + name + "!";
```

where name is now a Str.

We know that the + operator is left-associative, which means that evaluating this expression is equivalent to evaluating

```
"Hello, " + name
```

and applying the + operator to the result and `"!"`. In other words, the expression is equivalent to

```
("Hello, " + name) + "!"
```

By breaking down the expression into its components, we can see that we have two different forms of +. In one case, we pass a string literal as the first operand and a `Str` as the second. In the other, the left operand is a `Str` obtained as the result of a concatenation, and the right operand is a string literal. Thus, in each case we are calling + on a `const char*` and a `Str` in some order.

In §12.3.3/218, we defined + with arguments of type `Str`, not `const char*`. However, we know from §12.2/213 that by defining a constructor that takes a `const char*`, we also defined a conversion operator from `const char*` to `Str`. Evidently, our `Str` class handles these expressions already. In each case, the compiler will convert the `const char*` argument to type `Str`, and then it will invoke `operator+`.

It is important to understand the implications of conversion operations. For example,

```
Str greeting = "Hello, " + name + "!";
```

gives `greeting` the same value as if we had written

```
Str temp1("Hello, ");                        // Str::Str(const char*)
Str temp2 = temp1 + name;      // operator+(const Str&, const Str&)
Str temp3("!")                               // Str::Str(const char*)
Str greeting = temp2 + temp3;  // operator+(const Str&, const Str&)
```

Seeing all these temporaries, we can imagine that this approach might be expensive. In practice, because of the perceived cost of generating temporaries, commercial `string` library implementations often take the more tedious route of defining specific versions of the concatenation operator for every combination of operands, rather than relying on automatic conversions.

12.3.5 Designing binary operators

It is important to appreciate the role of conversions in the design of binary operators. If a class supports conversions, then it is usually good practice to define binary operators as nonmember functions. By doing so, we preserve symmetry between the operands.

If an operator is a member of a class, then that operator's left operand cannot be the result of an automatic conversion. The reason for this restriction is so that when a programmer writes an expression such as x + y, the compiler does not have to examine every type in the entire program to discover whether it is possible to convert x to a type that has a member named `operator+`. Because of the restriction, the compiler (and the programmer) has to look only at nonmember `operator+` functions and at `operator+` functions that are members of the class of x.

The left operand of a nonmember operator, and the right operand of any operator, follow the same rules as any ordinary function argument: The operand can be of any type that can be converted to the parameter type. If we make the binary operator a member function, we have introduced an asymmetry with respect to its operands: The right operand can be the result of an automatic conversion, but the left operand cannot. Such asymmetries are fine for intrinsically asymmetric operators such as +=, but in the context of symmetric operands, they are confusing and error prone. It is almost always desirable to treat both operands of such operators equivalently, which we can arrange only by making the operator a nonmember function.

In the case of the assignment versions of binary operators, we want to constrain the left operand to be of the class type. Otherwise, what would happen? If we allowed conversions for the left operand, then we might convert that operand to the class type and assign a new value to the resulting temporary. Because that value would be a temporary object, once we completed the assignment we would have no way to access the object to which we had just assigned! Therefore, like the assignment operator itself, all of the compound-assignment operators should be members of the class.

12.4 Some conversions are hazardous

Recall that in §11.2.2/190, we defined as explicit the constructor that took a size. Now that we know that constructors that take a single argument define conversions, we can understand what happens when we make a constructor explicit: Doing so tells the compiler to use that constructor only to construct objects explicitly. The compiler will not use an explicit constructor to create objects implicitly by converting operands in expressions or function calls.

To understand why explicit constructors might be useful, let's assume that we did not declare the Vec constructor as explicit. Then we could implicitly build a Vec of a given size. We could use this implicit conversion when calling a function, such as our frame function from §5.8.1/93. Recall that that function takes a single parameter of type const vector<string>&, and produces a character picture that puts a frame around the input vector. Suppose that frame used Vec instead of vector, that we had not given Vec an explicit constructor, and that we were to execute

```
Vec<string> p = frame(42);
```

What would happen? What should happen? More important, how could a user figure out what will happen?

In this case, what would happen is that the user would get a framed picture with 42 empty rows. Was this behavior what the user intended? Isn't it more likely that the user thought that the program would put a frame around the value 42? This kind of call is, more likely than not, a mistake, and so our Vec class—and, for that matter, the standard vector class—makes the constructor that takes an integer value explicit.

In general, it is useful to make explicit the constructors that define the structure of the object being constructed, rather than its contents. Those constructors whose arguments become part of the object usually should not be explicit.

As an example, the `string` and `Str` classes have constructors that take a single `const char*` and are not `explicit`. Each constructor uses its `const char*` argument to initialize the value of its object. Because the argument determines the value of the resulting object, it is sensible to allow automatic conversions from a `const char*` in expressions or function calls.

On the other hand, the `vector` and `Vec` constructors that take a single argument of type `Vec::size_type` are `explicit`. These constructors use their argument value to determine how many elements to allocate. The constructor argument determines the structure of the object, but not its value.

12.5 Conversion operators

In §12.2/213, we saw that some constructors also define conversions. Class authors can also define explicit **conversion operators**, which say how to convert an object from its type to a target type. Conversion operators must be defined as members of a class. The name of a conversion operator is `operator` followed by the target type name. Thus, if a class has a member called `operator double`, that member says how to create a value of type `double` from a value of the class type. For example,

```
class Student_info {
public:
    operator double() const;
    // ...
};
```

would say how to create a `double` from a `Student_info` object. The meaning of this conversion would depend on the definition of the operator, which might be to convert the object to its corresponding final grade. The compiler would use this conversion operator any time we had an object of type `Student_info` but needed an object of type `double`. So, for example, if `vs` were a `vector<Student_info>`, we could calculate the average grade of all students as follows:

```
vector<Student_info> vs;
// fill up vs

double d = 0;
for (int i = 0; i != vs.size(); ++i)
    d += vs[i]; // vs[i] is automatically converted to double

cout << "Average grade: " << d / vs.size() << endl;
```

Conversion operators are most often useful when converting from a class type to a built-in type, but they can also be useful when converting to another class type for which we do not own the code. In either case, we cannot add a constructor to the target type, so we can define the conversion operator only as part of the class that we own.

In fact, we use this kind of conversion operator every time we write a loop that implicitly tests the value of an `istream`. As we discussed in §3.1.1/39, we can use an `istream` object where a condition is expected:

```
if (cin >> x) { /* ... */ }
```

which we saw was equivalent to

```
cin >> x;
if (cin) { /* ... */ }
```

We can now understand what happens in this expression.

As we know, the `if` tests a condition, which is an expression that yields a truth value. The precise type of such a truth value is `bool`. Using a value of any arithmetic or pointer type automatically converts the value to type `bool`, so we can use values of these types as the expression in a condition. Of course, `iostream` is neither a pointer nor an arithmetic type. However, the standard library defines a conversion from type `istream` to **void***, which is a pointer to `void`. It does so by defining `istream::operator void*`, which tests various status flags to determine whether the `istream` is valid, and returns either `0` or an implementation-defined nonzero `void*` value to indicate the state of the stream.

We have not previously used the `void*` type. We said in §6.2.2/114 that the `void` type could be used only in a few ways—the basis for a pointer being one of them. A pointer to `void` is sometimes called a universal pointer, because it is a pointer that can point to any type of object. Of course, you cannot dereference the pointer, because the type of the object to yield isn't known. But one thing that can be done with a `void*` is to convert it to `bool`, which is exactly how it is used in this context.

The reason that class `istream` defines `operator void*` rather than `operator bool` is to allow the compiler to detect the following erroneous usage:

```
int x;
cin << x;              // we should have written cin >> x;
```

If class `istream` were to define `operator bool`, this expression would use `istream::operator bool` to convert `cin` to `bool`, and then convert the resulting `bool` value to `int`, shift that value left by a number of bits equal to the value of `x`, and throw the result away! By defining a conversion to `void*`, rather than to an arithmetic type, the standard library still allows an `istream` to be used as a condition, but prevents it from being used as an arithmetic value.

12.6 Conversions and memory management

Many C++ programs interface to systems written in C or assembly language that use null-terminated arrays of characters to hold string data. As we saw in §10.5.2/180, the C++ standard library itself uses this convention to obtain the names of input and output files. Because of this convention, we might conclude that our `Str` class should provide a conversion from `Str` to a null-terminated array of characters. If we did so, then our users could (automatically) pass `Str`s to functions that operate on null-terminated arrays. Unfortunately, as we shall see, doing so is fraught with memory-management pitfalls.

Assuming that we wanted to provide a conversion from `Str` to `char*`, we'd probably want to provide both `const` and `nonconst` versions:

```
class Str {
public:
    // plausible, but problematic conversion operations
    operator char*();                    // added
    operator const char*() const;    // added

    // as before
private:
    Vec<char> data;
};
```

With this rewrite, `Str` users could write code such as

```
Str s;
// ...
ifstream in(s);        // wishful thinking: convert s and then open the stream named s
```

The only problem is that these conversions are almost impossible to implement well. We can't just return `data`, most obviously because it's the wrong type: `data` is a `Vec<char>`, and we need an array of `char`. More subtly, even if the types matched, returning `data` would violate class `Str`'s encapsulation: A user who obtained a pointer to `data` could use that pointer to change the value of the `string`. Just as bad, consider what happens when the `Str` is destroyed. If the user tries to use the pointer after the `Str` object no longer exists, then the pointer will point to memory that has been returned to the system and is no longer valid.

We can solve the encapsulation problem by providing only a conversion to `const char*`, but doing so does not prevent a user from destroying the `Str` and then using the pointer. We can solve this second problem by allocating new space for a copy of the characters from `data`, and returning a pointer to this newly allocated space. The user would then have to manage this space, freeing it when it is no longer needed.

As it turns out, this design won't work either. Conversions may happen implicitly, in which case the user has no pointer to destroy! Look again at

```
Str s;

ifstream is(s);        // implicit conversion—how can we free the array?
```

If the `Str` class had the proposed conversion, then when we passed s to the `ifstream` constructor, we would implicitly convert the `Str` to the `const char*` that the constructor expects. This conversion would allocate new space to hold a copy of the value of s. However, there is no explicit pointer to this space, and so the user cannot free it. Clearly, a design that mandates memory leaks cannot be right.

When we design a class, we want to avoid letting users trip up by writing innocuous-looking code that gets them in trouble. Before the C++ standard was finished, many library vendors offered various kinds of `string`s. Some surely provided implicit conversions to character arrays, but did so in a way that allowed users to make one or both of the potential errors outlined earlier.

The standard `string` library takes a different approach: It lets users get a copy of the `string` in a character array, but makes them do so explicitly. The standard `string` class provides three member functions for getting a `char` array from a `string`. The first, c_str(), copies the contents of the string into a null-terminated char array. The string class owns the array, and the user is expected not to delete the pointer. Data in the array are ephemeral, and will be valid only until the next call of a member function that might change the string. Users are expected either to use the pointer immediately or to copy the data into storage that they will manage. The second function, data(), is like c_str(), except that it returns an array that is not null terminated. Finally, the copy function takes a char* and an integer as arguments, and copies as many characters as indicated by the integer into space pointed to by the char*, which space the user must allocate and free. We leave the implementation of these functions as an exercise.

Note that both c_str and data share the pitfalls of the implicit conversion to const char*. On the other hand, because users must request the conversion explicitly, they are more likely to know about the functions that they call. This knowledge should include the pitfalls inherent in retaining a copy of the pointer. If the library allowed implicit conversions, it would be easier for users to stumble into these problems. They might not even be aware that they had caused a conversion to take place, so they might be less likely to understand why things failed when they did.

12.7 Details

Conversions are defined by nonexplicit constructors that take a single argument, or by defining a conversion operator of the form operator *type-name*(), where *type-name* names the type to which the class type can be converted. Conversion operators must be members. If two classes define conversions to each other's types, ambiguities can result.

friend declarations can occur anywhere within the class definition, and allow the friend to access private members of the class granting friendship.

```
template<class T>
class Thing {
    friend std::istream& operator>>(std::istream&, Thing&);
    // ...
};
```

As we will see in §13.4.2/246, classes can also be named as friends.

Template functions as members: A class may have template functions as members. The class itself might or might not be a template. A class that has a template member function effectively has an unbounded family of member functions with the same name. Template member functions are declared and defined as are any other template functions.

string operations
s.c_str()	Yields a const char* that points to a null-terminated array. The data in the array are valid only until the next string operation that might modify s. The user may not delete the pointer and should not hold a copy of it because the contents pointed to have a limited lifetime.
s.data()	Similar to s.c_str(), but the array is not null terminated.

s.copy(p, n)   Copies up to an integral number n of characters from s into space
                pointed to by the character pointer p. The user is responsible for ensur-
                ing that p points at space that is sufficient to hold n characters.

Exercises

12-0.   Compile, execute, and test the programs in this chapter.

12-1.   Reimplement the Str class, but choose an implementation strategy that requires that the
class manage the storage itself. For example, you might store an array of char and a
length. Consider what implications this change in design has for copy control. Also consider the cost of using Vec, (e.g., in storage overhead).

12-2.   Implement the c_str, data, and copy functions.

12-3.   Define the relational operators for Str. In doing so, you will want to know that the
<cstring> header defines a function called strcmp, which compares two character
pointers. The function returns a negative integer if the null-terminated character array
denoted by the first pointer is less than the second, zero if the two strings are equal, or a
positive value if the first string is greater than the second.

12-4.   Define the equality and inequality operators for Str.

12-5.   Implement concatenation for Str so as not to rely on conversions from const char*.

12-6.   Give Str an operation that will let us implicitly use a Str object as a condition. The test
should fail if the Str is empty, and should succeed otherwise.

12-7.   The standard string class provides random-access iterators to manipulate the string's
characters. Add iterators and the iterator operations begin and end to your Str class.

12-8.   Add the getline function to the Str class.

12-9.   Use class ostream_iterator to reimplement the Str output operator. Why didn't we
ask you to reimplement the input operator using class istream_iterator?

12-10.   Having seen in §12.1/212 how Str defined a constructor that takes a pair of iterators, we
can imagine that such a constructor would be useful in class Vec. Add this constructor to
Vec, and reimplement Str to use the Vec constructor instead of calling copy.

12-11.   If you add the operations listed in these exercises, then you can use this Str class in all the
examples in this book. Reimplement the operations on character pictures from Chapter 5
and the split functions from §5.6/87 and §6.1.1/103.

12-12.   Define the insert function that takes two iterators for the Vec and Str classes.

12-13.   Provide an assign function that could be used to assign the values in an array to a Vec.

12-14.   Write a program to initialize a Vec from a string.

12-15.   The read_hw function from §4.1.3/57 checked the stream from which it read to determine
whether the function had hit end-of-file, or had encountered an invalid input. Our Str
input operator does no such check. Why? Will it leave the stream in an invalid state?

13

Using inheritance
and dynamic binding

The last several chapters have explored how we can build our own data types. This ability is one of the foundations of object-oriented programming (OOP). This chapter will begin a look at the the other key components of OOP—inheritance and dynamic binding.

In Chapter 9, we described a small class intended to encapsulate the operations used to solve the grading problem from Chapter 4. This chapter will revisit that problem. This time, we'll assume that there's a change in specification: Students can take the course for undergraduate or graduate credit. Obtaining graduate credit requires that the students do some extra work. We'll assume that in addition to the homework and exams that all students must complete, graduate students also have to write a thesis. As we'll see, this change in problem specification lends itself to an object-oriented solution, which we'll use to explore the language features that C++ offers to support OOP.

Our objective is to write new classes that will mirror these new requirements. We'd also like our previous solution to the grading problem, from §9.6/166, to continue to work. That is, we'd like classes that allow us to generate the final grade report by reading a file of grade records and writing a formatted report using the original code.

13.1 Inheritance

In our grading problem we know that a record for graduate credit is the same as for undergraduate credit, except that it has additional properties related to the thesis. Such contexts are natural places for *inheritance*. Inheritance is one of the cornerstones of OOP. The basic idea is that we can often think of one class as being just like another, except for some extensions. In this problem, all students must complete the homework and exams, but some must also do a thesis. What we'd like is to define two classes: one to represent the core requirements and the other to represent the requirements for graduate credit.

We mostly know how to write the first of these classes: It is similar to our previous `Student_info` class, which we'll rename `Core` for reasons that will become fully apparent in §13.4/243. For now, what's useful to know is that `Core` no longer represents all kinds of students, but only those students who meet the core requirements for the course.

We'd like to reserve `Student_info` as a name that denotes any kind of student. In addition to its name change, we'll add a `private` utility function to our `Core` class to read the portion of a student's record that all students have in common:

```
class Core {
public:
    Core();
    Core(std::istream&);
    std::string name() const;
    std::istream& read(std::istream&);
    double grade() const;
private:
    std::istream& read_common(std::istream&);
    std::string n;
    double midterm, final;
    std::vector<double> homework;
};
```

Class `Grad` will capture the extra requirements for obtaining graduate credit:

```
class Grad: public Core {
public:
    Grad();
    Grad(std::istream&);
    double grade() const;
    std::istream& read(std::istream&);
private:
    double thesis;
};
```

This definition says that we're defining a new type named `Grad`, which *is derived from* or *inherits from* `Core`, or, equivalently, that `Core` *is a base class of* `Grad`. Because `Grad` inherits from `Core`, every member of `Core` is also a member of `Grad`—except for the constructors, the assignment operator, and destructor. The `Grad` class can add members of its own, as we do here with the data member `thesis` and the constructors for `Grad`. It can redefine members from the base class, as we do with the `grade` and `read` functions. However, a derived class cannot delete any of the base class' members.

The use of `public` in `public Core` says that the fact that `Grad` inherits from `Core` is part of its interface, rather than part of its implementation. That is, `Grad` inherits the `public` interface to `Core`, which becomes part of the `public` interface to `Grad`. The `public` members of `Core` are effectively `public` members of `Grad`. For example, if we have a `Grad` object, we can call its `name` member function to obtain the student's name, even though `Grad` does not define its own `name` function.

The `Grad` class differs from the `Core` class in that it keeps track of a grade for the thesis, and uses a different algorithm for calculating the final grade. Thus, `Grad` objects will have five data elements. Four of them are inherited from `Core`; the fifth is a `double` value named `thesis`. It will have two constructors and four member functions, two of which redefine the corresponding members of `Core`, and the `name` and `read_common` functions, which it inherits from `Core`.

13.1.1 Protection revisited

As it stands, all four data elements and the read_common function in Core are inaccessible to member functions in Grad. We said that the members of Core were private. Only the class and its friends may access private members. Unfortunately, in order to write the Grad versions of the grade and read functions, we need access to some of these private members. We can fix this problem by rewriting the Core class using a protection label that we have not seen before:

```
class Core {
public:
    Core();
    Core(std::istream&);
    std::string name() const;
    double grade() const;
    std::istream& read(std::istream&);
protected:
    std::istream& read_common(std::istream&);
    double midterm, final;
    std::vector<double> homework;
private:
    std::string n;
};
```

We still say that n is private, but now the read_common function and the midterm, final, and homework data members are **protected**. The protected label gives derived classes, such as Grad, access to the protected members of their constituent base-class objects, but keeps these elements inaccessible to users of the classes.

Because n is a private member of Core, only the members and friends of class Core may access n. Grad has no special access to n; it can access n only through public member functions of Core.

The read, name, and grade functions are public members of Core, and as such they are available to all users of class Core—including classes derived from Core.

13.1.2 Operations

To complete our classes, we need to implement four constructors: the default constructor and the constructor that takes an istream, once for each class. We must also implement six operations: the name and read_common operations in class Core, and the read and grade functions for both classes. We'll see how to write the constructors in §13.1.3/231.

Before writing our code, we need to think a bit about how student records will be structured. As before, we'll want to accommodate a variable number of homework assignments, so those grades must come at the end of each record. Therefore, we'll assume that our records will consist of a student's name followed by the midterm and final exam grades. If the record is for undergraduate credit, then the homework grades will follow immediately. If the record is for graduate credit, then the thesis grade will follow the final exam, but precede the homework grades.

With this information, we know how to write the operations on Core:

```
string Core::name() const { return n; }

double Core::grade() const
{
    return ::grade(midterm, final, homework);
}

istream& Core::read_common(istream& in)
{
    // read and store the student's name and exam grades
    in >> n >> midterm >> final;
    return in;
}

istream& Core::read(istream& in)
{
    read_common(in);
    read_hw(in, homework);
    return in;
}
```

The Grad::read function is similar, but reads the thesis before calling read_hw:

```
istream& Grad::read(istream& in)
{
    read_common(in);
    in >> thesis;
    read_hw(in, homework);
    return in;
}
```

Note that in the definition of Grad::read, we can refer to elements from the base class without any special notation, because these elements are also members of Grad. If we wanted to be explicit about the fact that the members were inherited from Core, we could use the scope operator to do so:

```
istream& Grad::read(istream& in)
{
    Core::read_common(in);
    in >> thesis;
    read_hw(in, Core::homework);
    return in;
}
```

Of course, the thesis member is unqualified because that member is a part of Grad and not a part of Core. We could have written Grad::thesis, but not Core::thesis.

The grade function changes to account for the effect of thesis. Our policy is that the student receives the lesser of the grade obtained on the thesis and the grade that would have been obtained if we just counted the exams and homework scores:

```
double Grad::grade() const
{
    return min(Core::grade(), thesis);
}
```

Here we want to call the `grade` function in the base class in order to calculate the score independently from the `thesis` grade. In this case, the use of the scope operator is essential. Had we written

```
    return min(grade(), thesis);
```

we would have (recursively) called the `Grad` version of `grade`, leading to disaster.

   We use the `min` function from `<algorithm>` to determine which grade to return. The `min` function operates like `max` except that it returns the smaller of its two operands. As with `max`, those operands must be of exactly the same type.

13.1.3 Inheritance and constructors

Before we write the constructors for `Core` and `Grad`, we need to understand how the implementation creates objects of a derived type. As with any class type, the implementation begins by allocating space for the object. Next, it runs the appropriate constructor to initialize the object. The fact that the object is of a derived type adds an extra step to the construction process in order to construct the base-class part of the object. Derived objects are constructed by

- Allocating space for the entire object (base-class members as well as derived members)
- Calling the base-class constructor to initialize the base-class part(s) of the object
- Initializing the members of the derived class as directed by the constructor initializer
- Executing the body of the derived-class constructor, if any

The only new part is how we select which base-class constructor to run. Not surprisingly, we use the constructor initializer to specify the base-class constructor that we want. The derived-class constructor initializer names its base class followed by a (possibly empty) list of arguments. These arguments are the initial values to use in constructing the base-class part; they serve to select the base-class constructor to run in order to initialize the base. If the initializer does not specify which base-class constructor to run, then the base-class default constructor is used to build the base-part of the object.

```
    class Core {
    public:
        // default constructor for Core
        Core(): midterm(0), final(0) { }

        // build a Core from an istream
        Core(std::istream& is) { read(is); }
        // ...
    };

    class Grad: public Core {
    public:
        // both constructors implicitly use Core::Core() to initialize the base part
        Grad(): thesis(0) { }

        Grad(std::istream& is) { read(is); }
        // ...
    };
```

The constructors for `Core` are identical to the ones in §9.5.1/165 and §9.5.2/166: They specify how to make a `Core` from nothing or from an `istream`. The constructors for `Grad` say how to create a `Grad` from these same values, that is, either from no argument or from an `istream&`. It is worth noting that there is no requirement that the derived-class constructors take the same argument(s) as the constructors for the base class.

The default constructor for `Grad` says that to make a `Grad` from nothing, the implementation should construct its `Core` part and set the `thesis` member to `0`. As it stands, most of this work is implicit: First, because the constructor initializer is empty, we implicitly invoke the default constructor for `Core` to initialize the `midterm`, `final`, `homework`, and `name` members. In the same fashion, the `Core` default constructor implicitly initializes `name` and `homework` through their default constructors, and explicitly initializes only `midterm` and `final`. The only explicit action that the default `Grad` constructor takes is to initialize the `thesis` member. Once this is done, there is no other work for the constructor to do, so the function body is empty.

We make a `Grad` from an `istream` in much the same way that we make a `Core` from an `istream`—namely, by calling the `read` member. Before doing so, though, we first (implicitly) invoke the base-class default constructor to initialize the base part of the object. Then, because this constructor is a member of class `Grad`, the `read` that is called is `Grad::read`. We don't bother to initialize `thesis` because the `read` function reads a value into `thesis` from `is`.

It is important to understand how derived-class objects are constructed. Executing

```
Grad g;
```

causes the system to allocate enough space to hold `Grad`'s five data elements, run the `Core` default constructor to initialize the data members in the `Core` part of g, and then run the default constructor for `Grad`. Similarly, if we execute

```
Grad g(cin);
```

then after allocating an appropriate amount of space, the implementation will run the `Core` default constructor, followed by the `Grad::Grad(istream&)` constructor to read values into the `name`, `midterm`, `final`, `thesis`, and `homework` members.

13.2 Polymorphism and `virtual` functions

We have not yet completely reimplemented the original `Student_info` abstraction. That abstraction relied on a nonmember function to support part of its interface: It used the `compare` function to compare two student records. This function is used by `sort` to arrange records in alphabetical order.

Our new comparison function is identical to the one we wrote in §9.3.1/162 except for the change in type name:

```
bool compare(const Core& c1, const Core& c2)
{
    return c1.name() < c2.name();
}
```

We compare two student records by comparing their names. We delegate the real work to the `string` library `<` operator. What is interesting about this code is that we can use it to compare both `Core` records and `Grad` records, or even to compare a `Core` record with a `Grad` record:

```
Grad g(cin);        // read a Grad record
Grad g2(cin);       // read a Grad record

Core c(cin);        // read a Core record
Core c2(cin);       // read a Core record

compare(g, g2);  // compare two Grad records
compare(c, c2);  // compare two Core records
compare(g, c);   // compare Grad record with a Core record
```

In each of these calls to `compare`, the `name` member of class `Core` will be run to determine the value to return from `compare`. Obviously, this is the right member to call for class `Core`, but what about for `Grad`? When we defined class `Grad`, we said that it is inherited from `Core`, and we did not redefine the `name` function. Thus, when we invoke `g.name()` for a `Grad` object `g`, we are invoking the `name` member that it inherited from `Core`. That function operates the same way on a `Grad` as it does on a `Core`: It fetches the underlying n field from the `Core` part of the object.

The reason that we can pass a `Grad` object to a function expecting a `Core&` is that we said that `Grad` is inherited from `Core`, so every `Grad` object has a `Core` part:

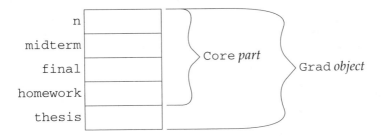

Because every `Grad` object has a `Core` part, we can bind `compare`'s reference parameters to the `Core` portions of `Grad` objects, exactly as we can bind them to plain `Core` objects. Similarly, we could have defined `compare` to operate on pointers to `Core` or on objects of type `Core` (as opposed to a reference to `Core`). In either case, we could still call the function on behalf of a `Grad` object. If the function took pointers, we could pass a pointer to `Grad`. The compiler would convert the `Grad*` to a `Core*`, and would bind the pointer to the `Core` part of the `Grad` object. If the function took a `Core` object, then what would be passed is just the `Core` portion of the object. There can be striking differences in behavior, depending on whether we pass an object itself, or a reference or pointer to the object—as we shall now see.

13.2.1 *Obtaining a value without knowing the object's type*

Our `compare` function does the right thing when we call it with a `Grad` object as an argument because the `name` function is shared by both `Grad` and `Core` objects. What if we wanted to compare students, not on the basis of their names, but on the basis of their final grades? For example, instead of producing a listing of final grades sorted by name, we might need to produce a listing sorted by final grade.

As a first cut at solving this problem, we'd write a function that is similar to `compare`:

```
bool compare_grades(const Core& c1, const Core& c2)
{
    return c1.grade() < c2.grade();
}
```

The only difference is that here we're invoking the `grade` function rather than the `name` function. This difference turns out to be significant!

The difference is that `Grad` redefines the meaning of the `grade` function, and we have done nothing to distinguish between these two versions of `grade`. When we execute the `compare_grades` function, it will execute the `Core::grade` member, just as `compare` executes `Core::name`. In this case, if we are operating on a `Grad` object, then the version from `Core` gives the wrong answer, because the `grade` functions in `Core` and `Grad` behave differently from each other. For `Grad` objects, we must run `Grad::grade` in order to account for the `thesis`.

What we need is a way for `compare_grades` to invoke the right `grade` function, depending on the *actual* type of object that we pass: If `c1` or `c2` refers to a `Grad` object, then we want the `Grad` version of `grade`; if the object is of type `Core`, then we want the one from `Core`. We want to make that decision at *run time*. That is, we want the system to run the right function based on the actual type of the objects passed to the function, which is known only at run time.

To support this kind of run-time selection, C++ provides **virtual** functions:

```
class Core {
public:
    virtual double grade() const;    // virtual added
    // ...
};
```

We now say that `grade` is a `virtual` function. When we call `compare_grades`, the implementation will determine the version of `grade` to execute by looking at the actual types of the objects to which the references `c1` and `c2` are bound. That is, it will determine which function to run by inspecting each object that we passed as an argument to `compare_grades`. If the argument is a `Grad` object, it will run the `Grad::grade` function; if the argument is a `Core` object, it will run the `Core::grade` function.

The `virtual` keyword may be used only inside the class definition. If the functions are defined separately from their declarations, we do not repeat `virtual` in the definitions. Thus, the definition of `Core::grade()` need not change. Similarly, the fact that a function is `virtual` is inherited, so we need not repeat the `virtual` designation on the declaration of `grade` within the `Grad` class. We do have to recompile our code with the new `Core` class definition. Once we have done so, then because the base-class version is `virtual`, we get the behavior that we need.

13.2.2 *Dynamic binding*

This run-time selection of the `virtual` function to execute is relevant only when the function is called through a reference or a pointer. If we call a `virtual` function on behalf of an object (as opposed to through a reference or pointer), then we know the exact type of the object at compile time. The type of an object is fixed: It is what it is, and does not vary at run time. In contrast, a reference or pointer to a base-class object may refer or point to a base-class object, or to an object of a type derived from the base class, meaning that the type of the reference or pointer and the type of the object to which a reference or pointer is bound may differ at run time. It is in this case that the `virtual` mechanism makes a difference.

For example, assume we rewrote `compare_grades` as follows:

```
//  incorrect implementation!
bool compare_grades(Core c1, Core c2)
{
    return c1.grade() < c2.grade();
}
```

In this version, we say that our parameters are objects, not references to objects. In this case, we always know the type of objects represented by `c1` and `c2`: They are `Core` objects. We can still call this function on behalf of a `Grad` object, but the fact that the argument had type `Grad` is immaterial. In this case, what happens is that what we pass is the *base* part of the object. The `Grad` object will be ***cut down*** to its `Core` part, and a copy of that portion of the `Grad` object will be passed to the `compare_grades` function. Because we said that the parameters are `Core` objects, the calls to `grade` are ***statically bound***—they are bound at compile time—to `Core::grade`.

This distinction between ***dynamic binding*** and static binding is essential to understanding how C++ supports OOP. The phrase *dynamic binding* captures the notion that functions may be bound at run time, as opposed to static bindings that happen at compile time. If we call a `virtual` function on behalf of an object, the call is statically bound—that is, it is bound at compile time—because there is no possibility that the object will have a different type during execution than it does during compilation. In contrast, if we call a `virtual` function through a pointer or a reference, then the function is dynamically bound—that is, bound at run time. At run time, the version of the `virtual` function to use will depend on the type of the object to which the reference or pointer is bound:

```
Core c;
Grad g;
Core* p;
Core& r = g;

c.grade();      //  statically bound to Core::grade()
g.grade();      //  statically bound to Grad::grade()
p->grade();     //  dynamically bound, depending on the type of the object to which p points
r.grade();      //  dynamically bound, depending on the type of the object to which r refers
```

The first two calls can be statically bound: We know that c is a Core object, and that at run time, c will still be a Core object. Therefore, the compiler can statically resolve this call, even though grade is a virtual function. In the third and fourth calls, however, we can't know the type of the object to which p or r refers until run time: They might be Core or Grad objects. Hence, the decision as to which function to run in these cases must be delayed until run time. The implementation makes that decision based on the type of the object to which p points or to which r refers.

The fact that we can use a derived type where a pointer or reference to the base is expected is an example of a key concept in OOP called ***polymorphism***. This word, from the Greek *polymorphos* (πολύμορφος), meaning "of many forms," was already in use in English in the mid-nineteenth century. In a programming context, it refers to the ability of one type to stand in for many types. C++ supports polymorphism through the dynamic-binding properties of virtual functions. When we call a virtual through a pointer or reference, we make a polymorphic call. The type of the reference (or pointer) is fixed, but the type of the object to which it refers (or points) can be the type of the reference (or pointer) or any type derived from it. Thus, we can potentially call one of many functions through a single type.

One final note about virtual functions: These functions must be defined, regardless of whether the program calls them. Nonvirtual functions may be declared but not defined, as long as the program does not call them. Many compilers generate mysterious error messages for classes that fail to define one or more virtual functions. If your program evokes a message from the compiler that you do not understand, and that message says that something is undefined, you should verify that you have defined all of your virtual functions. You are likely to find that the error goes away when you do so.

13.2.3 Recap

Before we continue, it is probably worth summarizing where we are, and making one slight additional change: We'll make the read function virtual as well. We'd like to be able to have the choice of which read function to run depend on the type of the object on which it is invoked. With that final change, let's look at our classes:

```
class Core {
public:
    Core(): midterm(0), final(0) { }
    Core(std::istream& is) { read(is); }

    std::string name() const;

    // as defined in §13.1.2/230
    virtual std::istream& read(std::istream&);
    virtual double grade() const;

protected:
    // accessible to derived classes
    std::istream& read_common(std::istream&);
    double midterm, final;
    std::vector<double> homework;
```

```
private:
    // accessible only to Core
    std::string n;
};

class Grad: public Core {
public:
    Grad(): thesis(0) { }
    Grad(std::istream& is) { read(is); }

    // as defined in §13.1.2/230; Note: grade and read are virtual by inheritance
    double grade() const;
    std::istream& read(std::istream&);
private:
    double thesis;
};

bool compare(const Core&, const Core&);
```

We have defined two classes to encapsulate our two kinds of students. The first class, Core, represents students meeting the core requirements for the course. Our second class inherits from Core, adding the requirements for completing a thesis. We can create Core or Grad objects in two ways. The default constructor creates a properly initialized, empty object; the other constructor takes an istream& and reads initial values from the specified stream. The operations let us read into an object, resetting its values, and let us fetch the student's name or final grade. Note that in this version, we have made both the grade and read functions virtual. Finally, our interface includes a global, nonmember compare function that compares two objects by comparing students' names.

13.3 Using inheritance to solve our problem

Now that we have classes that model our different kinds of students, we would like to use these classes to solve the grading problem from §9.6/166. That program read a file that contained student grade records, computed the final grade for each student, and wrote a formatted report in alphabetical order by student name. We'd like to solve the same problem, but do so for a file that contains records for both kinds of students.

Before solving the whole problem, we'll solve two simpler problems: We will write programs that can read files that consist entirely of one kind of record or the other. Both of these programs will look just like our original except for the type declarations:

```
int main()
{
    vector<Core> students;              // read and process Core records
    Core record;
    string::size_type maxlen = 0;

    // read and store the data
    while (record.read(cin)) {
        maxlen = max(maxlen, record.name().size());
        students.push_back(record);
    }
```

```
// alphabetize the student records
sort(students.begin(), students.end(), compare);

// write the names and grades
for (vector<Core>::size_type i = 0; i != students.size(); ++i) {
    cout << students[i].name()
         << string(maxlen + 1 - students[i].name().size(), ' ');
    try {
        double final_grade = students[i].grade(); // Core::grade
        streamsize prec = cout.precision();
        cout << setprecision(3) << final_grade
             << setprecision(prec) << endl;
    } catch (domain_error e) {
        cout << e.what() << endl;
    }
}
return 0;
}
```

We can write the same program to handle `Grad` records by changing the type definitions:

```
int main()
{
    vector<Grad> students;          // different type in the vector
    Grad record;                    // different type into which to read
    string::size_type maxlen = 0;

    // read and store the data
    while (record.read(cin)) {      // read from Grad, not Core
        maxlen = max(maxlen, record.name().size());
        students.push_back(record);
    }

    // alphabetize the student records
    sort(students.begin(), students.end(), compare);

    // write the names and grades
    for (vector<Grad>::size_type i = 0; i != students.size(); ++i) {
        cout << students[i].name()
             << string(maxlen + 1 - students[i].name().size(), ' ');
        try {
            double final_grade = students[i].grade(); // Grad::grade
            streamsize prec = cout.precision();
            cout << setprecision(3) << final_grade
                 << setprecision(prec) << endl;
        } catch (domain_error e) {
            cout << e.what() << endl;
        }
    }
    return 0;
}
```

Of course, the functions that are run in each instance depend on the type of `record`, and on the type of the objects contained in the `vector`. For example, the expression

```
record.read(cin)
```

calls `Core::read` or `Grad::read`, depending on the type of `record`. It is worth noting that this call is statically bound: The dependence on the type of `record` has nothing to do with the `virtual` nature of the `read` function. We are invoking the function on behalf of an object, not a pointer or reference to an object. Thus, `record` is either a `Core` or a `Grad`, depending on which version of the program is being run. However, once we define `record`, its type is fixed, and so the call to `record.read(cin)` is likewise bound at compile time. Similarly, the `grade` function that we call when generating output,

```
students[i].grade()
```

will be statically bound to the one from class `Core` when we run the first program, and to the one from `Grad` when we run the second program.

In both versions of the program, the uses of `name()` refer to the (nonvirtual) version defined in class `Core`. That function is inherited by `Grad`, so that when we run it for a `Grad` object, we are still running the version that we defined in `Core`. The `compare` function that we pass to `sort` operates on references to `Core`. When the version of the program that operates on `Grad` records runs, it will `compare` the `Core` parts.

Obviously, it is tedious to write separate versions of our program. What we really want to do is to write a single version that can handle either `Core` or `Grad` objects.

In order to write a single function that can read a file of either `Core` records or `Grad` records, we need to look closely at the code, and identify those places where the type of the record matters. In order to write a single version of the program, we will have to eliminate these type dependencies:

- The definition of the `vector` in which we store the elements as we read them
- The definition of the local temporary into which we read the records
- The `read` function
- The `grade` function

The remaining code is either type independent (the code to `sort` the `vector` or to iterate through it) or it is invariant between the `Grad` and `Core` versions (such as the name and `compare` functions). Because we defined the `grade` and `read` functions as `virtuals`, we have already solved the last two parts of our problem.

It turns out that the first two subproblems—what type to use for the local temporary and what type to store in the container—can be handled by the same strategy. It also turns out that there are two different approaches to solving these subproblems. The first approach is straightforward, so we'll look at it in the next section. The other solution represents a common, important C++ programming idiom, which we'll cover in §13.4/243.

13.3.1 Containers of (virtually) unknown type

The problem that we need to solve is to relax the type dependencies in the following:

```
vector<Core> students;     // must hold Core objects, not polymorphic types
Core record;               // Core object, not a type derived from Core
```

The type dependencies in this code should be fairly clear. When we define `record`, we say exactly what type of object `record` is: It is a `Core`, because that's what we said it was. Similarly, when we define `students`, we say that it is a `vector` that holds objects of type

Core. We'll have more to say about such containers in §13.6.1/249, but for now what's important is to realize that when we define a vector<Core>, we are saying that each object in the vector will be a Core object—not an object of a type derived from Core.

When we outlined the type dependencies in our two programs, we noted that we'd solved half the type issues because read and grade were virtual functions. The other half of the problem is that, as written, our programs make statically bound calls to these virtuals. In order to invoke the dynamic behavior that we need, we need to call read and grade through a pointer or reference to Core. That way, the type of the object bound can differ from the type of the pointer or reference. This observation leads us to a solution to all four subproblems: We can write the program to manage pointers instead of objects. We can have a vector<Core*>, and we can define record to be a pointer as well. In this way, we can obtain the dynamic behavior we need, while eliminating the type dependence involved in the definitions of the vector and our local temporary. Unfortunately, as we shall see, this solution pushes a lot of complexity onto our users. For example, the obvious try at a solution doesn't work at all:

```
int main()
{
    vector<Core*> students;

    Core* record;
    while (record->read(cin)) {          // crash!
        // ...
    }
}
```

The trouble with this program is that it fails horribly, because we never caused record to point to an object!

We can fix this problem, but only by requiring that our users actively manage the space consumed by the objects that they read from the file. Our users will also have to be able to detect what kind of records the program is reading. We'll assume that each record will contain an indicator to distinguish the kind of record that it contains: Records for graduate students will start with a G, and those for an undergraduate will start with a U.

Before we rewrite the program to use pointers, there is one more problem that we must solve: How do we sort a vector of pointers? The easy answer is that we'll need a new comparison function that takes two pointers to Core objects. The tricky part is that we cannot name this function compare. Recall that in §8.1.3/142 we discussed various subtleties in getting the right types for values that we pass as template arguments. For similar reasons, we cannot pass an overloaded function name as a template argument. If we did so, the compiler would have no way to determine which version of the function we wanted. Evidently, we'll need to write a comparison function that will give us a non-overloaded name to pass to sort:

```
bool compare_Core_ptrs(const Core* cp1, const Core* cp2)
{
    return compare(*cp1, *cp2);
}
```

Having written a specialized comparison function, we can now rewrite the program:

```
//  this code almost works; see §13.3.2/242
int main()
{
        vector<Core*> students;          // store pointers, not objects
        Core* record;                    // temporary must be a pointer as well
        char ch;
        string::size_type maxlen = 0;

        // read and store the data
        while (cin >> ch) {
            if (ch == 'U')
                record = new Core;       // allocate a Core object
            else
                record = new Grad;       // allocate a Grad object
            record->read(cin);           // virtual call
            maxlen = max(maxlen, record->name().size());// dereference
            students.push_back(record);
        }

        // pass the version of compare that works on pointers
        sort(students.begin(), students.end(), compare_Core_ptrs);

        // write the names and grades
        for (vector<Core*>::size_type i = 0;
            i != students.size(); ++i) {
            // students[i] is a pointer that we dereference to call the functions
            cout << students[i]->name()
                << string(maxlen + 1 - students[i]->name().size(), ' ');
            try {
                double final_grade = students[i]->grade();
                streamsize prec = cout.precision();
                cout << setprecision(3) << final_grade
                    << setprecision(prec) << endl;

            } catch (domain_error e) {
                cout << e.what() << endl;
            }
            delete students[i];          // free the object allocated when reading
        }
        return 0;
}
```

We have noted in comments the many differences between this code and our original. These changes all result from the fact that we must manipulate pointers and not objects.

The `while` loop changes to read the first character from the input, which we subsequently test to determine which kind of record we are about to read. Once we know what kind of object we need, we allocate an object of the appropriate type, and use that object to `read` from the standard input. The `read` function is `virtual`, so the right version will be called, depending on whether `record` points to a `Grad` or a `Core` object. In both cases, `read` will give the object the values from the next input record. Note that we must remember to dereference `record`, which is a pointer, to access `read`. The code to calculate the length of the longest name also changes to dereference the pointer, but otherwise the next few lines of code are unchanged.

When we get to the loop that does output, we have to remember that students[i] yields a pointer. Once we have fetched students[i], we have a pointer that must itself be dereferenced to get at the underlying object. As with the call to read, the call to grade is a virtual call, so the right version of grade is automatically invoked to calculate the grade, including a thesis if the object is a Grad and not otherwise. The final change is to remember to return to the implementation the space that the object consumed, which we do by calling delete on the pointer that students[i] contains.

13.3.2 Virtual destructors

Our program almost works. The only problem occurs when we delete the objects, as we do inside the output loop. When we allocated these objects, we allocated both Grad and Core objects, but we stored pointers to these objects as Core*, and not as Grad* pointers. Thus, when we delete them, we are deleting a pointer to Core, and never a pointer to Grad, even if the pointer actually points to a Grad object. Fortunately, this problem is easily fixed.

When we call delete on a pointer, two things happen: The destructor is run on the object, and the space that held the object is freed. When the program deletes the pointer in students[i], it could be pointing at either a Core object or a Grad object. Neither Core nor Grad explicitly defined a destructor, which means that when the delete runs, it will invoke the synthesized destructor and then return the space that the object consumed. The synthesized destructor will run the destructor for each data element in the class. But when the delete is executed, which destructor should the system run? Should the destructor destroy the members of a Core or a Grad? And when the space is freed, how much space should be returned—enough to hold a Core or a Grad?

These questions sound like the kind that the virtual mechanism can resolve—and indeed it can. In order to have a virtual destructor, the class must have a destructor, which we can then make virtual:

```
class Core {
public:
    virtual ~Core() { }
// as before
};
```

Now when we execute delete students[i], the destructor that will be run will depend on the type of object to which students[i] actually points. Similarly, the type of the memory that we return to the system will be determined by the type to which students[i] actually points.

Note that the body of the destructor is empty. The only work needed to destroy a Core is to destroy its members, and the system does this work automatically. Empty, virtual destructors are not uncommon. A virtual destructor is needed any time it is possible that an object of derived type is destroyed through a pointer to base. If there is no other reason for the destructor to be defined, then that destructor has no work to do and should be empty.

There is no need to update the `Grad` class to add a destructor. As with all `virtual` functions, the fact that the destructor is `virtual` is inherited. Because neither class has any explicit work to do in order to destroy objects, there is no need to redefine the destructor in the derived class. Because the derived class inherits the `virtual` property of its base-class destructor, all we have to do is recompile the program.

13.4 A simple handle class

Although the approach that we have just seen is straightforward, it has problems: The program has acquired a lot of extra complexity related to managing the pointers, and has added several pitfalls that could lead to bugs. Our users have to remember to allocate space for the records as they read them, and to remember to free that space when they no longer need the data. The code is constantly dereferencing the pointers to get at the underlying objects. Nevertheless, we have solved the problem of writing a program that can read a file that contains both kinds of records intermixed.

What we'd like to do is find a way to preserve the good properties of our simpler programs that dealt with either `Core` objects or `Grad` objects, and eliminate the problems inherent in our new solution, which can process both kinds of records. It turns out that there is a common programming technique, known as a ***handle class***, that will let us do so.

Our code became cluttered when we realized that we needed to be able to deal with objects whose type we could not know until run time. We knew that each object would be either a `Core`, or something derived from `Core`. Our solution used pointers, because we could allocate a pointer to `Core` and then make that pointer point to either a `Core` or a `Grad` object. The trouble with our solution is that it imposed error-prone bookkeeping on our users. We can't eliminate that bookkeeping, but we can hide it from our users by writing a new class that will encapsulate the pointer to `Core`:

```
class Student_info {
public:
    // constructors and copy control
    Student_info(): cp(0) { }
    Student_info(std::istream& is): cp(0) { read(is); }
    Student_info(const Student_info&);
    Student_info& operator=(const Student_info&);
    ~Student_info() { delete cp; }

    // operations
    std::istream& read(std::istream&);

    std::string name() const {
        if (cp) return cp->name();
        else throw std::runtime_error("uninitialized Student");
    }
    double grade() const {
        if (cp) return cp->grade();
        else throw std::runtime_error("uninitialized Student");
    }
```

```
        static bool compare(const Student_info& s1,
                            const Student_info& s2) {
            return s1.name() < s2.name();
        }

    private:
        Core* cp;
    };
```

The idea here is that a `Student_info` object can represent either a `Core` or a `Grad`. In that sense, it will act like a pointer. However, users of `Student_info` do not have to worry about allocating the underlying object to which the `Student_info` is bound. The class will take care of these tedious and error-prone aspects of our programs.

Each `Student_info` object will hold a pointer, called `cp`, that points to an object that has either type `Core` or a type derived from `Core`. As we'll see in §13.4.1/245, in the `read` function we'll allocate the object to which `cp` points. Therefore, both constructors initialize `cp` to `0`, indicating that the `Student_info` object is as yet unbound. In the constructor that takes an `istream`, we call the `Student_info::read` function. That function will allocate a new object of the appropriate type, and will give that object the value that it reads from the indicated `istream`.

We know from the rule of three (§11.3.6/201) that we will need a copy constructor, assignment operator, and destructor to manage the pointer. The work that the destructor must do is easy: It just has to destroy the object that the constructors allocated. Because we gave `Core` a `virtual` destructor in §13.3.2/242, the destructor for `Student_info` will operate correctly whether the object being destroyed is a `Grad` object or a `Core` object. We'll define the copy constructor and assignment operator in §13.4.2/246.

Because users will write programs in terms of `Student_info` objects rather than `Core` or `Grad` objects, the `Student_info` class must provide the same interface as the `Core` class. For both `name` and `grade`, there is nothing special for `Student_info` to do, and so these functions forward their work to the underlying `Core` or `Grad` object to which `cp` points.

However, `cp` could be `0`. It will be `0` if a user creates a `Student_info` object using the default constructor, and then does not read into it. If `cp` is `0`, we can't just forward the calls to the underlying object. Instead, we'll `throw` a `runtime_error` to indicate that a problem has occurred.

It is important to remember that the `Core::grade` function is `virtual`, which means that when we call it through `cp`, the version that is called at run time will depend on the type of object to which `cp` points. For example, if `cp` points to a `Grad` object, then we'll run the `Grad::grade` operation.

The only other function in the interface is the `compare` operation, which turns out to have a couple of interesting properties. First, recall that for the `Core` classes, `compare` was a global, nonmember function, whereas here, we implement it as a *static member function*. Static member functions differ from ordinary member functions in that they do not operate on an object of the class type. Unlike other member functions, they are associated with the class, not with a particular object. As such, they cannot access the nonstatic data members of objects of the class: There is no object associated with the function, so there are no members to use.

For our purposes, static member functions have one significant advantage: Their names are within the scope of their class. So, when we say that compare is a static member we are defining a function named Student_info::compare. Because the function has a qualified name, it does not overload the compare that we used to compare Core objects. Thus, our users will be able to call sort, passing Student_info::compare, and the compiler can know which function they want.

The other interesting thing about this function is its implementation. The function uses the Student_info::name function to get at the names stored in the records. It is worth thinking about what is happening here. The call to Student_info::name will call Core::name if cp is set. If cp is 0, then name will throw an exception, which propagates out to compare's caller. Because compare uses the public interface to Student_info, that function doesn't need to check cp directly. As with other user-level code, it passes that problem along to the Student_info class.

13.4.1 Reading the handle

The read function has three responsibilities: It must free the object, if any, to which this handle is bound. It must then decide what kind of object we are about to read, and it must allocate the right kind of object, which it can initialize from the stream it was given:

```
istream& Student_info::read(istream& is)
{
    delete cp;              // delete previous object, if any

    char ch;
    is >> ch;               // get record type

    if (ch == 'U') {
        cp = new Core(is);
    } else {
        cp = new Grad(is);
    }

    return is;
}
```

The read function starts by freeing the existing object (if any) to which the handle object was previously bound. We do not need to check whether cp is 0 before calling delete, because the language guarantees that it is harmless to delete a pointer with value 0. Having freed the old value, we are ready to read the new one. We start by reading and testing the first character on the line. Based on that character, we create an object of the appropriate type, initializing that object by running the appropriate constructor that takes an istream. These constructors call their own read functions to read values from the input stream into the newly created object. After the object is constructed, we store the pointer to it in cp. To finish up, we return the stream that we were given.

13.4.2 Copying handle objects

The copy constructor and assignment operator are necessary to manage the `Core` pointer. The constructor allocates this pointer as a side effect of calling `read`. When we copy a `Student_info`, we will want to allocate a new object and initialize it with the values from the object from which we are copying. However, there is a snag: What kind of object are we copying? There is no obvious way to know whether the `Student_info` object that we're copying points to a `Core` object or an object of a type derived from `Core`.

The way we solve this problem is to give `Core` and its derived classes a new `virtual` function. That function creates a new object that holds copies of the values in the original:

```
class Core {
    friend class Student_info;
protected:
    virtual Core* clone() const { return new Core(*this); }
    // as before
};
```

The `clone` function does exactly what we described, in a surprisingly succinct fashion. We allocate a new `Core` object and use `Core`'s copy constructor to give that new object the appropriate values. Remember that the `Core` class did not explicitly define a copy constructor. Nonetheless, we know from §11.3.5/201 that one exists: The compiler synthesized a default copy constructor, which copies each member from the existing `Core` object into the newly created one.

Because we created the `clone` function as an artifact of our implementation, we did not add it to the `public` interface of `Core`. The fact that `clone` is `protected` means that we must nominate `Student_info` as a `friend` of `Core`, so that `Student_info` objects can access the `clone` function. Class friendship is similar to the `friend` functions that we saw in §12.3.2/216. There, we learned that `friend` functions have access to the `private` and `protected` members of the class. Naming a class as a `friend` has the same effect as making all of the members of that class `friend`s. That is, by adding

```
    friend class Student_info;
```

to the definition of `Core`, we are saying that all the member functions in `Student_info` may access all the `private` and `protected` members of class `Core`.

Having added the `virtual` function `clone` to the base class, we have to remember to redefine the function in the derived class, so that when we `clone` a derived object, we will allocate a new `Grad` object:

```
class Grad {
protected:
    Grad* clone() const { return new Grad(*this); }
    // as before
};
```

As with `Core::clone`, we allocate a new object as a copy of `*this`, but here we return a `Grad*` rather than a `Core*`. Ordinarily, when a derived class redefines a function from the base class, it does so exactly: the parameter list and the return type are identical.

However, if the base-class function returns a pointer (or reference) to a base class, then the derived-class function can return a pointer (or reference) to a corresponding derived class.

We do not need to nominate `Student_info` as a friend of `Grad`, even though friendship is not inherited, because our `Student_info` class never refers to `Grad::clone` directly; it does so only through `virtual` calls to `Core::clone`, which it can access by virtue of its `friendship` with `Core`.

With these changes in place, we can now implement copying and assignment:

```
Student_info::Student_info(const Student_info& s): cp(0)
{
    if (s.cp) cp = s.cp->clone();
}
Student_info& Student_info::operator=(const Student_info& s)
{
    if (&s != this) {
        delete cp;
        if (s.cp)
            cp = s.cp->clone();
        else
            cp = 0;
    }
    return *this;
}
```

In the copy constructor, we initialize the pointer cp to 0, and conditionally call `clone` if there is something there to clone. If not, cp will remain equal to 0, indicating that the handle is unbound. Similarly, the assignment operator calls `clone` conditionally. Of course, we have other work to do in the assignment operator before calling `clone`. First we must guard against self-assignment, by testing whether the addresses of our two operands are the same. If we are assigning different objects, then we must free the object to which cp currently points before making cp point to the newly created object.

Neither the copy constructor nor the assignment operator does anything special if cp is 0, because it is perfectly legitimate to copy or assign an unbound handle.

13.5 Using the handle class

Having finished the handle class, we can now use it to allow our initial program from §9.6/166 to work with but one change:

```
int main()
{
    vector<Student_info> students;
    Student_info record;
    string::size_type maxlen = 0;

    // read and store the data
    while (record.read(cin)) {
        maxlen = max(maxlen, record.name().size());
        students.push_back(record);
    }
```

```
// alphabetize the student records
sort(students.begin(), students.end(), Student_info::compare);

// write the names and grades
for (vector<Student_info>::size_type i = 0;
    i != students.size(); ++i) {
    cout << students[i].name()
        << string(maxlen + 1 - students[i].name().size(), ' ');
    try {
        double final_grade = students[i].grade();
        streamsize prec = cout.precision();
        cout << setprecision(3) << final_grade
            << setprecision(prec) << endl;
    } catch (domain_error e) {
        cout << e.what() << endl;
    }
}
return 0;
}
```

The input loop now reads and processes two kinds of records. One kind of record represents a student who is completing only the core requirements for the course; the other kind represents a student who wants graduate credit. The loop works because the read function for Student_info reads either kind of record. That function first reads the character that says what kind of record we're about to read, and then allocates an object of the appropriate type, initializing the object from the input stream. It constructs the underlying Core or Grad object by reading the data, and stores a pointer to the newly created object in record. We copy the Student_info object into the vector, which copies the object as a side effect of running the Student_info copy constructor.

The next step is to sort the data, which we do by invoking sort, passing it the Student_info::compare function. That function calls the base-class name function to compare the names in the objects.

The output loop remains unchanged. On each trip through the loop, students[i] denotes a Student_info object. That object contains a pointer to an object that is either a Core or a Grad. When we call the grade function for Student_info, that function will use the pointer to call the (virtual) grade function on the underlying object. The type of object to which the handle points will determine which version to call at runtime.

Finally, the objects that were allocated inside the read for the Student_info function will be automatically freed when we exit main. On exiting main, the vector will be destroyed. The destructor for vector will destroy each element in students, which will cause the destructor for Student_info to be run. When that destructor runs, it will delete each of the objects allocated in read.

13.6 Subtleties

Although the ideas behind inheritance and dynamic binding are powerful, they can appear mysterious, at least at first. Now that we've seen examples that use these ideas, let's look at some of the associated subtleties that often cause trouble.

13.6.1 Inheritance and containers

In section §13.3.1/239, we noted that when we say that we want to store Core objects in a container, we're saying that the container will hold Core objects and nothing but Core objects. This assertion might have been surprising: It might seem that we should be able to store Core objects or objects derived from Core in the container. However, if we think about our own implementation of Vec from Chapter 11, we know that at some point, the Vec has to allocate storage for the objects that it contains. When we allocate that storage, we say which exact type to allocate. There is no virtual-like mechanism that determines what kind of object is needed and allocates enough space to hold that object.

What may be more surprising is what would happen if we persisted in defining a vector<Core> into which we intended to place either Core objects or Grad objects. The answer is that we could do so, but the results would probably be a surprise; for example

```
vector<Core> students;
Grad g(cin);                    // read a Grad
students.push_back(g);          // store the Core part(!) of g in students
```

We are allowed to store the Grad object in students, because we can use a Grad object wherever a reference to a Core object is required. The push_back function takes a reference to the vector's element type, so we can pass g to push_back. However, when we put the object into students, only the Core portion of g is copied! As in §13.2.2/235, this behavior is actually what we asked for, although it can be surprising—especially when encountered for the first time. What will happen is that push_back will expect that it was given a Core object, and will construct a Core element, copying only the Core parts of the object, ignoring whatever is specific to the Grad class .

13.6.2 Which function do you want?

It is important to realize that when a base- and derived-class function have the same name, but they don't match exactly in number and types of parameters, they behave as if they were completely unrelated functions. For example, we might add to our hierarchy an accessor function that we could use to change a student's final exam-grade. For Core students, this function should set only the final grade; for Grad students, the function should take two parameters, the second one being used to set the thesis:

```
void Core::regrade(double d) { final = d; }
void Grad::regrade(double d1, double d2) { final = d1; thesis = d2; }
```

If r is a reference to a Core, then

```
r.regrade(100);           // ok, call Core::regrade
r.regrade(100, 100);      // compile error, Core::regrade takes a single argument
```

This second call is an error even if r refers to an object of type Grad. The type of r is a reference to Core, and the version of regrade in Core takes one value of type double.

What may be more surprising is what happens if r is a reference to a Grad:

```
r.regrade(100);           // compile error, Grad::regrade takes two arguments
r.regrade(100, 100);      // ok, call Grad::regrade
```

Now when we look for a function to call, r is a Grad. The regrade function that applies to Grad objects takes two arguments. Even though there is a base-class version that takes a single argument, that version is effectively hidden by the existence of regrade in the derived class. If we want to run the version from the base class, we must call it explicitly:

```
r.Core::regrade(100);      // ok, call Core::regrade
```

If we want to use regrade as a virtual function, we must give it the same interface in the base and derived classes, which we can do by giving the Core version an extra, unused parameter with a default argument:

```
virtual void Core::regrade(double d, double = 0) { final = d; }
```

13.7 Details

Inheritance allows us to model classes that are similar to one another with exceptions:

```
class base {
public:
      // common interface
protected:
      // implementation members accessible to derived classes
private:
      // implementation accessible to only the base class
};

// public interface of base is part of the interface for derived
class derived: public base { ... };
```

Classes that derive from the base class may redefine operations from the base class and may add members of their own. Classes can also inherit privately:

```
class priv_derived: private base { ... };
```

which is rare and normally is used for implementation convenience only.

An object of a (publicly) derived type can be used where an object, reference, or pointer to a base class object is expected.

Derivation chains can be several layers deep:

```
class derived2: public derived { ... };
```

Objects of type derived2 have a derived part, which in turn has a base part. Thus, derived2 objects have the properties of derived and base class objects.

Derived-class objects are constructed by allocating enough space for the entire object, constructing the base-class part(s), and then constructing the derived class. Which derived constructor is run depends, as usual, on the arguments used in creating the derived-class object. That constructor, through its constructor-initializer list, can pass arguments to be used when constructing its immediate base class. If the constructor initializer does not explicitly initialize its base, then the base's default constructor is run.

Dynamic binding refers to the ability to select at run time which function to run based on the actual type of the object on which the function is called. Dynamic binding is in effect for calls to `virtual` functions made through a pointer or a reference. The fact that a function is `virtual` is inherited, and need not be repeated in the derived classes.

Derived classes are not required to redefine their `virtual` functions. If a class does not redefine a `virtual`, then it inherits the nearest definition for that function. However, any `virtual` functions that the class does contain must be defined. It is often a source of mysterious error messages from compilers to declare but not define a `virtual` function.

Overriding: A derived-class member function overrides a function with the same name in the base class if the two functions have the same number and types of parameters and both (or neither) are `const`. In that case, the return types must also match, except that as in §13.4.2/246, if the base-class function returns a pointer (or reference) to a class, the derived-class function can return a pointer (or reference) to a derived class. If the argument lists don't match, the base- and derived-class functions are effectively unrelated.

`virtual` destructors: If a pointer to the base class is used to `delete` an object that might actually be a derived-class object, then the base class needs a `virtual` destructor. If the class has no other need for a destructor, then the `virtual` destructor still must be defined and should be empty:

```
class base {
public:
    virtual ~base() { }
};
```

As with any other function, the `virtual` nature of the destructor is inherited by the derived classes, and there is no need to redefine the destructor in the derived classes.

Constructors and `virtual` functions: While an object is under construction, its type is the type of the class that is being constructed—even if the object is part of a derived-class object. Thus, calls to `virtual` functions from inside a constructor are statically bound to the version for the type being constructed.

Class `friendship`: A class can designate another as its `friend`; doing so grants friendship to all the member functions of the other class. Friendship is neither inherited nor transitive; friends of friends and classes derived from friends have no special privileges.

Static members exist as members of the class, rather than as an instance in each object of the class. Therefore, the `this` keyword is not available in a `static` member function. Such functions may access only `static` data members. There is a single instance of each `static` data member for the entire class, which must be initialized, usually in the source file that implements the class member functions. Because the member is initialized outside the class definition, you must fully qualify the name when you initialize it:

value-type class-name : : *static-member-name* = *value* ;

says that the `static` member named *static-member-name* from the class *class-name* has type *value-type* and is given the initial value *value*.

Exercises

13-0. Compile, execute, and test the programs in this chapter.

13-1. Annotate the `Core` and `Grad` constructors to write the constructor's name and argument list when the constructor is executed. For example, you should add a statement such as

```
cerr << "Grad::Grad(istream&)" << endl;
```

to the `Grad` constructor taking an `istream&` parameter. Then write a small program that exercises each constructor. Predict beforehand what the output will be. Revise your program and predictions until your predictions match what is actually written.

13-2. Given the `Core` and `Grad` classes defined in this chapter, indicate which function is called for each of these invocations:

```
Core* p1 = new Core;
Core* p2 = new Grad;
Core s1;
Grad s2;

p1->grade();
p1->name();

p2->grade();
p2->name();

s1.grade();
s1.name();

s2.name();
s2.grade();
```

Check whether you are correct by adding output statements to the `name` and `grade` functions that indicate which function is being executed.

13-3. The class that we built in Chapter 9 included a `valid` member that allowed users to check whether the object held values for a student record or not. Add that functionality to the inheritance-based system of classes.

13-4. Add to these classes a function that will map a numeric grade to a letter grade according to the grading policy outlined in §10.3/177.

13-5. Write a predicate to check whether a particular student met all the relevant requirements. That is, check whether a student did all the homework, and if a graduate student, whether the student wrote a thesis.

13-6. Add a class to the system to represent students taking the course for pass/fail credit. Assume that such students need not do the homework, but might do so. If they do, the homework should participate in determining whether they passed or failed, according to the normal formula. If they did no homework, then the grade is the average of their midterm and final grades. A passing grade is 60 or higher.

13-7. Add a class to the system to represent students auditing the course.

13-8. Write a program to generate a grade report that can handle all four kinds of students.

13-9. Describe what would happen if the assignment operator in §13.4.2/247 failed to check for self-assignment.

14

Managing memory (almost) automatically

When we built our `Student_info` handle class in Chapter 13, we combined two separable abstractions. Not only was that class an interface to the operations on student records, but it also managed a pointer to an implementation object. Combining two independent abstractions into a single class is often a sign of weak design.

What we'd like is to be able to define a class that is similar to `Student_info`, but that is strictly an interface class. Such interface classes are common in C++, especially when they interface to an inheritance hierarchy. We will arrange for our interface class to delegate the implementation details to another class, which behaves like a pointer but also manages the underlying memory. Once we have separated the interface class from the pointerlike class, we should be able to use a single pointerlike class with multiple interface classes.

As we'll see, we can also use classes such as these to improve the performance of programs that manage memory often. By arranging for several pointerlike objects to refer to a single underlying object where appropriate, we can avoid copying objects unnecessarily.

Much of this chapter revolves around the answer to a single question: What does it mean to copy an object? At first glance, this question seems to have an obvious answer: A copy is a distinct object that has all the properties of the original object. However, the moment it becomes possible for one object to refer to another, the question becomes more complicated: If an object x refers to an object y, does copying x cause y to be copied too?

Sometimes the answer to this latter question is obvious: If y is a member of x, the answer must be yes, and if x is nothing more than a pointer that happens to point to y, the answer is no. In this chapter we'll define three different versions of our pointerlike class, each of which differs from the others in how it defines copying.

These questions about copying, and the very idea of a pointerlike class, are fairly abstract notions. Because we will implement these abstractions, it is not surprising that this chapter is by far the most abstract in the book. As a result, it is likely to require—and repay—careful study.

14.1 Handles that copy their objects

Let's think again about the grading problem that we solved in Chapter 13. In solving that problem, we needed to store and process a collection of objects representing different types of students. These objects were of one of two types related by inheritance, with the possibility of more types being added later. Our first solution, in §13.3.1/239, used pointers to let us store a mixed collection of objects. Each of these pointers might point to a `Core` object, or to an object of a type derived from `Core`. User code was responsible for allocating the objects dynamically, and for remembering to free them. The program was cluttered with details related to managing the pointers, and was generally tricky.

The problem is that a pointer is a primitive, low-level data structure. Programming with pointers is notoriously error prone. Many of the problems with pointers arise because pointers are independent of the objects to which they point, leading to pitfalls:

- Copying a pointer does not copy the corresponding object, leading to surprises if two pointers inadvertently point to the same object.
- Destroying a pointer does not destroy its object, leading to memory leaks.
- Deleting an object without destroying a pointer to it leads to a dangling pointer, which causes undefined behavior if the program uses the pointer.
- Creating a pointer without initializing it leaves the pointer unbound, which also causes undefined behavior if the program uses it.

In §13.5/247, we solved the grading problem again, this time using the `Student_info` handle class. Because this class managed the pointers, our users' code dealt with `Student_info` objects, rather than with pointers. However, the `Student_info` class was intimately tied to the `Core` hierarchy: It contained operations that mirrored those in the `public` interface of the `Core` classes.

What we want to do now is to separate these abstractions. We'll still use `Student_info` to provide the interface, but it will rely on another class to manage the "handle." That is, this other class will manage the pointers to the implementation objects. The behavior of this new type can and will be independent of the type of the objects to which the handle can be attached.

14.1.1 A generic handle class

Because we want our class to be independent of the type of object that it manages, we already know that our class must be a template. Because we want it to encapsulate the handle behavior, we will call it `Handle`. The properties that our class will provide are:

- A `Handle` is a value that refers to an object.
- We can copy a `Handle` object.
- We can test a `Handle` object to determine whether it is bound to another object.
- We can use a `Handle` to trigger polymorphic behavior when it points to an object of a class that belongs to an inheritance hierarchy. That is, if we call a `virtual` function through our class, we want the implementation to choose the function to run dynamically, just as if we'd called the function through a real pointer.

Our `Handle` will have a restricted interface: Once you attach a `Handle` to an object, the `Handle` class will take over memory management for that object. Users should attach only one `Handle` to any object, after which they should not access the object directly through a pointer; all access should be through the `Handle`. These restrictions will allow `Handles` to avoid the problems inherent in built-in pointers. When we copy a `Handle` object, we'll make a new copy of the object, so that each `Handle` points to its own copy. When we destroy a `Handle`, it will destroy the associated object, and doing so will be the only straightforward way to free the object. We'll allow users to create unbound `Handles`, but we will throw an exception if the user attempts to access the object to which an unbound `Handle` refers (or, more accurately, doesn't refer). Users who want to avoid the exception can test to see whether the `Handle` is bound.

These properties are like the ones that we implemented in the `Student_info` class. The `Student_info` copy constructor and assignment operator called `clone` to copy the associated `Core` object. The `Student_info` destructor destroyed the `Core` object as well. The operations that used the underlying object checked before doing so to ensure that the `Student_info` was bound to a real object. What we want is a class that encapsulates this behavior, but that we can use to manage an object of any type:

```
template <class T> class Handle {
public:
    Handle(): p(0) { }
    Handle(const Handle& s): p(0) { if (s.p) p = s.p->clone(); }
    Handle& operator=(const Handle&);
    ~Handle() { delete p; }

    Handle(T* t): p(t) { }

    operator bool() const { return p; }
    T& operator*() const;
    T* operator->() const;

private:
    T* p;
};
```

The `Handle` class is a template class, so that we can create `Handles` that refer to any type. Each `Handle<T>` object holds a pointer to an object; the other operations manage this pointer. Aside from variable-name changes, the first four functions are identical to their versions in `Student_info`. The default constructor sets the pointer to zero to indicate that the `Handle` is unbound. The copy constructor (conditionally) calls the associated object's `clone` function to create a new copy of the object. The `Handle` destructor frees the object. The assignment operator, like the copy constructor, (conditionally) calls `clone` to create a new copy of the object:

```
template<class T>
Handle<T>& Handle<T>::operator=(const Handle& rhs)
{
    if (&rhs != this) {
        delete p;
        p = rhs.p ? rhs.p->clone() : 0;
    }
    return *this;
}
```

The assignment operator, as usual, starts by checking for self-assignment, doing nothing if the test succeeds. If the test fails, we continue by freeing the object that we had been managing, and then making a copy of the right-hand object. The statement that does the copy uses the conditional operator (§3.2.2/45) to decide whether it's safe to call `clone`. If `rhs.p` is set, we call `rhs.p->clone` and assign the resulting pointer to p. Otherwise, we set p to 0.

Because `Handle` models pointer behavior, we need a way to bind the pointer to an actual object, which we do in the constructor that takes a `T*`. That constructor remembers the pointer that it was given, thus binding the `Handle` to the object to which t points. For example, if we define

```
Handle<Core> student(new Grad);
```

we construct a `Handle` object named `student` that contains a `Core*` pointer, which we initialize to point to the object of type `Grad` that we just created:

Finally, we define three operator functions. The first of these, `operator bool()` lets users test the value of a `Handle` in a condition. The operation returns `true` if the `Handle` is bound to an object, and `false` otherwise. The other two define `operator*` and `operator->`, which give access to the object bound to the `Handle`:

```
template <class T>
T& Handle<T>::operator*() const
{
    if (p)
        return *p;
    throw runtime_error("unbound Handle");
}

template <class T>
T* Handle<T>::operator->() const
{
    if (p)
        return p;
    throw runtime_error("unbound Handle");
}
```

Applying the built-in unary * operator to a pointer yields the object to which the pointer points. Here we define our own *, so that * of a `Handle` object yields the value that results from applying the built-in * operator to the pointer member of that `Handle` object. Given our `student` object, `*student` will yield the result of applying * to `student.p` (assuming we could access the p member). In other words, the result of `*student` will be a reference to the `Grad` object that we created when we initialized `student`.

The -> operator is a bit more complicated. Superficially, -> looks like a binary operator, but in fact it behaves differently from ordinary binary operators. Like the scope or dot operators, the -> operator is used to access a member whose name appears in its right operand from an object named by its left operand. Because names are not expressions, we have no direct access to the name that our user requested. Instead, the language requires that we define `->` to return a value that can be treated as a pointer. When we define `operator->`, we are saying that if `x` is a value of type that defines `operator->` then

```
x->y
```

is equivalent to

```
(x.operator->())->y
```

In this case, `operator->` returns the pointer that its object holds. So for `student`,

```
student->y
```

is equivalent to

```
(student.operator->())->y
```

which, because of the way we defined `operator->`, is equivalent to

```
student.p->y
```

(ignoring the fact that protection would not ordinarily allow us to access `student.p` directly). Thus, the `->` operator has the effect of forwarding calls made through a `Handle` object to the underlying pointer that is a member of the `Handle` object.

One of our objectives was for `Handle` to preserve the polymorphic behavior associated with built-in pointers. Having seen the definitions of `operator*` and `operator->`, we can see that we have reached our goal. These operations yield either a reference or a pointer, through which we obtain dynamic binding. For example, if we execute `student->grade()`, we're calling `grade` through the `p` pointer inside `student`. The particular version of `grade` that is run depends on the type of the object to which `p` points. Assuming that `student` still points to the `Grad` object to which it initially pointed, this call would be to `Grad::grade`. Similarly, `operator*` yields a reference, so evaluating `(*student).grade()` calls `grade` through a reference, and the implementation will decide which particular function to call at run time.

14.1.2 Using a generic handle

We could use `Handle`s to rewrite the pointer-based grading program from §13.3.1/241:

```
int main()
{
    vector< Handle<Core> > students;        // changed type
    Handle<Core> record;                    // changed type
    char ch;
    string::size_type maxlen = 0;

    // read and store the data
    while (cin >> ch) {
        if (ch == 'U')
            record = new Core;              // allocate a Core object
        else
            record = new Grad;              // allocate a Grad object
```

```
        record->read(cin);   //  Handle<T>::->, then virtual call to read
        maxlen = max(maxlen, record->name().size()); // Handle<T>::->
        students.push_back(record);
    }

    // compare must be rewritten to work on const Handle<Core>&
    sort(students.begin(), students.end(), compare_Core_handles);

    // write the names and grades
    for (vector< Handle<Core> >::size_type i = 0;
         i != students.size(); ++i) {
        // students[i] is a Handle, which we dereference to call the functions
        cout << students[i]->name()
                << string(maxlen + 1 - students[i]->name().size(), ' ');
        try {
            double final_grade = students[i]->grade();
            streamsize prec = cout.precision();
            cout << setprecision(3) << final_grade
                    << setprecision(prec) << endl;
        } catch (domain_error e) {
            cout << e.what() << endl;
        }
        // no delete statement
    }
    return 0;
}
```

This program stores `Handle<Core>` objects instead of `Core*` objects and so, as we did in §13.3.1/240, we'll need to write a non-overloaded comparison operation that operates on `const Handle<Core>&` that we can pass to `sort`. We leave the implementation as an exercise, but assume that it is named `compare_Core_handles`.

Because our `Handle` class uses the `clone` member of the object to which it is attached, we'll also need to change our `Core` class (§13.4.2/246) to allow `Handle<Core>` to use that `clone` member, either by making `Handle<Core>` a `friend` or by making the `clone` member `public`.

The only other differences are in the output loop. Dereferencing `students[i]` yields a `Handle`, which has an `operator->` that we use to access the `name` and `grade` functions through the underlying `Core*`. For example, `students[i]->grade()` uses the overloaded `->`, so it effectively calls `students[i].p->grade()`. Because `grade` is `virtual`, we'll run the version that is appropriate to the type of the object to which `students[i].p` points. Moreover, because `Handle` takes care of memory management for us, we no longer need to `delete` the objects to which the elements of `students` refer.

More important, we can also reimplement `Student_info`, which can now become a pure interface class, delegating the work of managing pointers to `Handle`:

```
class Student_info {
public:
    Student_info() { }
    Student_info(std::istream& is) { read(is); }
    // no copy, assign, or destructor: they're no longer needed

    std::istream& read(std::istream&);
```

```
        std::string name() const {
            if (cp) return cp->name();
            else throw std::runtime_error("uninitialized Student");
        }

        double grade() const {
            if (cp) return cp->grade();
            else throw std::runtime_error("uninitialized Student");
        }
        static bool compare(const Student_info& s1,
                            const Student_info& s2) {
            return s1.name() < s2.name();
        }
private:
    Handle<Core> cp;
};
```

In this version of `Student_info`, `cp` is a `Handle<Core>` rather than a `Core*`. Therefore, we no longer need to implement the copy-control functions, because the `Handle`
manages the underlying object. The other constructors operate as before. The `name` and
`grade` functions look the same, but their execution relies on the conversion to `bool`,
which is invoked in the test on `cp` and in the overloaded `operator->` from the `Handle`
class, which is used to get at the functions on the underlying objects.

   To complete our reimplementation, we need to write the `read` function:

```
    istream& Student_info::read(istream& is)
    {
        char ch;
        is >> ch;         // get record type

        // allocate new object of the appropriate type
        // use Handle<T>(T*) to build a Handle<Core> from the pointer to that object
        // call Handle<T>::operator= to assign the Handle<Core> to the left-hand side
        if (ch == 'U')
            cp = new Core(is);
        else
            cp = new Grad(is);

        return is;
    }
```

This code looks like the earlier `Student_info::read` function, but its execution is quite
different. Most obviously, the `delete` statement is gone, because the assignment to `cp`
will free the object if appropriate. To understand this code, we need to trace through it
carefully. For example, when we execute `new Core(is)`, we get a `Core*` object, which
we implicitly convert to a `Handle<Core>` using the `Handle(T*)` constructor. That
`Handle` value is then assigned to `cp` using the `Handle` assignment operator, which automatically `delete`s the object, if any, to which the `Handle` previously referred. This
assignment constructs and destroys an extra copy of the `Core` object that we created, a
copy that we will now see how to avoid.

14.2 Reference-counted handles

At this point, we have achieved our goal of separating the work of managing pointers from our interface class. We can use `Handles` to implement a wide variety of interface classes, none of which would have to worry about memory management. However, our `Handle` class still has the problem that copying or assigning objects copies the underlying data, even when it does not need to do so. The reason being that `Handle` always copies the object to which the `Handle` is bound.

In general, we would like to be able to decide whether we want to make such copies. For example, we might want objects that are copies of one another to share their underlying information. Such classes do not need or want valuelike behavior. Other classes may not have any way of changing state once an object is created. In such cases, there is no reason to copy the underlying object. Copying such objects would waste time and space. To support these kinds of classes, we'd like a kind of `Handle` that does not copy the underlying object when the `Handle` itself is copied. Of course, if we allow multiple `Handles` to be bound to the same underlying object, we'll still need to free that object at some point. The obvious point at which to free the object is when the last `Handle` that points to it goes away.

To this end, we will use a ***reference count***, which is an object that keeps track of how many objects refer to another object. Each target object will have a reference count associated with it. We will arrange to increment the reference count each time we create a new handle that refers to our target object, and to decrement the reference count each time a referring object goes away. When the last referring object goes away, the reference count will become zero. At that point we'll know that it is safe to destroy the target object.

This technique can save a lot of unneeded memory management and copying of data. We'll first build a new class, called `Ref_handle`, which will show how to add reference counts to our `Handle` class. Then, in the next two sections, we'll explore how reference counting can help us define classes that behave like values while sharing representations.

To add reference counting to a class, we have to allocate a counter, and change the operations that create, copy, and destroy the objects so that they update the counter appropriately. Each object to which we have a `Ref_handle` will have a reference count associated with it. The only question is where to store the counter. In general, we don't own the source code for the types from which we want to make `Ref_handles`, so we can't just add the counter to the object class type itself. Instead, we'll add another pointer to our `Ref_handle` class to keep track of the count. Each object to which we have attached a `Ref_handle` will also have an associated reference count that tracks how many copies we have made of that object:

```
template <class T> class Ref_handle {
public:
    // manage reference count as well as pointer
    Ref_handle(): refptr(new size_t(1)), p(0) { }
    Ref_handle(T* t): refptr(new size_t(1)), p(t) { }
    Ref_handle(const Ref_handle& h): refptr(h.refptr), p(h.p) {
        ++*refptr;
    }
```

```
    Ref_handle& operator=(const Ref_handle&);
    ~Ref_handle();

    // as before
    operator bool() const { return p; }
    T& operator*() const {
        if (p)
            return *p;
        throw std::runtime_error("unbound Ref_handle");
    }
    T* operator->() const {
        if (p)
            return p;
        throw std::runtime_error("unbound Ref_handle");
    }
private:
    T* p;
    std::size_t* refptr;        // added
};
```

We have added a second data member to our `Ref_handle` class, and updated the constructors to initialize that new member. The default constructor and the constructor that takes a `T*` create new `Ref_handle` objects, so they allocate a new reference count (of type `size_t`) and set the value of that counter to 1. The copy constructor doesn't create a new object. Instead, it copies the pointers from the `Ref_handle<T>` object that it was passed, and increments the reference count to indicate that there is one more pointer to the `T` object than there was previously. Thus, the new `Ref_handle<T>` object points to the same `T` object, and to the same reference count, as the `Ref_handle<T>` object from which we copy. So, for example, if `X` is a `Ref_handle<T>` object, and we create `Y` as a copy of `X`, then the situation looks like this:

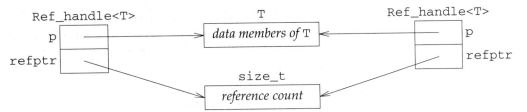

The assignment operator also manipulates the reference count instead of copying the underlying object:

```
template<class T>
Ref_handle<T>& Ref_handle<T>::operator=(const Ref_handle& rhs)
{
    ++*rhs.refptr;
    // free the left-hand side, destroying pointers if appropriate
    if (--*refptr == 0) {
        delete refptr;
        delete p;
    }
```

```
//  copy in values from the right-hand side
refptr = rhs.refptr;
p = rhs.p;
return *this;
}
```

As always, it is important to protect against self-assignment, which we do by incrementing the reference count of the right-hand side before decrementing the reference count of
the left-hand side. If both operands refer to the same object, the net effect will be to leave
the reference count unchanged, while ensuring that it will not reach zero unintentionally.

If the reference count goes to zero when we decrement it, then the left operand is the
last Ref_handle bound to the underlying object. Because we are about to obliterate the
value of the left operand, we are about to delete the last reference to that object. Therefore, we must delete the object, and its corresponding reference count before we overwrite the values in refptr and p. We delete both p and refptr because both were
dynamically allocated objects; thus, we must free them to avoid a memory leak.

Having deleted the pointers, if needed, we then copy the values from the right-hand
side into the left-hand side and, as usual, return a reference to the left operand.

The destructor, like the assignment operator, checks whether the Ref_handle object
being destroyed is the last one bound to its T object. If so, the destructor deletes the
objects to which the pointers point:

```
template<class T> Ref_handle<T>::~Ref_handle()
{
    if (--*refptr == 0) {
        delete refptr;
        delete p;
    }
}
```

This version of Ref_handle works well for classes that can share state between copies
of different objects, but what about classes, such as Student_info, that want to provide
valuelike behavior? For example, if we used the Ref_handle class to implement
Student_info, then after executing, say,

```
Student_info s1(cin);      //  initialize s1 from the standard input
Student_info s2 = s1;      //  "copy" that value into s2
```

the two objects s1 and s2 would refer to the same underlying object, even though it
might appear that s2 is a copy of s1. If we do anything to change the value of one of
these objects, we change the value of the other as well.

Our original Handle class defined in §14.1.1/255 provided valuelike behavior because
it always copied the associated object by calling clone. It should be easy to see that our
new Ref_handle class never calls clone at all. Because Ref_handle never calls
clone, handles of this type never copy the objects to which they are attached. On the
other hand, this version of Ref_handle certainly has the advantage of avoiding needless
copying of data. The trouble is that it does so by avoiding *all* copying, needless or not.
What can we do?

14.3 Handles that let you decide when to share data

So far, we have seen two possible definitions for our generic handle class. The first version always copies the underlying object; the second never does so. A more useful kind of handle is one that lets the program that uses it decide when it wants to copy the target object and when it doesn't. Such a handle class preserves the performance of Ref_handle, and allows the class author to provide the valuelike behavior of Handles. Such a handle will preserve the useful properties of built-in pointers, but avoids many of the pitfalls. Thus, we'll call this final handle class Ptr, to capture the notion that it is a useful substitute for built-in pointers. In general, our Ptr class will copy the object if we are about to change its contents, but only if there is another handle attached to the same object. Fortunately, the reference count gives us a way to tell whether our handle is the only one attached to its object.

The fundamentals of our Ptr class are the same as the Ref_handle class that we developed in §14.2/260. All we need to do is to add one more member function to that class to give control to the user:

```
template<class T> class Ptr {
public:
    // new member to copy the object conditionally when needed
    void make_unique() {
        if (*refptr != 1) {
            --*refptr;
            refptr = new size_t(1);
            p = p? p->clone(): 0;
        }
    }

    // the rest of the class looks like Ref_handle except for its name
    Ptr(): refptr(new size_t(1)), p(0) { }
    Ptr(T* t): refptr(new size_t(1)), p(t) { }
    Ptr(const Ptr& h): refptr(h.refptr), p(h.p) { ++*refptr; }

    Ptr& operator=(const Ptr&);      // implemented analogously to §14.2/261
    ~Ptr();                          // implemented analogously to §14.2/262
    operator bool() const { return p; }
    T& operator*() const;            // implemented analogously to §14.2/261
    T* operator->() const;           // implemented analogously to §14.2/261

private:
    T* p;
    std::size_t* refptr;
};
```

This new make_unique member does just what we want: If the reference count is 1, it does nothing; otherwise, it uses the clone member of the object to which the handle is bound to make a copy of that object, and sets p to point to the copy. If the reference count is not 1, there must be at least one other Ptr that refers to the original object. We therefore decrement the reference count associated with the original (which might reduce it to 1 but not to 0). We then create a new reference count for our handle, and for others that might be created in the future as copies of it. Because so far there is only one Ptr attached to the copy that we're making, we initialize the counter to 1. Before calling `clone`, we check whether the pointer to the object from which we're copying is bound to an actual object. If so, we call the `clone` function to copy that object. When we're done, we'll know that this `Ptr` is the only one that is attached to the object to which p points. That object is either the same one as before (if the original reference count was one) or a copy of it (if the reference count was greater than one).

We can use this latest revision of `Ptr` in the handle-based `Student_info` implementation in §14.1.2/258. When we do, we'll discover that we don't need to change this implementation of `Student_info` at all, because none of our operations changes the value of the object without also replacing it. The only `Student_info` operation that changes the value is the `read` function, but that function always assigns a newly created value to its `Ptr` member. When it does so, the `Ptr` assignment operator will either free the old value or keep it around, depending on whether there are other objects that refer to the old value. In either case, the object into which we read will have a new `Ptr` object and will, therefore, be the only user of that object. If our users write code such as

```
Student_info s1;
read(cin, s1);            // give s1 a value
Student_info s2 = s1;     // copy that value into s2
read(cin, s2);            // read into s2; changes only s2 and not s1
```

then the value of `s2` is reset in the `read` call, but the value of `s1` is unchanged.

On the other hand, had we added the `virtual` version of the `regrade` function described in §13.6.2/249 to the `Core` hierarchy, and given `Student_Info` a corresponding interface function, then that function would need to change to call `make_unique`:

```
void Student_info::regrade(double final, double thesis)
{
    // get our own copy before changing the object
    cp.make_unique();

    if (cp)
        cp->regrade(final, thesis);
    else throw runtime_error("regrade of unknown student");
}
```

14.4 An improvement on controllable handles

Useful as our controllable handle might be, it doesn't quite do all we want. For example, suppose we want to use it to reimplement the `Str` class from Chapter 12. As we saw in §12.3.4/219, we implicitly copy a lot of characters to form the new `Str`s that result from concatenating two existing `Str` objects. By reference-counting the `Str` class, we might think that we can avoid at least some of these copies:

```
// does this version work?
class Str {
    friend std::istream& operator>>(std::istream&, Str&);
```

```
    public:
        Str& operator+=(const Str& s) {
            data.make_unique();
            std::copy(s.data->begin(), s.data->end(),
                      std::back_inserter(*data));
            return *this;
        }

        // interface as before
        typedef Vec<char>::size_type size_type;

        // reimplement constructors to create Ptrs
        Str(): data(new Vec<char>) { }
        Str(const char* cp): data(new Vec<char>)   {
            std::copy(cp, cp + std::strlen(cp),
                      std::back_inserter(*data));
        }

        Str(size_type n, char c): data(new Vec<char>(n, c)) { }
        template<class In> Str(In i, In j): data(new Vec<char>) {
            std::copy(i, j, std::back_inserter(*data));
        }

        // call make_unique as necessary
        char& operator[](size_type i) {
            data.make_unique();
            return (*data)[i];
        }
        const char& operator[](size_type i) const { return (*data)[i]; }
        size_type size() const { return data->size(); }
    private:
        // store a Ptr to a vector
        Ptr< Vec<char> > data;
    };
    // as implemented in §12.3.2/216 and §12.3.3/219
    std::ostream& operator<<(std::ostream&, const Str&);
    Str operator+(const Str&, const Str&);
```

We have preserved the interface to `Str`, but we have fundamentally changed the implementation. Instead of holding a `vector` directly in each `Str` object, we store a `Ptr` to the vector. This design allows multiple `Str`s to share the same underlying character data. The constructors initialize this `Ptr` by allocating a new `vector` initialized with the appropriate values. The code for the operations that read, but do not change, `data` are unchanged from our previous version. Of course, these operations now operate on a `Ptr`, so there is an indirection through the pointer stored in the `Ptr` to get at the underlying characters that make up the `Str`. The interesting operations are the ones that change the `Str`, such as the input operator, the compound concatenation operator, and the nonconst version of the subscript operator.

For example, look at the implementation of `Str::operator+=`. It wants to append data to the underlying `vector`, so it calls `data.make_unique()`. Once it has done so, the `Str` object has its own copy of the underlying data, which it can modify freely.

14.4.1 *Copying types that we can't control*

Unfortunately, the definition of make_unique has a serious problem:

```
template<class T>
void Ptr<T>::make_unique()
{
    if (*refptr != 1) {
        --*refptr;
        refptr = new size_t(1);
        p = p? p->clone(): 0;              // here is the problem
    }
}
```

Look at the call to p->clone. Because we are using a Ptr< vector<char> >, this call will try to call the clone function that is a member of vector<char>. Unfortunately, no such function exists!

Yet the clone function has to be a member of the class to which we are attaching a Ptr, because only in that way can it be a virtual function. In other words, making clone a member is critically important to making it possible for Ptr to work across all members of an inheritance hierarchy; yet doing so is impossible, because we can't change the definition of the Vec class. That class is designed to implement a subset of the interface to the standard vector class. If we add a clone member, we'll no longer have a subset because we'll have added a member that vector does not have. What can we do?

Solutions to tough problems such as this one often involve what we jokingly call the fundamental theorem of software engineering: *All problems can be solved by introducing an extra level of indirection.* The problem is that we are trying to call a member function that does not exist, and we have no way to cause the member function to exist. The solution, then, is not to call the member function directly but to define an intermediary global function that we can both call and create. We will still call this new function clone

```
template<class T> T* clone(const T* tp)
{
    return tp->clone();
}
```

and change our make_unique member to call it

```
template<class T>
void Ptr<T>::make_unique()
{
    if (*refptr != 1) {
        --*refptr;
        refptr = new size_t(1);
        p = p? clone(p): 0;  // call the global (not member) version of clone
    }
}
```

It should be clear that introducing this intermediary function does not change the behavior of make_unique. It still calls clone, which still calls the clone member of the object that is being copied. However, make_unique now works through a level of indirection:

It calls the nonmember `clone` function, which in turn calls the `clone` member for the object to which p points. For classes such as `Student_info` that define `clone`, this indirection buys us nothing. But for classes such as `Str` that hold `Ptr`s to types that do not provide a `clone` function, the indirection is exactly what we need to make the whole thing work. For these latter types, we can define yet another intermediary function:

```
// the key to making Ptr< Vec<char> > work
template<>
Vec<char>* clone(const Vec<char>* vp)
{
    return new Vec<char>(*vp);
}
```

The use of `template<>` at the beginning of this function indicates that the function is a **template specialization**. Such specializations define a particular version of a template function for the specific argument type. By defining this specialization, we are saying that `clone` behaves differently when we give it a pointer to a `Vec<char>` than it behaves when we give it any other pointer type. When we pass `clone` a `Vec<char>*` argument, the compiler will use this specialized version of `clone`. When we pass other types of pointers, it will instantiate the general template form of `clone`, which calls the member `clone` for the pointer that it was passed. Our specialized version uses the `Vec<char>` copy constructor to construct a new `Vec<char>` from the one that we gave it. It is true that this specialization of `clone` does not offer virtual behavior, but we do not need it to do so because there are no classes derived from `Vec`.

What we have done, then, is to moderate our reliance on the `clone` member by recognizing that the member might not exist. By introducing the extra indirection, we have made it possible to specialize the `clone` template to do whatever is appropriate to copy an object of a particular class, be it to use a `clone` member, to call a copy constructor, or something else entirely. In the absence of a specialization, the `Ptr` class will use the `clone` member, but it will do so only if there is a call to `make_unique`. In other words

- If you use `Ptr<T>` but you don't use `Ptr<T>::make_unique`, then it doesn't matter whether `T::clone` is defined.
- If you use `Ptr<T>::make_unique`, and `T::clone` is defined, `make_unique` will use `T::clone`.
- If you use `Ptr<T>::make_unique`, and you don't want to use `T::clone` (perhaps because it doesn't exist), you can specialize `clone<T>` to do whatever you want.

The extra indirection has made it possible to control the behavior of `Ptr` in great detail. All that remains is the hard part—deciding what you wanted to do in the first place.

14.4.2 When is a copy necessary?

One last part of this example is worth reviewing in detail. Look back at the definitions of the two versions of `operator[]`. One of them calls `data.make_unique`; the other doesn't. Why the difference?

The difference relates to whether the function is a `const` member. The second version of `operator[]` is a `const` member function, which means that it promises not to change the contents of the object. It keeps this promise by returning a `const char&` to its caller. Therefore, there is no harm in sharing its underlying `Vec<char>` object with other `Str` objects. After all, the user can't use the value obtained to change the value of the `Str`.

In contrast, the first version of `operator[]` returns a `char&`, which means that a user could use this return value to change the contents of the `Str`. If the user does so, we want to limit the change to this `Str` and not propagate the change to any other `Str`s that might happen to share the underlying `Vec`. We defend against the possibility of changing the value of any other `Str` objects by calling `make_unique` on the `Ptr` before returning a reference to a character of the `Vec`.

14.5 Details

Template specializations look like the template definitions that they are specializing, but they omit one or more of the type parameters, replacing them with specific types instead. The myriad uses of template specializations are beyond the scope of this book, but you should know that they exist, and that they are useful for making decisions about types during compilation.

Exercises

14-0.   Compile, execute, and test the programs in this chapter.

14-1.   Implement the comparison operation that operates on `Ptr<Core>`.

14-2.   Implement and test the student grading program using `Ptr<Core>` objects.

14-3.   Implement the `Student_info` class to use the final version of `Ptr`, and use that version to implement the grading program from §13.5/247.

14-4.   Reimplement the `Str` class to use the final version of `Ptr`.

14-5.   Test the reimplemented `Str` class by recompiling and rerunning programs that use `Str`, such as the version of `split` and the picture operations that use a `Vec<Str>`.

14-6.   The `Ptr` class really solves two problems: maintaining reference counts, and allocating and deallocating objects. Define a class that does reference counting and nothing else; then use that class to reimplement the `Ptr` class.

15

Revisiting character pictures

Inheritance is most useful in modeling large, complex systems, which are well beyond the scope of any introductory book. One of the reasons that we are so fond of the character-picture example that we introduced in §5.8/91 is that such pictures lend themselves to an object-oriented solution, yet we can implement them in only a few hundred lines of code. We have used this example for many years, refining our code and simplifying the presentation. In reviewing the example for this book, we were able to remove nearly half the code by using the standard library and our generic handle class from Chapter 14.

In §5.8/91, we wrote several functions that represented a character picture as a `vector<string>`, a strategy that entailed copying characters whenever we constructed a new picture. Copying all those characters wastes time and space. For example, if we were to concatenate two copies of a picture, we would then store three copies of each character: one for the original, and one for each side of the newly concatenated picture.

Even more important, the solution in §5.8/91 discards all structural information about the pictures. We have no idea how a given picture was formed. It might have been the initial input from our user, or it might have been created by applying one or more operations to simpler pictures. Some potentially useful operations require preserving a picture's structure. For example, if we want to be able to change the frame characters in a picture, we can do so only if we know which components of a picture were framed and which ones were not. We cannot look only for instances of the frame characters, because these characters might, coincidentally, have been part of an initial input picture.

As we'll see in this chapter, by using inheritance and our generic handle class, we will be able to preserve the structural information inherent in a picture, while at the same time reducing the space consumption of our system dramatically.

15.1 Design

We are trying to solve two distinct problems. One is a design problem—we'd like to keep structural information about how a picture was created. The other is an implementation problem—we want to store fewer copies of the same data. Both problems result from our decision to store a picture as a `vector<string>`, so we must revisit that decision.

We can solve the implementation problem by managing our data with the Ptr class that we developed in Chapter 14. That class will let us store the actual character data in a single object, and then arrange for multiple pictures to share that same object. For example, if we frame a given picture, we will no longer have to copy the characters of the picture that we're framing. Instead, class Ptr will manage a reference count associated with the data, which will indicate how many other pictures are using those data.

The design problem is harder to solve. Each picture that we create has a structure, which we want to retain. We form a picture either from an initial collection of characters, or through one of three operations: frame, to produce a framed picture; and hcat or vcat, to create pictures that are concatenated horizontally or vertically.

In other words, we have four similar kinds of pictures. Despite their similarity, we create them differently, and we would like to keep track of the differences.

15.1.1 Using inheritance to model the structure

Our problem is a perfect match for inheritance: We have various kinds of data structures that are similar to one another, but that differ in ways that we sometimes want to take into account. Each of our data structures is a kind of picture, which implies that inheritance is a sensible way to represent these data structures. We can define a common base class that models the common properties of every kind of picture, and then derive from that base class a separate class for each specific kind of picture that we want to support.

We'll call the derived classes String_Pic, for pictures created from strings that our user gives us; Frame_Pic, for a picture created by framing another picture; and HCat_Pic and VCat_Pic, for pictures that are the result of concatenating two other pictures horizontally or vertically respectively. By relating these classes through inheritance, we can use virtual functions to write code that doesn't always need to know the precise kind of picture on which it is operating. That way, our users can still use any of our operations without knowing which kind of picture is being manipulated. We will derive each of these classes from a common base class, which we shall call Pic_base, resulting in the following inheritance hierarchy:

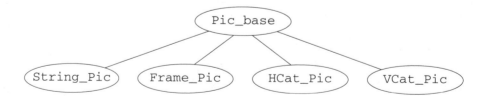

The next question to resolve is whether to make the inheritance hierarchy visible to our users. There seems to be little reason to do so. None of our operations deals with specific kinds of pictures; instead, they all deal with the abstract notion of a picture. So, there is no need to expose the hierarchy. Moreover, because we intend to use a reference-counting strategy, our users will find it more convenient if we hide the inheritance and associated reference counting.

Instead of making our users deal directly with `Pic_base` and its associated derived classes, we'll define a picture-specific interface class. Our users will access that class, freeing them from having to be aware of any of our implementation's details. In particular, using an interface class will hide the inheritance hierarchy, along with the fact that our class relies on `Ptr`. Apparently, then we'll need to define six classes: the interface class, the base class for our inheritance hierarchy, and the four derived classes. We'll call the interface class `Picture`. Internally, `Picture` will use a `Ptr` to manage its data.

What kind of `Ptr`? That is, what type of objects will the `Ptr` manage? It will manage our implementation class, `Pic_base`. Thus, class `Picture` will have a single data member, which will have type `Ptr<Pic_base>`. But the objects that will be bound to the `Ptr` will always be objects of one of the derived types. Thus, when we create (and destroy) `Pic_base` objects we will do so through a `Pic_base` pointer but the objects will be of derived type. As we saw in §13.3.2/242 this design means that we'll need to give `Pic_base` a virtual destructor. We'll make the destructor `public`, so that `Ptr` can use it.

We said that we intend to conceal our use of `Pic_base` and its related hierarchy, so that users will manipulate these objects only indirectly through class `Picture`, and will not access any of these classes directly. It turns out that the most straightforward way to hide these classes is to rely on the normal protection mechanisms. By giving these classes an empty `public` interface, we can let the compiler enforce our decision that all interactions with our pictures will be through class `Picture`.

To make these decisions concrete, let's write code that captures what we know so far:

```
// private classes for use in the implementation only
class Pic_base { };

class String_Pic: public Pic_base { };
class Frame_Pic: public Pic_base { };
class VCat_Pic: public Pic_base { };
class HCat_Pic: public Pic_base { };

// public interface class and operations
class Picture {
public:
    Picture(const std::vector<std::string>& =
        std::vector<std::string>());
private:
    Ptr<Pic_base> p;
};
```

Each `Picture` object will hold a (private) `Ptr<Pic_base>` object. Class `Pic_base` is the common base class for the four classes that will represent our four kinds of pictures. The `Ptr` class will manage the reference counts to allow us to share the underlying `Pic_base` objects. We will implement each operation on a `Picture` by forwarding that operation through the `Ptr` to the underlying derived-class object. We haven't thought yet about what these operations will be, so for now we've left the bodies of `Pic_base` and its derived classes empty.

So far, the `Picture` class is pretty simple: The only operation is to create a `Picture` from a `vector` of `string`s. We use a default argument (§7.3/127) to make that `vector` optional. If a user constructs a `Picture` with no argument, then the compiler will supply `vector<string>()` as an argument automatically, which yields a `vector<string>` with no elements. Therefore, the effect of the default argument is to allow us to use a definition such as

```
Picture p;              // an empty Picture
```

to create a `Picture` with no rows.

Next, we need to think about how to represent our other `Picture` operations. We know that we want to implement `frame`, `hcat`, and `vcat`. What we must decide is how to do so, and whether these operations should be members of class `Picture`. The operations do not change the state of the `Picture` on which they operate, so there is no strong reason to make them members. Moreover, there is a strong reason not to do so: As we saw in §12.3.5/220, by making them nonmembers we can allow conversions.

For example, because the `Picture` constructor that we have already written is not `explicit`, users will be able to write

```
vector<string> vs;
Picture p = vs;
```

and the implementation will convert `vs` into a `Picture` for us. If we wish to allow this behavior—and we do—then we should also allow users to write expressions such as `frame(vs)`. If `frame` were a member, then users would not be able to write the seemingly equivalent `vs.frame()`. Remember that conversions are not applied to the left operand of the `.` operator, so this call would be interpreted as invoking the (nonexistent) `frame` member of `vs`.

Moreover, we believe that our users will find it convenient to use an expression syntax to build up complicated pictures. We consider it clearer to write,

```
hcat(frame(p), p)
```

than to write

```
p.frame().hcat(p)
```

because the first example reflects the symmetry of `hcat`'s arguments and the second example conceals it.

In addition to the functions that let us build `Pictures`, we will want to define an output operator that can write the contents of a `Picture`. These decisions let us flesh out the rest of our interface design:

```
Picture frame(const Picture&);
Picture hcat(const Picture&, const Picture&);
Picture vcat(const Picture&, const Picture&);
std::ostream& operator<<(std::ostream&, const Picture&);
```

15.1.2 The `Pic_base` class

The next step in our design is to fill in the details of the `Pic_base` hierarchy. If we look back at our original implementation, we'll see that we used the `size` function from `vector<string>` to determine how many `strings` were in a given picture, and we wrote a separate `width` function (§5.8/91), which proved useful in padding the output. When we think about how we will display a picture, we see that we are likely to need to be able to perform these same operations on our classes that are derived from `Pic_base`. These operations will need to be `virtual`, so that we can ask any kind of `Pic_base` how many rows it has and how wide its widest row is. Furthermore, because our users will use the output operator to write the contents of a particular `Pic_base`, we can infer that we'll need another `virtual` function to display a given `Pic_base` on a given `ostream`.

The only one of these operations that needs significant insight is `display`. It is easy to decide that one of the parameters to `display` should be the stream on which to write its output, but figuring out what other parameters `display` might take requires that we think carefully about how it will operate. When we write a `Picture`, that `Picture` will comprise one or more component parts, each of which is an object of a class derived from `Pic_base`. If we think about writing a horizontally concatenated picture, it will be apparent that each row of the output from a single `Picture` might involve writing the corresponding row for more than one subpicture. In particular, we cannot write the entire contents of one subpicture, and then the entire contents of the other. Instead, we have to write the contents of each subpicture a row at a time, interleaved with the corresponding rows of the other subpictures. We can conclude, therefore, that the `display` function needs a parameter that says which row to write.

Similarly, when we `display` the left-hand part of a horizontally concatenated picture, we'll need to tell the corresponding subpicture to pad each row to use the full `width()` of itself on each line. We'll also need to tell a picture that is contained within a `Frame_Pic` to pad to its widest extent. On the other hand, if we're displaying a `Picture` that contains only a `String_Pic`, or a vertically concatenated `Picture` composed only of `String_Pics`, then padding the output results only in writing a lot of unneeded trailing blanks. So, as an optimization, we'll pass `display` a third argument that indicates whether to pad the output.

These observations lead us to decide that the `display` function will take three arguments: the stream on which to generate the output, the number of the row to write, and a `bool` that will indicate whether to pad the picture to its full width. With these decisions, we can fill in the details of the `Pic_base` family of classes:

```
class Pic_base {
    // no public interface (except for the destructor)
    typedef std::vector<std::string>::size_type ht_sz;
    typedef std::string::size_type wd_sz;

    virtual wd_sz width() const = 0;
    virtual ht_sz height() const = 0;
    virtual void display(std::ostream&, ht_sz, bool) const = 0;
public:
    virtual ~Pic_base() { }
};
```

We start by defining shorthand names for the `size_types` that we'll need in our implementation. Thinking ahead, we can see that the underlying data will still be a `vector<string>`, so the `size_type` member of `vector<string>` will be the right type to represent the height of a picture, and the one from `string` will be the one we need for the width. We'll abbreviate these types as `ht_sz` and `wd_sz` respectively.

The other task is to define our `virtual` functions for the base class, which you'll notice take a new form: In each case we say `= 0` where the body would appear. This syntax indicates our intention that there be no other definition of this `virtual` function. Why did we define these functions this way?

To answer this question, let's begin by thinking about what the definitions would look like if we tried to write them. In our design, `Pic_base` exists only to act as the common base class for our concrete picture classes. We will create objects of these concrete types as a result of executing one of the `Picture` operations, or in response to a user's creating a `Picture` from a `vector<string>`. None of these operations directly creates or manipulates `Pic_base` objects. If there are never any `Pic_base` objects, then what would it mean to take the `height` or `width` of a `Pic_base` object (as opposed to doing so for an object of a type derived from `Pic_base`)? These operations are needed only for the derived classes, in which there always will be a concrete picture. For a `Pic_base` itself, there is nothing of which to take the `height` or `width`.

Instead of forcing us to concoct an arbitrary definition for these operations, the C++ language lets us say that there will be no definition for a given `virtual` function. As a side effect of declining to implement the `virtual` function, we also promise that there will never be objects of the associated type. There may still be objects of types derived from this type, but there are no objects of its exact type.

The way that we specify that we don't intend to implement a `virtual` function is to say `= 0`, as we did on `height`, `width`, and `display`. Doing so makes it a ***pure virtual function***. By giving a class even a single pure `virtual` function, we are also implicitly specifying that there will never be objects of that class. Such classes are called ***abstract base classes***, because they exist only to capture an abstract interface for an inheritance hierarchy. They are purely abstract: There are no objects of the base class itself. Once we give a class any pure `virtual`s, the compiler will enforce our design by preventing us from creating any objects of an abstract class.

15.1.3 The derived classes

As with `virtual` itself, the fact that a function is a pure `virtual` is inherited. If a derived class defines all of its inherited pure `virtual` functions, it becomes a concrete class, and we can create objects of that class. However, if the derived class fails to define even a single pure `virtual` function that it inherits, then the abstract nature is also inherited. In this case the derived class is itself abstract, and we will not be able to create objects of the derived class. Because each of our derived classes is intended to model a concrete class, we know that we have to redefine all of the `virtual`s in each of the derived classes.

The only other things we have to think about right now are what data each of our derived classes will contain, and the associated question of how we will construct objects of each type. We designed these classes to model the structure of how a picture was formed. The type of a picture object tells us how it was created: A `String_Pic` is created from character data that a user supplied to us; a Frame_Pic results from running frame on another Picture; and so on. In addition to knowing how an object was created, we also need to store the object(s) from which it was created. For a String_Pic, we'll need to remember the characters that the user gave us, which we can do in a vector<string>. We create a Frame_Pic by framing another Picture, so we'll need to store the Picture that was framed. Similarly, we create HCat_Pics and VCat_Pics by combining two other Pictures. These classes will store the Pictures used in creating the resultant new object.

Before settling on a design that stores Pictures in the Pic_base derived classes, we should think through the implications of this design a bit more deeply. Class Picture is an interface class intended for use by our users. As such, it captures the interface to our problem domain but not the implementation. Specifically, it does not have height, width, or display operations. If we think a bit about how these functions might be implemented, we'll see that we'll need access to the corresponding operations on the Picture(s) stored in each of the derived types. For example, to calculate height of a VCat_Pic, we need to add the heights of the two Pictures from which it was formed. Similarly, we'll obtain the width by finding the maximum of the widths of the two component Pictures.

An implication of storing a Picture in each of the derived classes is that we'll have to give class Picture functions that duplicate the Pic_base operations. Doing so obscures our initial design intent, which was that class Picture should be concerned with interface not implementation. We can maintain our design by realizing that what we need in the derived classes is not an interface object but an implementation object. This realization implies that instead of storing a Picture, we should store a Ptr<Pic_base>. This design keeps a clean separation between interface and implementation, while still maintaining our intention to reference count our implementation objects to avoid unnecessary data duplication.

Although our design is clean, enough indirection is involved that a picture may help:

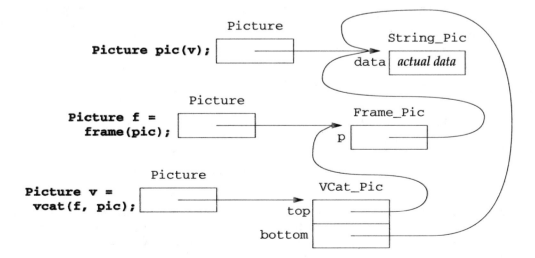

Here we assume that we are generating three `Pictures`. The first `Picture` represents a
`String_Pic` object that holds the data that we got from the user. The second one represents a `Frame_Pic` object that we constructed by calling `frame` on the initial `Picture`.
Finally, we construct a `Picture` that represents the output of `vcat` run on the two previous `Pictures`. Each `Picture` has a single data member, which is a `Ptr<Pic_base>`.
That `Ptr` points to an object of the appropriate `Pic_base` derived type. Each such object,
in turn, contains either the `vector` that holds a copy of the data we got from the user, or
one or two `Ptrs` that point to the `Pic_base` objects used to create the `Picture`. Not
shown in this diagram are the reference counts associated with the `Ptr` objects, because
we assume that the `Ptr` class is doing its job, and we can ignore the details of that job.

What's different from what we did in Chapter 5 is that only `String_Pic` contains any
characters. The others hold one or two `Ptrs`. Therefore, we won't copy any characters
when we create `f` or `v`. Instead, the `Ptr` will be yet another reference to the `Ptrs` in the
`Pictures` that are used in creating a new `Picture`, and the `Ptr` class will take care of
the reference counting for us. So, when we call `frame(pic)`, the effect is to create a new
`Frame_Pic` object, and to point its `Ptr` at the same `String_Pic` that is stored in `pic`.
Similarly, the `VCat_Pic` contains two `Ptrs` pointing to the `Frame_Pic` and the
`String_Pic` respectively. We will not destroy any of these `Pic_base` objects; doing so
is the responsibility of the `Ptr` class. It will arrange to destroy each `Pic_base` object
when the last `Ptr` that refers to each object has gone away.

At this point, we should capture these design decisions in code. We know what data
each object will contain, and we know what our operations will be:

```
class Pic_base {
    // no public interface (except for the destructor)
    typedef std::vector<std::string>::size_type ht_sz;
    typedef std::string::size_type wd_sz;

    // this class is an abstract base class
    virtual wd_sz width() const = 0;
    virtual ht_sz height() const = 0;
    virtual void display(std::ostream&, ht_sz, bool) const = 0;

public:
    virtual ~Pic_base() { }
};

class Frame_Pic: public Pic_base {
    // no public interface
    Ptr<Pic_base> p;
    Frame_Pic(const Ptr<Pic_base>& pic): p(pic) { }

    wd_sz width() const;
    ht_sz height() const;
    void display(std::ostream&, ht_sz, bool) const;
};
```

Here we say that `Frame_Pic` inherits from `Pic_base`, and declare our intention to
define class-specific versions of each of the three `virtuals` from that base class. Thus,
`Frame_Pic` will not be an abstract class, and we will be able to create `Frame_pic` objects.

It is worth noting that we have declared these virtuals in the private section of the class. Doing so lets the compiler enforce our design decision that only class Picture and operations on Pictures can access the Pic_base hierarchy. Of course, because these virtuals are private, we may need to revisit the class definition to include friend declarations for class Picture, or the associated operations, as needed.

The Frame_Pic constructor needs only to copy the Ptr from the object that is being framed, which it does in the constructor initializer. The constructor body is empty, because there is no other work to do.

Continuing with our other derived classes, the concatenation classes will operate similarly to Frame_Pic: Each class will need to remember its two constituent pictures. How they were concatenated, vertically or horizontally, will be implicit in the type itself:

```
class VCat_Pic: public Pic_base {
    Ptr<Pic_base> top, bottom;
    VCat_Pic(const Ptr<Pic_base>& t, const Ptr<Pic_base>& b):
        top(t), bottom(b) { }

    wd_sz width() const;
    ht_sz height() const;
    void display(std::ostream&, ht_sz, bool) const;
};

class HCat_Pic: public Pic_base {
    Ptr<Pic_base> left, right;
    HCat_Pic(const Ptr<Pic_base>& l, const Ptr<Pic_base>& r):
        left(l), right(r) { }

    wd_sz width() const;
    ht_sz height() const;
    void display(std::ostream&, ht_sz, bool) const;
};
```

The String_Pic class differs slightly from the others in that it stores a copy of the vector<string> that contains the picture's data:

```
class String_Pic: public Pic_base {
    std::vector<std::string> data;
    String_Pic(const std::vector<std::string>& v): data(v) { }

    wd_sz width() const;
    ht_sz height() const;
    void display(std::ostream&, ht_sz, bool) const;
};
```

We still copy the underlying characters from our user's vector parameter v into our own member, which is called data. This is the only place in our entire program that copies characters. Everywhere else, we copy only Ptr<Pic_base> objects, which copies pointers and manipulates reference counts.

15.1.4 Copy control

Perhaps the most interesting aspect of our design is what isn't here. There are no copy constructors, assignment operators, or destructors. Why?

The reason is that the synthesized defaults work. The `vector` class takes care of managing the space for the initial copy of the characters that our user gives us as part of creating a new `Picture`. If we copy or assign two `Pictures` that refer to `String_Pics`, or we destroy a `Picture`, then the `Ptr` operations will do the right thing to manage the `Picture` objects, and arrange to delete the underlying `String_Pic` at the right time. More generally, the `Ptr` class takes care of copying, assigning, and destroying the `Ptr` members in the other `Pic_base` classes—and in class `Picture` itself.

15.2 Implementation

At this point we have a pretty good design of both our interface and the implementation. The `Picture` class and the associated operations on `Pictures` will manage the user interface. The `Picture` constructor and the operations will create objects of one of the types derived from `Pic_base`. We'll use `Ptr<Pic_base>` to manage the underlying space, thus avoiding extraneous copies of the data. It is now time to implement the interface operations and each of the derived classes.

15.2.1 Implementing the user interface

We'll start by implementing the interface class and operations. What we know so far is

```
class Picture {
public:
    Picture(const std::vector<std::string>& =
        std::vector<std::string>());
private:
    Ptr<Pic_base> p;
};

Picture frame(const Picture&);
Picture hcat(const Picture&, const Picture&);
Picture vcat(const Picture&, const Picture&);
std::ostream& operator<<(std::ostream&, const Picture&);
```

Let's think first about the operations that create new `Pictures`. Each of these operations creates an object of an appropriate class derived from `Pic_base`. That object will copy the `Ptr` from the `Picture(s)` on which the operation executes. We will bind a `Picture` to this newly created `Pic_base` object, and return that `Picture`. For example, if p is a `Picture`, then `frame(p)` should create a new `Frame_Pic` that is attached to the `Pic_base` from p. It will then generate a new `Picture` that is attached to the new `Frame_pic`. Let's start here:

```
Picture frame(const Picture& pic)
{
    Pic_base* ret = new Frame_Pic(pic.p);
    // what do we return?
}
```

We start by defining a local pointer to `Pic_base`, which we initialize by creating a new `Frame_Pic` that copies the `Ptr` object inside `pic`. There are now two problems. The easy one is that the `Frame_Pic` constructor is `private`. As we saw in §15.1.3/276, each of the `Pic_base` classes is hidden. We don't want users to know about these classes, so we defined only `private` operations to let the compiler enforce this design decision. We can solve this problem by making the `frame` operation a `friend` of class `Frame_Pic`.

The other problem is more subtle: We have created a new object of type `Frame_pic`, but what we need is an object of type `Picture`. More generally, we can imagine that `hcat`, `vcat`, and other functions that we might subsequently write will generate objects of other types derived from `Pic_base`, and that they will do so in contexts in which we really want objects of type `Picture`. The point is that `frame` and related operations return `Pictures`, not `Pic_bases`. Fortunately, we know from §12.2/213 that we can convert one type to another if we provide an appropriate constructor. In this case, the appropriate constructor is one that constructs a `Picture` from a `Pic_base*`:

```
class Picture {
    Ptr<Pic_base> p;
    Picture(Pic_base* ptr): p(ptr) { }
    // as before
};
```

Our constructor initializes `p` with the pointer to `Pic_base` that we were given. Remember that class `Ptr` has a constructor that takes a `T*`, which in this case is a `Pic_base*`. The initializer `p(ptr)` invokes this `Ptr::Ptr(T*)` constructor, passing it `ptr`. Once we have this `Picture` constructor, we can complete the `frame` operation:

```
Picture frame(const Picture& pic)
{
    return new Frame_Pic(pic.p);
}
```

We've eliminated the local `Pic_base` object because we don't need it. Instead, we create a new `Frame_Pic` object, the address of which is automatically converted to a `Picture`, which we `return` from the function. Completely understanding this little function requires a good grasp of the subtleties involved when using automatic conversions and copy constructors. The single statement in this function has the same effect as

```
// create the new Frame_Pic
Pic_base* temp1 = new Frame_Pic(pic.p);

// construct a Picture from a Pic_base*
Picture temp2(temp1);

// return the Picture, which will invoke the Picture copy constructor
return temp2;
```

Like `frame`, the concatenation functions rely on our new `Picture` constructor:

```
Picture hcat(const Picture& l, const Picture& r)
{
    return new HCat_Pic(l.p, r.p);
}

Picture vcat(const Picture& t, const Picture& b)
{
    return new VCat_Pic(t.p, b.p);
}
```

In each case, we construct an object of the appropriate type, bind a `Ptr<Pic_base>` to it, construct a `Picture` from the `Ptr<Pic_base>`, and return a copy of that `Picture`. Of course, for these functions to compile, we'll need to add the appropriate `friend` declarations to the `HCat_Pic` and `VCat_Pic` classes.

To construct a `Picture` from a `vector<string>`, we adopt the same strategy that we used for the other kinds of pictures:

```
Picture::Picture(const vector<string>& v): p(new String_Pic(v)) { }
```

Again, we create a new `String_Pic` object, but this time we use it directly to initialize `p`, instead of returning it. Of course, we will have to remember to make `Picture` a friend of `String_Pic`, so that it can access the `String_Pic` constructor.

It is important to realize how this constructor differs from the `frame`, `hcat`, and `vcat` functions. Each of these other functions is defined to return a `Picture`, and in each one we use a pointer to a class derived from `Pic_base` in the `return` statement. Therefore, we implicitly used the `Picture(Pic_base*)` constructor to create a `Picture` to return. In the `Picture` constructor that we've just written, we are still creating a pointer to a class derived from `Pic_base`—in this case, class `String_pic`—but now we're using this pointer to initialize member `p`, which has type `Ptr<Pic_base>`. Doing so uses the `Ptr(T*)` constructor in class `Pic_base`, not the `Picture(Pic_base*)` constructor, because we're constructing a `Ptr<Pic_base>`, not a `Picture`.

To complete the implementation of our interface functions, we must define the output operator. This operation is also straightforward: We need to iterate through the underlying `Pic_base`, and call `display` to write each line of the output:

```
ostream& operator<<(ostream& os, const Picture& picture)
{
    const Pic_base::ht_sz ht = picture.p->height();
    for (Pic_base::ht_sz i = 0; i != ht; ++i) {
        picture.p->display(os, i, false);
        os << endl;
    }
    return os;
};
```

We initialize `ht` by calling the (`virtual`) height function for the underlying `Pic_base`, so that we do not have to recompute the height each time through the loop. Remember that `p` is actually a `Ptr<Pic_base>`, and that `Ptr` has overloaded `->` to implement references through the `Ptr` as references through the pointer that the `Ptr` contains. We iterate ht times through the underlying `Pic_base`, each time calling the (`virtual`) display function, asking it to write the current row. The third argument (`false`) indicates that `display` need not pad the output. If we need padding to write one of the interior `Pictures`, the inner `display` functions will indicate that padding is needed. At this stage, we can't yet tell if padding is necessary. We write `endl` to end each line of output, and when we're done, we return `os`.

As with the other operations that we have implemented, we will have to remember to add a `friend` declaration to class `Pic_base` to allow `operator<<` to access its `display` and `height` members.

15.2.2   The `String_Pic` class

Having completed the interface class and operations, we can turn our attention to the derived classes. We'll start with `String_Pic`:

```
class String_Pic: public Pic_base {
    friend class Picture;
    std::vector<std::string> data;
    String_Pic(const std::vector<std::string>& v): data(v) { }

    ht_sz height() const { return data.size(); }
    wd_sz width() const;
    void display(std::ostream&, ht_sz, bool) const;
};
```

We have implemented the `height` function, but otherwise the `String_Pic` class is unchanged from the one that we described in §15.1.3/277. The `height` function is trivial: It forwards the request to the `size` member of `vector`.

To determine the `width` of a `String_Pic`, we need to look at each element in `data` to see which is the longest:

```
Pic_base::wd_sz String_Pic::width() const
{
    Pic_base::wd_sz n = 0;
    for (Pic_base::ht_sz i = 0; i != data.size(); ++i)
        n = std::max(n, data[i].size());
    return n;
}
```

Except for the type names, this function looks like the original `width` function from §5.8/91. Because a `String_Pic` holds a `vector<string>`, we should not be surprised at this similarity.

The `display` function is more complicated. It has to iterate through the underlying `vector`, writing the `string` associated with the requested row number.

What about padding? Note that this function might be called directly from the output operator, as would happen if the `Picture` we were writing pointed to a `String_Pic`— or it might be called indirectly, as part of writing a larger `Picture` of which this `String_Pic` is a part. In the latter case, the `display` function may be asked to pad the output to make each row fill the same size in the overall output. The amount of padding will vary for each `string`, and will be whatever is needed to consume as many spaces in the output as the number needed for the longest string. In other words, we'll need to pad from the length of this string to the width() of this String_Pic. A bit of fore-thought should convince us that we're likely to need to pad other pictures too. For now, we'll assume that we have a pad function that takes an output stream and the start and (one past) the end positions to pad with blanks. We'll implement this function shortly.

Another complexity arises from the fact that the row number passed to display may exceed the height of this String_Pic. One way in which this situation could happen is if the String_Pic is part of a horizontally concatenated Picture in which one side is shorter than the other. Our Pictures line up at the top border, but they may be of different heights. Thus, we will need to check whether the row we're asked to write is in range. With this analysis complete, we can now write the code:

```
void String_Pic::display(ostream& os, ht_sz row, bool do_pad) const
{
    wd_sz start = 0;

    // write the row if we're still in range
    if (row < height()) {
        os << data[row];
        start = data[row].size();
    }

    // pad the output if necessary
    if (do_pad)
        pad(os, start, width());
}
```

We first check whether the row we were asked to write is in range—that is, whether row is less than the height() of this String_Pic. If so, then we write it and set start to indicate how many characters we wrote in the process. Regardless of whether we wrote a row, we check whether we are supposed to pad the output. If so, we pad from start to the overall width() of this String_Pic. If the row is out of range, then start is 0, so we write an entire row of blanks.

15.2.3 Padding the output

We can now think about our padding function. Because we want to access this function from each of the derived classes, we'll define the pad operation as a function member of Pic_base that is both static and protected:

```
class Pic_base {
    // as before
protected:
    static void pad(std::ostream& os, wd_sz beg, wd_sz end) {
        while (beg != end) {
            os << " ";
            ++beg;
        }
    }
};
```

This function takes an `ostream` on which to write blanks, and two values that control how many blanks to write. When a display function needs to call `pad`, it will pass the current column number and one past the last column number that needs to be filled in by the current `display` operation. The `pad` function will fill this range with blanks.

Note the use of the `static` keyword on the declaration of `pad`. As we saw in §13.4/244, this use of `static` indicates that `pad` is a static member function. Such functions differ from an ordinary member function in that they are not associated with an object of the class type.

It may also be surprising that we can define a member function for an abstract base class. After all, if there can be no objects of the base class, why should there be member functions? However, remember that each derived object contains a base-class part. Each derived class also inherits any member functions defined in the base. Thus, a base-class function will execute on the base-class portion of a derived object. In this particular case, the function that we are defining is a `static` member, so the question of access to members of the base is moot. But it is important to realize that abstract classes may define data members, and (ordinary) member functions, as well as `static` ones. These functions will access the base-class objects that are part of derived objects.

Static members (both functions and static data members, which we can also define) are useful in that they let us minimize the names that are defined globally. Our `pad` function is a good example. We can imagine many abstractions that have the notion of padding. In this book we talked about padding in the context of writing a formatted report of student grades, as well as in the context of writing `Pictures`. If the `Picture` class were to define `pad` as a global function, then we would not also be able to define a `pad` function for `Student_info`, or vice versa. By making `pad` a `static` member, we allow for the fact that other abstractions in our program might have the notion of padding. As long as each class defines what `pad` means only in the context of the class, these mutually independent notions of padding can coexist within our program.

15.2.4 The `VCat_Pic` class

Implementing the concatenation classes is not hard. We'll start with `VCat_Pic`:

```
class VCat_Pic: public Pic_base
{
    friend Picture vcat(const Picture&, const Picture&);
    Ptr<Pic_base> top, bottom;
    VCat_Pic(const Ptr<Pic_base>& t, const Ptr<Pic_base>& b):
        top(t), bottom(b) { }

    wd_sz width() const
        { return std::max(top->width(), bottom->width()); }
    ht_sz height() const
        { return top->height() + bottom->height(); }
    void display(std::ostream&, ht_sz, bool) const;
};
```

We added the appropriate `friend` declaration for the `vcat` operation, and implemented the `height` and `width` functions inline. If a picture is concatenated vertically, its `height` is the sum of its two components' heights, and the `width` is the greater of the two components' widths.

The `display` function is not much harder:

```
void VCat_Pic::display(ostream& os, ht_sz row, bool do_pad) const
{
    wd_sz w = 0;
    if (row < top->height()) {
        // we are in the top subpicture
        top->display(os, row, do_pad);
        w = top->width();
    } else if (row < height()) {
        // we are in the bottom subpicture
        bottom->display(os, row - top->height(), do_pad);
        w = bottom->width();
    }
    if (do_pad)
        pad(os, w, width());
}
```

First, we define a variable `w`, which will contain the width of the current row, in case we need it for padding. Next, we check whether we're in the `top` component, by testing `row` against the `height()` of the `top` picture. If we're in that range, then we invoke `display` to write the `top` component, passing the `bool` that we were given to indicate whether to pad the output. Remember, `display` is `virtual`, so this call will invoke whatever the appropriate `display` function is for the kind of `Pic_base` to which `top` actually refers. Once we've written the given `row`, we remember its width in `w`.

If we're not in `top`, we might be in `bottom`. If we get to this `else` test, then we know that `row` is greater than `top->height()`, so we now check whether `row` is within the overall range of this picture. If so, it must be in the `bottom` picture. As we did for `top`, we call `display` on `bottom` to write the picture, offsetting the `row` number to adjust for having already written as many rows as are in `top`. Having written the row from the `bottom` picture, we remember its width. If we're out of range, `w` remains 0.

When we're done writing the row, we check whether padding is needed. If so, we `pad` from the width that we remembered in `w` to the full width of our own picture.

15.2.5 The HCat_Pic class

Not surprisingly, the `HCat_Pic` class looks a lot like `VCat_Pic`:

```
class HCat_Pic: public Pic_base {
    friend Picture hcat(const Picture&, const Picture&);
    Ptr<Pic_base> left, right;
    HCat_Pic(const Ptr<Pic_base>& l, const Ptr<Pic_base>& r):
        left(l), right(r) { }

    wd_sz width() const { return left->width() + right->width(); }
    ht_sz height() const
        { return std::max(left->height(), right->height()); }
    void display(std::ostream&, ht_sz, bool) const;
};
```

Because we're concatenating two pictures side by side, this time the width is the sum of the components' widths, and the height is the greater of the two heights. Here, the display function is simpler than the corresponding one from VCat_Pic, because we delegate managing whether the row is in range to the component pictures:

```
void HCat_Pic::display(ostream& os, ht_sz row, bool do_pad) const
{
    left->display(os, row, do_pad || row < right->height());
    right->display(os, row, do_pad);
}
```

First we write the requested row from left by calling display, asking it to write the given row. We pad this row if we were asked to pad our own output, or if we're on a row that is within the range of the right-hand picture (in which case we must pad each row of the left-hand picture to ensure that the corresponding row of the right-hand picture begins at the right place in the output line). If the row is out of range for left, then the display function executed on left will deal with that problem. Similarly, we delegate writing the requested row from right to the display function on right. This time we pass along the do_pad value that we were given, because there is no reason to force padding on the right-hand side.

15.2.6 The Frame_Pic class

The only derived class we have left to implement is Frame_Pic:

```
class Frame_Pic: public Pic_base {
    friend Picture frame(const Picture&);
    Ptr<Pic_base> p;
    Frame_Pic(const Ptr<Pic_base>& pic): p(pic) { }

    wd_sz width() const { return p->width() + 4; }
    ht_sz height() const { return p->height() + 4; }
    void display(std::ostream&, ht_sz, bool) const;
};
```

The height and width operations forward their calculations to the picture that was framed. We add 4 to these values, to account for the borders and the space that separates the border from the interior, framed picture.

The display function is tedious but not hard:

```
void Frame_Pic::display(ostream& os, ht_sz row, bool do_pad) const
{
    if (row >= height()) {

        // out of range
        if (do_pad)
            pad(os, 0, width());

    } else {
        if (row == 0 || row == height() - 1) {
```

```
                        // top or bottom row
                        os << string(width(), '*');
              } else if (row == 1 || row == height() - 2) {
                        // second from top or bottom row
                        os << "*";
                        pad(os, 1, width() - 1);
                        os << "*";
              } else {
                        // interior row
                        os << "* ";
                        p->display(os, row - 2, true);
                        os << " *";
              }
        }
}
```

First we check whether the requested row is in range; if not and we're being asked to pad, we do so, filling the entire row with blanks. If we're in range, there are three cases: We're writing the top or bottom border, we're writing the mostly blank line that separates the border from the interior picture, or we're writing a row from the interior picture.

We know that we're dealing with the top or bottom border if the row number is 0 or height() - 1. In this case, we write a row that consists entirely of asterisks to form the border. If we're one row in from the border, then we want to write an asterisk, followed by the appropriate number of blanks, followed by another asterisk. Finally, we might be in an interior row of the picture. In this case, we want to write that row of the border, which is an asterisk followed by a blank, and then the interior picture, followed by another blank and asterisk for the right-hand border. We write the interior picture by calling display, offsetting the row value to account for the border that we have already written. In the call to display, we indicate that the interior picture should pad the output so that when we write the right-hand border, it will be straight.

15.2.7 Don't forget `friends`

The only work that remains is to add the appropriate friend declarations to Picture and Pic_base. We've already noted that we need to add a friend declaration to class Picture for each of the Picture operations. After all, these operations all use the Ptr inside Picture, and need permission to access that member. What may be less obvious is the collection of friends that we need to add to class Pic_base:

```
// forward declaration, described in §15.3/288
class Picture;

class Pic_base {
        friend std::ostream& operator<<(std::ostream&, const Picture&);
        friend class Frame_Pic;
        friend class HCat_Pic;
        friend class VCat_Pic;
        friend class String_Pic;
```

```
        // no public interface (except for the destructor)
        typedef std::vector<std::string>::size_type ht_sz;
        typedef std::string::size_type wd_sz;

        // this class is an abstract base class
        virtual wd_sz width() const = 0;
        virtual ht_sz height() const = 0;
        virtual void display(std::ostream&, ht_sz, bool) const = 0;
    public:
        virtual ~Pic_base() { }

    protected:
        static void pad(std::ostream& os, wd_sz, wd_sz);
    };

    class Picture {
        friend std::ostream& operator<<(std::ostream&, const Picture&);
        friend Picture frame(const Picture&);
        friend Picture hcat(const Picture&, const Picture&);
        friend Picture vcat(const Picture&, const Picture&);

    public:
        Picture(const std::vector<std::string>& =
            std::vector<std::string>());
    private:
        Picture(Pic_base* ptr): p(ptr) { }
        Ptr<Pic_base> p;
    };

    // operations on Pictures
    Picture frame(const Picture&);
    Picture hcat(const Picture&, const Picture&);
    Picture vcat(const Picture&, const Picture&);
    std::ostream& operator<<(std::ostream&, const Picture&);
```

The first `friend` declaration in `Pic_base` should be easy to understand. The output operator invokes both the `height()` and `display()` functions, so it must be granted access to these members. What may be more surprising is the `friend` declarations for the classes that inherit from `Pic_base`. Don't they have access to the members of `Pic_base` through inheritance? Yes they do, in principle, but except for `pad`, all of the members of `Pic_base` are `private`. Why didn't we just make these other members `protected`, as we did with the `pad` function? The answer is that it wouldn't have solved the problem.

A member of a derived class (such as `Frame_pic`) can access the `protected` members of the base-class parts of objects of its own class (such as `Frame_pic`), or of other classes derived from it, but it cannot access the `protected` members of base-class objects that stand alone—that is, that are not part of a derived-class object. Therefore, member functions of class `Frame_pic`, which is derived from class `Pic_base`, can access `protected` members of the `Pic_base` parts of `Frame_pic` objects, or objects of classes derived from `Frame_pic`, but they cannot access `protected` members of stand-alone `Pic_base` objects directly.

One might think that this restriction would be irrelevant to our program. After all, class `Pic_base` is an abstract base class, so there can be no stand-alone objects of that class. However, the access rules apply to any attempt to access a member of what appears to be a stand-alone `Pic_base` object, even if at run time the object is of a derived class.

For example, consider the `height` function in class `Frame_pic`:

```
ht_sz Frame_Pic::height() const { return p->height() + 4; }
```

This function uses the expression `p->height()`, which implicitly calls the `operator->` member of class `Ptr` (§14.3/263) to obtain a pointer. This pointer has type `Pic_base*`; we dereference it to access the `height` member of the corresponding object. Because the pointer's type is `Pic_base*`, the compiler will check protection as if we were trying to access a member of a `Pic_base` object, even though the actual object will be of a type derived from `Pic_base`. Therefore, even if we made `height` a `protected` member, we would still have to include `friend` declarations to allow this access. Each of the derived classes in our hierarchy turns out to require `friend` declaration for similar reasons.

This rule may be surprising, but its logic is straightforward: If the language granted derived objects access to the `protected` members of a base-class object, then it would be trivial to subvert the protection mechanisms. If we needed access to a `protected` member of a class, we could define a new class that inherited from the class that we wanted to access. Then we could define the operation that needed access to the `protected` member as a member of that newly derived class. By doing so, we could override the original class designer's protection strategy. For this reason, `protected` access is restricted to members of the base-class part of a derived-class object, and does not allow direct access to the members of base-class objects.

15.3 Details

Abstract base classes have one or more pure `virtual` functions:

```
class Node {
    virtual Node* clone() const = 0;
};
```

says that `clone` is a pure `virtual` function, and, by implication, that `Node` is an abstract base class. It is not possible to create objects of an abstract class. A class can be made abstract through inheritance: If the class fails to redefine even a single inherited pure `virtual`, then the derived class is also abstract.

Forward declarations: The requirement to define names before using them (§0.8/6) causes trouble in writing families of classes that refer to one another. To avoid this trouble, you can declare just the name of the class by writing

```
class class-name;
```

thereby saying that *class-name* names a class, but not describing the class itself.

We used such a forward declaration for class `Picture` in §15.2.7/286. The `Picture` class contains a member of type `Ptr<Pic_base>`, and the `Pic_base` class has a `friend` declaration for `operator<<` that uses the type `const Picture&`. Therefore, these two classes refer to each other.

Such mutual type dependencies can yield programs that are impossible to implement. For example:

```
class Yang;            // forward declaration

class Yin {
     Yang y;
};

class Yang {
     Yin y;
};
```

Here, we have said that every `Yin` object contains a `Yang` object, which contains a `Yin` object, and so on. Implementing such types would require infinite memory.

The mutual dependency in our picture classes does not cause such problems, because class `Picture` does not contain a member of type `Pic_base` directly. Instead, it has a member of type `Ptr<Pic_base>`, which contains a `Pic_base*`. Using pointers in this way avoids infinitely nested objects.

Moreover, in the case of a pointer (or reference), the compiler does not actually need to know the details of the type until operations are invoked through the pointer (or reference). Because the declaration of `operator<<` uses the `const Picture&` type only to declare a parameter type, the compiler needs to know only that the name `Picture` names a type. The details of that type aren't needed until we define `operator<<`.

Exercises

15-0. Compile, execute, and test the programs in this chapter.

15-1. Test your system by writing a program that executes

```
Picture p = // some initial starting picture
Picture q = frame(p);
Picture r = hcat(p, q);
Picture s = vcat(q, r);
cout << frame(hcat(s, vcat(r, q))) << endl;
```

15-2. Reimplement the `Frame_Pic` class so that the frame uses three different characters: one for the corners, another for the top and bottom borders, and a third for the side borders.

15-3. Give users the option to specify what characters to use for these border characters.

15-4. Add an operation to `reframe` a `Picture`, which changes the frame characters. The operation should change all of the frames in the interior picture.

15-5. Reimplement `HCat_Pic` so that when pictures of a different size are concatenated, the shorter one is centered in the space consumed by the longer one. That is, if we horizontally concatenate two pictures, one of which is four lines long and the other is two lines long, the first and last rows of the output picture will be blank on the side of the shorter picture. What can we now conclude about the necessity of the tests between `row` and `0`.

15-6.   The Vec and Str classes that we developed in Chapters 11 and 12 are powerful enough to be used to implement Pictures. Reimplement the material in this chapter to use Vec<Str> instead of vector<string>, and test your implementation.

16

Where do we go from here?

We have come to the end of the main part of our book. This ending may seem premature: There are still significant parts of the language, and large parts of the library, that we have not described. However, we have chosen to stop at this point for two important reasons.

The first reason is that we have already presented tools that you can use to solve a wide range of programming problems. We believe that your best strategy at this point is to practice using these tools on your own problems before you learn about any more new tools. It might even be a good idea to begin by rereading this entire book, doing all the exercises that you didn't do the first time around.

If you are looking for ideas about programming style or technique, we recommend our previous book, *Ruminations on C++* (Addison-Wesley, 1997), which contains a mixture of stylistic essays and programming examples.

The second reason is that once you have written enough programs that use the material that we have covered so far, you will no longer need the detailed tutorial style that we have adopted in this book. Instead, you will have gained enough C++ programming experience that you will be able to take advantage of books that contain more detailed information, and less explanation, than this one.

16.1 Use the abstractions you have

There is an old story about a visitor who has become lost in New York, with tickets in hand to a piano recital. Stopping a passerby, the visitor asks, "Excuse me. Can you tell me how to get to Carnegie Hall?" The answer: "Practice!"

It is important to understand—thoroughly—how to use the abstractions that you have available before you try to learn about new ones. The abstractions that you have include the ones from the standard library, and others that you may have had to create as you solve programming problems. By combining ideas from the standard library, which we can apply to a wide variety of problems, with ideas that solve problems in a particular application domain, we can write useful programs with surprisingly little effort. In particular, if we design our own abstractions well, we should be able to use them to solve problems that we had not considered when we designed them.

We can find an example of this ideal in the classes that we wrote in Chapter 13 to store student grades and in Chapter 15 to generate character pictures. We have used the character-picture classes in a variety of forms for years. In contrast, we wrote the student-record classes from scratch for this book. Only when we were thinking about what to say in this chapter did we realize that we could combine these two abstractions in a particularly nice way.

The combination uses character pictures to write a histogram of students' grades. The point, of course, is that such a visual display lets us see anomalies much more quickly than does a mere table of numbers. The basic idea is to convert each final grade into a string of = symbols whose length is proportional to the grade. For example, with appropriate input, we might generate the following output:

```
* * * * * * * * * * * * * * * * * * * * * * * * * * * * * *
*                                                         *
*  James      ===============                             *
*  Kevin      ================                            *
*  Lynn       =================                           *
*  MaryKate   ================                            *
*  Pat        ============                                *
*  Paul       ====================                        *
*  Rhia       =================                           *
*  Sarah      =====================                       *
*                                                         *
* * * * * * * * * * * * * * * * * * * * * * * * * * * * * *
```

From this histogram, it is immediately obvious that Pat is having trouble keeping up with the course.

What is nice about this example is how small it is, and how directly the solution mirrors the problem:

```
Picture histogram(const vector<Student_info>& students)
{
    Picture names;
    Picture grades;

    // for each student
    for (vector<Student_info>::const_iterator it = students.begin();
            it != students.end(); ++it) {

        // create vertically concatenated pictures of the names and grades
        names = vcat(names, vector<string>(1, it->name()));
        grades = vcat(grades,
             vector<string>(1, " " + string(it->grade() / 5, '=')));
    }

    // horizontally concatenate the name and grade pictures to combine them
    return hcat(names, grades);
}
```

Our histogram function takes a (const reference to a) vector of Student_info objects, each of which represents a student. From these records, we will create two Pictures, one of which, names, contains all the students' names; the other, grades, contains a row that corresponds to each student's final grade. When we've processed every student, we horizontally concatenate the two pictures, lining up each student with the corresponding grade. Because each picture is conceptually a rectangle, this horizontal concatenation automatically accounts for the different lengths of the students' names.

The `main` program builds up the `vector`, in familiar fashion, by reading a file of student records. When it's done, it calls `histogram` to generate the `Picture`, frames it, and then uses the output operator to write it:

```
int main()
{
    vector<Student_info> students;
    Student_info s;

    // read the names and grades
    while (s.read(cin))
        students.push_back(s);

    // put the students in alphabetical order
    sort(students.begin(), students.end(), Student_info::compare);

    // write the names and histograms
    cout << frame(histogram(students)) << endl;
    return 0;
}
```

The most important new idea in this example is that it contains no new ideas! What made it easy was being so familiar with the ideas that we have already covered that we can combine them in ways that we had not anticipated. This kind of familiarity comes only with practice.

16.2 Learn more

Eventually, you are going to need to know more details about the language and library. For that matter, our ideal of learning nothing new until you understand thoroughly everything that we have presented so far—like most ideals—is probably not entirely attainable in practice. At some point, you are going to encounter a question about C++ that this book does not answer, so you will need to turn elsewhere for advice.

For this purpose, two books stand out. The first, Bjarne Stroustrup's *The C++ Programming Language, Third Edition* (Addison-Wesley, 1998), is the most complete single source of information about C++. It covers the entire language and library, and tells you everything you need to know—and probably more—about all aspects of both. The second, Matthew Austern's *Generic Programming and the STL* (Addison-Wesley, 1999), discusses the standard library's algorithms and data structures in much more detail than either our book or Stroustrup's. Moreover, it is authoritative, because although Austern was not the original author or implementer of this part of the library—that honor goes to Alex Stepanov—he has been working closely with Stepanov for the past several years, and is one of the main driving forces behind the further evolution of that library.

Together, this book, *Ruminations on C++*, and the books by Stroustrup and Austern comprise well over 2,000 pages. We are, therefore, reluctant to recommend any additional reading. However, if your appetite is truly voracious, we suggest that you visit `http://www.accu.org`. There, you will find reviews of more than 2,000 books, many of which are related to C++. They also have the good taste to give their highest recommendations to *Ruminations on C++* and the books by Stroustrup and Austern.

As you look for reading material, keep in mind that books on the shelf do not make you a better programmer. Ultimately, the only way to improve your programming is to write programs. Have fun!

Exercises

16-0. Compile, execute, and test the programs in this chapter.

16-1. Write a self-reproducing program. Such a program is one that does no input, and that, when run, writes a copy of its own source text on the standard output stream.

Appendix A

Language details

This appendix serves two purposes: It includes some additional low-level details, and it summarizes in one place the expressions and statements of the language, including some that we have not used elsewhere in this book. The low-level material relates primarily to the complexities of C++'s declarator syntax, and the details of the built-in arithmetic types, both of which the language inherits from the C programming language. These details are not necessary for understanding the programs in this book, and indeed are not necessary to writing good C++ programs. However, there are many programs that do require knowledge of these details, so it may be useful to review them.

In this appendix we describe syntax as follows: `constant-width` symbols stand for themselves, *italic* words stand for syntactic categories, ... means zero or more repetitions of the item that immediately precedes it, and phrases enclosed in italic brackets *[ ]* are optional. Moreover, we use italic curly braces *{ }* for grouping, and | to show alternatives. For example,

> *declaration-stmt: decl-specifiers [declarator [initializer]] [, declarator [initializer]]... ;*

means that a *declaration-stmt* consists of *decl-specifiers*, followed by zero or more *declarators*, each optionally followed by an *initializer*, followed by a semicolon.

A.1 Declarations

Declarations can be hard to understand, especially if they declare several names with different types or deal with functions that return pointers to functions. For example, in §10.1.1/171, we saw that

```
int* p, q;
```

defines p as an object of type "pointer to int" and q as an object of type int, and in §10.1.2/173, we saw that

```
double (*get_analysis_ptr())(const vector<Student_info>&);
```

declares get_analysis_ptr as a function, with no arguments, that returns a pointer to a function with a const vector<Student_info>& argument that returns double.

You can clarify such declarations by rewriting them, for example, as

```
int* p;
int q;
```

and

```
//  define analysis_fp as a name for the type of a function that takes a
//  const vector<Student_info>& argument and returns a double
typedef double (*analysis_fp)(const vector<Student_info>&);
analysis_fp get_analysis_ptr();
```

Unfortunately, that strategy won't save you from having to read confusing declarations in other people's programs.

In general, a declaration looks like

declaration-stmt: decl-specifiers [declarator [initializer]] [, declarator [initializer]]... ;

It declares a name for each of its *declarators*. These names are meaningful from where they are declared to the end of the declaration's scope. Some declarations are also definitions. Names may be declared multiple times but must be defined only once. A declaration is a definition if it allocates storage or defines a class or function body.

C++ inherits its declaration syntax from C. The key to understanding declarations is to realize that each declaration begins with a sequence of *decl-specifiers* that collectively specify a type and other attributes of what is being declared. Zero or more *declarators*, each of which may have an associated *initializer*, follow the *decl-specifiers*. Each declarator ascribes to a name a type that depends on the specifiers and on the declarator's form.

The first step in understanding any declaration is to locate the boundary between the specifiers and the declarators. Doing so is surprisingly simple: All the specifiers are keywords or names of types, so the specifiers end just before the first symbol that isn't one of those. For example, in

```
const char * const * const * cp;
```

the first symbol that is neither a keyword nor the name of a type is `*`, so the specifiers are `const char`, and the (only) declarator is `* const * const * cp`.

As another example, consider the arcane declaration from §10.1.2/173:

```
double (*get_analysis_ptr())(const vector<Student_info>&);
```

The boundary here is easy to find: `double` names a type, and the open parenthesis that follows it is neither a keyword nor the name of a type. Therefore, the *decl-specifiers* part is just `double`, and the declarator is the rest of the declaration, not including the semicolon.

A.1.1 Specifiers

We can divide the *decl-specifiers* into three broad categories: type specifiers, storage-class specifiers, and miscellaneous specifiers:

decl-specifiers: { type-specifier | storage-class-specifier | other-decl-specifier } ...

However, this division serves only to aid understanding, because there is no corresponding division in declarations themselves: *decl-specifiers* can appear in any order.

Type specifiers determine the type that underlies any declaration. We discuss the built-in types themselves in §A.2/299.

> *type-specifier:* char | wchar_t | bool | short | int | long | signed |
>   unsigned | float | double | void | *type-name* | const | volatile
>
> *type-name: class-name* | *enum-name* | *typedef-name*

The const specifier says that objects of the type may not be modified. volatile tells the compiler that the variable may change in ways outside the definition of the language and that aggressive optimizations should be avoided.

Note that const can appear both as part of the specifiers, thus modifying the type, and as part of the declarator, specifying a const pointer. There is never any ambiguity because a const that is part of a declarator always follows a *.

Storage-class specifiers determine the location and lifetime of a variable:

> *storage-class-specifiers:* register | static | extern | mutable

The register specifier suggests that the compiler should try to optimize performance by putting the object into a register if possible.

Ordinarily, local variables are destroyed on exit from the block in which they were declared; static variables are preserved across entry and exit from a scope.

The extern specifier indicates that the current declaration is not a definition, implying that there is a corresponding definition elsewhere.

The mutable storage class is used only for class *data-members*, and allows those *data-members* to be modified even if they are members of const objects.

Other declaration specifiers define properties that are not related to types:

> *other-decl-specifier:* friend | inline | virtual | typedef

The friend specifier (§12.3.2/216 and §13.4.2/246) overrides protection.

inline is a specifier for function definitions and is a hint to the compiler to lay the code down inline if possible. The definition of the function must be in scope when the call is to be expanded, so it is usually a good idea to put the body of an inline function into the same header that declares the function.

The virtual specifier (§13.2.1/234) may be used only with member functions, and denotes a function for which calls can be dynamically bound.

The typedef specifier (§3.2.2/43) defines a synonym for a type.

A.1.2 Declarators

A declaration declares one entity for each declarator, giving that entity a name, and implicitly giving the entity the storage class, type, and other attributes as specified by the specifiers. The specifiers and declarator together determine whether the name names an object, array, pointer, reference, or function. For example,

```
int *x, f();
```

declares that x is a pointer to `int` and f is a function returning `int`. It is the declarators `*x` and `f()` that make the distinction between the types of x and f.

> *declarator:* [`*` [`const`] | `&`] ... *direct-declarator*

> *direct-declarator: declarator-id* | (*declarator*) |
>> *direct-declarator* (*parameter-declaration-list*) |
>> *direct-declarator* [*constant-expression*]

A *declarator-id* is an *identifier*, possibly qualified:

> *declarator-id:* [*nested-name-specifier*] *identifier*

> *nested-name-specifier:* { *class-or-namespace-name* `::` } ...

If a declarator is a *direct-declarator* that consists only of a *declarator-id*, then it specifies that the identifier being declared has the properties implied by the *decl-specifiers*, without further modification. For example, in the declaration

```
int n;
```

the declarator is n, which is a *direct-declarator* that consists only of a *declarator-id*, so by implication, n has type `int`.

If a declarator has one of the other possible forms, then you can determine the type of the identifier as follows: First, let T be the type implied by the *decl-specifiers*, ignoring non-type properties such as `friend` or `static`, and let D be the declarator. Then repeat the following steps until you have reduced D to a *declarator-id*, at which point T is the type you seek:

1. If D has the form `(D1)`, then replace D with D1.
2. If D has the form `* D1` or `* const D1`, replace T with "pointer to T" or "constant pointer to T" (*not* "pointer to constant T"), depending on whether the `const` is present. Then replace D with D1.
3. If D has the form D1 (*parameter-declaration-list*), replace T with "function returning T" with arguments as defined by the *parameter-declaration-list*, and replace D with D1.
4. If D has the form D1 [*constant-expression*], then replace T with "array of T" that has the number of elements given by the *constant-expression*, and replace D with D1.
5. Finally, if the declarator has the form `& D1`, then replace T with "reference to T" and D with D1.

As an example, consider the declaration

```
int *f();
```

We start with T and D being `int` and `*f()`, so D has the form `*D1`, where D1 is `f()`.

You might think that D could have either of the forms D1() or *D1. However, if D had form D1(), then D1 would have to be `*f`, and D1 would also have to be a *direct-declarator* (because the grammar at the beginning of this section allows only a *direct-declarator* to precede ()). If we look at the definition of *direct-declarator*, however, we see that it cannot contain a `*`. Therefore, D can only be `*f()`, which has the form `*D1`, where D1 is `f()`.

Now that we have determined that D1 is f(), we know that we must replace T with "pointer to T," which is "pointer to int," and replace D with f().

We have not yet reduced D to a *declarator-id*, so we must repeat the process. This time, D1 can only be f, so we replace T with "function returning T," which is "function returning pointer to int with no arguments," and we replace D with f.

At this point we have reduced D to a *declarator-id*, so we're done. We have determined that the declaration

```
int *f();
```

declares f to have type "function with no arguments returning pointer to int."

As another example, the declaration

```
int* p, q;
```

has two declarators, *p and q. For each declarator, T is int. For the first declarator, D is *p, so we transform T to "pointer to int," and D to p. The declaration, therefore, gives p the type "pointer to int."

We analyze the second declarator independently, with T again being int and D being q. At this point it should be obvious that the declaration gives q the type int.

Finally, let's analyze the arcane example from §10.1.2/173:

```
double (*get_analysis_ptr())(const vector<Student_info>&);
```

The analysis proceeds in the following five stages:

1. T: double   D: (*get_analysis_ptr())(const vector<Student_info>&)
2. T: function returning double with const vector<Student_info>& argument
                                          D: (*get_analysis_ptr())
3. T: function returning double... (as before)   D: *get_analysis_ptr()
4. T: pointer to function returning double...   D: get_analysis_ptr()
5. T: function returning pointer to function returning double... D: get_analysis_ptr

In other words, we learn that get_analysis_ptr is a function that returns a pointer to a function that returns a double result, and takes a const vector<Student_info>& as its argument. We leave unwinding const vector<Student_info>& as an exercise.

Fortunately, few function declarations are this confusing; most of them look like

declarator: declarator-id (parameter-declaration-list)

By far the most common difficult case is a function that returns a pointer to function.

A.2 Types

Types pervade C++ programs. Every object, expression, and function has a type, and the type of an entity determines its behavior. With a single exception (the type of an object within an inheritance hierarchy that is accessed through a pointer or reference), the type of every entity is known at compile time.

In C++, types can be thought of as ways of structuring and accessing memory as well as ways of defining operations that can be performed on objects of the type. That is, types specify both properties of data and operations on that data.

Although this book concentrates on using and building higher-level data structures, it is important to understand the primitive types used to build them. These primitive types represent common abstractions that are close to the hardware, such as numbers (integral and floating point), characters (including wide characters for international character sets), truth values, and machine addresses (pointers, references, and arrays). Literals, also often called constants, represent integer, floating-point, Boolean, character, or string values. This section reviews and expands on facilities related to the built-in types.

A.2.1 Integral types

C++ inherits from C a bewildering variety of integral types, including integers, Boolean, and character types. Because C++ is intended to be able to run efficiently on a wide variety of hardware, it leaves many of the details of its fundamental types up to the implementation rather than defining those types precisely.

A.2.1.1 Integer

There are three distinct signed integer types and three distinct unsigned integer types:

```
short int                    int                      long int
unsigned short int           unsigned int             unsigned long int
```

The `short` and `long` types can be abbreviated by dropping the keyword `int`. The keywords, if there are more than one, can appear in any order.

Each of these types is capable of representing any integer within an implementation-defined range. Each type but the first must offer a range at least as generous as that of the type that precedes it. The ranges for `short int` and `int` must be at least ± 32767 ($\pm(2^{15}-1)$), and the range for `long int` must be at least ± 2147483647 ($\pm(2^{31}-1)$).

Every signed integral type has a corresponding unsigned type. Every unsigned type represents integers modulo 2^n, where n depends on the type and the implementation. Analogous to the signed types, the n that corresponds to every unsigned type except `unsigned char` must be at least as large as the n for the preceding type. Moreover, every unsigned type must be capable of holding every non-negative value in the range of the corresponding signed type, and each signed type is required to have the same internal representation as the corresponding unsigned type for the values that they have in common. It follows from these requirements that the four unsigned types must have an extra bit that corresponds to signed types' sign bits, meaning that the unsigned types must correspond to values of n that are at least 8, 16, 16, and 32 respectively.

Compilers are allowed to use either one's- or two's-complement representation for the signed types.

The standard library defines a type called `size_t` that is a synonym for one of the unsigned types. It is guaranteed to be large enough to hold the size of the largest possible object, including arrays. Its type is defined in the system header `<cstddef>`.

Integer literals: An integer literal is a sequence of digits, optionally preceded by a base indicator, and optionally followed by a size indicator. Pedantically speaking, integer literals do not have signs, so that -3 is an expression, not a literal.

If the literal begins with `0x` or `0X`, then the integer is represented in hexadecimal, and the "digits" can include any of `AaBbCcDdEeFf` as well as the usual decimal digits. If the literal begins with a `0` that is not followed by `x` or `X`, then the integer is represented in octal, and the "digits" can include only `01234567`.

The size indicator is `u`, `l`, `ul`, or `lu`, in either upper- or lowercase. If it is `lu` or `ul`, then the literal has type `unsigned long`. If it is `u`, then the literal has type `unsigned` if the value will fit; otherwise, it has type `unsigned long`. If it is `l`, then the literal has type `long` if the value will fit; otherwise, it has type `unsigned long`.

If there is a base indicator but no size indicator, then the type is the first of `int`, `unsigned`, `long`, and `unsigned long` into which the value will fit. If there is neither a size nor a base indicator, then the type is `int` if the value will fit, and `long` otherwise.

These rules imply that the type of an integer literal often depends on the implementation. Fortunately, integer literals in well-written programs tend to be small, so these details don't matter most of the time. Nevertheless, we have mentioned them in case you need to refer back to them.

A.2.1.2 Boolean

Expressions that are treated as conditions have type `bool`. The possible values of type `bool` are `true` and `false`. It is possible to use a number or a pointer as a truth value. In such contexts, zero is considered `false`, and any other value is considered `true`.

When a `bool` value is used as a number, `false` is treated as `0` and `true` as `1`.

Boolean literals: The only Boolean literals are `true` and `false`, each of which has type `bool`, with the obvious meaning.

A.2.1.3 Character

In C++, characters are just tiny integers. In particular, they can be used in arithmetic expressions in the same way as integers.

As is the case with integers, characters can be signed or not, so there are distinct `signed char` and `unsigned char` types. Every implementation's range for `signed char` is required to be able to contain every character in the machine's basic character set, as well as being at least ± 127 ($\pm(2^7 - 1)$).

In addition, there is a plain `char` type, which, although it is a distinct type, is required to have the same representation as one of the other two types. It is up to the implementation to determine which of those types it should be. As usual, the choice is intended to reflect which representation is most natural for the machine.

There is also a "wide character" type, called `wchar_t`, which must contain at least 16 bits, and is intended to be used for representing characters in languages such as Japanese, which have many more characters than the Latin alphabet provides. The `wchar_t` type is required to behave the same way as one of the other integral types. The particular other type involved depends on the implementation and is normally chosen to yield the most efficient representation.

Character literals: A character literal, of which ′a′ is an example, is typically a single character surrounded by single quotes. It has type char, which, as we know from §A.2.1.3/301, is really a kind of integer. Every implementation defines a correspondence between characters, such as a, and their integral values. Most programs have no reason to depend on that correspondence, because programmers can write literals such as ′a′ to mean "the integer that corresponds to the character a." Because the correspondence varies from one implementation to another, programmers should not depend on arithmetic properties of characters. For example, there is no assurance that ′a′+1 is equal to ′b′. Digits, however, are guaranteed to have contiguous values. For example, ′3′ + 1 is always equal to ′4′ (but not necessarily equal to 4).

String literals, A string literal, of which "Hello, world!" is an example, is a sequence of zero or more characters surrounded by double quotes. The type of a string literal is const char*. The compiler inserts a null character at the end of every string literal.

Two string literals that are separated only by whitespace are automatically concatenated to form a longer string literal. This behavior allows string literals that span more than a single line to be written more conveniently.

A.2.1.4 Character representations

We said that a character literal is typically a single character surrounded by single quotes, and that a string literal is typically a sequence of characters surrounded by double quotes. The reason for the "typically" is that there are some exceptions to the general rule. These exceptions apply equally to character literals and string literals:

- To represent a quote of the same kind that began the literal, you must precede it by another backslash, as in ′\′′, or "the \"quotes\"", to make it clear that the quote does not end the literal. For convenience, you can precede the other kind of quote by a backslash as well, as in ′\"′.
- To represent a backslash, you must precede it by a backslash, as in ′\\′, so that the compiler will not think that the backslash is there to give special meaning to the character following it.
- There are rules having to do with international character sets, which are beyond the scope of this book, but which affect the meaning of programs with two or more consecutive question marks in their text. To make it possible to avoid consecutive question marks, C++ allows \? to represent a question mark, so that you can write literals such as "What?\?" without consecutive question marks.
- A number of control characters, which affect output in various ways, have printable representations inside literals: newline (\n), horizontal tab (\t), vertical tab (\v), backspace (\b), carriage return (\r), form feed (\f), and alert (\a). Their actual effect when written on an output device depends on the implementation.
- If you really need a character with a particular internal representation, you can represent it as \x followed by hexadecimal digits (in upper- or lowercase), or by \ followed

by up to three octal digits. So, for example, `'\x20'` and `'\40'` both represent the character whose internal representation is decimal 32 (20 in hex, 40 in octal). On implementations based on the ASCII character set, this character is the same as `' '`. The most common use of this representation—and the only one you will see in many programs—is that `'\0'` is the character whose value is zero.

A.2.2 Floating point

C++ has three floating-point types, called `float`, `double`, and `long double` in order of nondecreasing precision. The implementation is allowed to implement `float` with the same precision as `double`, or `double` with the same precision as `long double`. Every implementation is required to offer at least six significant (decimal) digits in the `float` type and ten in the `double` and `long double` types. Most implementations offer only six significant digits for `float` and fifteen for `double`.

Floating-point literals: A floating-point literal is a nonempty sequence of digits with an exponent at the end, a decimal point somewhere in it, or both. Like integer literals, floating-point literals do not begin with a sign; `-3.1` is an expression, not a literal. The decimal point may be at the beginning, middle, or end of the sequence of digits, or it may be omitted entirely if there is an exponent. The exponent is `e` or `E`, followed by an optional sign, and one or more digits. The exponent is always interpreted in decimal.

For example, `312E5` and `31200000.` represent the same number, but `31200000` is an integer literal, not a floating-point literal. As another example, `1.2E-3` represents the same number as `.0012` or, for that matter, `0.000012e+2`.

Floating-point literals normally have type `double`. If you want a literal to have type `float`, you can append `f` or `F`; if you want it to have type `long double`, you can append `l` or `L`.

A.2.3 Constant expressions

A *constant-expression* is an expression of integral type with a value that is known at compile time. The operands in a *constant-expression* can contain only literals, enumerators, `const` variables, or `static` data members of integral type that are initialized from *constant-expressions* or `sizeof` expressions. The expressions may not contain functions, class objects, pointers, or references and are not allowed to use assignment, increment, decrement, function-call, or comma operators.

A *constant-expression* can appear wherever a constant is expected. Examples include dimensions in array declarations (§10.1.3/174), labels in `switch` statements (§A.4/309), and initializers for enumerators (§A.2.5/305).

A.2.4 Conversions

Conversions happen as needed to bring the operands of each operator to a common type. When there is a choice, conversions that preserve information are preferred over those that lose information. Moreover, conversion to unsigned types is preferred to conversion to signed types, all arithmetic on short integers or characters implies conversion to int or longer, and floating-point arithmetic implies conversion to double or longer.

The simplest conversions are promotions. Promotions allow values of a smaller type (e.g., char) to be promoted to a larger, related type (e.g., int); they preserve the sign of the initial value. Integral promotions convert values of char, signed char, unsigned char, short, and unsigned short to int, if the values will fit, and to unsigned int otherwise. Wide characters and enumeration types (§A.2.5/305) are promoted to the smallest int that can represent all the values in the underlying type. The types int, unsigned int, long, and unsigned long are tried in order, bool is promoted to int, and float is promoted to double.

Conversion of an integral type to a floating-point type preserves as much precision as can be represented on the machine hardware.

Converting a larger signed value (e.g., long) to a shorter value (e.g., short) is implementation defined. Converting a larger unsigned value to a shorter value is modulo 2^n, where n is the number of bits in the shorter type. Converting a floating-point value to an integral type truncates by discarding the fractional part. The behavior is undefined if the truncated value doesn't fit.

Pointers, integral types, and floating-point values can be converted to bool. If the value is 0 then the resulting bool is false, otherwise, it is true. bools can be converted to the other types; true is converted as a value of 1 and false as 0.

A *constant-expression* (§A.2.3/303) that evaluates to 0 may be converted to a pointer.

Any pointer can be converted to a void*. Also, a pointer to nonconst can be converted to a pointer to const—similarly for a nonconst reference. A pointer or reference to an object of a type that was publicly derived may be converted to a pointer or reference to any of its base classes.

Arithmetic conversions: Because the operands can be integral or floating point, and signed or unsigned, it can be a little tricky to figure out the type of the result of an arithmetic operation. The rules for doing so are called the ***usual arithmetic conversions***, and work as follows:

- If either operand is floating point, the result is floating point, with the precision of the most precise operand.
- Otherwise, if either operand is unsigned long, then so is the result.
- Otherwise, if one operand is long int and the other is unsigned (any unsigned type but unsigned long, which would force the result to be unsigned long by the previous rule), then the result depends on the implementation: If the range of long int contains the range of unsigned int, then the result is long int; otherwise, it is unsigned int.
- Otherwise, if either operand is long int, the result is long int.
- Otherwise, the operands must both be signed integers of int type or shorter, and the result is int.

One consequence of these rules is that the result of an arithmetic operation is never short or char, either signed or unsigned. All arithmetic is done only on int or wider types.

A.2.5 Enumerated types

An enumerated type specifies a set of integral values. Objects of the type may take on only values specified by the type:

```
enum enum-name {
        enumerator [ , enumerator ] ...
};
```

*enum-name*s are *type-name*s and can be used where a *type-name* is expected.

Variables of the *enum-name* type can have values only from the list of *enumerator*s:

enumerator: identifier [= constant-expression]

Unless specified, the values of enumerated types correspond to consecutive integers, starting from zero. It is also possible to state explicit values for the enumerators. The initializers must have integral (§A.2.1/300) type, and a value that the compiler can determine during compilation (§A.2.3/303). If a value of an enumerated type is used in a context that requires an integer, the value will be converted automatically.

A.2.6 Overloading

More than one function can have the same name, provided that the functions differ in type or number of parameters.

Calling an overloaded function implies a compile-time check to determine which of the set of overloaded functions should be called. The function to call is determined by comparing the actual arguments at the call with the types of the formal parameters. The function that best matches the actual arguments is selected. To be the best match, a function must be a better match than the others on one or more arguments and no worse in any argument.

The best match for any particular argument is defined as follows:
- An exact match (the argument types are identical) is best.
- A match using promotions (§A.2.4/303) is better than a match using built-in conversions, which is better than a match using conversions defined by a class type (§12.2/213 and §12.5/222).

It is an error if there is more than one function that best matches the call.

A.3 Expressions

C++ inherits a rich expression syntax from C, to which it adds operator overloading (§A.3.1/308). Operator overloading allows program authors to define the argument and return types and meaning of operators, but not their precedence, valence (number of operands), or associativity, nor the meaning of built-in operators on operands of built-in types. In this section we will describe—with a few additions—the operators as they apply to built-in types.

Every operator yields a value, the type of which depends on the types of its operands. In general, if the operands have the same type, that is the type of the result. Otherwise, standard conversions are performed to bring the types to a common type (§A.2.4/303).

An *lvalue* is a value that denotes a nontemporary object, hence it has an address. Certain operations are valid only for lvalues, and some operations yield lvalues. Every expression yields a value; some expressions also yield lvalues.

Only four operators guarantee the order of evaluation for their operands:

&&   The right operand is evaluated only if the left operand is `true`.

|| The right operand is evaluated only if the left operand is `false`.

? :   Only one expression after the condition will be evaluated. The expression after the ? is evaluated if the condition is `true`; otherwise, the expression after the : is evaluated. The result is the expression that was evaluated; it is an lvalue if both expressions were lvalues of the same type.

,   The left operand is evaluated first and discarded; the result is the right operand.

For the other operators, aside from precedence rules, order of evaluation is not guaranteed. That is, the compiler is permitted to evaluate operands in any order. Parentheses can be used to override the default precedence, but explicit temporaries are required to control the order of evaluation completely.

Each operator has a specified precedence and associativity. In the following table, we summarize all the operators in order by precedence. When several operators are grouped together, they share the same precedence and associativity. Each grouping introduces a new level of precedence. This table expands the one first presented in Chapter 2 and includes all the operators:

terminal	Identifier or literal constant; identifiers are lvalues, literals are not.
`C::m`	The member m from class C.
`N::m`	The member m from namespace N.
`::m`	The name m at global scope.
`x[y]`	The element in object x indexed by y. Yields an lvalue.
`x->y`	The member y of the object pointed to by x. Yields an lvalue.
`x.y`	The member y of object x. Yields an lvalue if x is an lvalue.
`f(args)`	Call function f passing *args* as argument(s).
`x++`	Increments the lvalue x. Yields the original value of x.
`x--`	Decrements the lvalue x. Yields the original value of x.
`*x`	Dereferences the pointer x. Yields the object pointed to as an lvalue.
`&x`	The address of the object x. Yields a pointer.
`-x`	Unary minus. May be applied only to expressions of numeric type.
`!x`	Logical negation. If x is zero, then `!x` is `true`, otherwise `false`.
`~x`	Ones complement of x. x must be an integral type.
`++x`	Increments the lvalue x. Yields the incremented value as an lvalue.
`--x`	Decrements the lvalue x. Yields the decremented value as an lvalue.
`sizeof(e)`	The number of bytes, as a `size_t`, consumed by expression e.
`sizeof(T)`	The number of bytes, as a `size_t`, consumed by objects of type T.
`T(args)`	Constructs a T object from *args*.

`new T`	Allocates a new, default-initialized object of type `T`.
`new T(`*args*`)`	Allocates a new object of type `T` initialized by *args*.
`new T[n]`	Allocates an array of n default-initialized objects of type `T`.
`delete p`	Frees object pointed to by p.
`delete [] p`	Frees the array of objects pointed to by p.

`x * y`	Product of x and y.
`x / y`	Quotient of x and y. If both operands are integers, the implementation chooses whether to round toward 0 or $-\infty$.
`x % y`	`x - ((x / y) * y)`.

| `x + y` | Sum of x and y, if both operands are numeric. If one operand is a pointer and the other is integral, yields a pointer to a position y elements after x. |
| `x - y` | Result of subtracting y from x if operands are numeric. If x and y are pointers, yields the distance, in elements, between them. |

| `x >> y` | For integral x and y, x shifted right by y bits; y must be non-negative. If x is an `istream`, reads from x into y and returns lvalue x. |
| `x << y` | For integral x and y, x shifted left by y bits; y must be non-negative. If x is an `ostream`, writes y into x and returns lvalue x. |

| `x` *relop* `y` | Relational operators yield a `bool` indicating the truth of the relation. The operators (<, >, <=, and >=) have their obvious meanings. If x and y are pointers, they must point to the same object or array. |

| `x == y` | Yields a `bool` indicating whether x equals y. |
| `x != y` | Yields a `bool` indicating whether x is not equal to y. |

| `x & y` | Bitwise and. x and y must be integral. |

| `x ^ y` | Bitwise exclusive or. x and y must be integral. |

| `x | y` | Bitwise or. x and y must be integral. |

| `x && y` | Yields a `bool` indicating whether both x and y are `true`. Evaluates y only if x is `true`. |

| `x || y` | Yields a `bool` indicating whether either x or y is `true`. Evaluates y only if x is `false`. |

| `x = y` | Assigns the value of y to x. Yields x as its (lvalue) result. |
| `x` *op*`= x` | Compound assignment operators. Equivalent to x = x *op* y, where *op* is an arithmetic, bitwise, or shift operator. |

| `x ? y1 : y2` | Yields y1 if x is `true`; y2 otherwise. Only one of y1 or y2 is evaluated. y1 and y2 must be of the same type. If y1 and y2 are lvalues, the result is an lvalue. The operator is right-associative. |

| `throw x` | Signal an error by throwing value x. The type of x determines which handler will catch the error. |

| `x , y` | Evaluates x, discards the result, then evaluates y. Yields y. |

A.3.1 Operators

Most of the built-in operators may be overloaded. The throw, scope, dot, and conditional operator (the ? : operator) may not be overloaded. All of the other operators may be. §11.2.4/192 describes how to define an overloaded operator.

The postfix increment/decrement operator is distinguished from the prefix version by being defined as taking a dummy, unused parameter. That is, to overload the postfix operators, we write

```
class Number {
public:
    Number operator++(int) { /* function-body */ }
    Number operator--(int) { /* function-body */ }
};
```

The most commonly overloaded operators include the assignment and index operator, the shift operators used to do input–output with ostreams and istreams, and the operators used to implement iterators summarized in §B.2.5/317.

A.4 Statements

Like most programming languages, C++ distinguishes between declarations, expressions, and statements. In appropriate contexts, declarations and statements can be nested within other declarations and statements, but neither can be nested inside an expression. Every statement ultimately appears inside the definition of a function, where it forms part of what happens when that function is called.

Unless otherwise specified, the statements that constitute a function are executed in the order in which they appear. Exceptions include loops; calls to functions; the goto, break, and continue statements; and the try and throw statements associated with exception handling.

Statements are written in free form. Beginning a new line in midstatement does not affect the statement's meaning. Most statements end with semicolons—the main exception is the block (which begins with { and ends with }).

;   Null statement; has no effect when executed.

e;   Expression statement; evaluates e for its side effects.

{ }   Statement block; executes statements in the block in sequence.
      Variables defined in the block are destroyed at the end of the block.

if (*condition*) *statement1*
      Evaluates *condition* and executes *statement1* if *condition* is true.

if (*condition*) *statement1* else *statement2*
      Evaluates the *condition* and executes *statement1* if *condition* is true; otherwise executes *statement2*. Each else is associated with the nearest unmatched if.

while (*condition*) *statement*
      Tests *condition* and executes *statement* so long as *condition* is true.

do *statement* while (*condition*);
> Executes *statement* and then tests *condition*. Continues executing *statement* until *condition* is false.

for (*init-stmt condition*; *expression*) *statement*
> Executes *init-stmt* once on entry to the loop and then tests *condition*. If *condition* is true, executes *statement* and then executes *expression*. Continues testing *condition*, followed by *statement* and *expression*, until *condition* is false.
>
> If *init-stmt* is a declaration, then the scope of the variable is the for *statement* itself.

switch (*expression*) *statement*
> In practice, *statement* is almost always a block that includes labeled statements with labels of the form

        case *value*:

> where each *value* must be a distinct integral constant expression (§A.2.3/303). In addition, the label

        default:

> may appear, but no more than once.
>
> Executing a switch statement evaluates *expression* and jumps to the case label whose value matches it. If there is no match, control passes to the default: label, if any, or to the point immediately after the entire switch statement.
>
> Because case labels are just labels, control will flow from one to the next unless the programmer takes explicit action to prevent it from doing so. The usual such action is to use a break statement before each case label after the first.

break;
> Jumps to the point immediately after the end of the nearest enclosing while, for, do, or switch statement.

continue;
> Jumps back to the beginning of the next iteration (including the test) in the nearest enclosing for, while, or do statement. If the nearest enclosing statement is a for statement, the next iteration includes the *expression* in the for-statement as well. For example,

```
for (int i = 0; i < 10; ++i) {
    if (i % 3 == 0)
        continue;
    cout << i << endl;
}
```

> writes $1, 2, 4, 5, 7$, and 8, with each value on a separate line.

goto *label*;
> Behaves similarly to such statements in other languages. The target of a goto is a label, which is an identifier followed by a colon. Labels can have the same names as other entities without ambiguity. The scope of a label is the entire function in which it appears, which implies that it is possible to jump from outside a block to inside it. However, such a jump cannot bypass the initialization of a variable.

`try  {` *statements* `} catch  (`*parameter-1*`)  {` *statements-1* `}`
          [`catch  (`*parameter-2*`)  {` *statements-2* `}]* ...

Executes code in *statements* that might `throw` an exception, which should be handled by the one or more `catch` clauses that follow.

The `catch` clause handles exceptions whose thrown value is of similar type to the type of *parameter-n* by executing code in *statements-n*. Similar here means that the thrown value has the same type as the parameter or a type derived from the parameter's type.

If the `catch` has the form `catch (...)`, then the clause catches any otherwise uncaught exception.

If there is no appropriate `catch` that matches the type of the exception, then the exception propagates out of the function to the nearest enclosing `try`. If there is no appropriate `try`, then the program terminates.

`throw` *expression* ;

Terminates the program or transfers control to a `catch` clause of a `try` statement whose execution is in progress. Passes *expression* whose type determines which `catch` clause can handle the exception. If no appropriate `try` statement is currently being executed, the program terminates.

Exceptions are often class objects, and are usually thrown in one function and caught in another.

Appendix B

Library summary

The standard library is a major contribution to the standardization of C++. Throughout this book, we have relied on the library to write succinct, idiomatic C++ programs. This chapter reviews the library facilities that we used, and describes some generally useful facilities that we did not have occasion to use. Each section presents a library class or family of related classes by showing and explaining how to use the relevant facilities.

In general, the standard library introduces names into namespace `std`. Programs that use standard-library facilities must therefore either prefix such names by `std::` or make them generally available with `using`-declarations. In this appendix, we will not explicitly mention the need to do so. Accordingly, for example, we shall refer to `cout` rather than to `std::cout`.

Our examples generally assume the following meanings for the names shown:

n	A variable or expression that yields a value of any of the integral types
t	A value of type `T`
s	A `string` value
cp	A pointer to the initial element of a null-terminated character array
c	A `char` value
p	A predicate, which is a function that returns `bool` or a value convertible to `bool`
os	An output stream
is	An input stream
strm	An input or output stream
b	An iterator that denotes the beginning of a sequence
e	An iterator that denotes (one past) the end of a sequence
d	An iterator that denotes a destination
it	An iterator that denotes an element

B.1 Input–output

Objects of classes `istream`, `ostream`, `ifstream`, and `ofstream` denote sequential streams, with an object being bound to a single stream at any one time. Objects of these types cannot be copied or assigned; therefore, the only way to pass a stream to or from a function is through a pointer or a reference.

Fundamentals

```
#include <iostream>
```
Declares input–output classes and associated operations.

```
cout
cerr
clog
```
Objects of type `ostream` bound to the standard output (`cout`) and error (`cerr`, `clog`) streams. Output to `cout` and `clog` is buffered by default; output to `cerr` is unbuffered by default.

`cin`   An object of type `istream` bound to the standard input stream.

Reading and writing

`is >> t`   Conventionally, reads a value from `is` into `t` after skipping whitespace. The input must be in a form suitable for conversion to the type of `t`, which must be a nonconst lvalue. Unsuitable input causes the request to fail, leaving `is` in failure state until a call is made to `is.clear()`. The library defines the input operator for the built-in types and `string`; class authors are encouraged to follow suit.

`os << t`   Conventionally, sends the value of `t` to `os` in a format appropriate to the type of `t`. The library defines `<<` for built-in types and `string`; class authors are encouraged to follow suit.

`is.get(c)` Reads the next character, even if it is a whitespace character, from `is` into `c`.

`is.unget()`
Backs up the stream `is` by one character. Useful when we want to read until we hit a particular character, and then want to leave that character on the stream for subsequent processing. Only one character of pushback memory is guaranteed.

Iterators

```
#include <iterator>
```
Declares input and output stream iterators.

```
istream_iterator<T> in(is);
```
Defines `in` as an input iterator that reads values of type `T` from `is`.

```
ostream_iterator<T> out(os, const char* sep = "");
```
Defines `out` as an output iterator that writes values of type `T` on the stream `os`, writing `sep` as separator value after each element. By default, the separator is a null string, but it can be a string literal (§10.2/176) or a pointer to a null-terminated array of characters.

File streams

```
#include <fstream>
```
Declares facilities for input–output to streams that are attached to files.

```
ifstream is(cp);
```
Defines `is` and attaches it to the file named (in an implementation-dependent manner) by `cp`. Class `ifstream` is derived from `istream`.

```
ofstream os(cp);
```
> Defines `os` and attaches it to the file named by `cp`. Class `ofstream` is derived from `ostream`.

Controlling output format

```
#include <ios>
```
> Defines the `streamsize` type, which is a signed integral type that is appropriate to represent the sizes of input–output buffers.

```
os.width()
os.width(n)
```
> Returns the width (as a `streamsize`) previously associated with `os`. Sets the width to n if given. The next item written on that stream will be padded on the left to the stream's width, after which the width will be reset to 0.

```
os.precision()
os.precision(n)
```
> Returns the precision (as a `streamsize`) previously associated with `os`. Sets the precision to n if given. Subsequent floating-point values written on that stream will appear with the given number of significant digits.

Manipulators

```
#include <iomanip>
```
> Declares manipulators other than `endl`, which is declared in `<iostream>`.

```
os << endl
```
> Ends the current output line and flushes the stream associated with `os`.

```
os << flush
```
> Flushes the stream associated with `os`.

```
os << setprecision(n)
os << setw(n)
```
> Equivalent to `os.precision(n)` and `os.width(n)` respectively.

Errors and end-of-file

```
strm.bad()
```
> Returns a `bool` indicating whether the last operation on `strm` failed as a result of invalid data.

```
strm.clear()
```
> Attempts to reset `strm` so that it can be used after an invalid operation. Throws `ios::failure` if `strm` cannot be reset.

```
strm.eof()
```
> Returns a `bool` indicating whether `strm` has hit end-of-file.

```
strm.fail()
```
> Returns a `bool` indicating whether the last operation on `strm` failed as a result of hardware or other system-level problems.

```
strm.good()
```
> Returns a `bool` indicating whether the last operation on `strm` succeeded.

B.2 Containers and iterators

This book covers the sequential containers `vector` and `list`, the associative container `map`, and class `string`, which shares many container properties. All containers that provide a particular operation use similar interfaces for the operation. We summarize the common operations, followed by operations peculiar to specific containers.

Programmers who want to use sequential containers should use `vector`, unless there is a reason to do otherwise. The most common such reason is a desire to insert or delete many elements other than at the end of the container, an operation that the `list` class supports much more efficiently than the `vector` class does.

B.2.1 Common container operations

All containers and the `string` class offer the following interface:

container<T>::`iterator`
container<T>::`const_iterator`
> Iterator types associated with *container*<T>. Objects of either type can be used to read the values of the container's elements; objects of type *container*<T>::`iterator` can be used to modify the elements as well.

container<T>::`reference`
container<T>::`const_reference`
> Synonyms for `T&` and `const T&`, respectively.

container<T>::`reverse_iterator`
container<T>::`const_reverse_iterator`
> Iterator types that access the container's elements in reverse order.

container<T>::`size_type`
> An unsigned integral type with room for the size of the largest container .

container<T>::`value_type`
> Synonym for `T`.

`c.begin()`
`c.end()`
> Iterators that denote the first element, if any, and one past the last element of `c`. Both of these functions yield values that have `c`'s `const_iterator` or `iterator` type, depending on whether `c` is `const`.

`c.rbegin()`
`c.rend()`
> Iterators (of `c`'s `const_reverse_iterator` or `reverse_iterator` type, depending on whether `c` is `const`) that access `c`'s elements in reverse order.

container<T> `c;`
> Defines `c` as an empty *container*, with `c.size() == 0`.

container<T> `c2(c);`
> Defines `c2` as a *container*, with `c2.size() == c.size()`. Each element of `c2` is a copy of the corresponding element of `c`.

`c = c2`   Replaces `c`'s elements with copies of `c2`'s elements. Returns `c` as an lvalue.
`c.size()`   The number of elements in `c`.
`c.empty()` Returns `true` if `c` is empty, `false` otherwise.

c.clear() Empties the container c. Equivalent to c.erase(c.begin(), c.end()).
           After the operation completes, c.size() == 0. Returns void.

B.2.2 Sequential containers

In addition to the common container operations, string and the sequential containers
(vector and list) also support the following operations:

container<T> c(n, t);
           Defines c to have n elements, each of which is a copy of t.
container<T> c(b, e);
           Defines c and initializes it with a copy of the elements in the sequence
           denoted by the input iterators b and e.
c.insert(it, t)
c.insert(it, n, t)
c.insert(it, b, e)
           Inserts elements into c immediately before it. If c is a vector or string,
           the operation invalidates all iterators that refer to or after the insertion point
           and may cause reallocation, invalidating all iterators into c. Note that for
           vector and string, this operation may be slow if it is far from the end.
                The first form of insert inserts a copy of t, and returns an iterator that
           refers to the newly inserted element. The second form inserts n copies of t,
           and returns void. The third form inserts copies of the elements in the
           sequence denoted by the input iterators b and e, and returns void. The
           iterators b and e must not refer to elements of c.
c.erase(it)
c.erase(b, e)
           Removes the element denoted by it, or the elements in the range [b, e),
           from c, invalidating all iterators referring to erased elements. If c is a vec-
           tor or string, then all iterators referring to elements after the erasure are
           also invalidated. Returns an iterator that refers to the position immediately
           after the erasure. Note that erase on a vector or string is slow if the
           erasure is far from the end of the container.
c.assign(b, e)
           Replaces c's elements with the elements in the sequence denoted by the
           input iterators b and e.
c.front() Returns a reference to the first element of c. Undefined if c is empty.
c.back() Returns a reference to the last element of c. Undefined if c is empty.
c.push_back(t)
           Appends a copy of t to c, increasing the size of c by one. Returns void.
c.pop_back()
           Removes the last element from c. Returns void. Undefined if c is empty.
inserter(c, it)
           Returns an output iterator that inserts values into c starting immediately
           before the position denoted by it. Declared in <iterator>.

`back_inserter(c)`

> Returns an output iterator that can append new values to the end of `c` by calling `c.push_back`. Declared in `<iterator>`.

B.2.3 Additional sequential operations

Some operations are supported only on those containers for which the operations can be done efficiently. These include the following:

`c[n]`

> A reference to the `n`th element of `c`, where the initial element has position `0`. The reference is `const` if `c` is `const`, and nonconst otherwise. Undefined if `n` is out of range. Valid only for `vector` and `string`.

`c.push_front(t)`

> Inserts a copy of `t` at the beginning of `c`, increasing the size of `c` by one. Returns `void`. Not valid for `string` or `vector`.

`c.pop_front()`

> Removes the first element from `c`. Returns `void`. Undefined if `c` is empty. Valid only for `list`.

`front_inserter(c)`

> Returns an output iterator that can insert new values at the front of `c` by calling `c.push_front`. Declared in `<iterator>`.

B.2.4 Associative containers

Associative containers are optimized for fast access based on a key. In addition to the general container operations outlined in §B.2.1/314, associative containers also provide the following:

container`<T>::key_type`

> The type of the *container*'s key. An associative container with keys of type `K` and elements of type `V` has a `value_type` of `pair<const K, V>`, not `V`.

container`<T> c(cmp);`

> Defines `c` as an empty associative container that uses the predicate `cmp` to order the elements.

container `c(b, e, cmp);`

> Defines `c` as an associative container, initialized with a copy of the values in the sequence denoted by the input iterators `b` and `e`, that uses `cmp` to order the elements.

`c.insert(b, e)`

> Inserts elements into `c` from the sequence denoted by the input iterators `b` and `e`. The `map` container inserts only those elements whose keys are not already in `c`.

`c.erase(it)`

> Removes the element denoted by the iterator `it` from `c`. Returns `void`.

`c.erase(b, e)`

> Removes elements in the range `[b, e)` from `c`. Returns `void`.

```
c.erase(k)
```
      Removes all elements with key k from c. Returns the number removed.

`c.find(k)`   Returns an iterator referring to the element with key equal to k. Returns c.end() if no such element exists.

B.2.5 Iterators

The standard library relies heavily on iterators to make its algorithms data-structure independent. Iterators are an abstraction of pointers, in that they provide operations that allow access to container elements analogous to what pointers allow on array elements.

The standard algorithms are written to assume that iterators meet requirements that the library classifies into *iterator categories*. Every library algorithm that uses iterators of a particular category can work with every library- or user-defined class that provides iterators that fall into that category.

- **Output**: It is possible to use the iterator to advance through the container one element at a time, and to write each element visited once and only once. Example: Class ostream_iterator is an output iterator; and the copy algorithm requires only the output-iterator properties for its third argument.
- **Input**: It is possible to use the iterator to advance through the container one element at a time, and to read each element as often as needed before advancing to the next element. Example: Class istream_iterator is an input iterator, and the copy algorithm requires only input-iterator properties for its first two arguments.
- **Forward**: It is possible to use the iterator to advance through the container one element at a time, to revisit elements to which previously remembered iterators refer, and to read or write each element as often as needed. Example: replace is an algorithm that requires forward-iterator properties.
- **Bidirectional**: It is possible to use the iterator to move through the container one element at a time, either forward or backward. Example: list and map provide bidirectional iterators, and reverse is an algorithm that requires bidirectional iterators.
- **Random access**: It is possible to move through the container using all the operations supported by pointers. Example: vector, string, and built-in arrays support random-access iterators. The sort algorithm requires random-access iterators.

All iterator categories support testing for (in)equality. Random-access iterators support all the relational operations.

Iterator categories can be thought of as cumulative, in the sense that every forward iterator is also an input iterator and an output iterator, every bidirectional iterator is also a forward iterator, and every random-access iterator is also a bidirectional iterator. Thus, any algorithm that accepts any iterator type as an argument will accept a random-access iterator. Class ostream_iterator and the insert iterator adaptors provide output iterators, and thus can be used only by algorithms that require only output-iterator operations.

All iterators support the following operations:

```
++p
p++
```
      Advances p to the next position in the container. ++p returns p as an lvalue after advancing it; p++ returns a copy of p's previous value.

`*p`	The element to which p refers. For output iterators, `*p` may be used only as the left operand of `=`, and each distinct value of p may be used in this way only once. For input iterators, `*p` may be used only for reading; and the act of incrementing p invalidates all copies that might have been made of p's previous value. For all other iterator types, `*p` yields a reference to the value stored in the container element to which p refers, and p remains valid as long as the element to which p refers continues to exist.
`p == p2`	Yields `true` if p is equal to p2; `false` otherwise.
`p != p2`	Yields `true` if p is not equal to p2; `false` otherwise.

All iterators other than output iterators also support

`p->x`	Equivalent to `(*p).x`

Bidirectional and random-access iterators also support decrement operations:

`--p`	
`p--`	Advances p backward to refer to the previous element. `--p` returns p as an lvalue after advancing it; `p--` returns a copy of p's previous value.

Random-access iterators provide all of the "pointer" operations, including the following:

`p + n`	If `n >= 0`, then the result is an iterator that refers to a point n positions beyond p. The operation is undefined if fewer than $n - 1$ elements follow the element denoted by p. If `n < 0`, then the result is an iterator that refers to the element `-n` positions before the element denoted by p. The operation is undefined unless this element is within range of the container.
`n + p`	Equivalent to `p + n`.
`p - n`	Equivalent to `p + (-n)`.
`p2 - p`	Defined only if p and p2 refer to positions in the same container. If $p2 \geq p$, yields the number of elements in the range `[p, p2)`. Otherwise, yields the negation of the number of elements in the range `[p2, p)`. The result has type `ptrdiff_t` (§10.1.4/175).
`p[n]`	Equivalent to `* (p + n)`.
`p < p2`	`true` if p denotes an earlier position in the container than that denoted by p2. Undefined if p and p2 do not refer to positions in the same container.
`p <= p2`	Equivalent to `(p < p2) || (p == p2)`.
`p > p2`	Equivalent to `p2 < p`.
`p >= p2`	Equivalent to `p2 <= p`.

B.2.6 `vector`

The `vector` class provides dynamically allocated, type-independent arrays, and supports random-access iterators. In addition to the common sequential-container operations (§B.2.1/314 and §B.2.2/315), `vector` also supports the following:

```
#include <vector>
```
Declares the `vector` class and associated operations.

```
v.reserve(n)
```
Reallocates v so that it can grow to accommodate at least n elements without further reallocation.

```
v.resize(n)
```
Reallocates v to hold n elements. Invalidates all iterators referring to elements of v. Preserves the first n elements. If the new size is less than the old, excess elements are destroyed. If the new size is greater than the old, new elements are value-initialized (§9.5/164).

B.2.7 list

The `list` class provides dynamically allocated, type-independent, doubly linked lists, and supports bidirectional iterators (unlike `vector`, which supports random-access iterators). In addition to the general operations on sequential containers (§B.2.1/314 and §B.2.2/315), `list` also supports the following:

```
#include <list>
```
Declares the `list` class and associated operations.

```
l.splice(it, l2)
```
Inserts all the elements of l2 into l immediately before the position denoted by it, and removes those elements from l2. Invalidates all iterators and references into l2. After completion, `l.size()` is the sum of the original sizes of l and l2, and `l2.size() == 0`. Returns `void`.

```
l.splice(it, l2, it2)
l.splice(it, l2, b, e)
```
Inserts the element denoted by it2, or the elements in the sequence denoted by [b, e), into l immediately before the position denoted by it, and removes those elements from l2. The element denoted by it2, or the elements in the range [b, e), must be entirely within l2. Invalidates iterators and references to the `spliced` elements. Returns `void`.

```
l.remove(t)
l.remove_if(p)
```
Removes from l all elements with value equal to t, or for which the predicate p yields `true`. Returns `void`.

```
l.sort(cmp)
l.sort()   Sorts l using <, or the predicate cmp if supplied, to compare elements.
```

B.2.8 string

The `string` class provides variable-length character strings and random-access iterators to access their characters. Although `strings` aren't true containers, they support the container operations shown previously (§B.2.1/314 and §B.2.2/315) and can be used with the algorithms (§B.3/321). In addition, the `string` class also supports the following:

```
#include <string>
```
Declares the `string` class and associated operations.
```
string s(cp);
```
Defines s as a `string` initialized to a copy of the characters denoted by `cp`.

`os << s`   Writes the characters in s onto `os`. Returns a reference to `os`.

`is >> s`   Reads a word from `is` into s, obliterating s's previous contents. Returns a reference to `is`. Words are delimited by a whitespace (space, tab, newline).
```
getline(is, s)
```
Reads the input stream `is` up to and including the next newline, and stores the characters read, excluding the newline, in s, obliterating s's previous contents. Returns a reference to `is`.

`s += s2`   Appends s2 to s and returns a reference to s.

`s + s2`   Returns the result of concatenating s and s2.

`s relop s2`   Returns a `bool` indicating whether the relational operation is `true`. The `string` library defines all the relational and equality operators: `<`, `<=`, `>`, `>=`, `==`, and `!=`. Two `strings` are equal if their respective elements are equal. If one `string` is a prefix of the other, then the shorter is less than the longer. Otherwise, the result is determined by comparing the first pair of respective characters at which the `strings` differ.
```
s.substr(n, n2)
```
Returns a new `string` that holds n2 characters copied from s, starting at position n. Undefined if `n > s.size()`. Copies characters in the range from n to the end of s if n + n2 is greater than `s.size()`.

`s.c_str()`   Yields a `const` pointer to a null-terminated character array that contains a copy of the characters in s. The array persists only until the next `nonconst` member function is called on s.

`s.data()`   Like `c_str`, but the array is not null terminated
```
s.copy(cp, n)
```
Copies up to the first n characters, without null termination, from s into a user-supplied character array denoted by `cp`. It is the caller's responsibility to ensure that there is room for at least n characters.

B.2.9 `pair`

Class `pair<K, V>` provides an abstraction for a pair of values of type K and V respectively. The operations on `pair<K, V>` include the following:
```
#include <utility>
```
Declares the `pair` class and associated operations.

`x.first`   The first element of the `pair` named x.

`x.second`   The second element of the `pair` named x.
```
pair<K, V> x(k, v);
```
Defines x as a new `pair` composed of elements with types K and V, and values k and v, so that `x.first` has type K and `x.second` has type V. Note that to declare a `pair` explicitly, you must know the types of its members.

`make_pair(k, v)`

> Generates a new `pair<K, V>` with element values k and v. Note that it is not necessary to know the types of k and v to use this form.

B.2.10 `map`

Class `map` provides dynamically allocated, type-independent associative arrays. It uses `pair` as an auxiliary class to store the (name, value) pairs that are the `map`'s elements. Iterators are bidirectional. Each `map` holds values of type V associated with keys of type `const K`. Accordingly, the value stored in an element of a `map` can be changed, but the key cannot be changed. In addition to the general container operations (§B.2.1/314) and those on associative containers (§B.2.4/316), `map` also supports the following:

`#include <map>`

> Declares the `map` class and associated operations.

`map<K, V, P> m(cmp);`

> Defines m as a new, empty `map`, which holds values of type V associated with keys of type `const K`, and uses predicate `cmp` of type P to compare elements when inserting them into the `map`.

`m[k]`

> Yields a reference to the value in m at the position indexed by k. If no such element exists, then a value-initialized element (§9.5/164) of type V is inserted into the `map`. Because evaluating `m[k]` can potentially change m's contents, m must not be `const`.

`m.insert(make_pair(k, v))`

> Inserts value v into m at the position indicated by the key k. If a value already exists with key k, then the associated value is not changed. Returns a `pair<map<K, V>::iterator, bool>` with a `first` component that refers to the element with the given key, and a `second` component that indicates whether a new element was inserted. Note that `make_pair` generates a `pair<K, V>`, which is converted by `insert` to a `pair<const K, V>`.

`m.find(k)`   Returns an iterator referring to the element, if any, with key k. Returns `m.end()` if no such element exists.

`*it`

> Yields a `pair<const K, V>`, which contains the key, and the value with which that key is associated, at the position denoted by `it`. Accordingly, `it->first` has type `const K`, and represents the key, and `it->second` has type V and represents the corresponding value.

B.3 Algorithms

The standard library includes many generic algorithms, which are written to operate on iterators, thereby gaining independence from the particular data structures on which they operate and the types stored therein. Note that associative containers have iterators that refer to compound types such as `pair<const K, V>`. Therefore, using these algorithms with associative containers requires careful thought.

Most algorithms operate on sequences delimited by pairs of iterators in which the first iterator denotes the first element in the sequence and the second denotes one past the last element. Except as noted, all algorithms are defined in the `<algorithm>` header.

```
#include <algorithm>
```
Includes declarations for generic algorithms.

`accumulate(b, e, t)`

`accumulate(b, e, t, f)`

Defined in the `<numeric>` header. Creates a temporary object *obj* with the same type and value as `t`. For each input iterator `it` in the range `[b, e)`, evaluates *obj* = *obj* + `*it` or *obj* = `f`(*obj*, `*it`), depending on which form of `accumulate` was called. The result is a copy of *obj*. Note that because + may be overloaded, even the first form of `accumulate` may operate on types other than the built-in arithmetic types. For example, we can use `accumulate` to concatenate all the `string`s in a container.

`binary_search(b, e, t)`

Returns a `bool` indicating whether the value `t` is in the (sorted) sequence delimited by the forward iterators `b` and `e`.

`copy(b, e, d)`

Copies the values in the sequence denoted by the input iterators `b` and `e` into the destination indicated by output iterator `d`. The function assumes that enough space exists in the destination to hold the values being copied. Returns a value that denotes a position one past the last destination element.

`equal(b, e, b2)`

`equal(b, e, b2, p)`

Returns a `bool` indicating whether the elements in the sequence denoted by the input iterators `b` and `e` are equal to the elements in a sequence of the same size beginning at the input iterator `b2`. Uses the predicate `p` for the test, or the `==` operator if `p` is not supplied.

`fill(b, e, t)`

Sets the elements in the sequence denoted by the input iterators `b` and `e` to the value `t`. Returns `void`.

`find(b, e, t)`

`find_if(b, e, p)`

Returns an iterator denoting the first occurrence of the value `t`, or for which the predicate `p` is `true` (if `p` is supplied), in the sequence denoted by the input iterators `b` and `e`. Returns `e` if no such element exists.

`lexicographical_compare(b, e, b2, e2)`

`lexicographical_compare(b, e, b2, e2, p)`

Returns a `bool` indicating whether the sequence of elements in the range `[b, e)` is less than the sequence of elements in the range `[b2, e2)`, using the predicate `p` for element comparisons, or the `<` operator if `p` is not supplied. If one of the sequences is a prefix of the other, then the shorter sequence is considered to be less than the other. Otherwise, the result is determined by comparing the first pair of respective elements at which the sequences differ. Iterators `b`, `e`, `b2`, and `e2` need only be input iterators.

`max(t1, t2)`
`min(t1, t2)`

Returns the larger (for `max`) or smaller (for `min`) of `t1` and `t2`, both of which must be of the same type.

`max_element(b, e)`
`min_element(b, e)`

Returns an iterator denoting the largest (smallest) element in the sequence denoted by the forward iterators `b` and `e`.

`partition(b, e, p)`
`stable_partition(b, e, p)`

Partitions the sequence denoted by the bidirectional iterators `b` and `e` so that elements for which the predicate `p` is `true` are at the front of the container. Returns an iterator to the first element for which the predicate is `false`, or `e` if the predicate is `true` for all elements. The `stable_partition` function maintains the input order among the elements in each partition.

`remove(b, e, t)`
`remove_if(b, e, p)`

Rearranges the elements in the sequence denoted by the forward iterators `b` and `e` so that elements whose values do not match `t`, or for which the predicate `p` returns `false` (if `p` is supplied), are coalesced at the beginning of the associated sequence. Returns an iterator one past the unremoved elements.

`remove_copy(b, e, d, t)`
`remove_copy_if(b, e, d, p)`

Like `remove`, but it puts a copy of the elements that do not match `t`, or for which the predicate `p` is `false`, (if `p` is supplied), into the destination denoted by the output iterator `d`. Returns a value one past the last destination element. The destination is assumed to be large enough to hold the values copied. The elements in the sequence denoted by the iterators `b` and `e` are not moved. Thus, `b` and `e` need only be input iterators.

`replace(b, e, t1, t2)`
`replace_copy(b, e, d, t1, t2)`

Replaces each element with value `t1` by the value `t2` in the sequence denoted by the forward iterators `b` and `e`. Returns `void`. The second form copies the elements, replacing `t1` with `t2`, into the sequence denoted by the output iterator `d` and returns a value one past the last destination element. For the copy version `b` and `e` need only be input iterators.

`reverse(b, e)`
`reverse_copy(b, e, d)`

The first form reverses the elements in the sequence denoted by the bidirectional iterators `b` and `e` by swapping pairs of elements, and returns `void`. The second form stores the reversed sequence in the destination starting at the output iterator `d`, and returns a value one past the last element copied

into the destination. As usual, the destination must have enough room to
hold the values in the sequence.

search(b, e, b2, e2)
search(b, e, b2, e2, p)

Returns a forward iterator positioned on the first occurrence, in the
sequence denoted by the forward iterators b and e, of the subsequence
denoted by the forward iterators b2 and e2. Uses the predicate p for the
test, or the == operator if p is not supplied.

transform(b, e, d, f)
transform(b, e, b2, d, f)

If b2 is not supplied, f must take one argument; transform calls the function f on the elements in the sequence denoted by the input iterators b and
e. If b2 is supplied, f must take two arguments, which are taken pairwise
from the sequence denoted by b and e and the sequence of the same length
beginning at the input iterator b2. In either case, transform puts the
sequence of results from the function into the destination denoted by the
output iterator d, and returns a value one past the last destination element.
As usual, the destination is assumed to be large enough to hold the generated elements. Note that d is permitted to be equal to b or b2 (if supplied),
in which case the result replaces the given input sequence.

sort(b, e)
sort(b, e, p)
stable_sort(b, e)
stable_sort(b, e, p)

Sorts, in place, the sequence defined by the random-access iterators b and e.
Uses the predicate p for the test, or the < operator if p is not supplied. The
stable_sort functions maintain the input order among equal elements.

unique(b, e)
unique(b, e, p)

Rearranges the sequence delimited by the forward iterators b and e so that
the first instance of each subsequence of consecutive equal elements is
moved to the beginning of the container. Returns an iterator positioned on
the first element that should not be considered as part of the result (or e if all
consecutive pairs of input elements are unequal). Uses the predicate p for
the test, or == if p is not supplied.

unique_copy(b, e, d, p)

Copies the sequence delimited by input iterators b and e into the sequence
beginning at the position denoted by the output iterator d, eliminating any
adjacent duplicates in the process. Returns d after incrementing it by the
number of elements copied. As usual, assumes d is large enough to hold the
elements. Uses the predicate p for the test, or == if p is not supplied.

Index

H

.h file name suffix, 66
half-open range, 28, 31, 33, 90, 104
Handle, 254–255
handle, 253–254
  class, 243, 247
  object, copy a, 246
hardware failure, 40
hash table, 136
hazardous conversion, 221
hcat, 95, 272, 280
HCat_Pic, 270, 277, 284
header
  file, 66
  file, standard, 66
  guard, 67
  standard, 2
height, 273
Hello, world! program, 1
hexadecimal, 301–302
hierarchy, Pic inheritance, 270
histogram, 292
histogram, 292
horizontal
  concatenation, 94, 277, 280, 284
  tab (\t), 302
http://www.acceleratedcpp.com, xiv, 1
http://www.accu.org, 294

I

if, 23, 308
#ifndef directive, 67
ifstream, 180, 186, 312
ignorance, selective, xii, 80
#include directive, 2, 66, 71
increment
  overloaded, 308
  postfix, 32, 98, 102, 306, 317
  prefix, 20, 32, 81, 98, 306, 317
indentation, 29
index, 45, 97, 109, 123, 137, 175, 185, 192, 316
  range, 47
inequality operator, 20, 81, 98
inheritance, 227, 250, 270
  and constructor, 231
  and container, 249
inheritance
  friend and, 247
  hierarchy, Pic, 270
initialization
  array, 176–177, 185

assignment and, 199
  default, 38, 164, 201
  order of, 165, 168
  value, 97, 125, 128, 137, 164, 201
initialize, 10, 13
initializer, 296
  constructor, 165, 168
inline member function, 162, 167
inline, 72, 297
input, 9, 15, 312
  error, 57
  iterator, 145, 150, 154, 317
  operator, 11, 37
  polymorphic, 236, 245, 259
  stream failure state, 57
  unsuccessful, 40
input–output, 312
  file, 180
  operator, 215
insert, 94, 97, 315–316, 321
inserter, 121, 315
instantiate, 141–142
int, 2, 22, 297, 300
integer, 300
  literal, 301
  range, 300
integral type, 300
interface, 10
  class, 253, 258, 270
  graphical user, xiii
invalid
  iterator, 83, 86
  pointer, 182
invalid_argument, 73
invalid_pointer, 182
invariant, 31, 38, 40, 150
  class, 206
  loop, 20
<iomanip>, 36, 313
<ios>, 36, 313
<iostream>, 2, 312
is_negative, 173
is_palindrome, 105
isalnum, 98, 107
isalpha, 98
isdigit, 98
islower, 99
ispunct, 99
isspace, 89, 98, 104
istream_iterator, 150, 312
isupper, 99
italic, bold, xiv
<iterator>, 102, 312
iterator, 79–81, 140, 143, 153
  adaptor, 102, 121